EDENSZERO

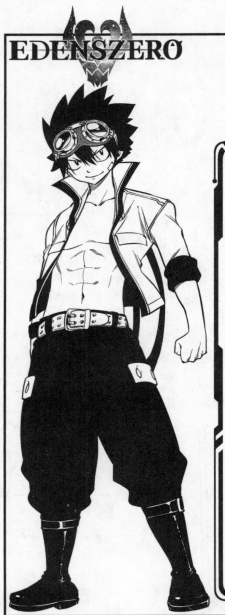

**Edens Zero
In-Depth Character File 1**

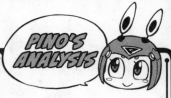

PINO'S ANALYSIS

Name: Shiki Granbell

Powers: Ether Gear (Satan Gravity)

Likes: Friends

Dislikes: Bugs

Attack: ☆☆☆☆

Defense: ☆☆☆

Marksmanship: ☆☆

Ether Power: ☆☆☆☆

Intelligence: ☆☆

Love for Friends: ☆☆☆☆☆

Memo

This is my Master. He uses a gravity
Ether Gear. He cares very much for
his friends and his goal is to make
lots of them. He appears to have an
intense hatred for bugs. I wonder if
something happened with them in
the past? He inherited the warship
Edens Zero from the Demon King
Ziggy and has set out on a quest to
find Mother.

CHAPTER 87: 4 ON 4

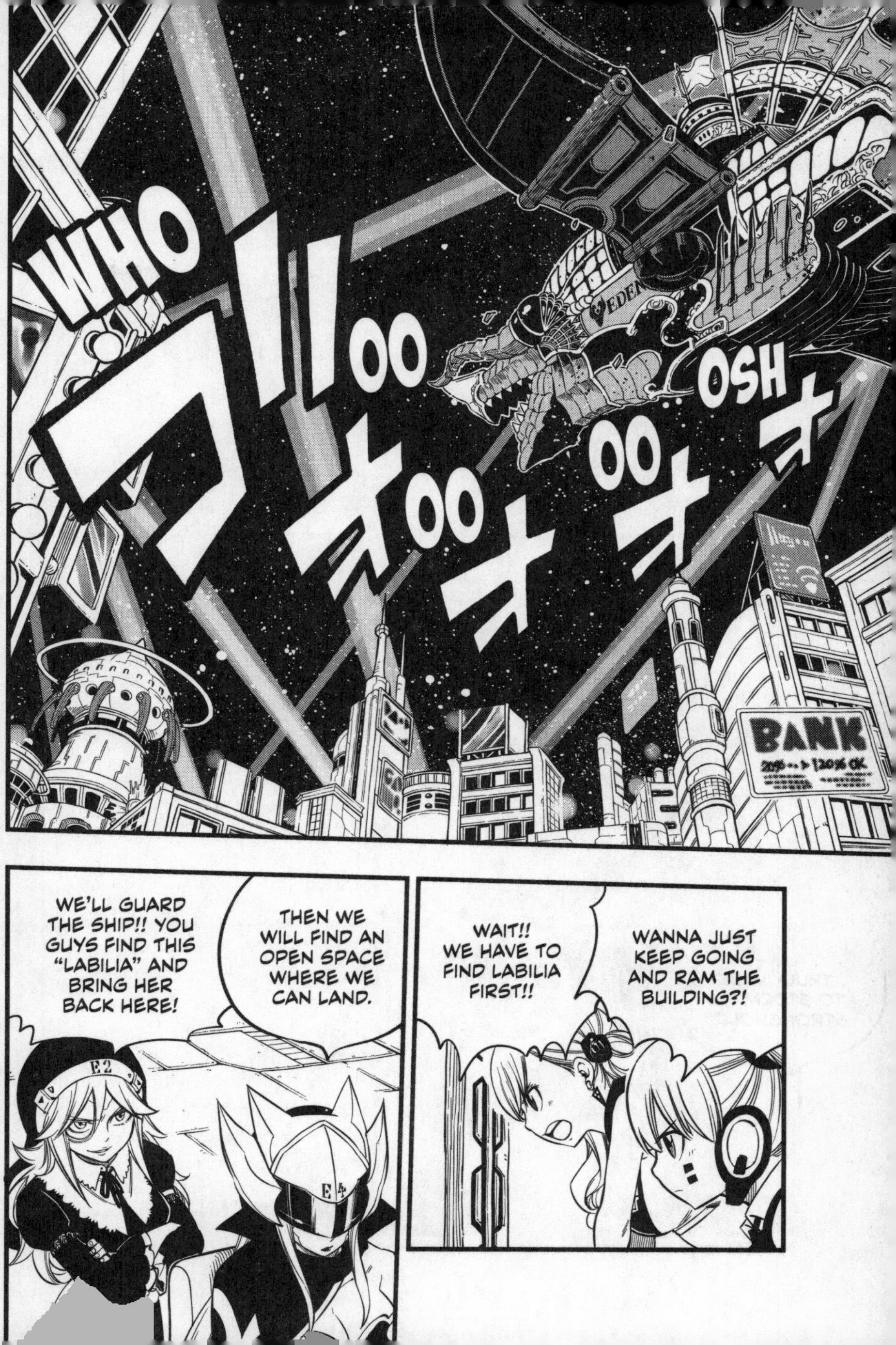
WHO
OO
OO
OO
OSH
BANK
WANNA JUST KEEP GOING AND RAM THE BUILDING?!
WAIT!! WE HAVE TO FIND LABILIA FIRST!!
THEN WE WILL FIND AN OPEN SPACE WHERE WE CAN LAND.
WE'LL GUARD THE SHIP!! YOU GUYS FIND THIS "LABILIA" AND BRING HER BACK HERE!

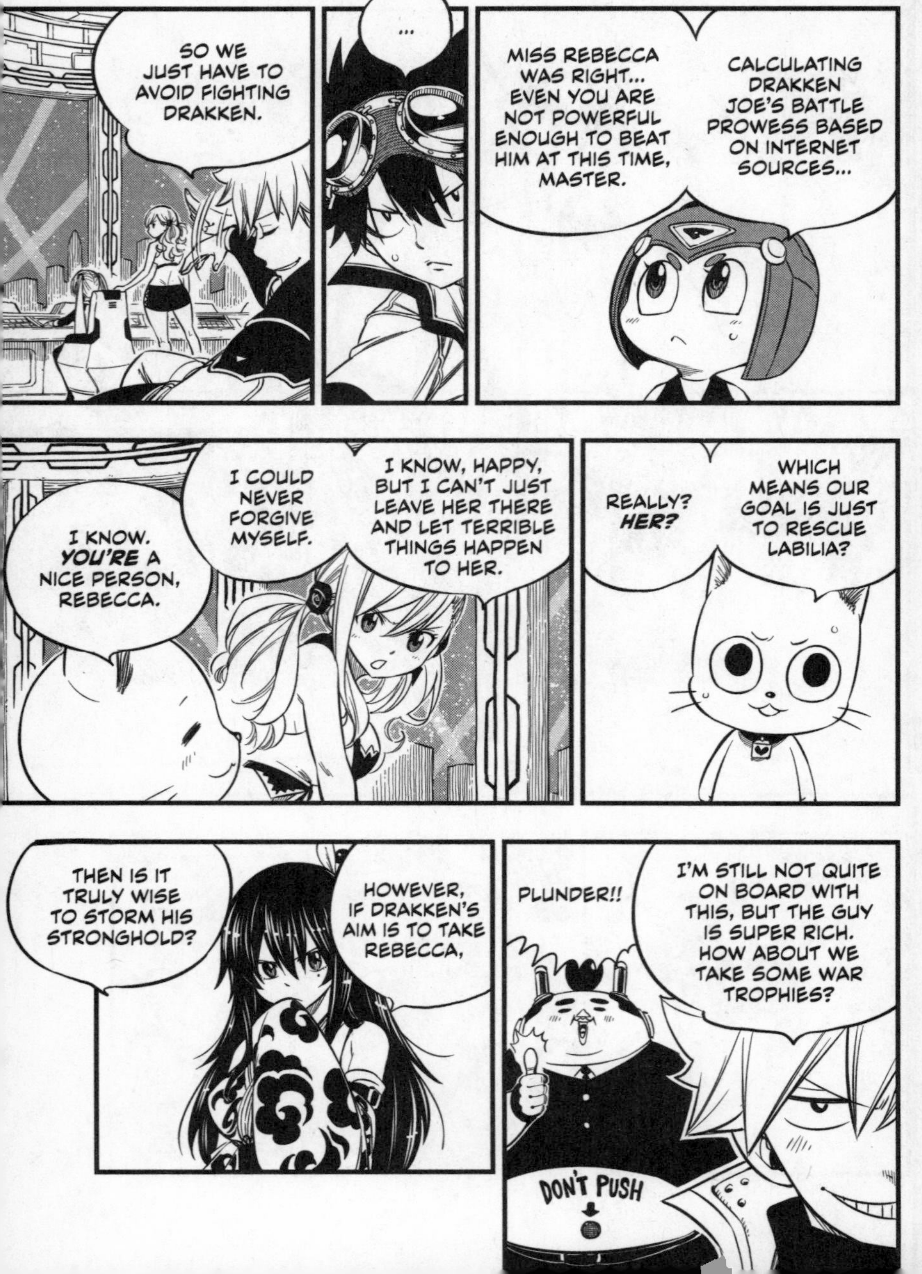
CALCULATING DRAKKEN JOE'S BATTLE PROWESS BASED ON INTERNET SOURCES...
MISS REBECCA WAS RIGHT... EVEN YOU ARE NOT POWERFUL ENOUGH TO BEAT HIM AT THIS TIME, MASTER.
...
SO WE JUST HAVE TO AVOID FIGHTING DRAKKEN.
WHICH MEANS OUR GOAL IS JUST TO RESCUE LABILIA?
REALLY? ***HER?***
I KNOW, HAPPY, BUT I CAN'T JUST LEAVE HER THERE AND LET TERRIBLE THINGS HAPPEN TO HER.
I COULD NEVER FORGIVE MYSELF.
I KNOW. ***YOU'RE*** A NICE PERSON, REBECCA.
I'M STILL NOT QUITE ON BOARD WITH THIS, BUT THE GUY IS SUPER RICH. HOW ABOUT WE TAKE SOME WAR TROPHIES?
PLUNDER!!
DON'T PUSH
HOWEVER, IF DRAKKEN'S AIM IS TO TAKE REBECCA,
THEN IS IT TRULY WISE TO STORM HIS STRONGHOLD?

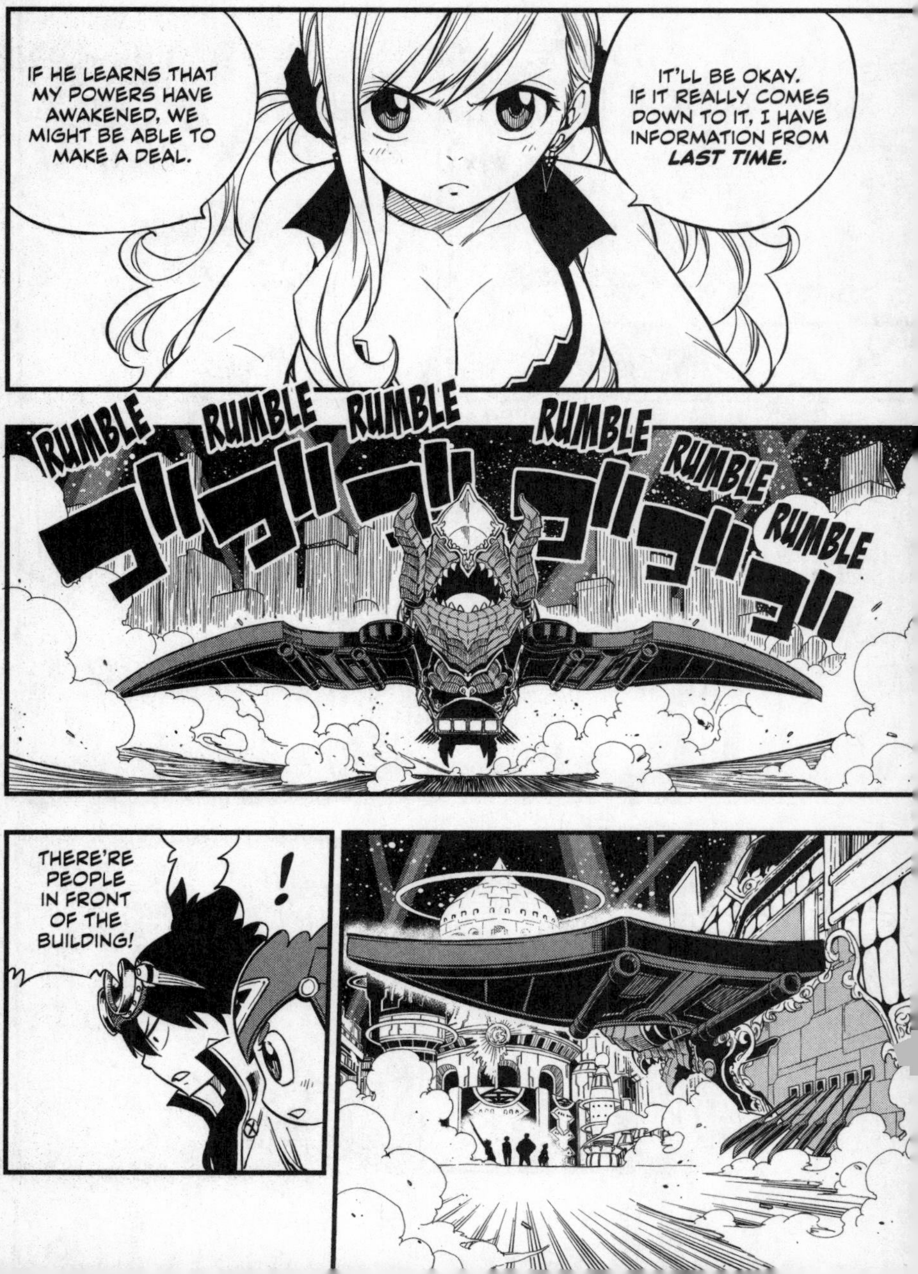
IT'LL BE OKAY. IF IT REALLY COMES DOWN TO IT, I HAVE INFORMATION FROM *LAST TIME.*
IF HE LEARNS THAT MY POWERS HAVE AWAKENED, WE MIGHT BE ABLE TO MAKE A DEAL.
RUMBLE RUMBLE RUMBLE RUMBLE RUMBLE RUMBLE
!
THERE'RE PEOPLE IN FRONT OF THE BUILDING!

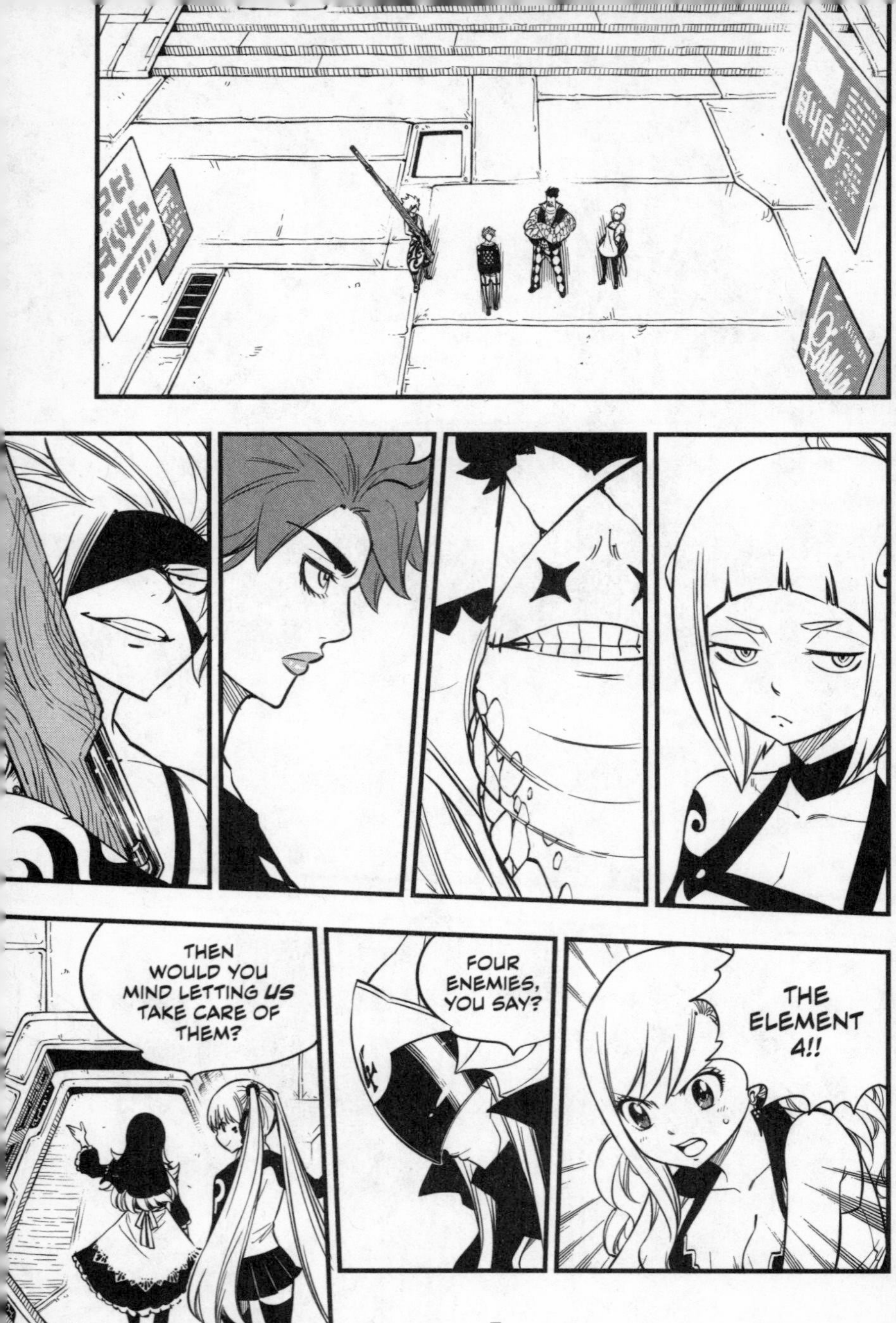
THE ELEMENT 4!!
FOUR ENEMIES, YOU SAY?
THEN WOULD YOU MIND LETTING *US* TAKE CARE OF THEM?

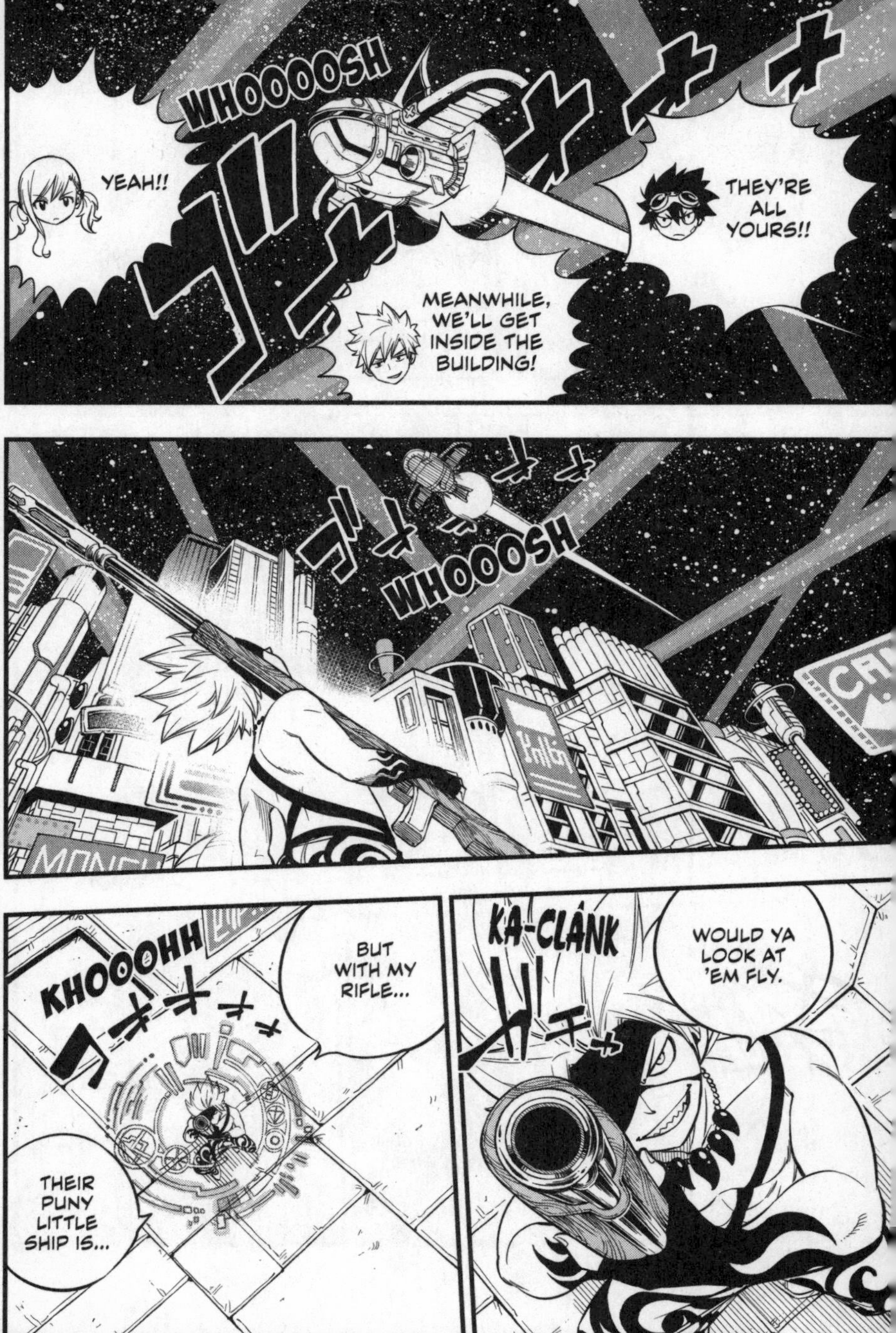
WHOOOOSH
THEY'RE ALL YOURS!!
YEAH!!
MEANWHILE, WE'LL GET INSIDE THE BUILDING!
WHOOOSH
KA-CLANK
WOULD YA LOOK AT 'EM FLY.
BUT WITH MY RIFLE...
KHOOOHH
THEIR PUNY LITTLE SHIP IS...

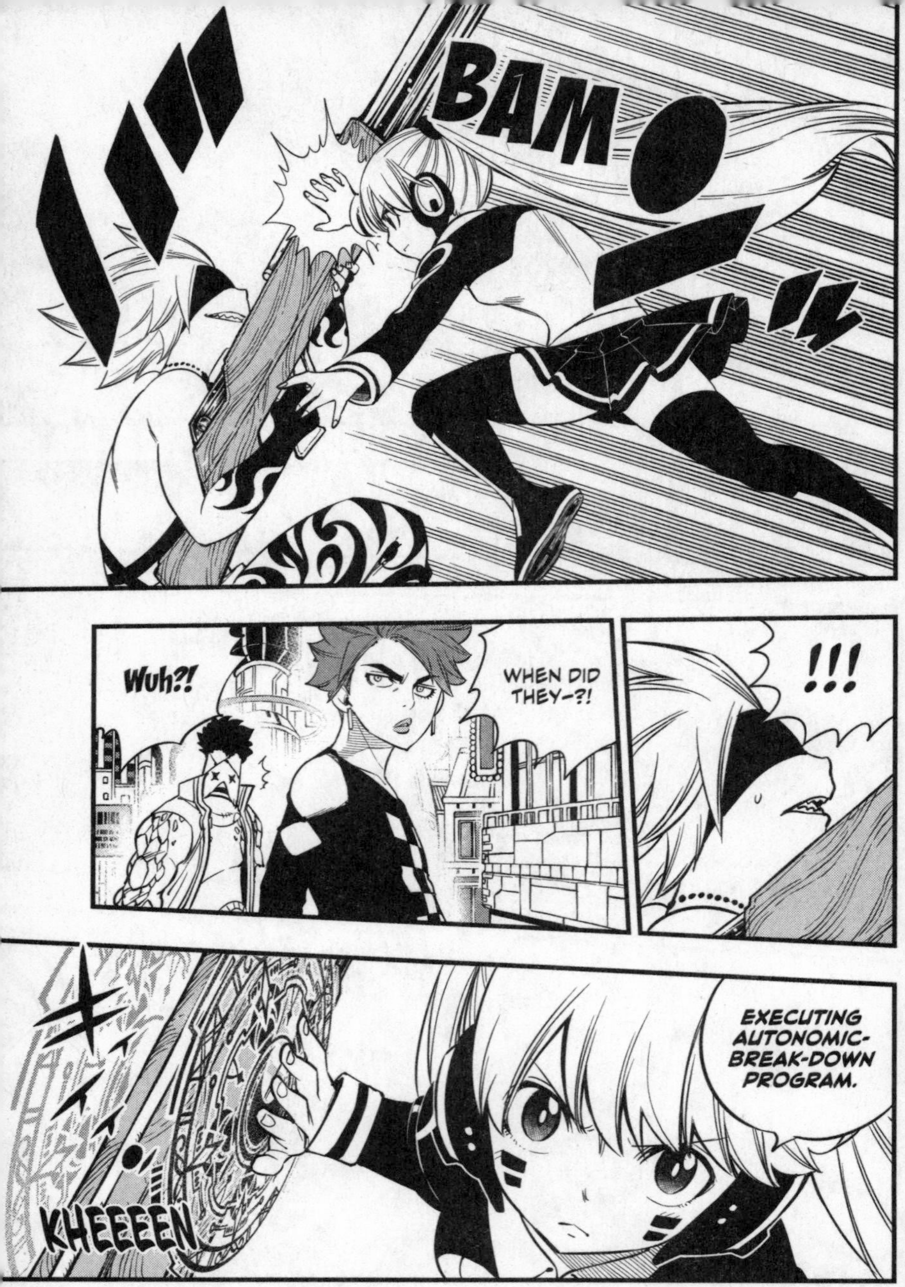
BAM
!!!
WHEN DID THEY-?!
Wuh?!
EXECUTING AUTONOMIC-BREAK-DOWN PROGRAM.
KHEEEEN

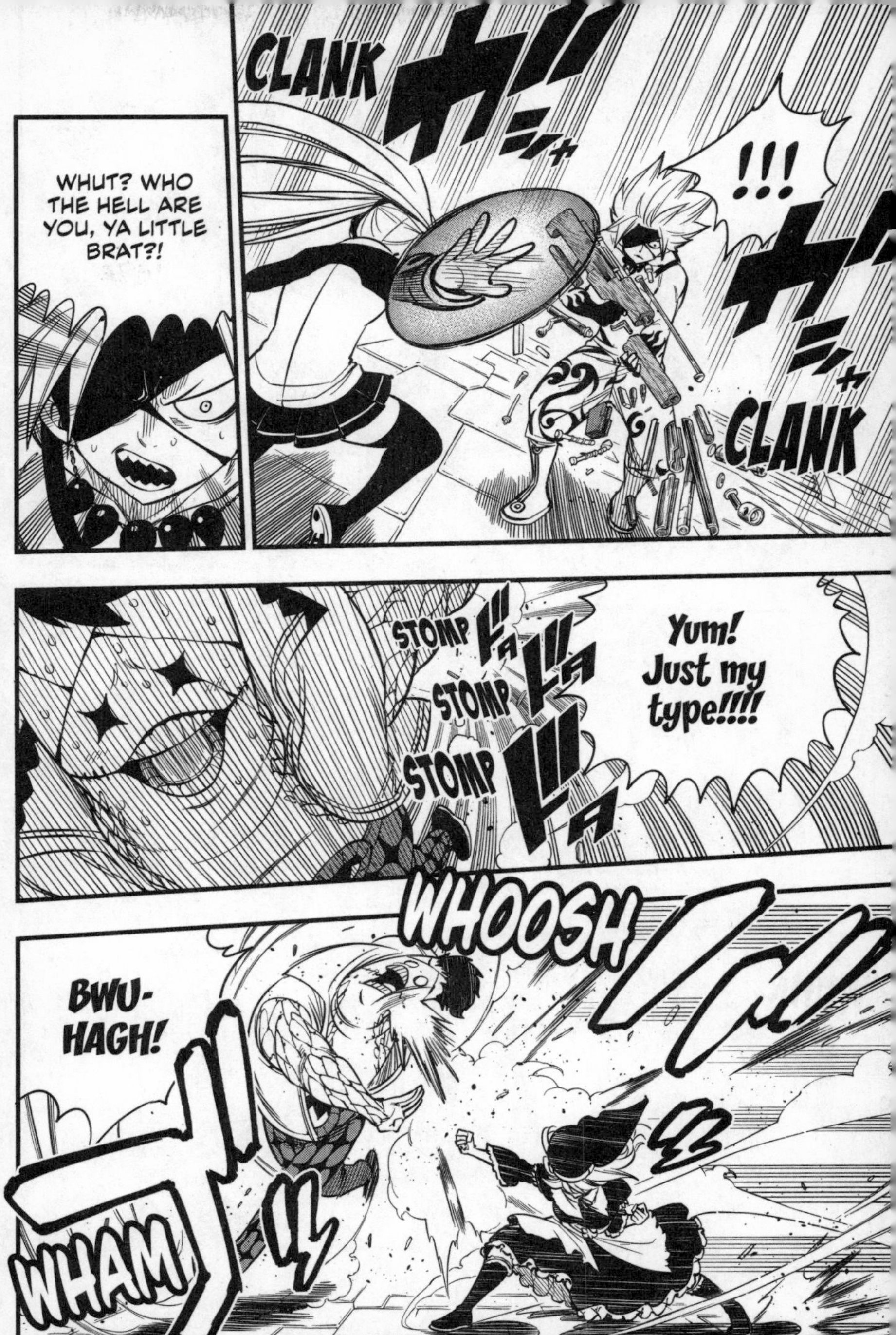
CLANK
!!!
CLANK
WHUT? WHO THE HELL ARE YOU, YA LITTLE BRAT?!
Yum! Just my type!!!!
STOMP
STOMP
STOMP
WHOOSH
BWU-HAGH!
WHAM

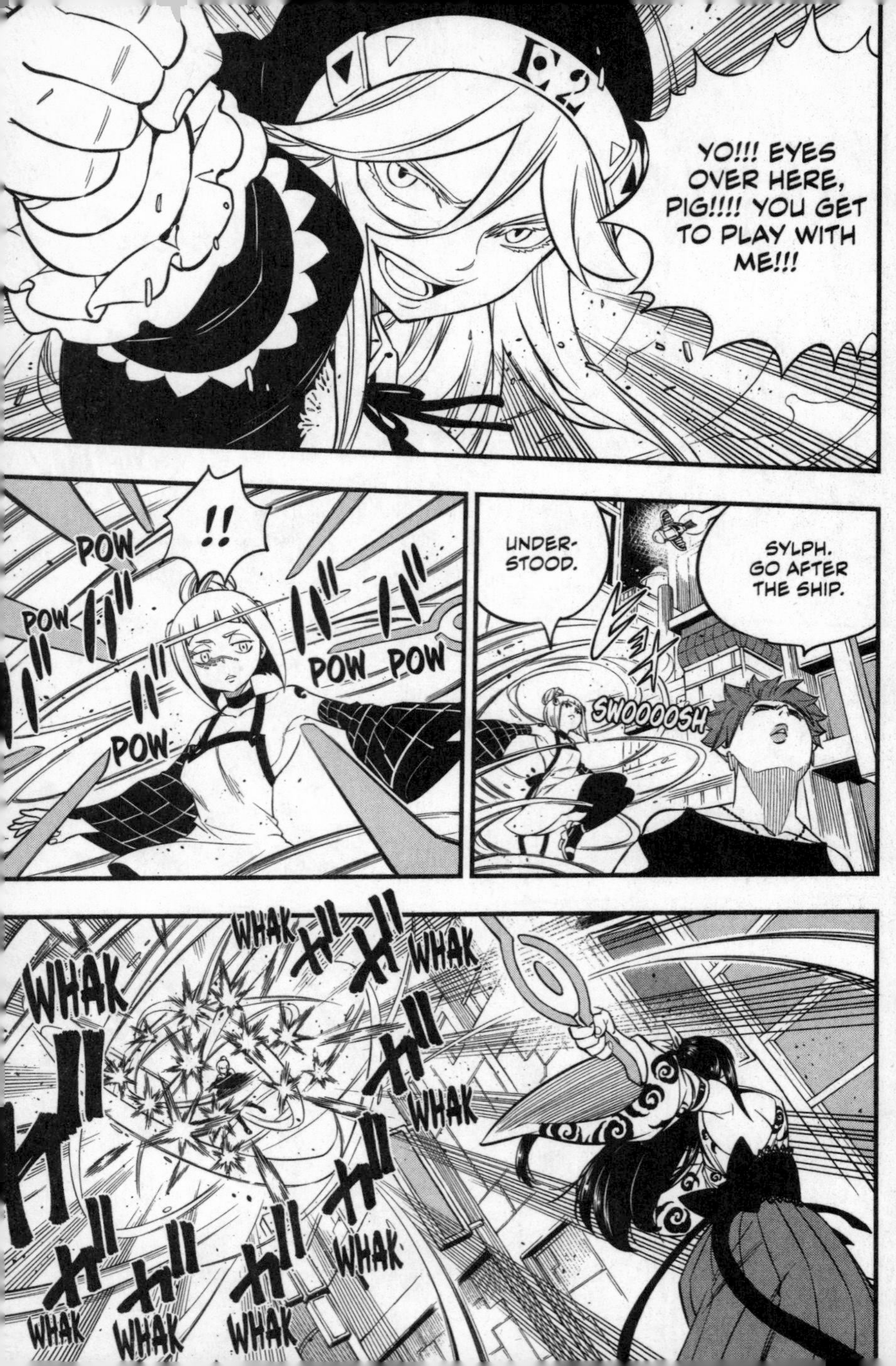
YO!!! EYES OVER HERE, PIG!!!! YOU GET TO PLAY WITH ME!!!
SYLPH. GO AFTER THE SHIP.
UNDER-STOOD.
SWOOOOSH
!!
POW
POW
POW POW
POW
WHAK
WHAK
WHAK
WHAK
WHAK
WHAK
WHAK
WHAK

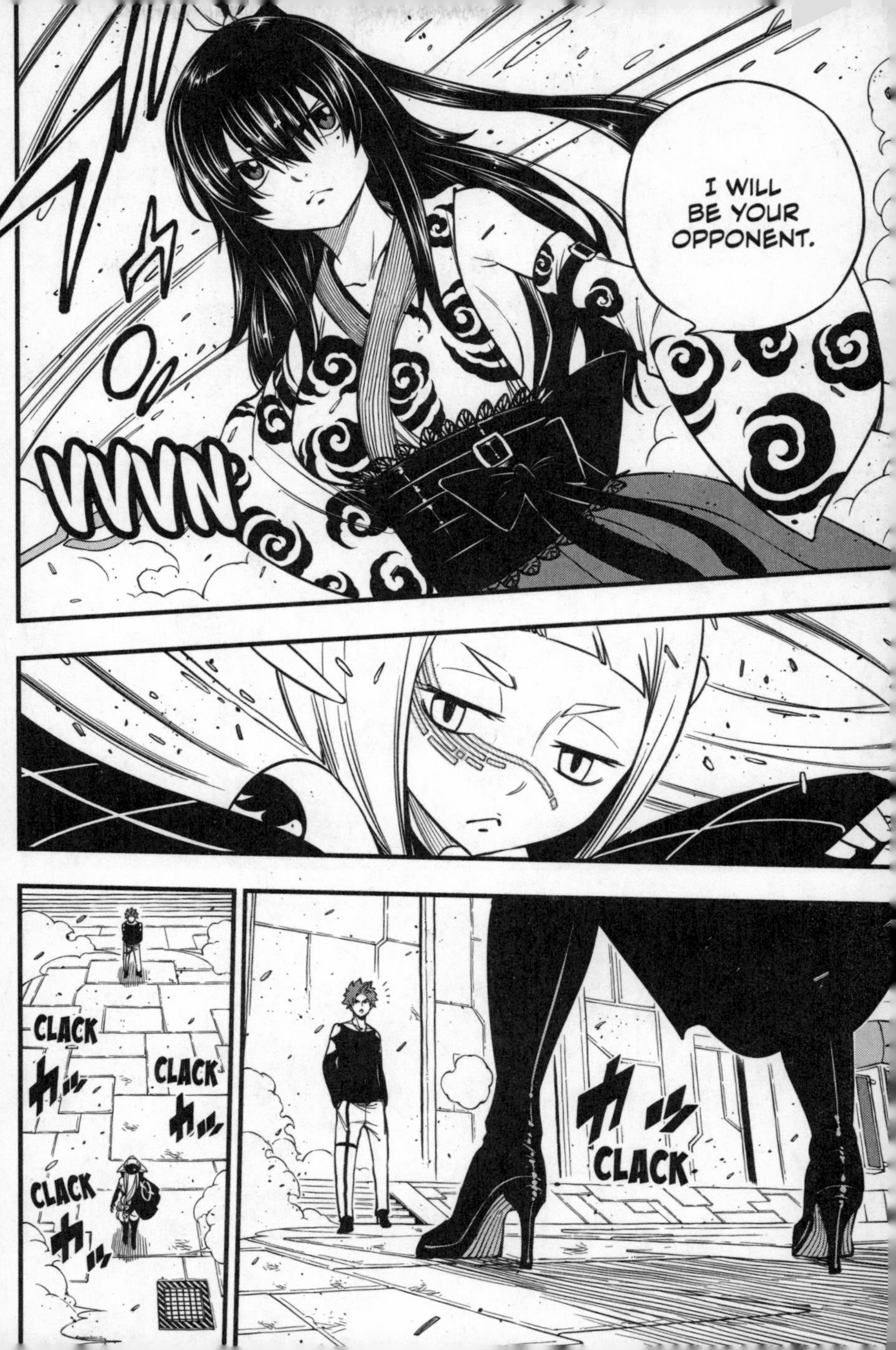
I WILL BE YOUR OPPONENT.
VVVN
CLACK
CLACK
CLACK
CLACK

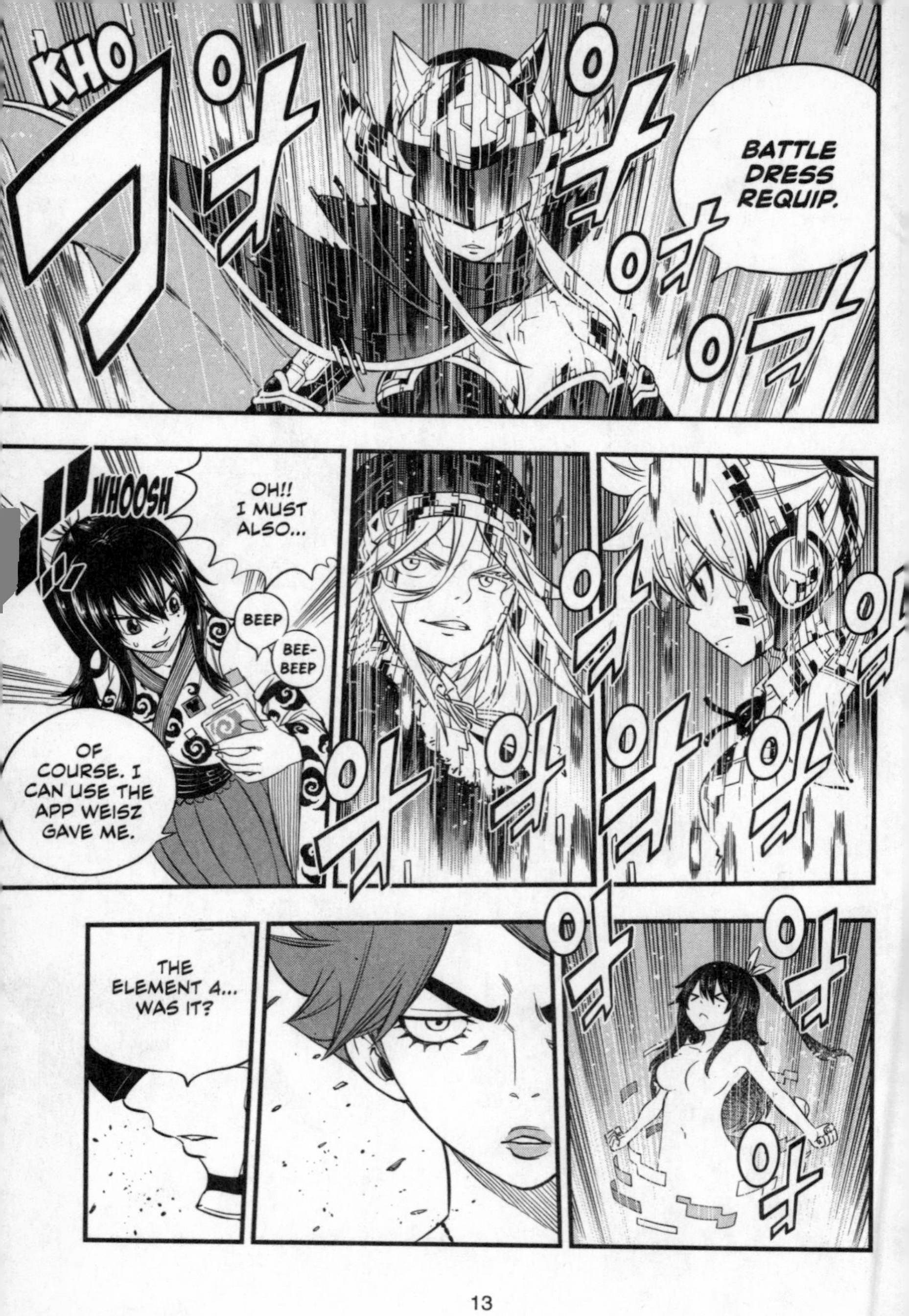
KHO
BATTLE DRESS REQUIP.
!!
WHOOSH
OH!! I MUST ALSO...
BEEP
BEE-BEEP
OF COURSE. I CAN USE THE APP WEISZ GAVE ME.
THE ELEMENT 4... WAS IT?

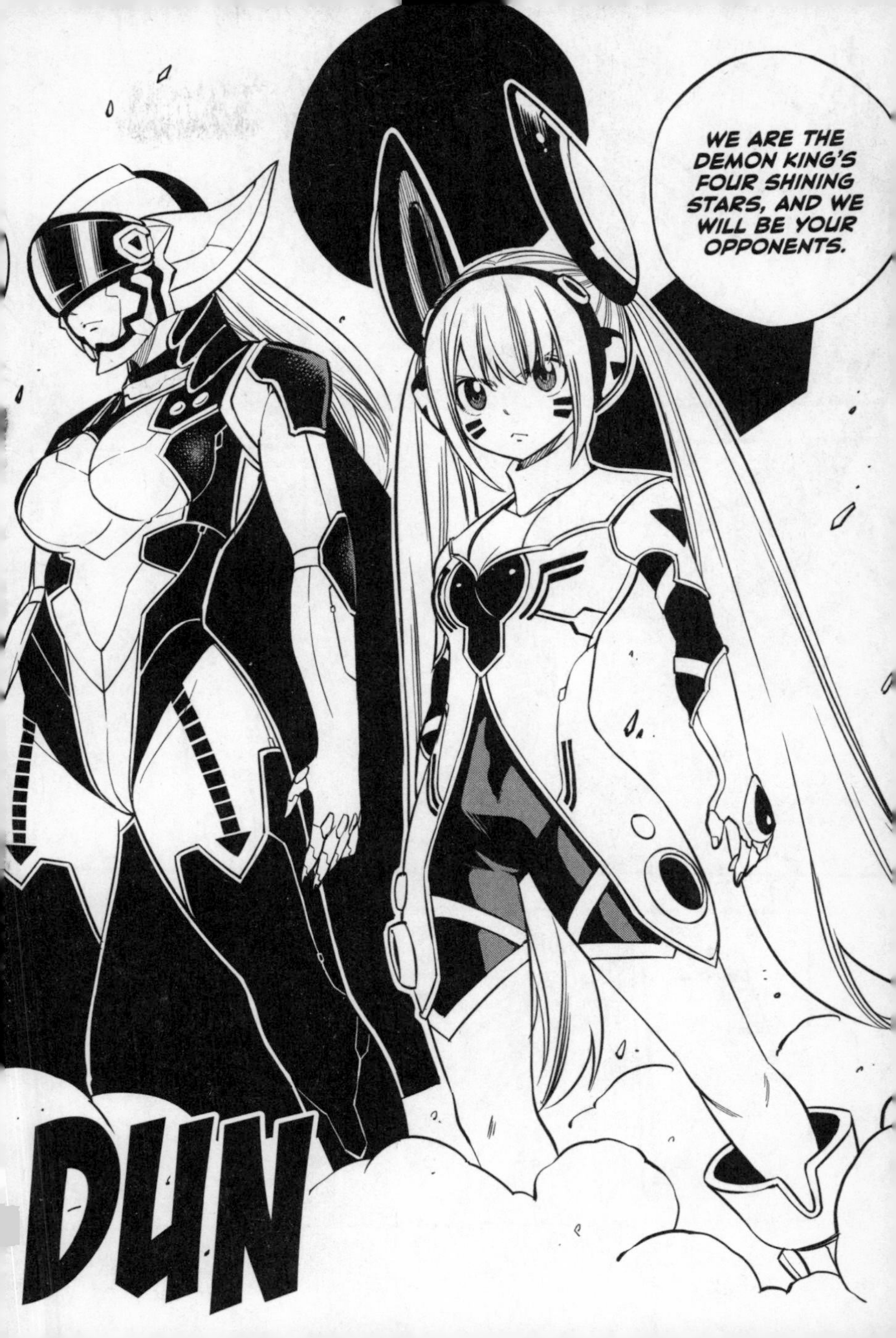
WE ARE THE DEMON KING'S FOUR SHINING STARS, AND WE WILL BE YOUR OPPONENTS.
DUN

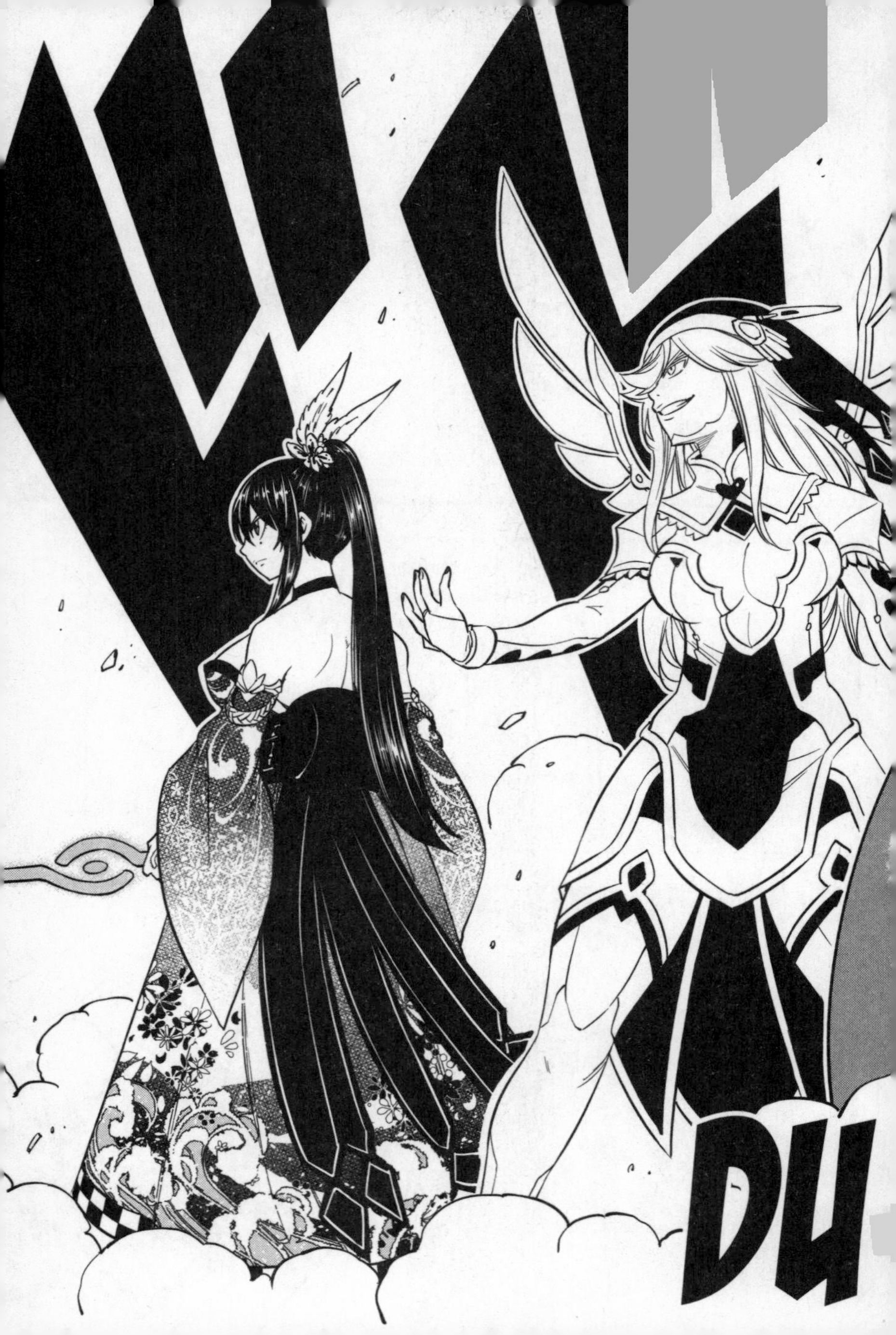
DU

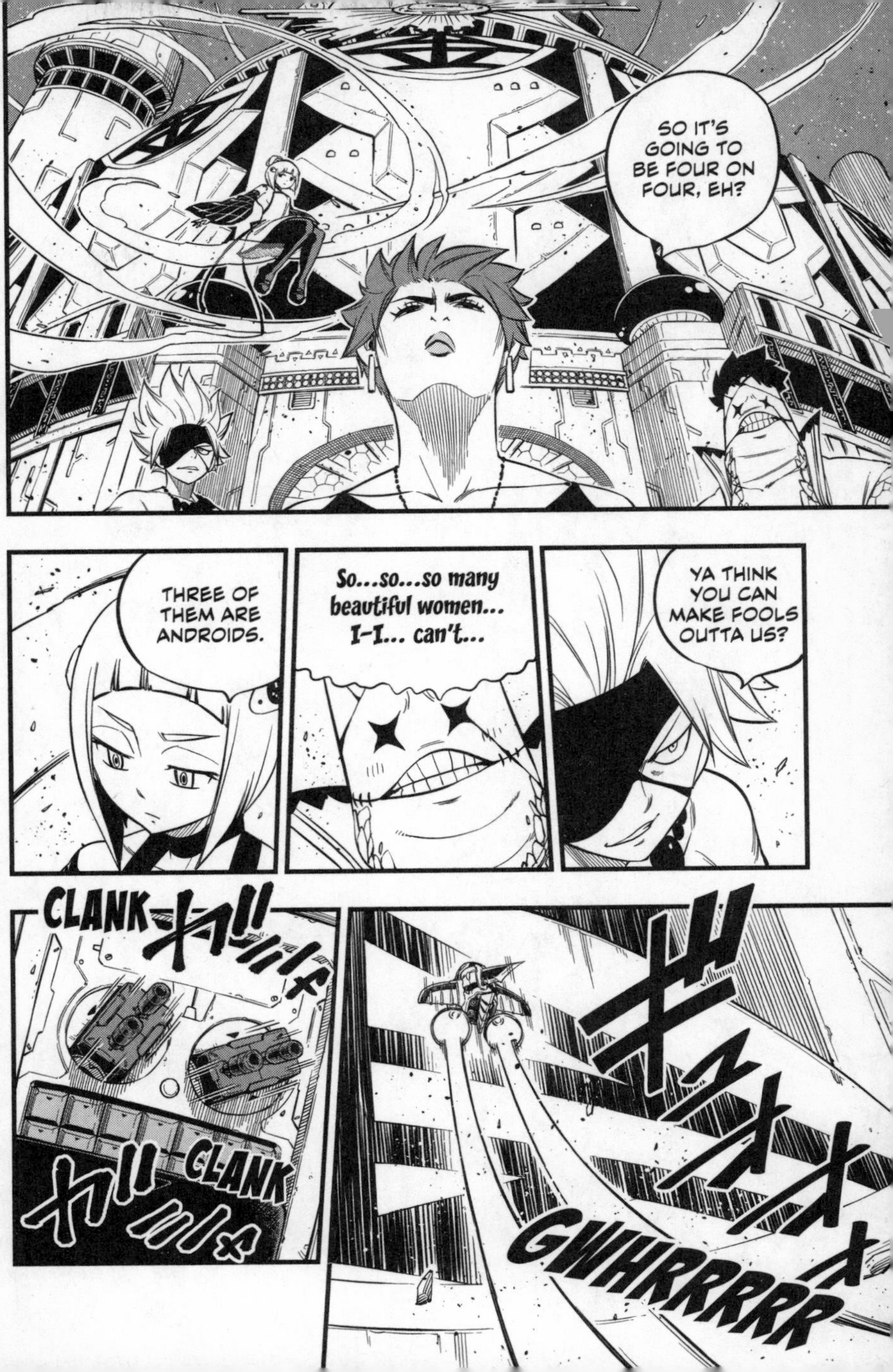
SO IT'S GOING TO BE FOUR ON FOUR, EH?
YA THINK YOU CAN MAKE FOOLS OUTTA US?
So...so...so many beautiful women... I-I... can't...
THREE OF THEM ARE ANDROIDS.
GWHRRRRRR
CLANK
CLANK

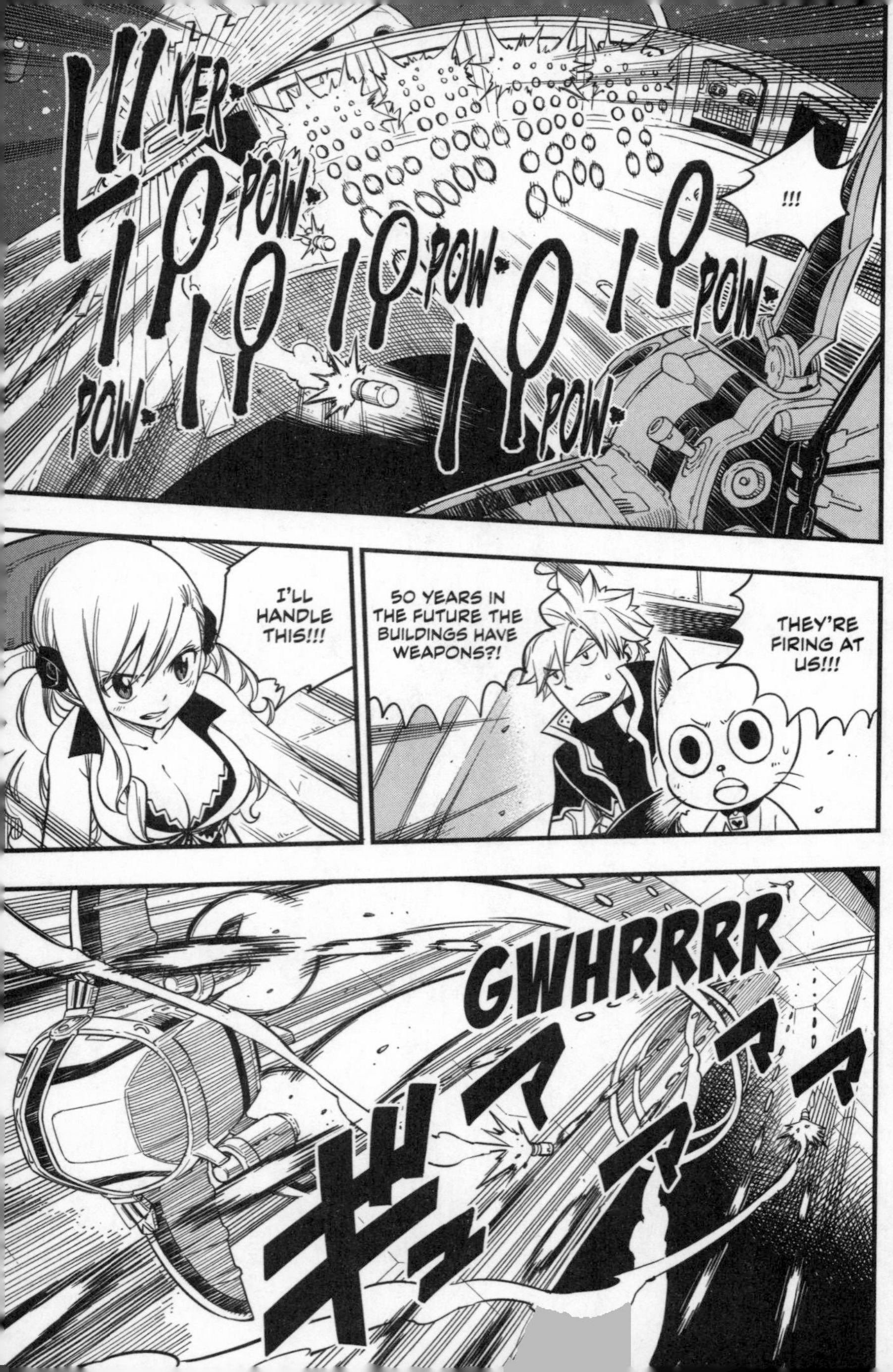
KER-
POW
POW
POW
POW
POW
POW
!!!
THEY'RE FIRING AT US!!!
50 YEARS IN THE FUTURE THE BUILDINGS HAVE WEAPONS?!
I'LL HANDLE THIS!!!
GWHRRRR

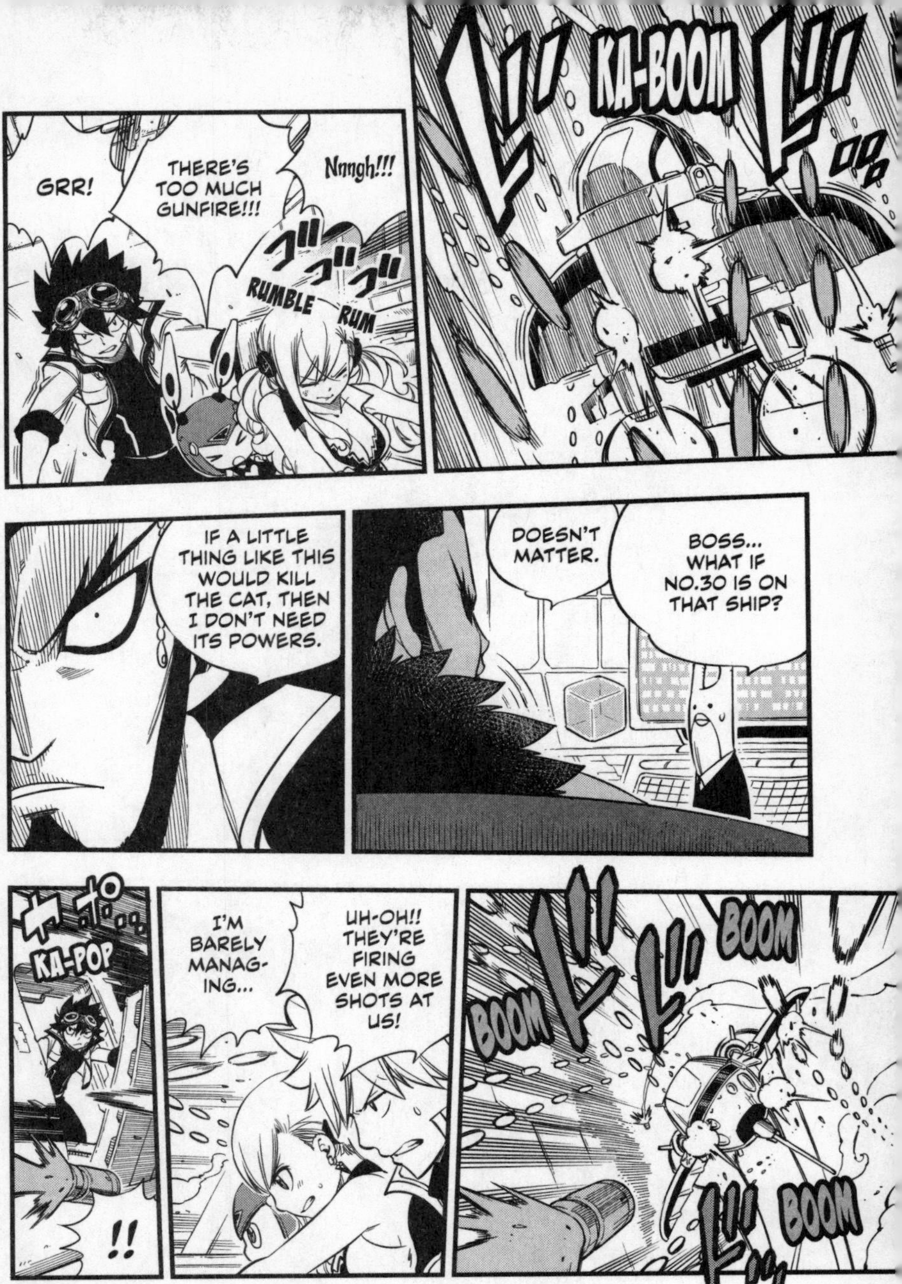
KA-BOOM
Nnngh!!!
THERE'S TOO MUCH GUNFIRE!!!
GRR!
RUMBLE
RUM
BOSS... WHAT IF NO.30 IS ON THAT SHIP?
DOESN'T MATTER.
IF A LITTLE THING LIKE THIS WOULD KILL THE CAT, THEN I DON'T NEED ITS POWERS.
BOOM
BOOM
BOOM
UH-OH!! THEY'RE FIRING EVEN MORE SHOTS AT US!
I'M BARELY MANAG-ING...
KA-POP
!!

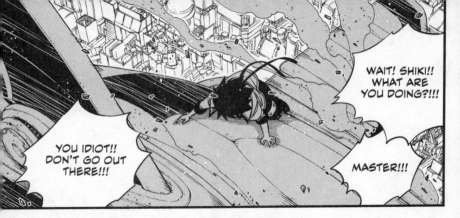

WAIT! SHIKI!! WHAT ARE YOU DOING?!!!

YOU IDIOT!! DON'T GO OUT THERE!!!

MASTER!!!

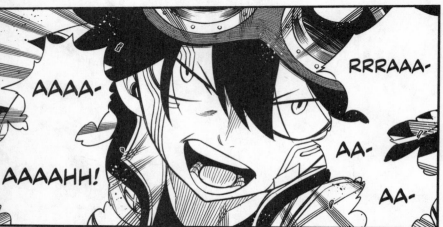

AAAA-

AAAAHH!

RRRAAA-

AA-

AA-

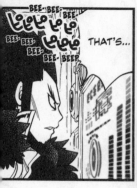

BEE-BEE-BEE
BEE-BEE-BEE
BEE-BEE-BEE
BEE-BEEP

THAT'S...

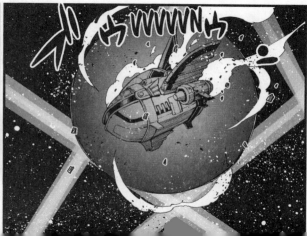

VVVVVVVVV

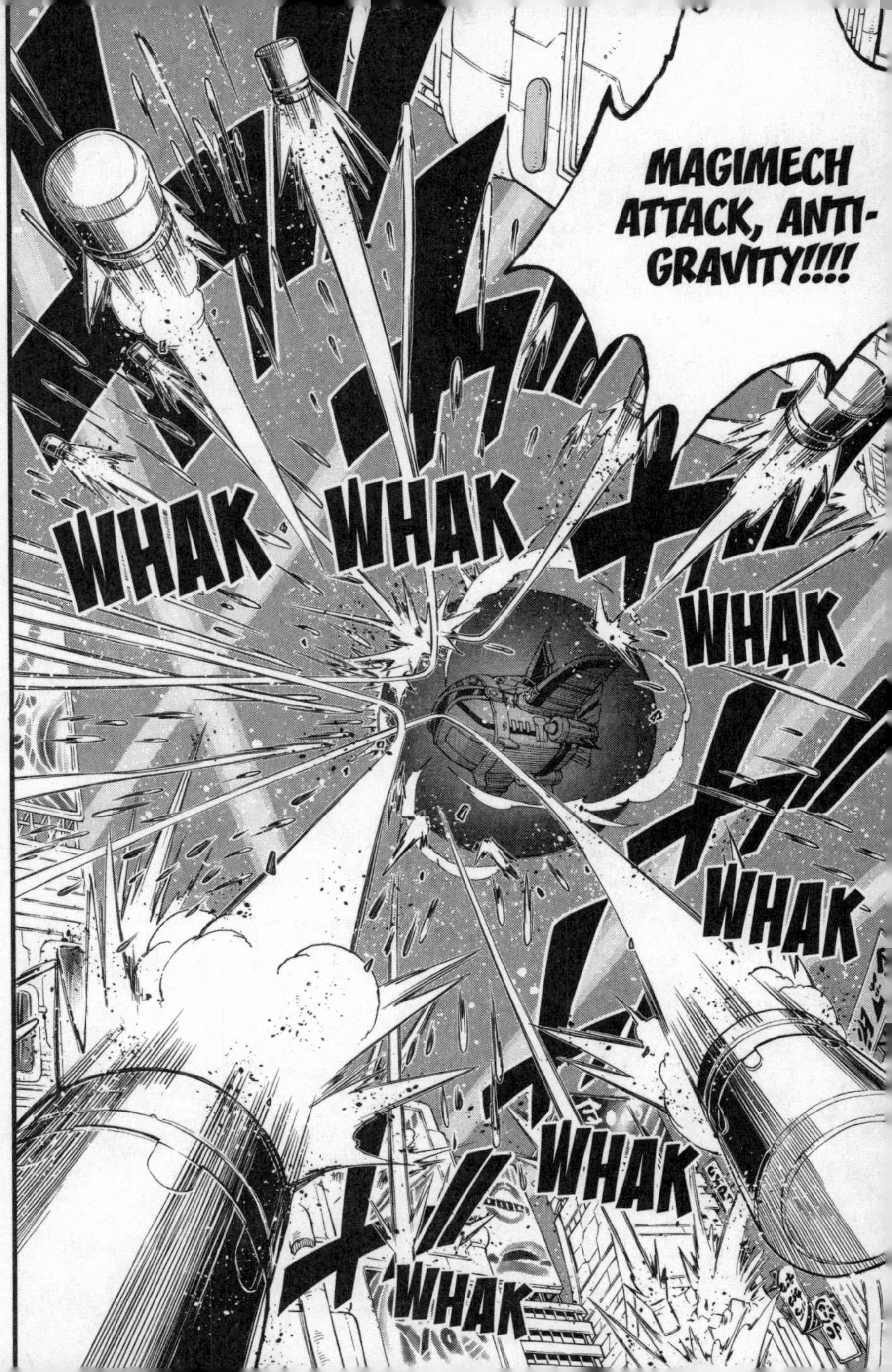
MAGIMECH ATTACK, ANTI-GRAVITY!!!!
WHAK
WHAK
WHAK
WHAK
WHAK
WHAK

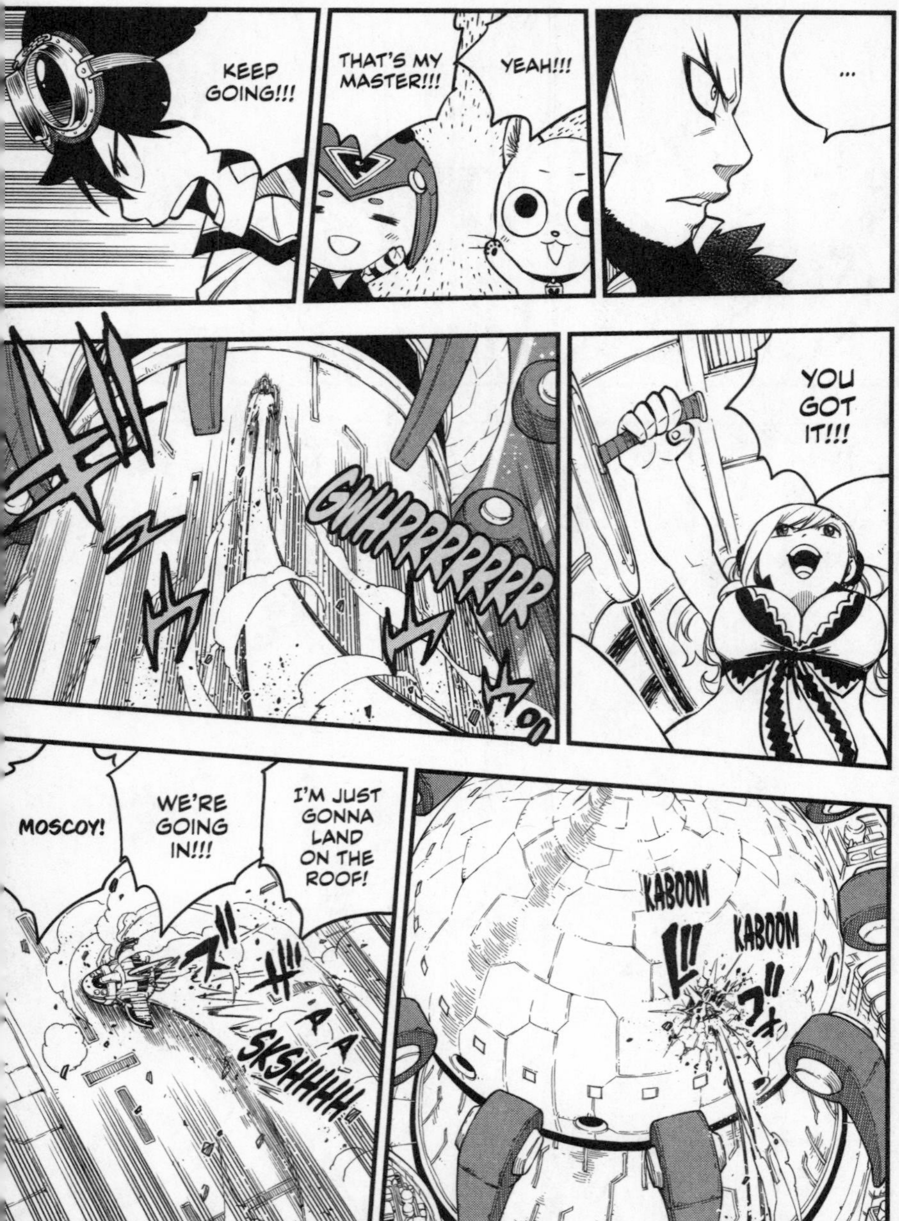
...
YEAH!!!
THAT'S MY MASTER!!!
KEEP GOING!!!
YOU GOT IT!!!
GWHRRRRRRRR
KABOOM
KABOOM
I'M JUST GONNA LAND ON THE ROOF!
WE'RE GOING IN!!!
MOSCOY!
SKSHHHH

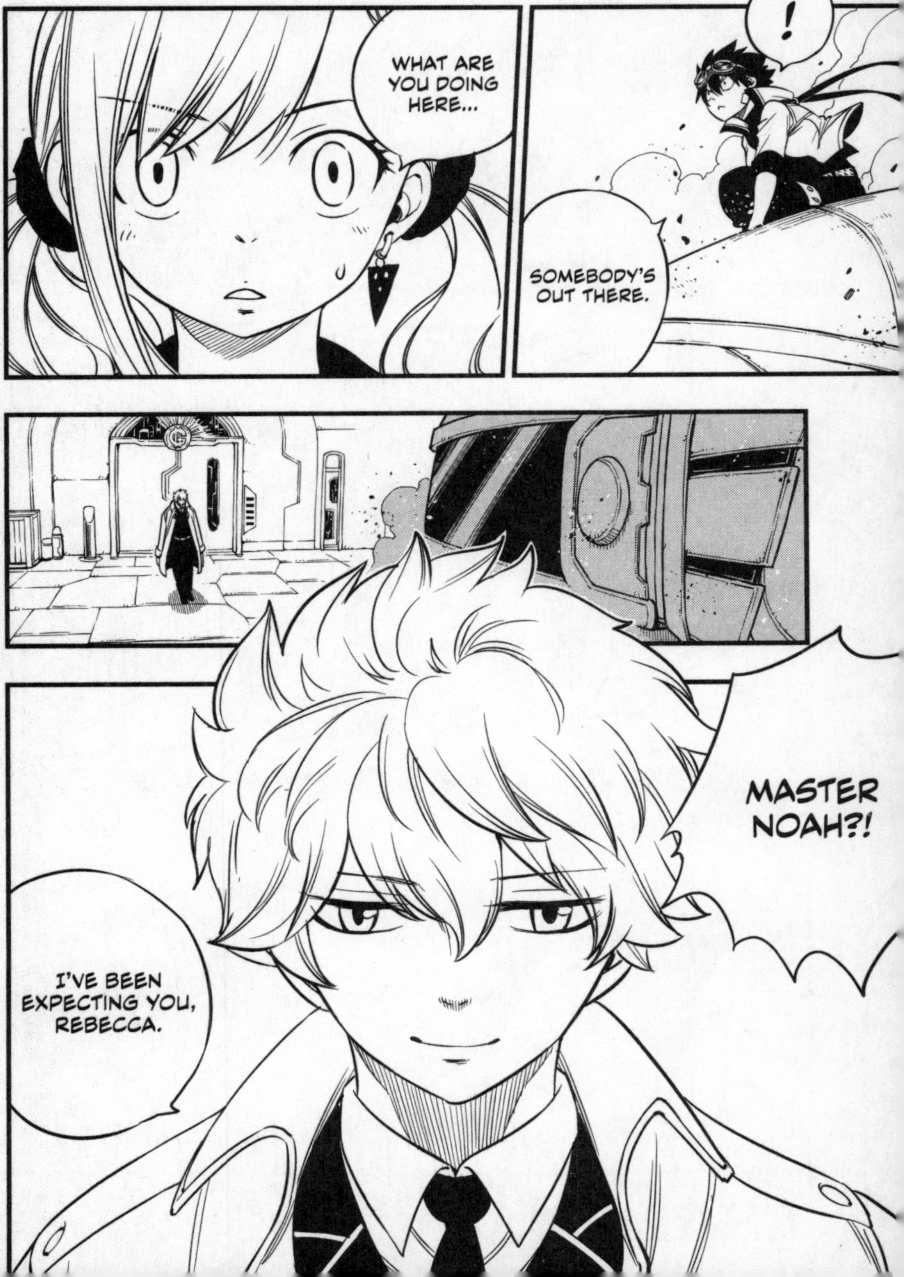
!
SOMEBODY'S OUT THERE.
WHAT ARE YOU DOING HERE...
MASTER NOAH?!
I'VE BEEN EXPECTING YOU, REBECCA.

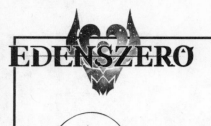

EDENS ZERO

Edens Zero
In-Depth Character File 2

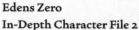

PINO'S ANALYSIS

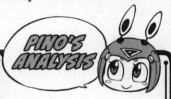

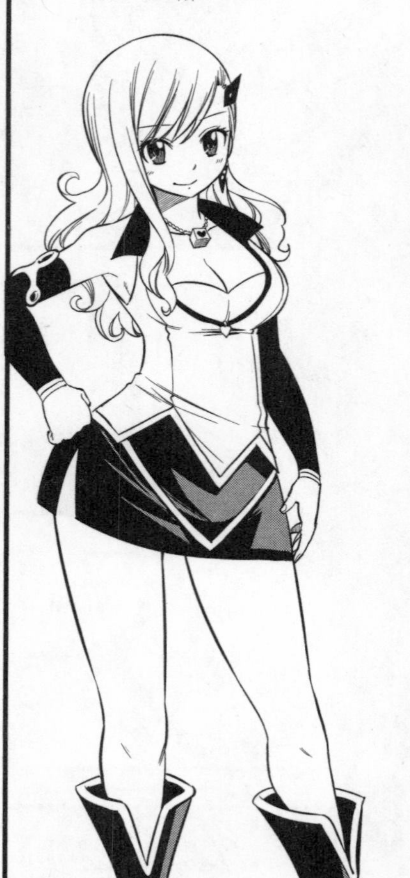

Name: Rebecca Bluegarden

Powers: Ether Gear (Cat Leaper)

Likes: Happy, cats, food

Dislikes: Labilia

Attack:	☆☆
Defense:	☆
Marksmanship:	☆☆☆☆☆
Ether Power:	☆☆☆☆
Intelligence:	☆☆☆
Leg Sexiness:	☆☆☆☆☆

Memo

She is a B-Cuber who uploads videos, but apparently her videos are not very popular. She has honed her kinetic eyesight through video games, so she has tremendous skill as a markswoman. She used her Cat Leaper power to come back in time from a bleak and desolate future.

CHAPTER 88: EYE OF GOD

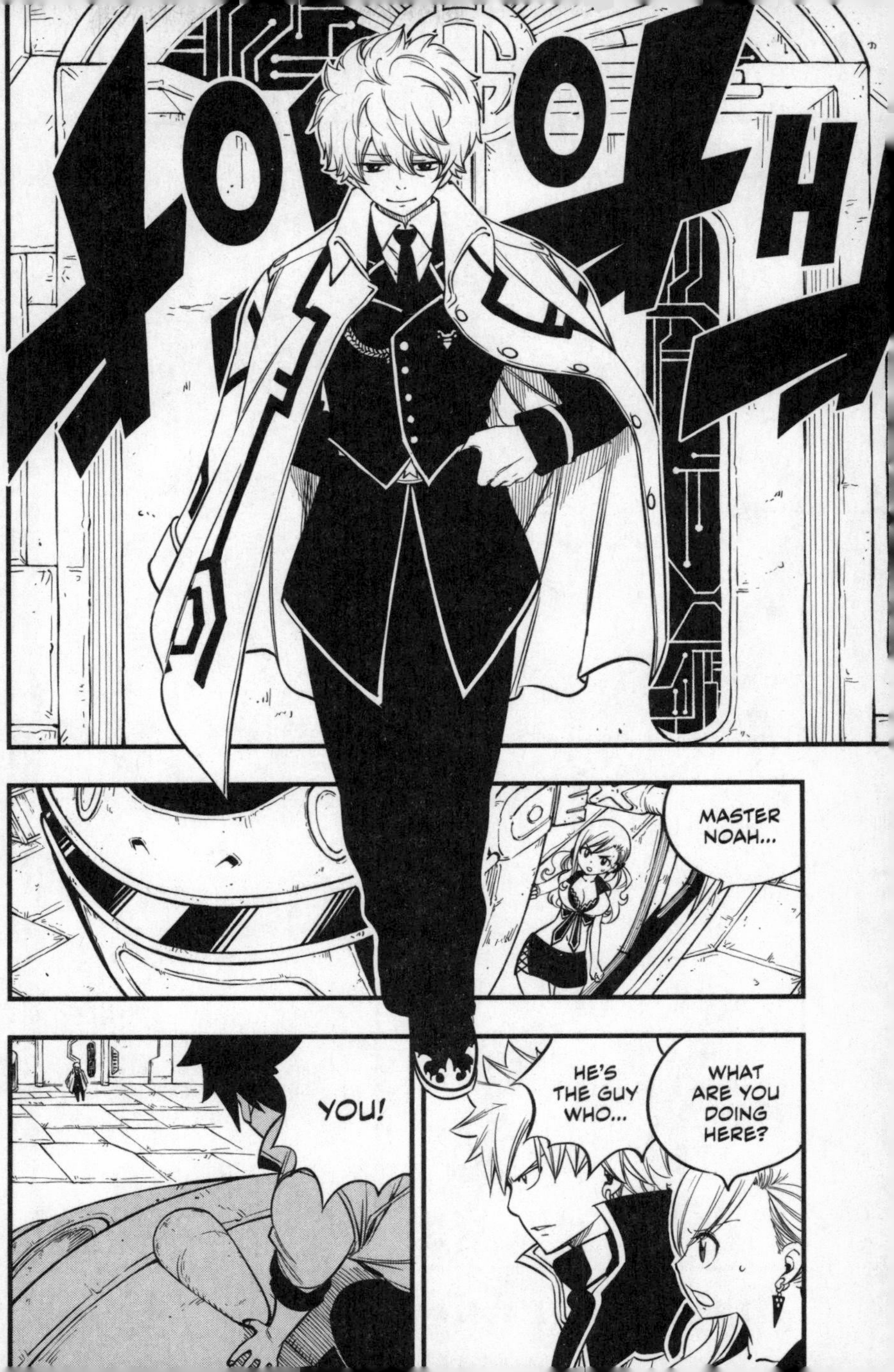
MASTER NOAH...
WHAT ARE YOU DOING HERE?
HE'S THE GUY WHO...
YOU!

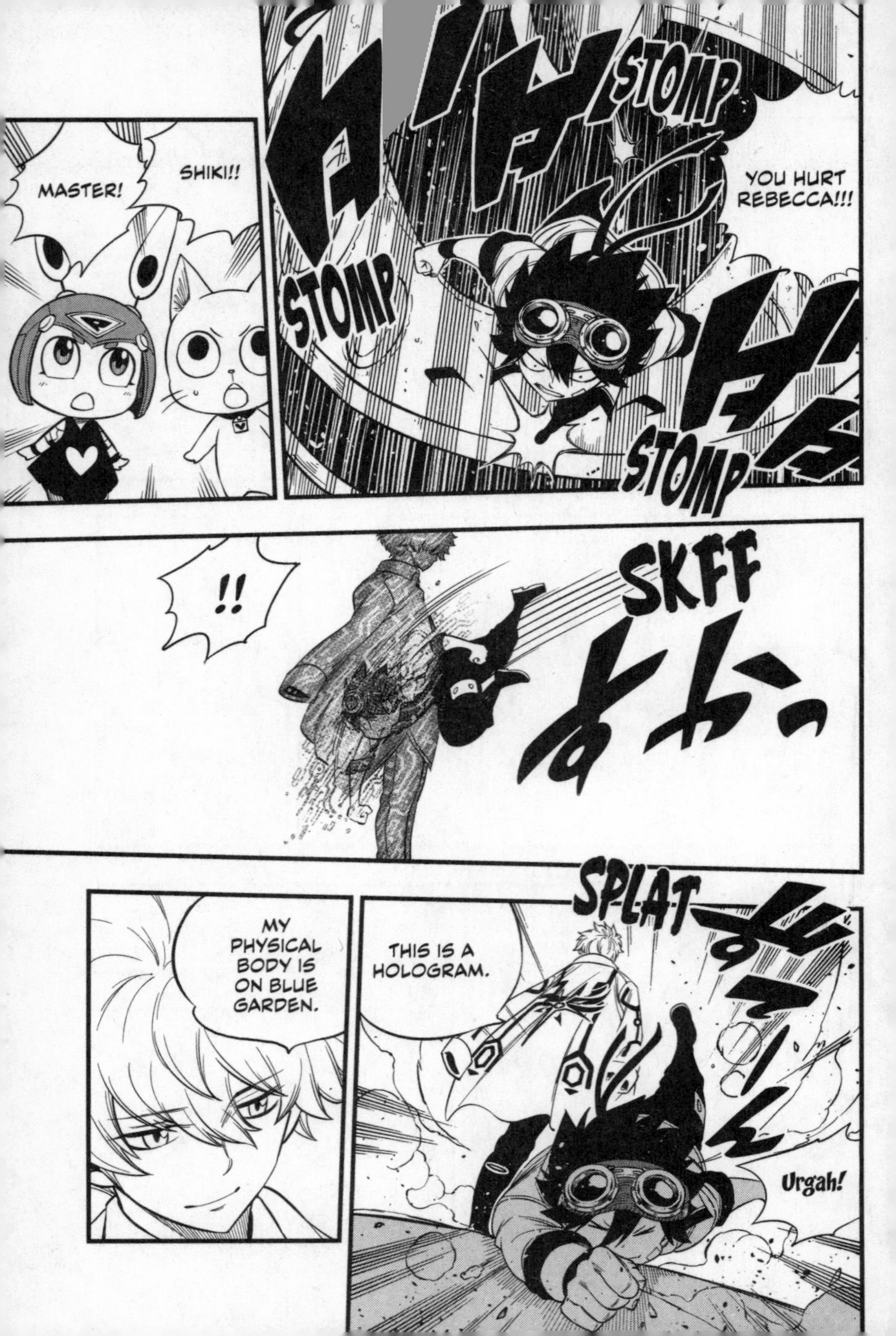
STOMP
YOU HURT REBECCA!!!
STOMP
STOMP
SHIKI!!
MASTER!
SKFF
!!
SPLAT
THIS IS A HOLOGRAM.
Urgah!
MY PHYSICAL BODY IS ON BLUE GARDEN.

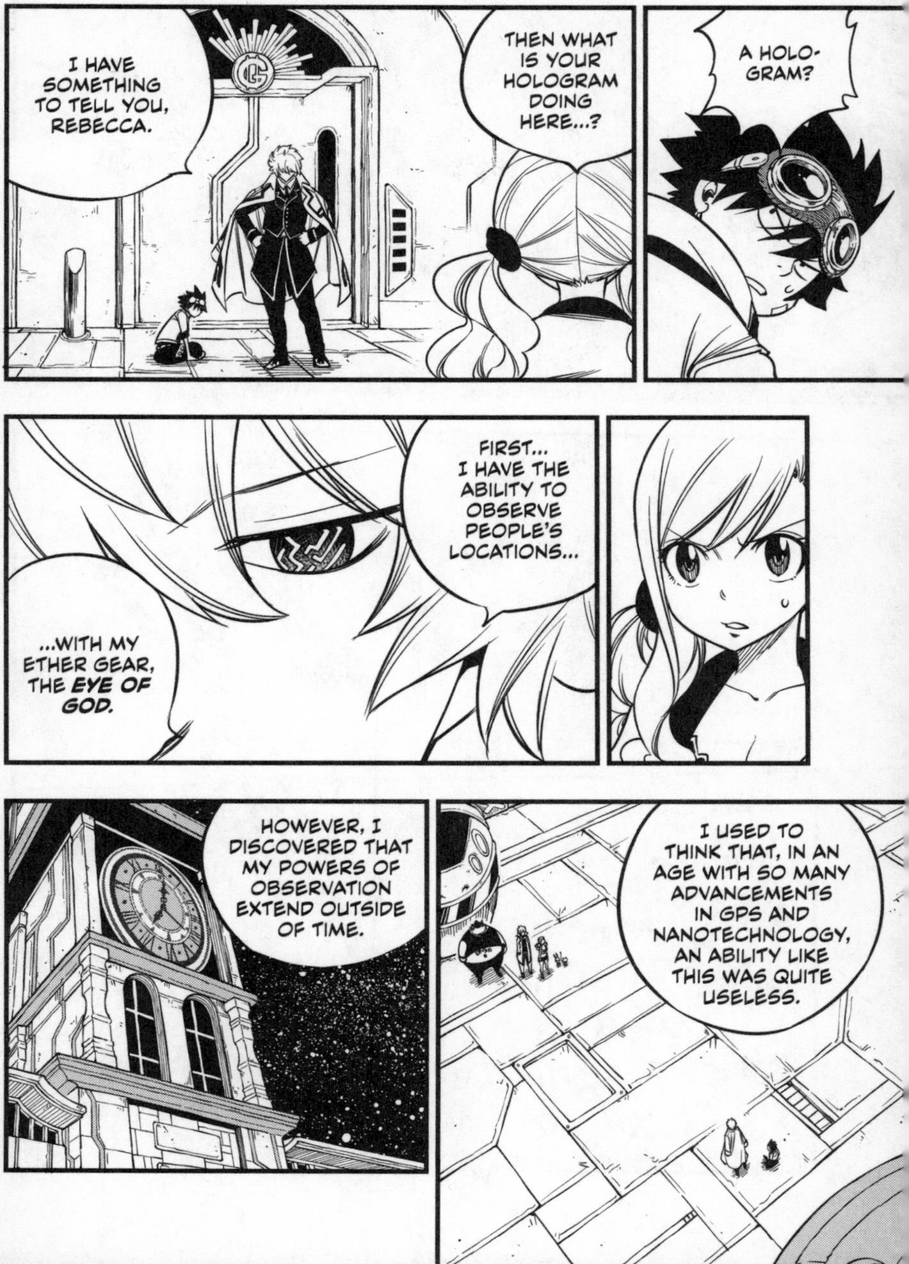
A HOLO-GRAM?
THEN WHAT IS YOUR HOLOGRAM DOING HERE...?
I HAVE SOMETHING TO TELL YOU, REBECCA.
FIRST... I HAVE THE ABILITY TO OBSERVE PEOPLE'S LOCATIONS...
...WITH MY ETHER GEAR, THE *EYE OF GOD.*
I USED TO THINK THAT, IN AN AGE WITH SO MANY ADVANCEMENTS IN GPS AND NANOTECHNOLOGY, AN ABILITY LIKE THIS WAS QUITE USELESS.
HOWEVER, I DISCOVERED THAT MY POWERS OF OBSERVATION EXTEND OUTSIDE OF TIME.

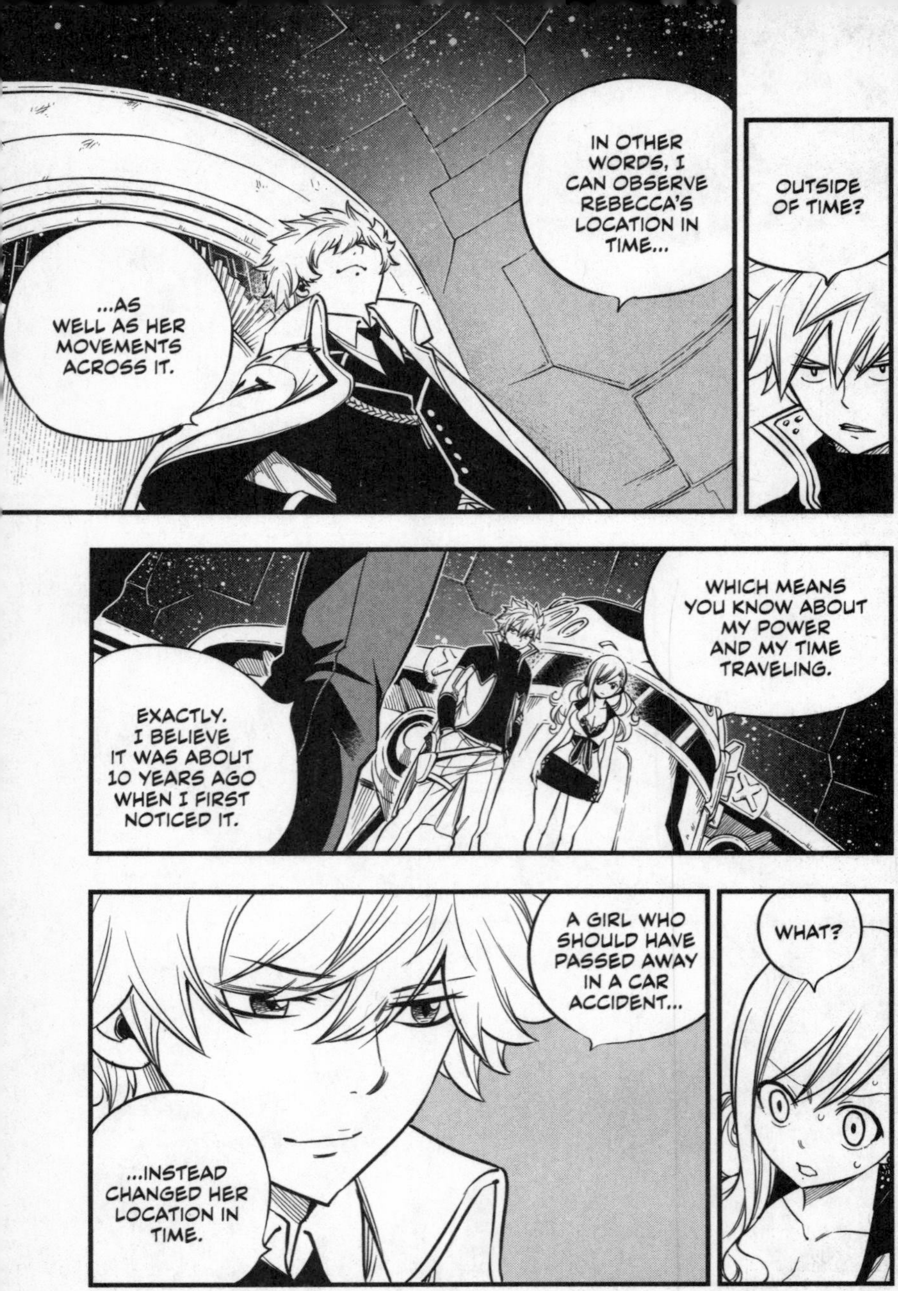
OUTSIDE OF TIME?
IN OTHER WORDS, I CAN OBSERVE REBECCA'S LOCATION IN TIME...
...AS WELL AS HER MOVEMENTS ACROSS IT.
WHICH MEANS YOU KNOW ABOUT MY POWER AND MY TIME TRAVELING.
EXACTLY. I BELIEVE IT WAS ABOUT 10 YEARS AGO WHEN I FIRST NOTICED IT.
WHAT?
A GIRL WHO SHOULD HAVE PASSED AWAY IN A CAR ACCIDENT...
...INSTEAD CHANGED HER LOCATION IN TIME.

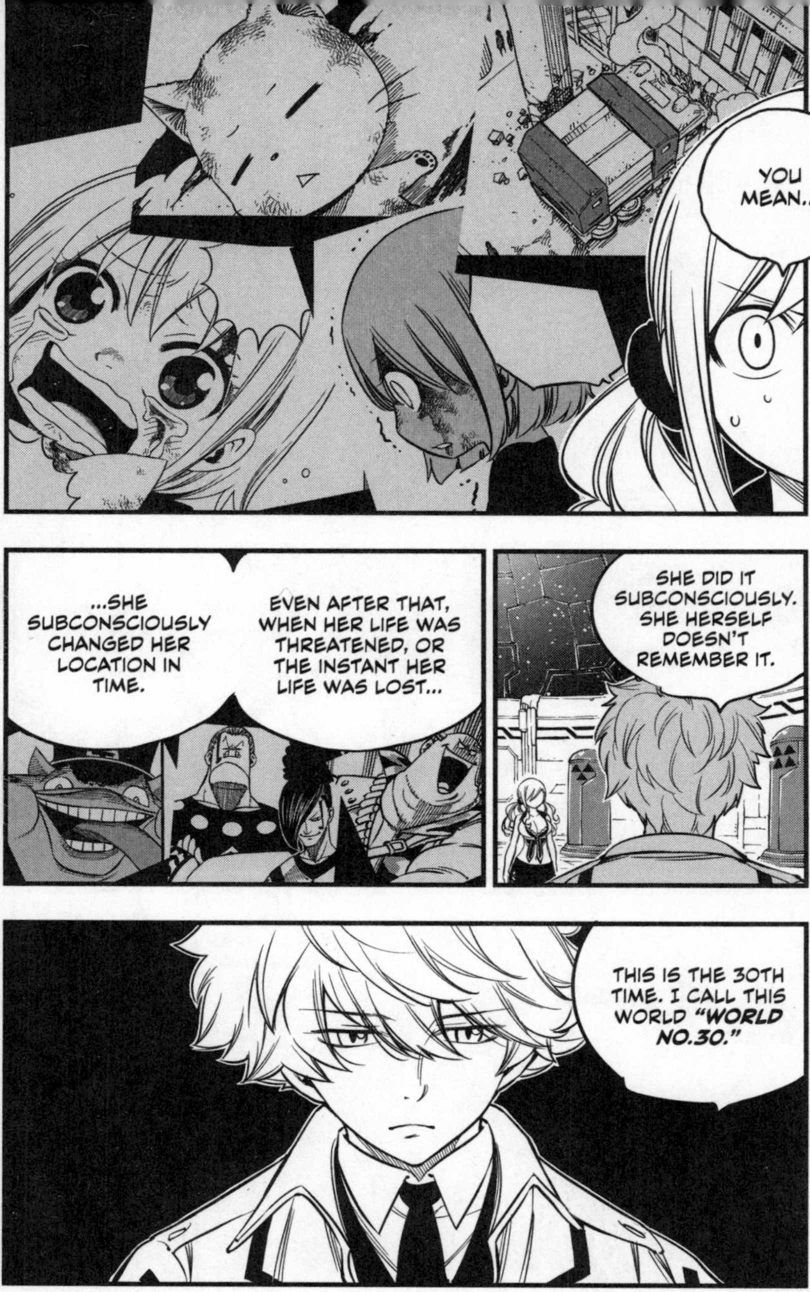
YOU MEAN...
SHE DID IT SUBCONSCIOUSLY. SHE HERSELF DOESN'T REMEMBER IT.
EVEN AFTER THAT, WHEN HER LIFE WAS THREATENED, OR THE INSTANT HER LIFE WAS LOST...
...SHE SUBCONSCIOUSLY CHANGED HER LOCATION IN TIME.
THIS IS THE 30TH TIME. I CALL THIS WORLD *"WORLD NO.30."*

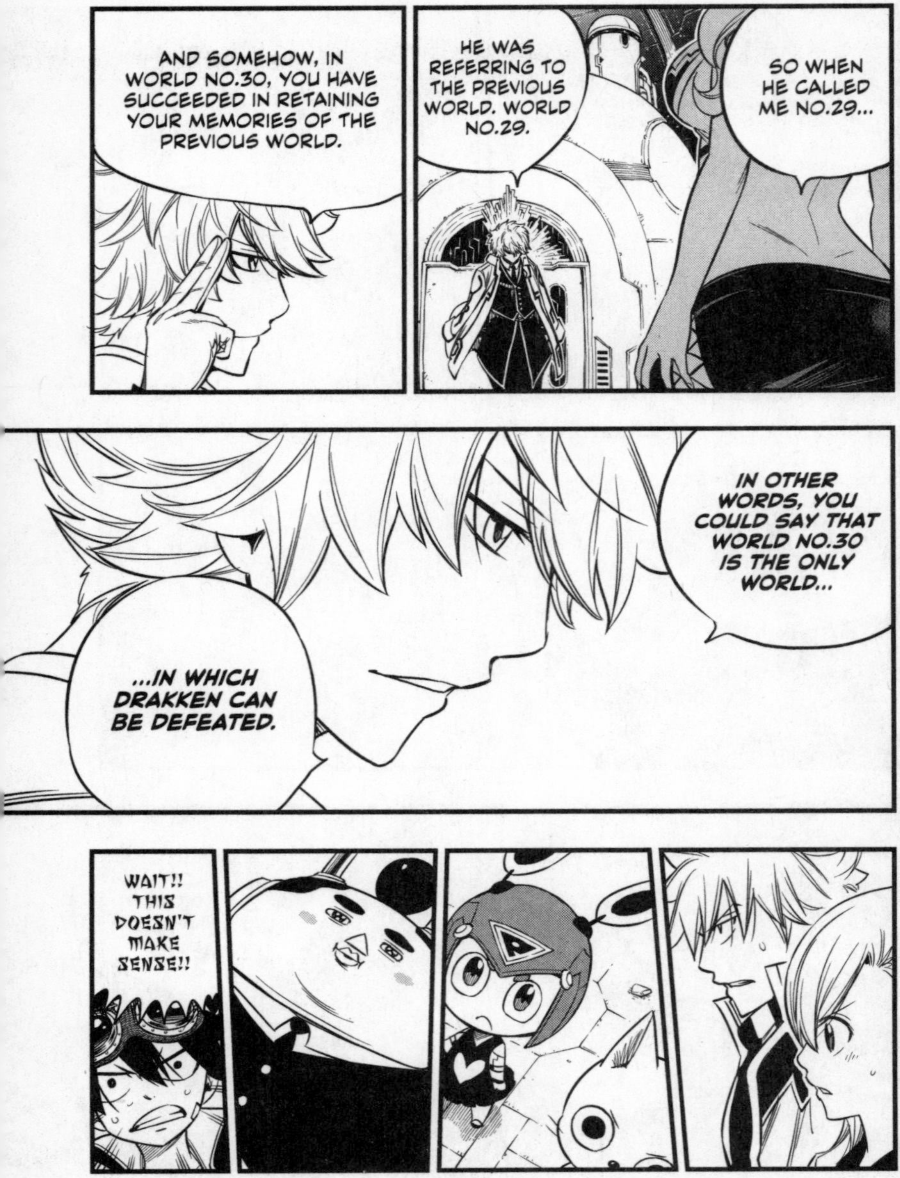
SO WHEN HE CALLED ME NO.29...
HE WAS REFERRING TO THE PREVIOUS WORLD. WORLD NO.29.
AND SOMEHOW, IN WORLD NO.30, YOU HAVE SUCCEEDED IN RETAINING YOUR MEMORIES OF THE PREVIOUS WORLD.
IN OTHER WORDS, YOU COULD SAY THAT WORLD NO.30 IS THE ONLY WORLD...
...IN WHICH DRAKKEN CAN BE DEFEATED.
WAIT!! THIS DOESN'T MAKE SENSE!!

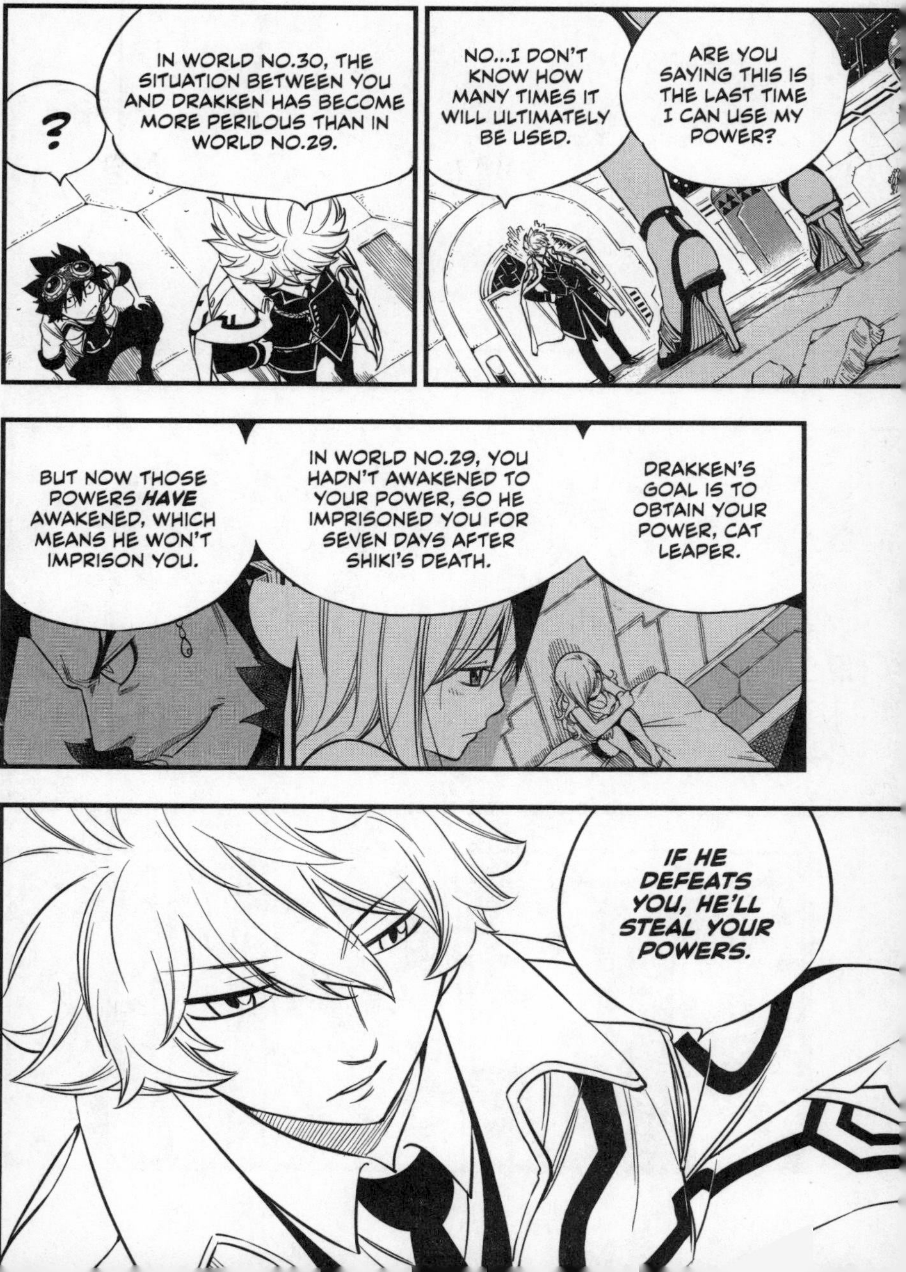
ARE YOU SAYING THIS IS THE LAST TIME I CAN USE MY POWER?
NO...I DON'T KNOW HOW MANY TIMES IT WILL ULTIMATELY BE USED.
IN WORLD NO.30, THE SITUATION BETWEEN YOU AND DRAKKEN HAS BECOME MORE PERILOUS THAN IN WORLD NO.29.
?
DRAKKEN'S GOAL IS TO OBTAIN YOUR POWER, CAT LEAPER.
IN WORLD NO.29, YOU HADN'T AWAKENED TO YOUR POWER, SO HE IMPRISONED YOU FOR SEVEN DAYS AFTER SHIKI'S DEATH.
BUT NOW THOSE POWERS *HAVE* AWAKENED, WHICH MEANS HE WON'T IMPRISON YOU.
IF HE DEFEATS YOU, HE'LL STEAL YOUR POWERS.

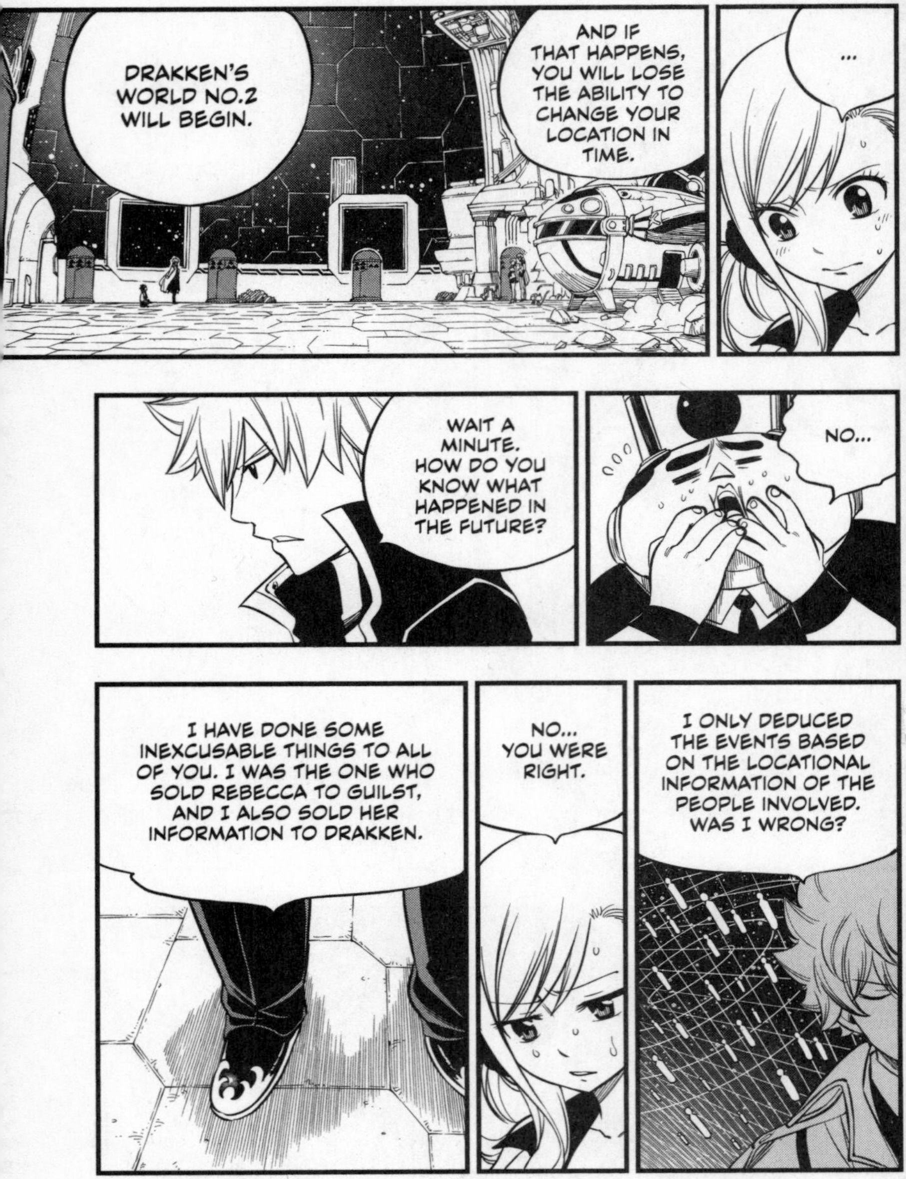

...
DRAKKEN'S WORLD NO.2 WILL BEGIN.
AND IF THAT HAPPENS, YOU WILL LOSE THE ABILITY TO CHANGE YOUR LOCATION IN TIME.
NO...
WAIT A MINUTE. HOW DO YOU KNOW WHAT HAPPENED IN THE FUTURE?
I ONLY DEDUCED THE EVENTS BASED ON THE LOCATIONAL INFORMATION OF THE PEOPLE INVOLVED. WAS I WRONG?
NO... YOU WERE RIGHT.
I HAVE DONE SOME INEXCUSABLE THINGS TO ALL OF YOU. I WAS THE ONE WHO SOLD REBECCA TO GUILST, AND I ALSO SOLD HER INFORMATION TO DRAKKEN.

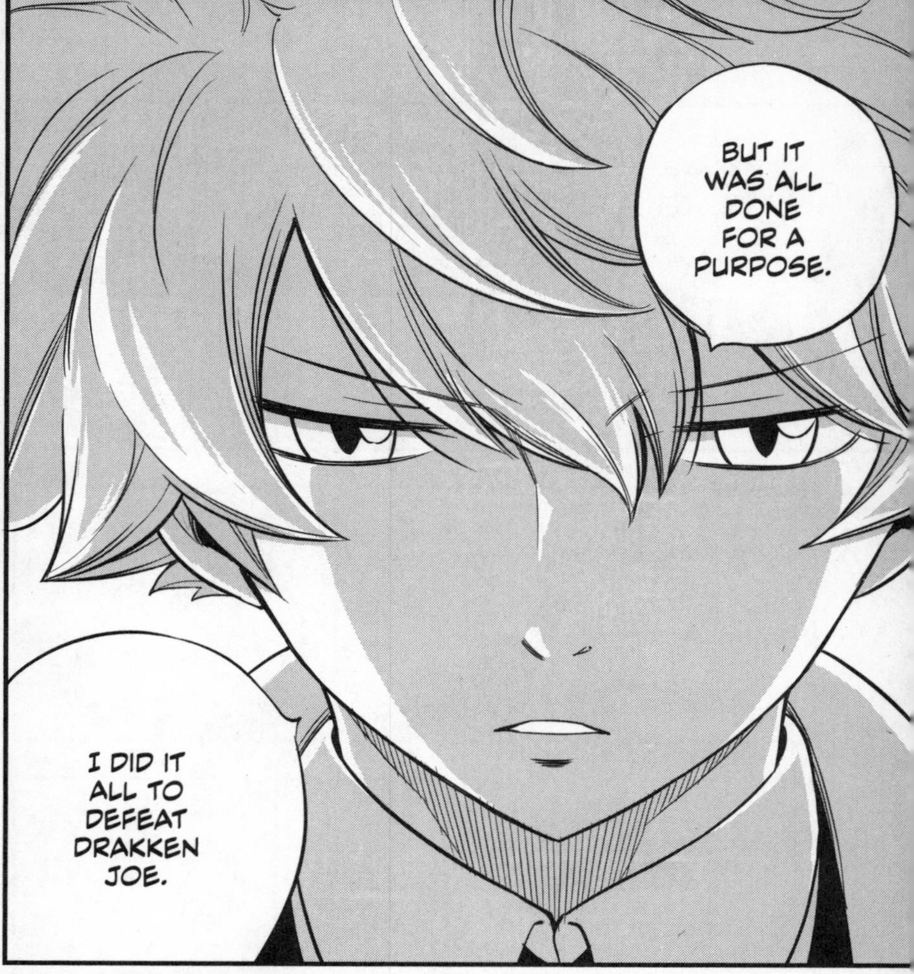
BUT IT WAS ALL DONE FOR A PURPOSE.
I DID IT ALL TO DEFEAT DRAKKEN JOE.

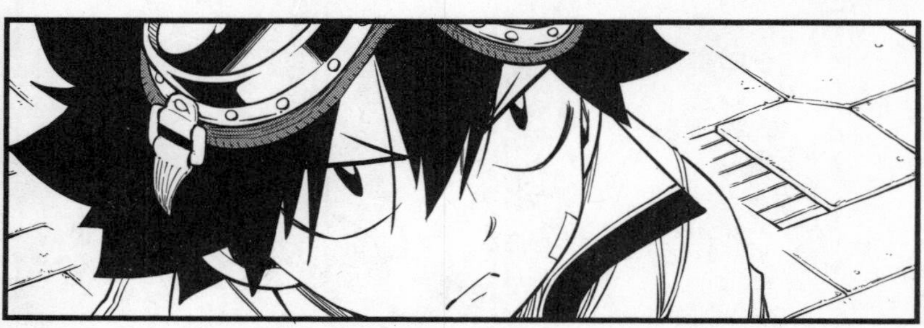

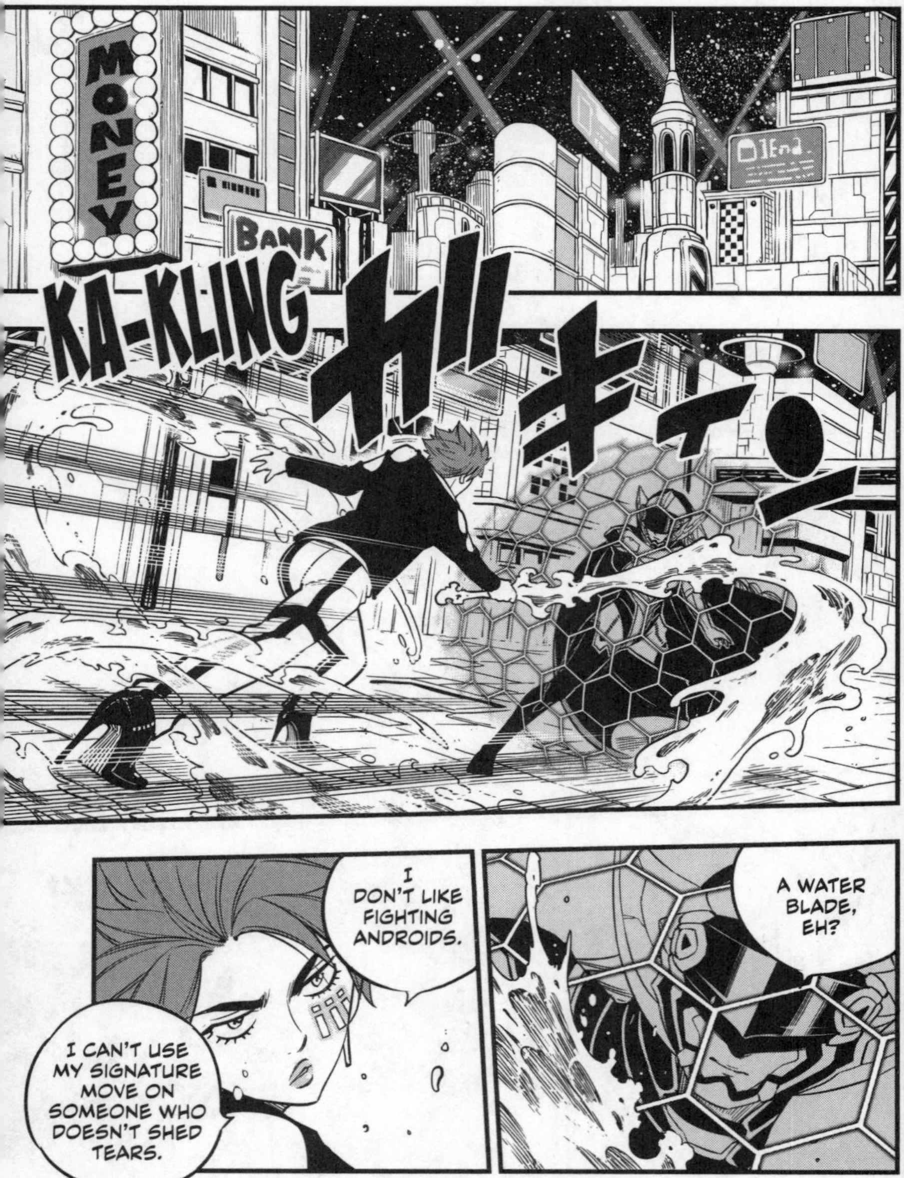
MONEY
BANK
KA-KLING
A WATER BLADE, EH?
I DON'T LIKE FIGHTING ANDROIDS.
I CAN'T USE MY SIGNATURE MOVE ON SOMEONE WHO DOESN'T SHED TEARS.

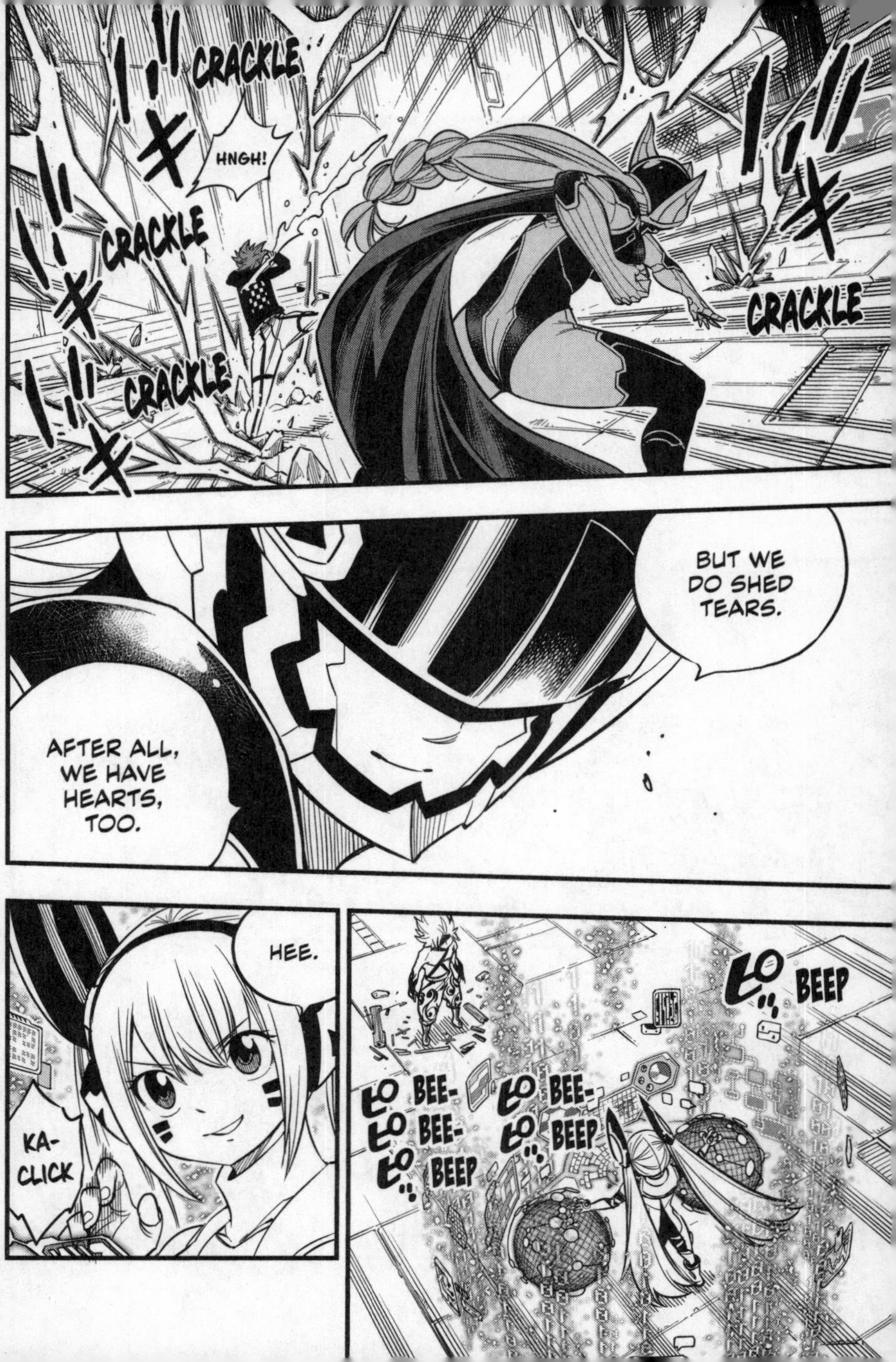

CRACKLE
CRACKLE
HNGH!
CRACKLE
CRACKLE
BUT WE DO SHED TEARS.
AFTER ALL, WE HAVE HEARTS, TOO.
BEEP
BEE- BEEP
BEE- BEE- BEEP
HEE.
KA-CLICK

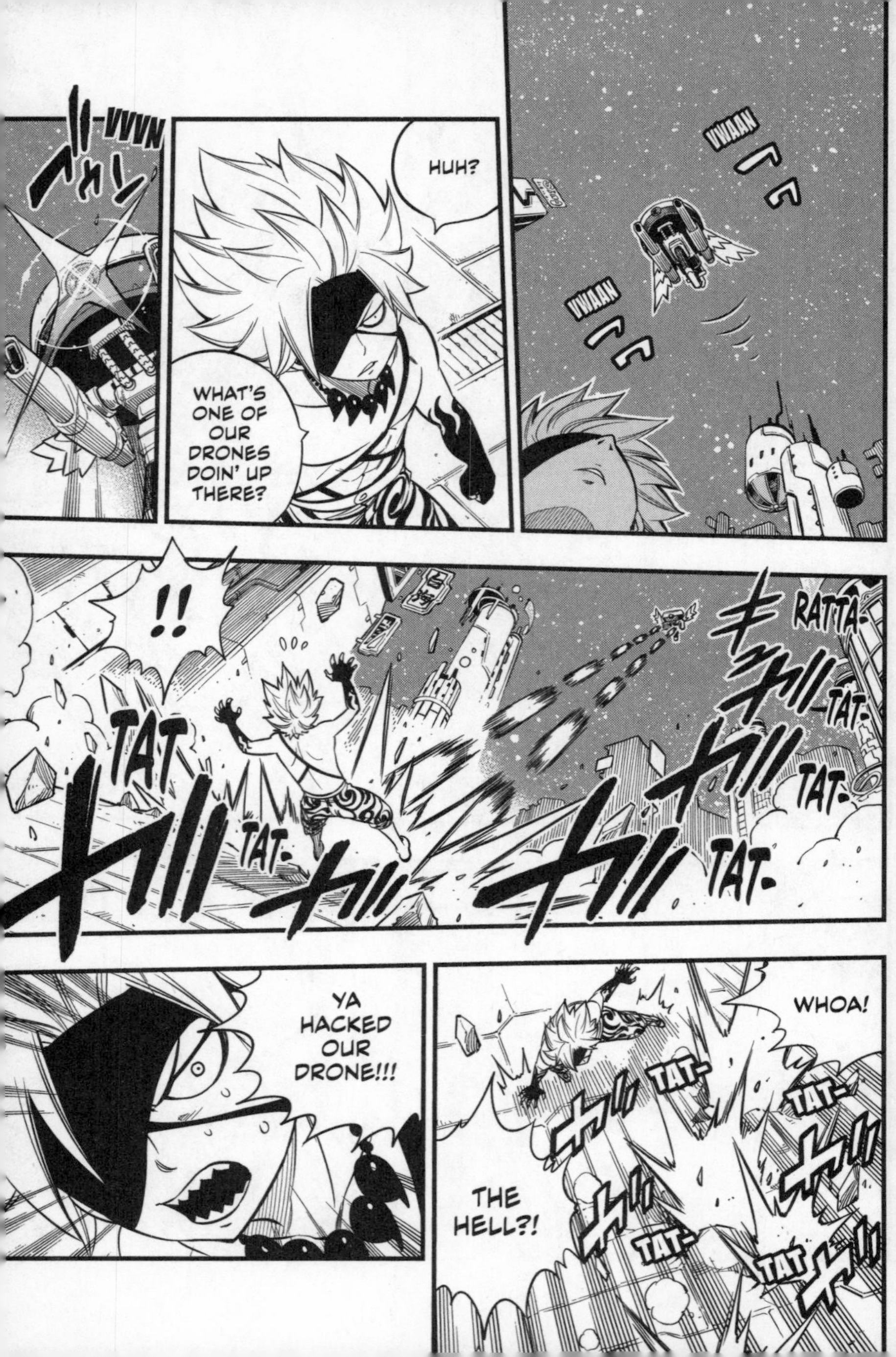
VWAAN
VWAAN
HUH?
WHAT'S ONE OF OUR DRONES DOIN' UP THERE?
VVVN
RATTA-
TAT-
TAT-
!!
TAT
TAT-
TAT-
WHOA!
TAT-
TAT-
THE HELL?!
TAT-
TAT
YA HACKED OUR DRONE!!!

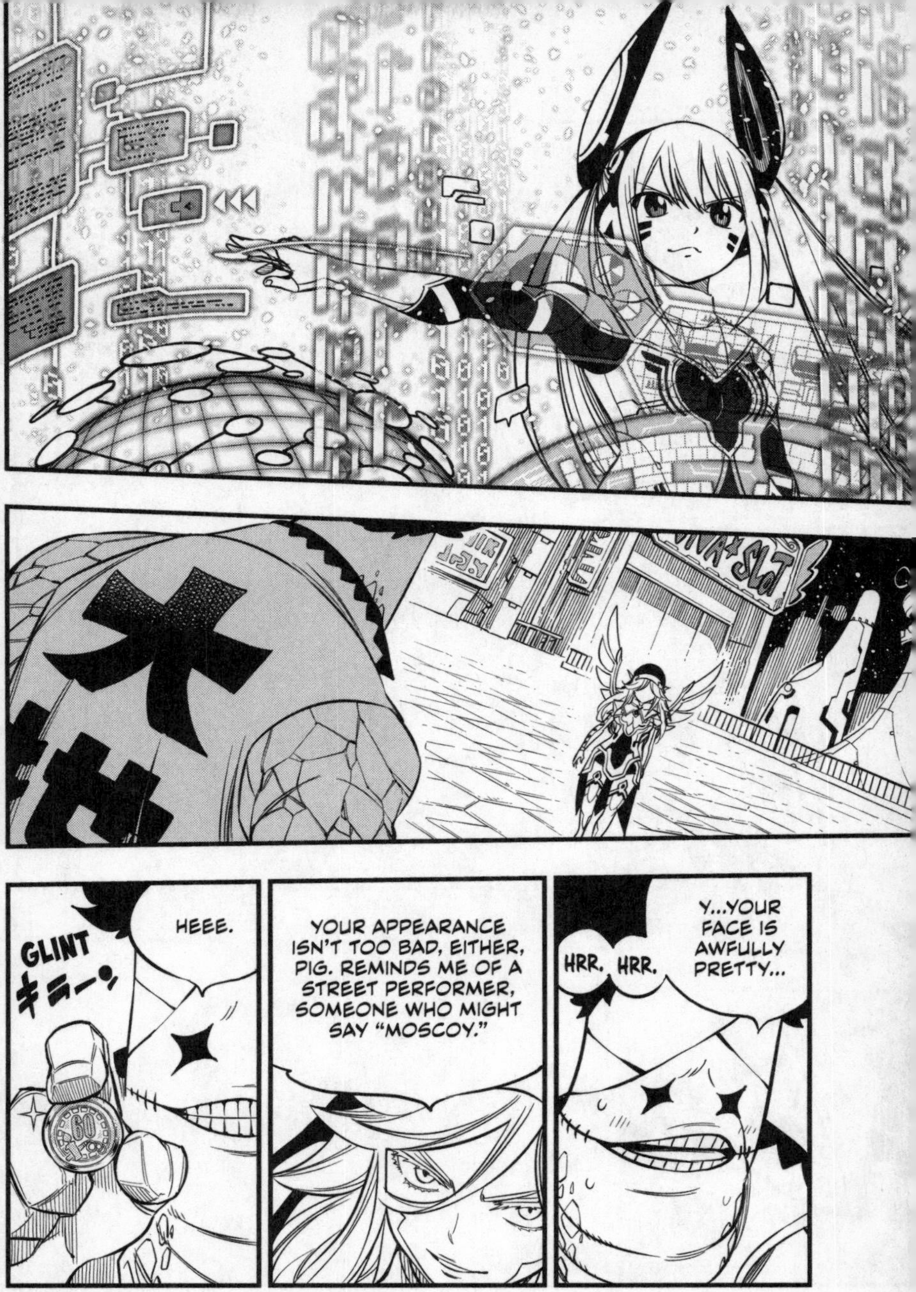
Y...YOUR FACE IS AWFULLY PRETTY...
HRR. HRR.
YOUR APPEARANCE ISN'T TOO BAD, EITHER, PIG. REMINDS ME OF A STREET PERFORMER, SOMEONE WHO MIGHT SAY "MOSCOY."
HEEE.
GLINT
キラー

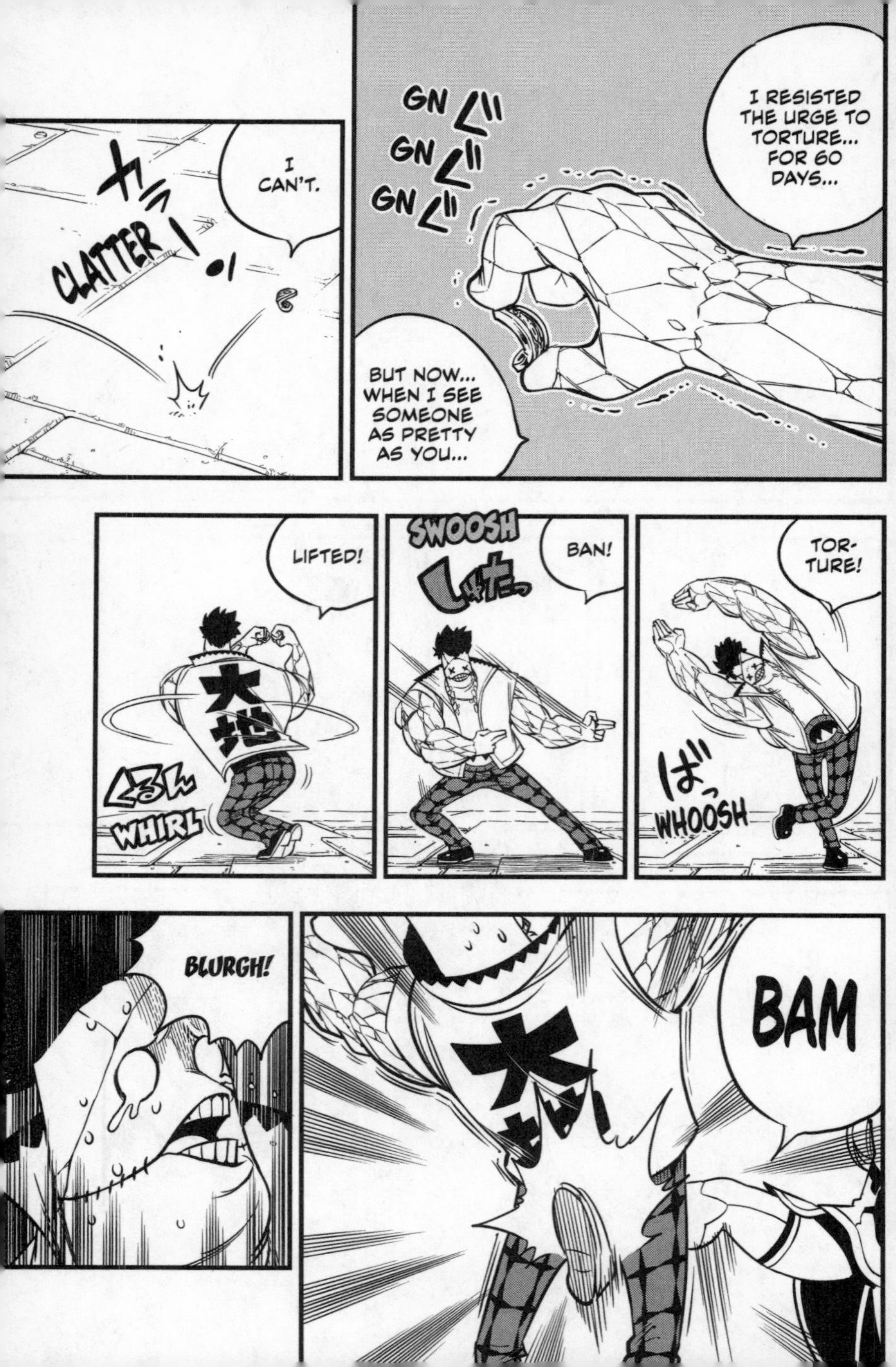
I RESISTED THE URGE TO TORTURE... FOR 60 DAYS...
GN
GN
GN
BUT NOW... WHEN I SEE SOMEONE AS PRETTY AS YOU...
I CAN'T.
CLATTER
TOR-TURE!
ばっ
WHOOSH
SWOOSH
BAN!
LIFTED!
くるん
WHIRL
BAM
BLURGH!

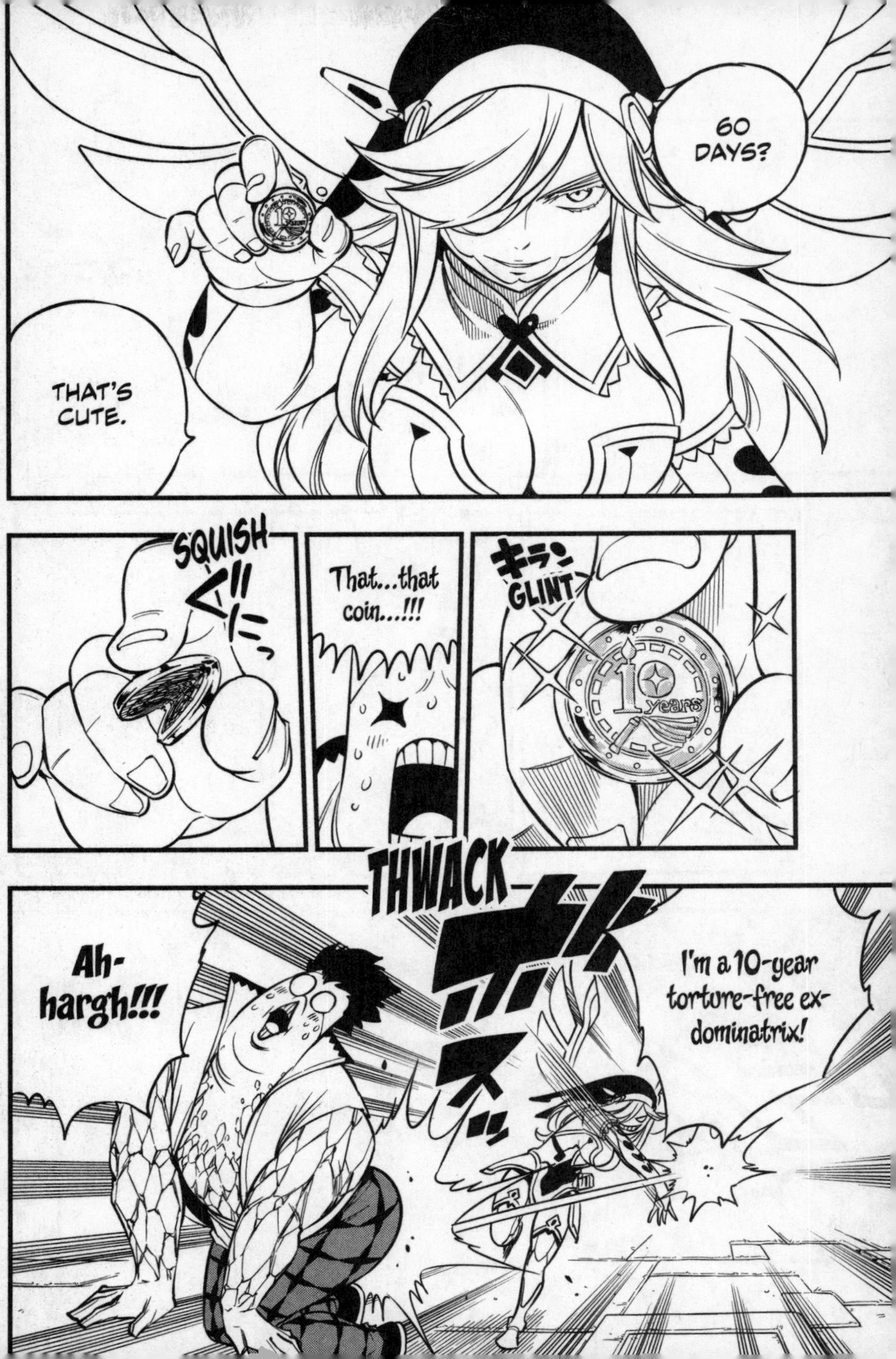
60 DAYS?
THAT'S CUTE.
キラン
GLINT
That...that coin...!!!
SQUISH
I'm a 10-year tortore-free ex-dominatrix!
THWACK
Ah-hargh!!!

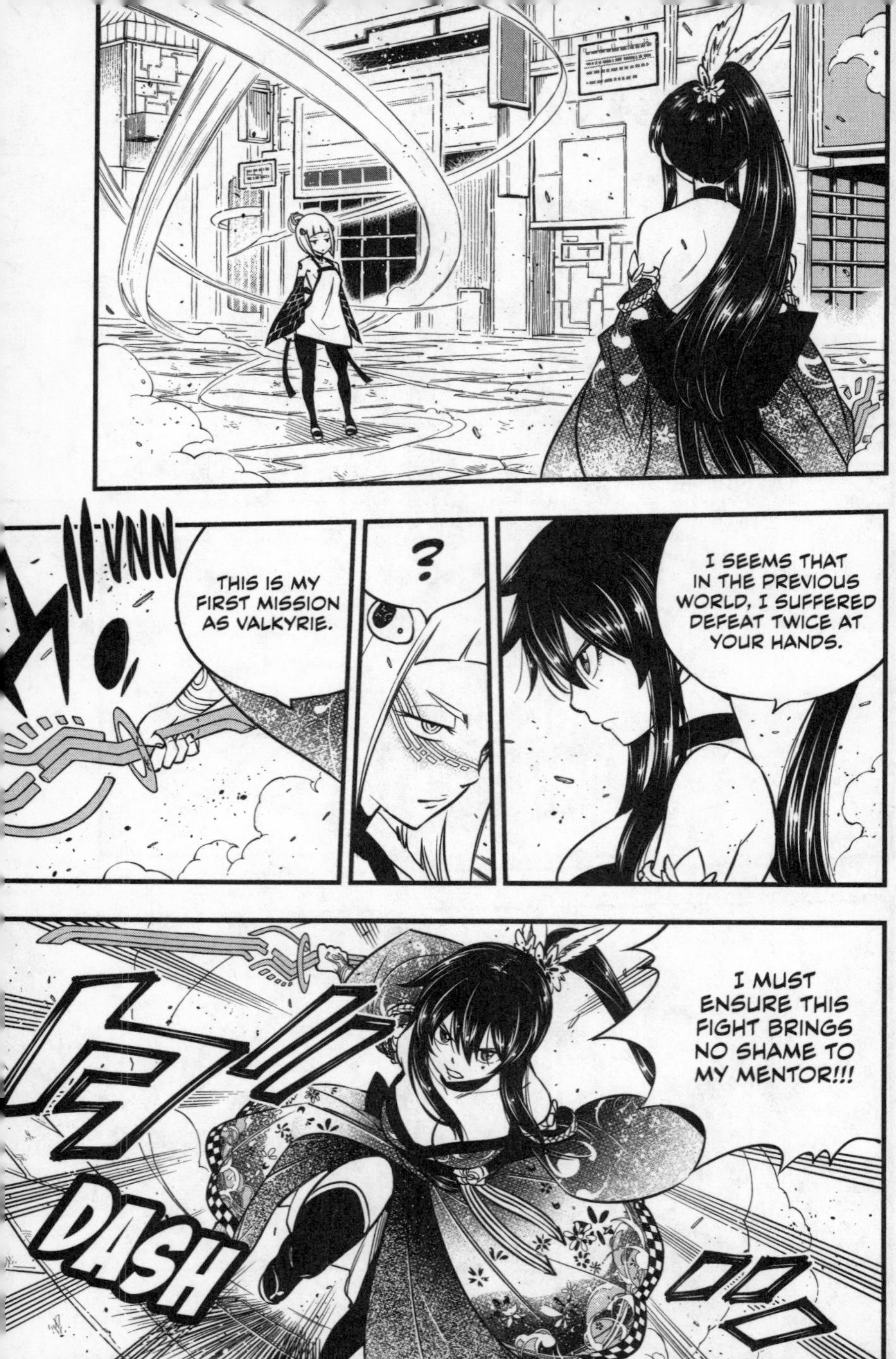
I SEEMS THAT IN THE PREVIOUS WORLD, I SUFFERED DEFEAT TWICE AT YOUR HANDS.
?
VNN
THIS IS MY FIRST MISSION AS VALKYRIE.
I MUST ENSURE THIS FIGHT BRINGS NO SHAME TO MY MENTOR!!!
DASH

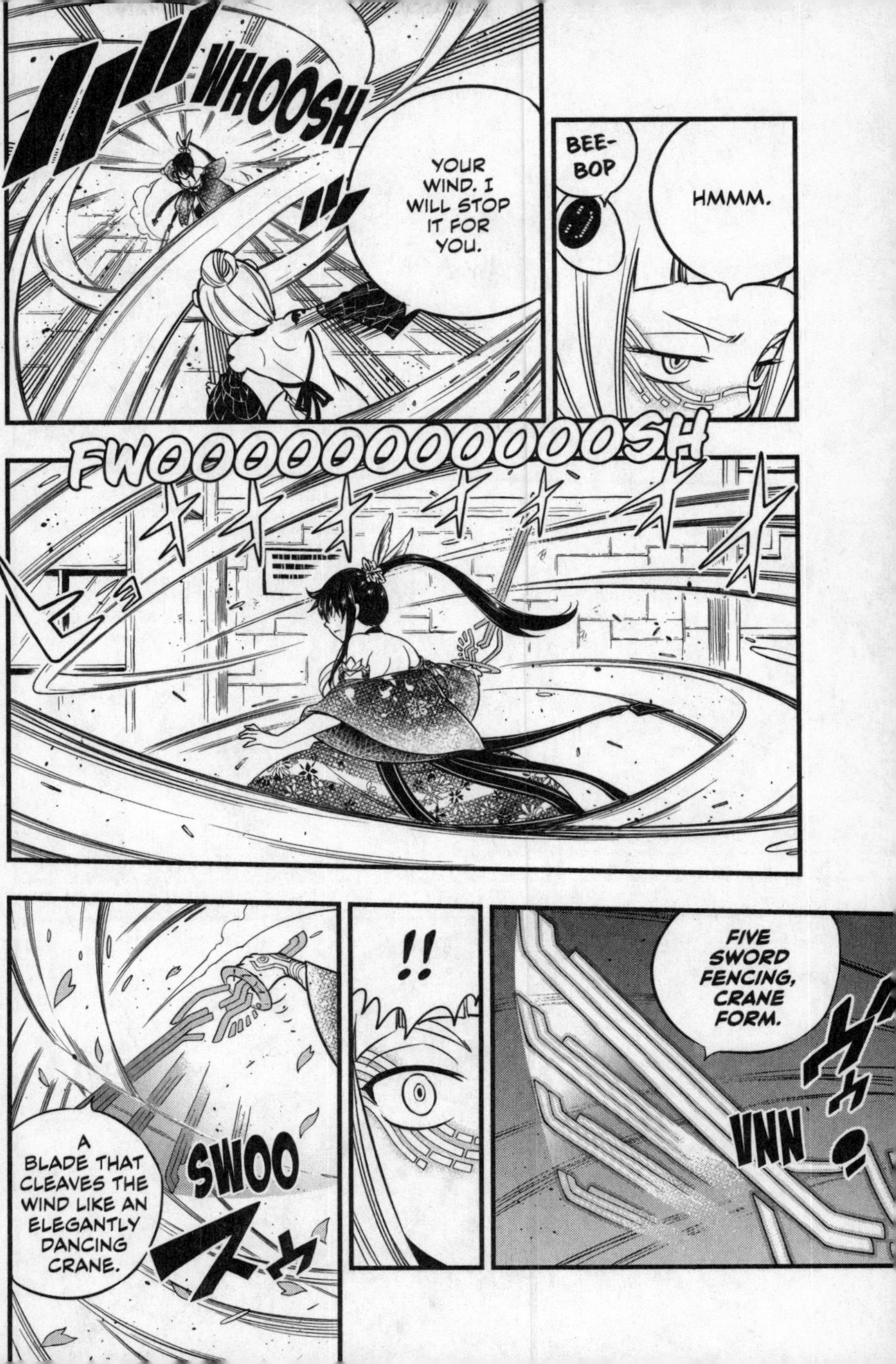
HMMM.
BEE-BOP
YOUR WIND. I WILL STOP IT FOR YOU.
WHOOSH
FWOOOOOOOOOOOSH
FIVE SWORD FENCING, CRANE FORM.
VNN
!!
SWOO
A BLADE THAT CLEAVES THE WIND LIKE AN ELEGANTLY DANCING CRANE.

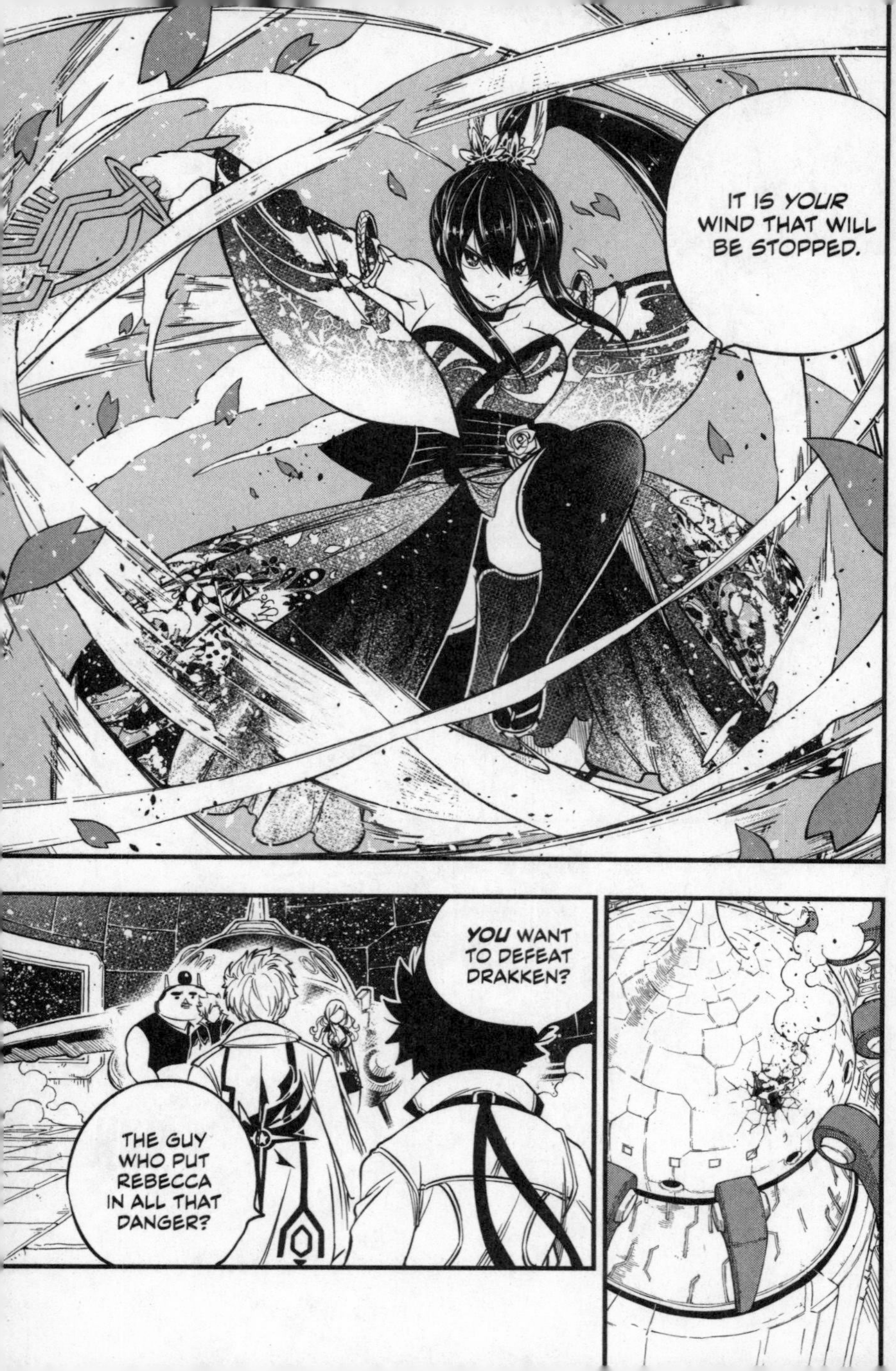
IT IS *YOUR* WIND THAT WILL BE STOPPED.
YOU WANT TO DEFEAT DRAKKEN?
THE GUY WHO PUT REBECCA IN ALL THAT DANGER?

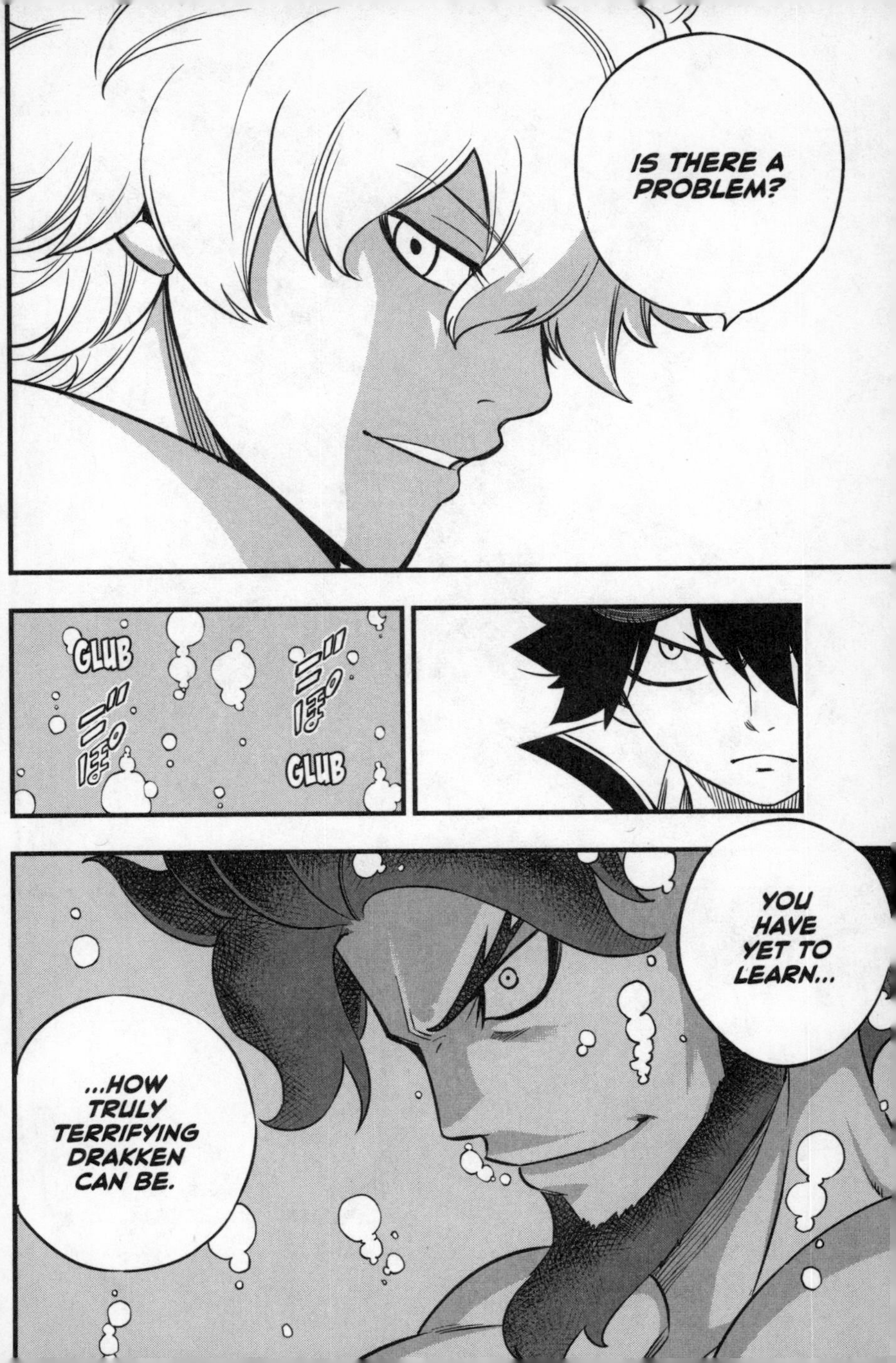
IS THERE A PROBLEM?
GLUB
GLUB
YOU HAVE YET TO LEARN...
...HOW TRULY TERRIFYING DRAKKEN CAN BE.

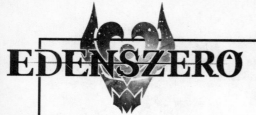

EDENS ZERO

Edens Zero
In-Depth Character File 3

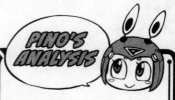

PINO'S ANALYSIS

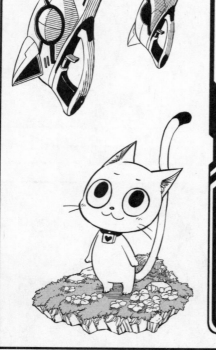

Name: Happy

Powers: Happy Blasters

(transforms into gun mode)

Likes: Rebecca, fish

Dislikes: Dogs

Attack: ☆

Defense: ☆

Marksmanship: ☆☆☆☆☆

Ether Power: ☆☆

Intelligence: ☆☆☆

Mechtitude: ☆☆☆

Memo

A cat from the planet Exceed. He could always speak the human language. When he was very young, he was an in accident and brought back to life as an android with an entirely mechanical body. He is Miss Rebecca's partner and transforms into guns when it is time for battle. He has a cute habit of saying, "Aye."

CHAPTER 89: HERMIT VS. FIE

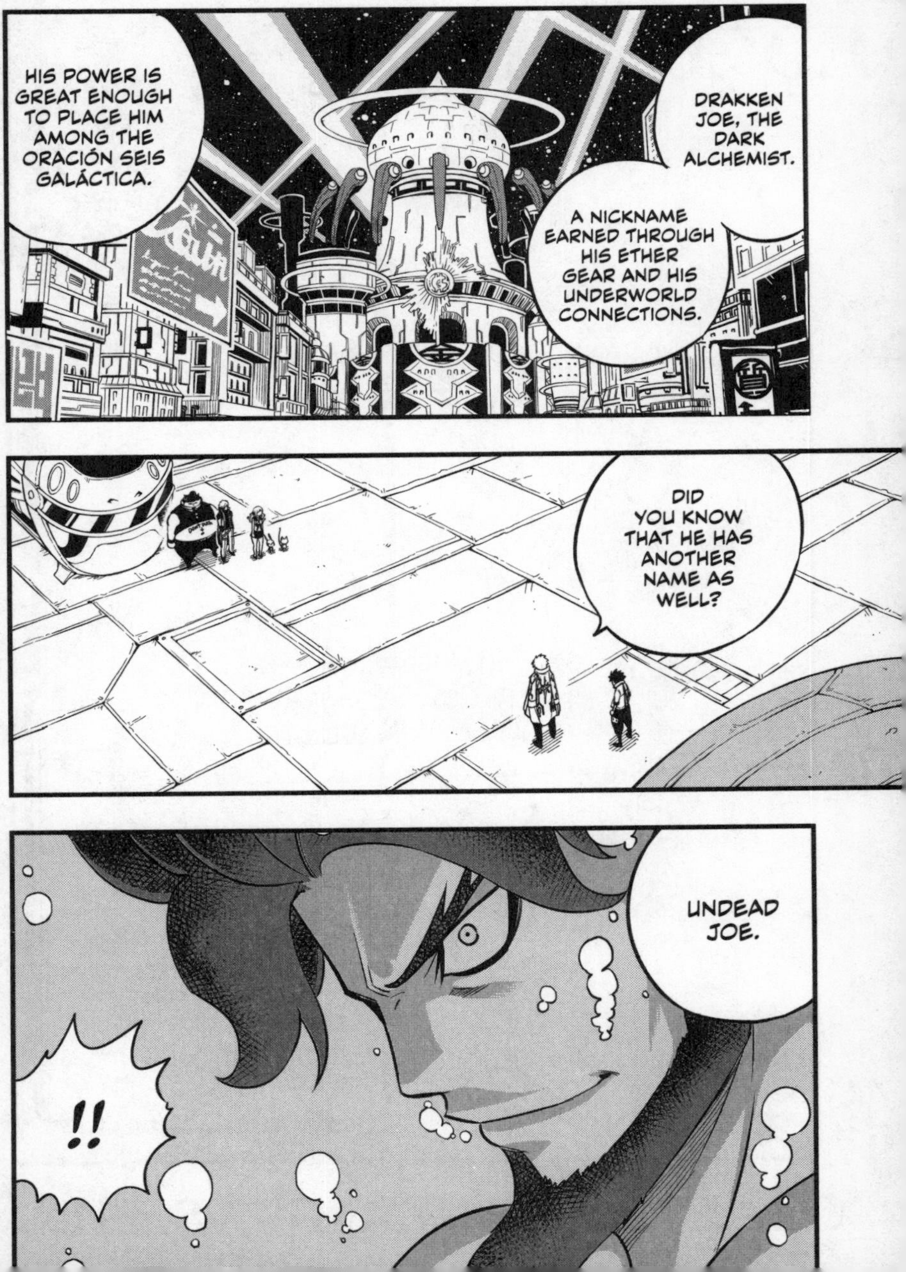
DRAKKEN JOE, THE DARK ALCHEMIST.
A NICKNAME EARNED THROUGH HIS ETHER GEAR AND HIS UNDERWORLD CONNECTIONS.
HIS POWER IS GREAT ENOUGH TO PLACE HIM AMONG THE ORACIÓN SEIS GALÁCTICA.
DID YOU KNOW THAT HE HAS ANOTHER NAME AS WELL?
UNDEAD JOE.
!!

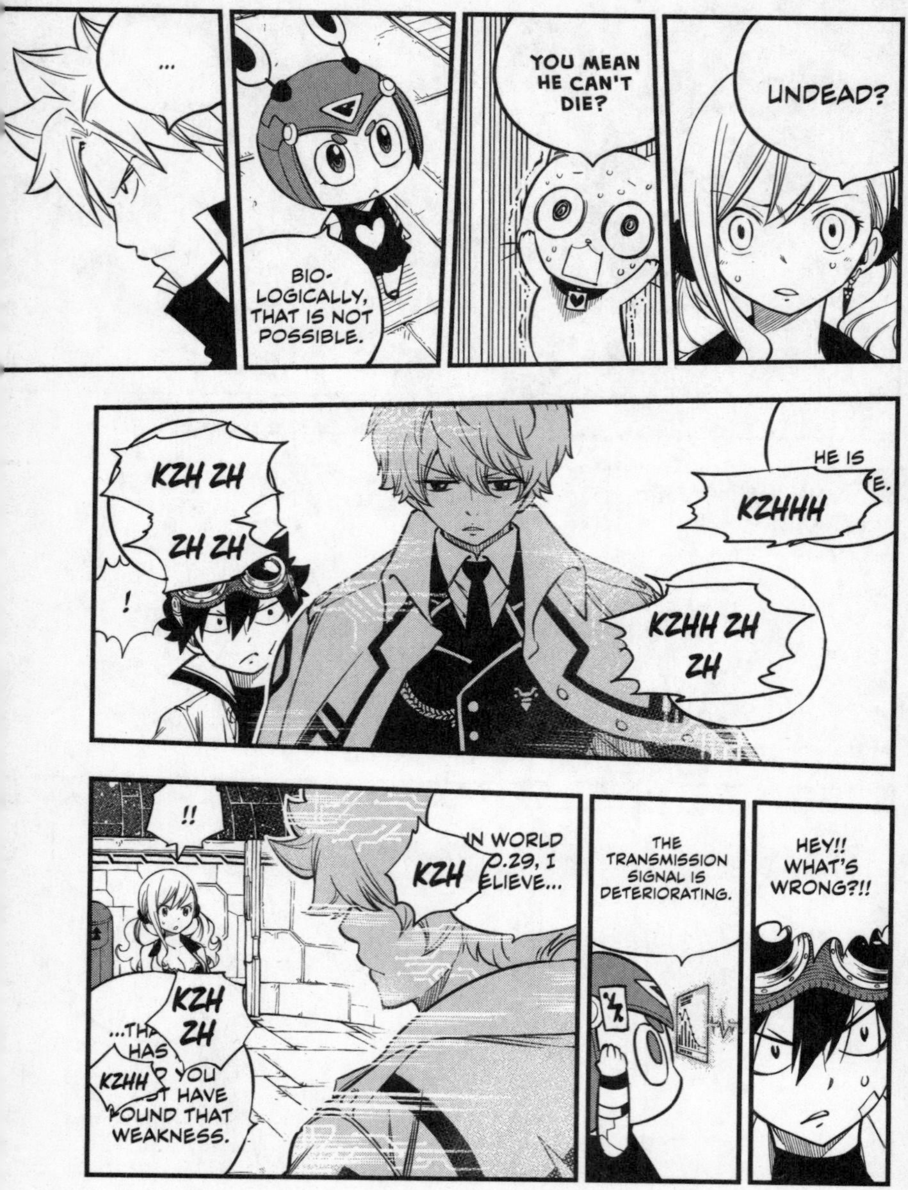
UNDEAD?
YOU MEAN HE CAN'T DIE?
BIO-LOGICALLY, THAT IS NOT POSSIBLE.
...
HE IS
E.
KZHHH
KZHH ZH ZH
KZH ZH ZH ZH
!
HEY!! WHAT'S WRONG?!!
THE TRANSMISSION SIGNAL IS DETERIORATING.
!!
IN WORLD .29, I ELIEVE...
KZH
KZH ZH
...THA HAS YOU ST HAVE OUND THAT WEAKNESS.
KZHH

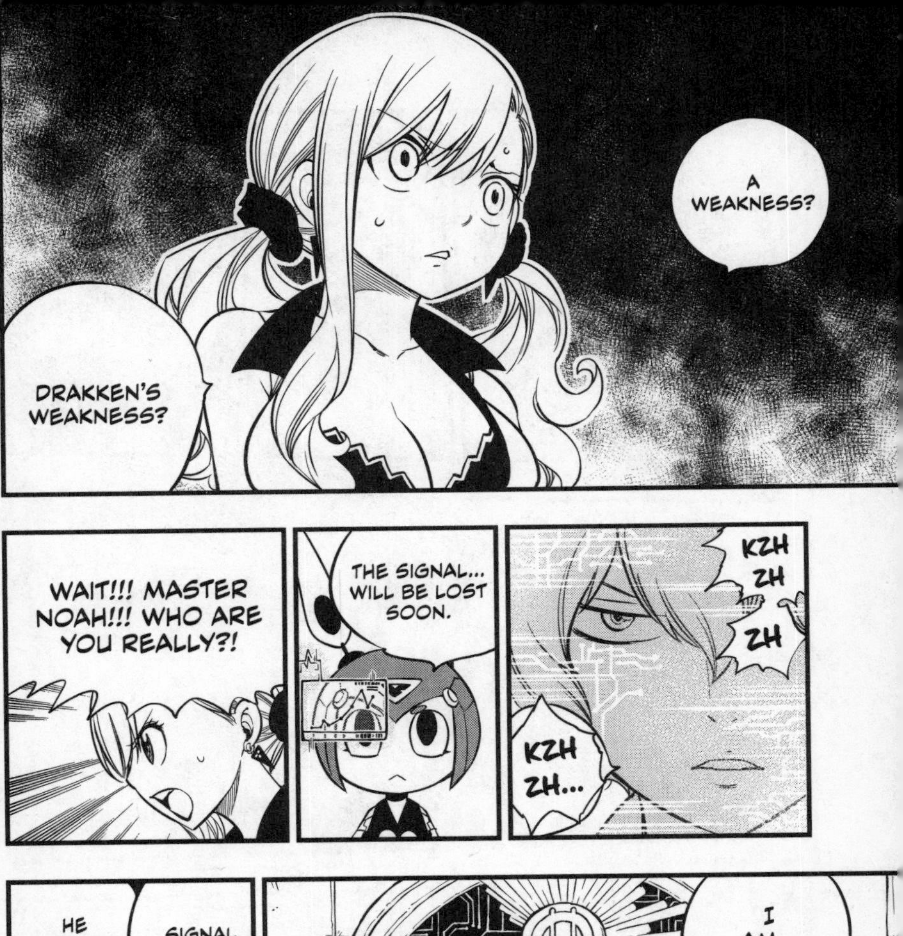
A WEAKNESS?
DRAKKEN'S WEAKNESS?
KZH ZH ZH
KZH ZH...
THE SIGNAL... WILL BE LOST SOON.
WAIT!!! MASTER NOAH!!! WHO ARE YOU REALLY?!
I AM...
PTSS
SIGNAL LOST.
HE DISAP-PEARED.

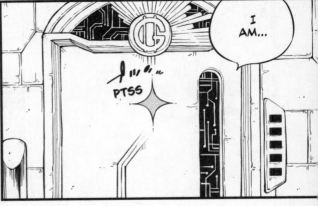

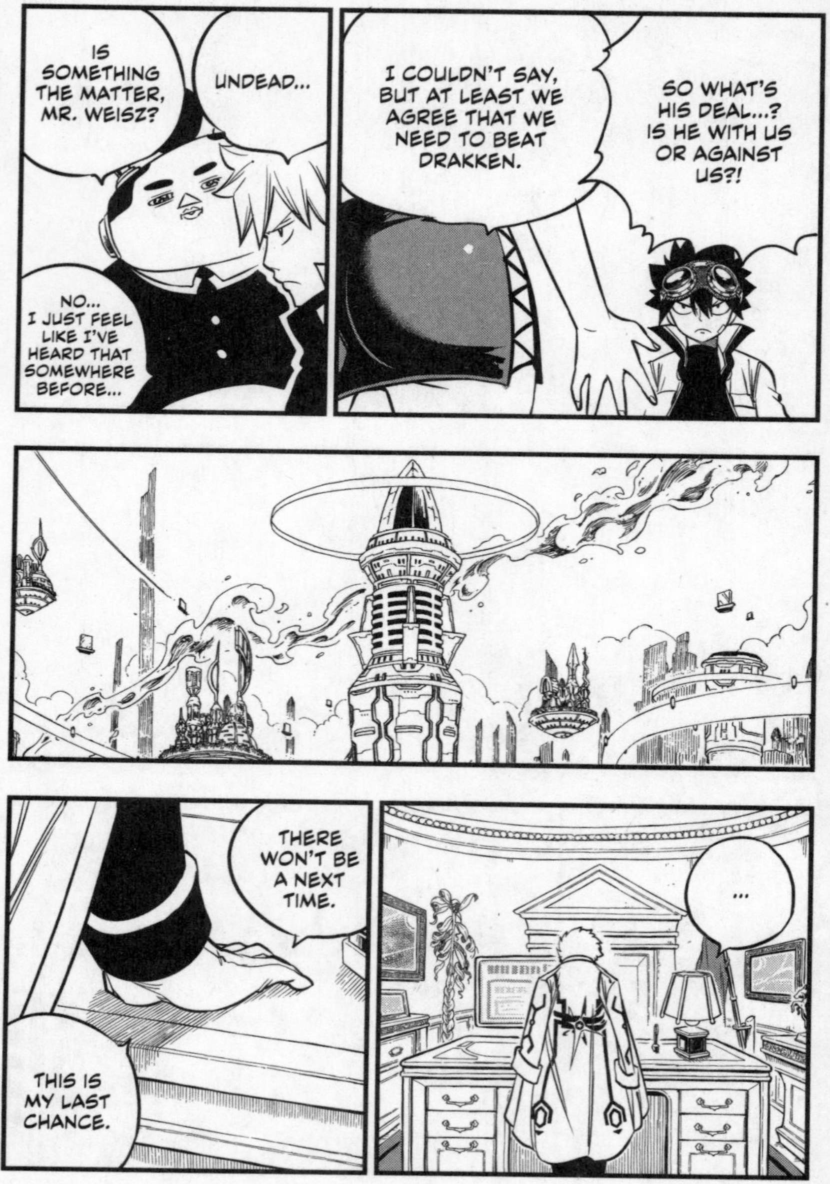
SO WHAT'S HIS DEAL...? IS HE WITH US OR AGAINST US?!
I COULDN'T SAY, BUT AT LEAST WE AGREE THAT WE NEED TO BEAT DRAKKEN.
UNDEAD...
IS SOMETHING THE MATTER, MR. WEISZ?
NO... I JUST FEEL LIKE I'VE HEARD THAT SOMEWHERE BEFORE...
...
THERE WON'T BE A NEXT TIME.
THIS IS MY LAST CHANCE.

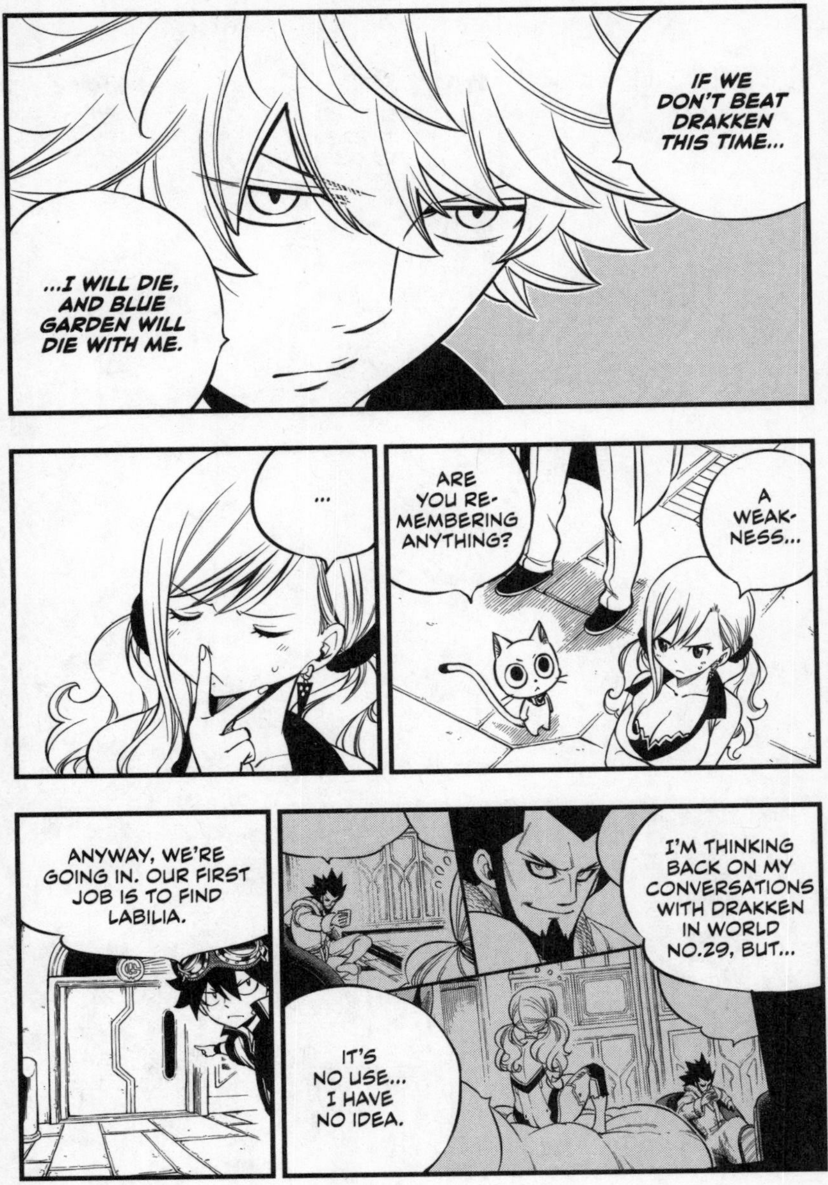
IF WE DON'T BEAT DRAKKEN THIS TIME...
...I WILL DIE, AND BLUE GARDEN WILL DIE WITH ME.
A WEAKNESS...
ARE YOU REMEMBERING ANYTHING?
...
I'M THINKING BACK ON MY CONVERSATIONS WITH DRAKKEN IN WORLD NO.29, BUT...
IT'S NO USE... I HAVE NO IDEA.
ANYWAY, WE'RE GOING IN. OUR FIRST JOB IS TO FIND LABILIA.

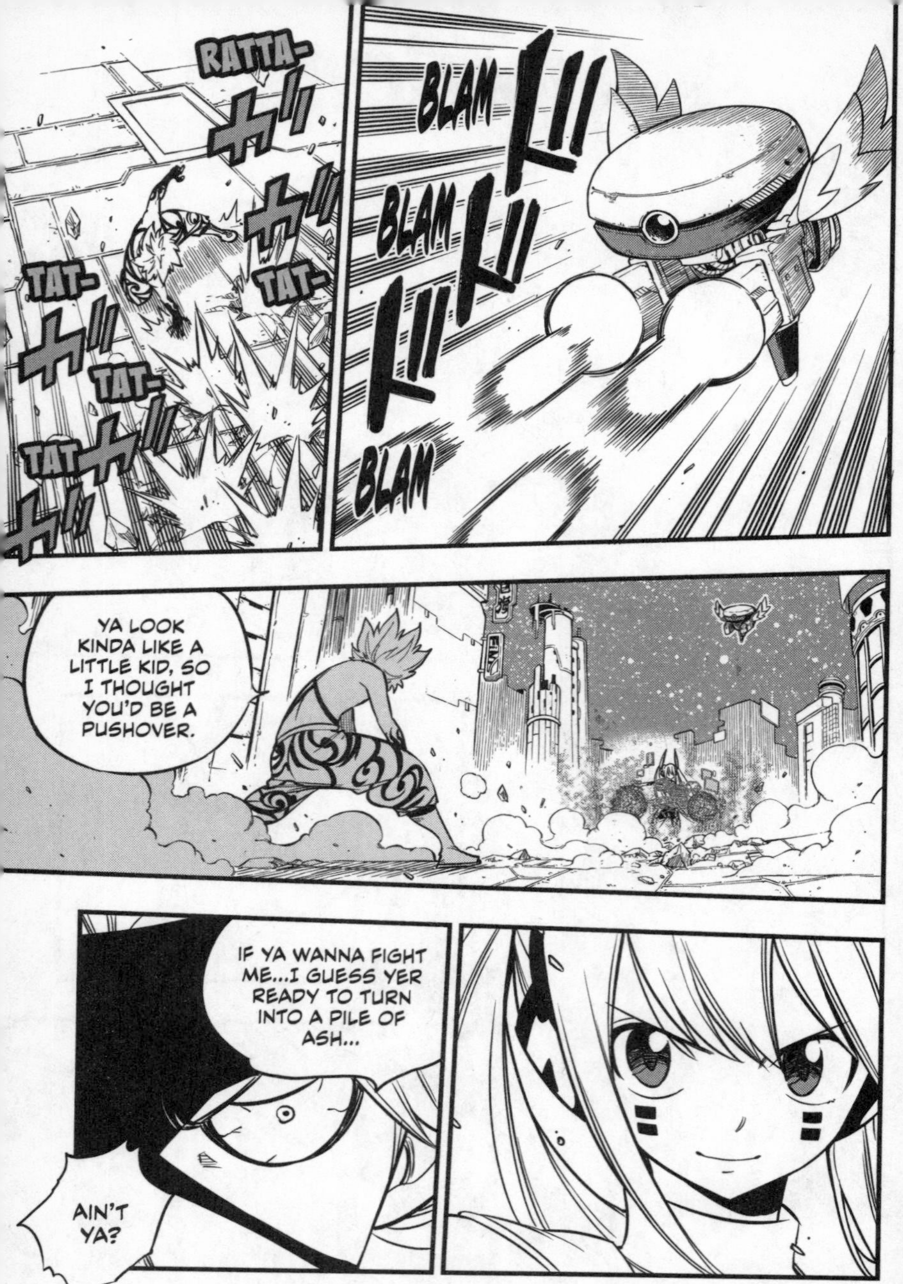

BLAM
BLAM
BLAM
RATTA-
TAT-
TAT-
TAT-
TAT
YA LOOK KINDA LIKE A LITTLE KID, SO I THOUGHT YOU'D BE A PUSHOVER.
IF YA WANNA FIGHT ME...I GUESS YER READY TO TURN INTO A PILE OF ASH...
AIN'T YA?

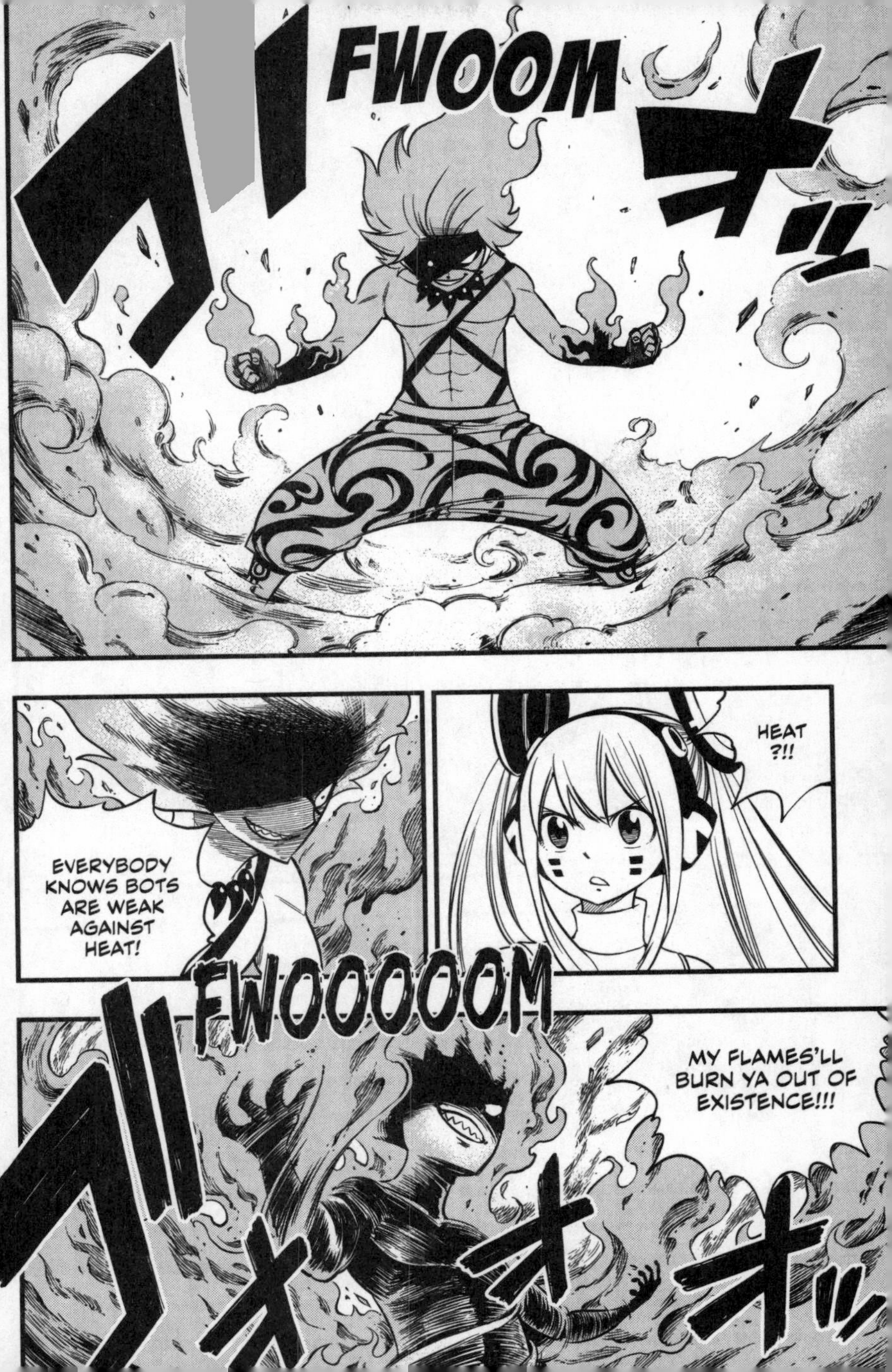
FWOOM
HEAT ?!!
EVERYBODY KNOWS BOTS ARE WEAK AGAINST HEAT!
FWOOOOOM
MY FLAMES'LL BURN YA OUT OF EXISTENCE!!!

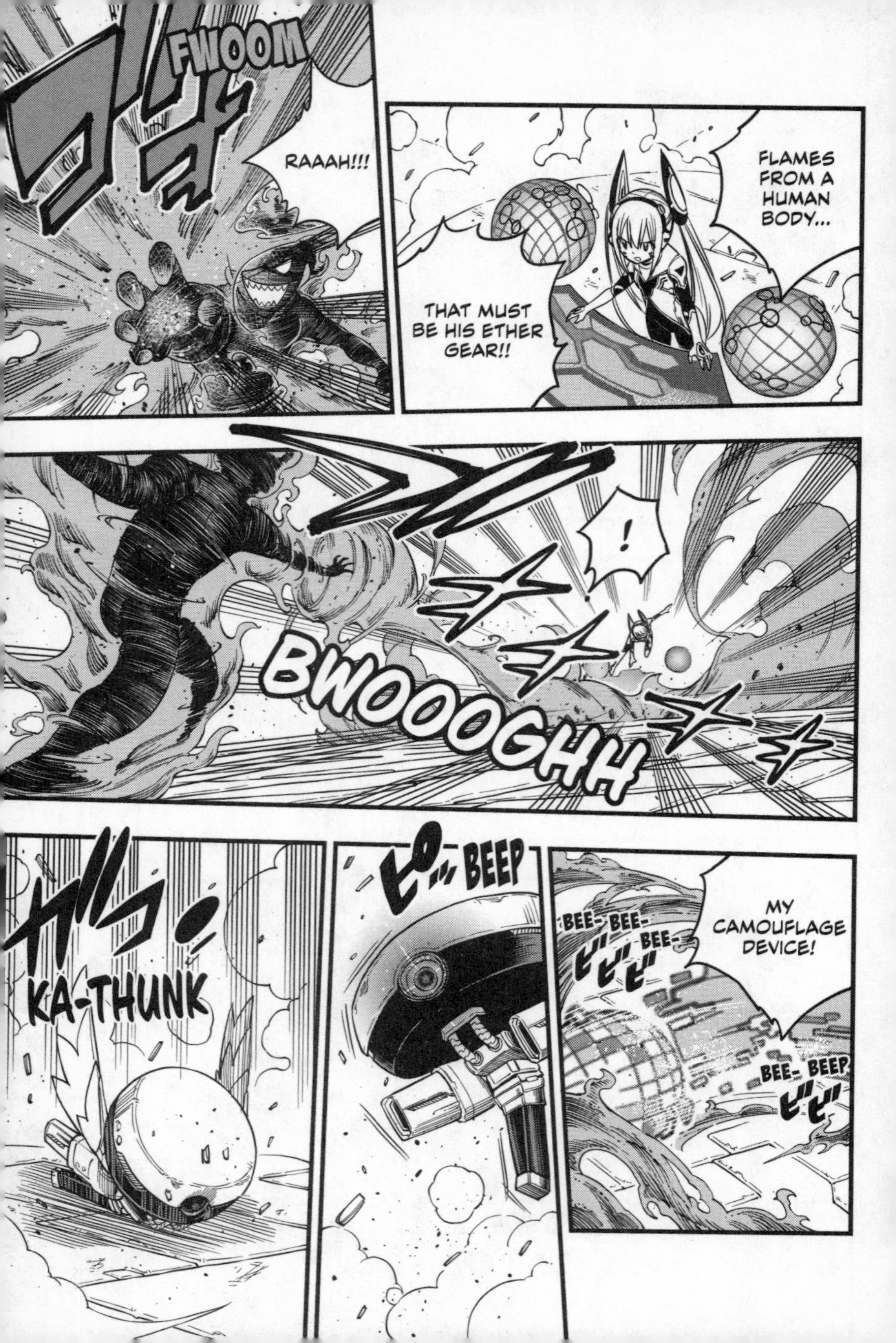
FLAMES FROM A HUMAN BODY...
THAT MUST BE HIS ETHER GEAR!!
FWOOM
RAAAH!!!
!
BWOOOGHH
MY CAMOUFLAGE DEVICE!
BEE- BEE- BEE-
BEE- BEEP
BEEP
KA-THUNK

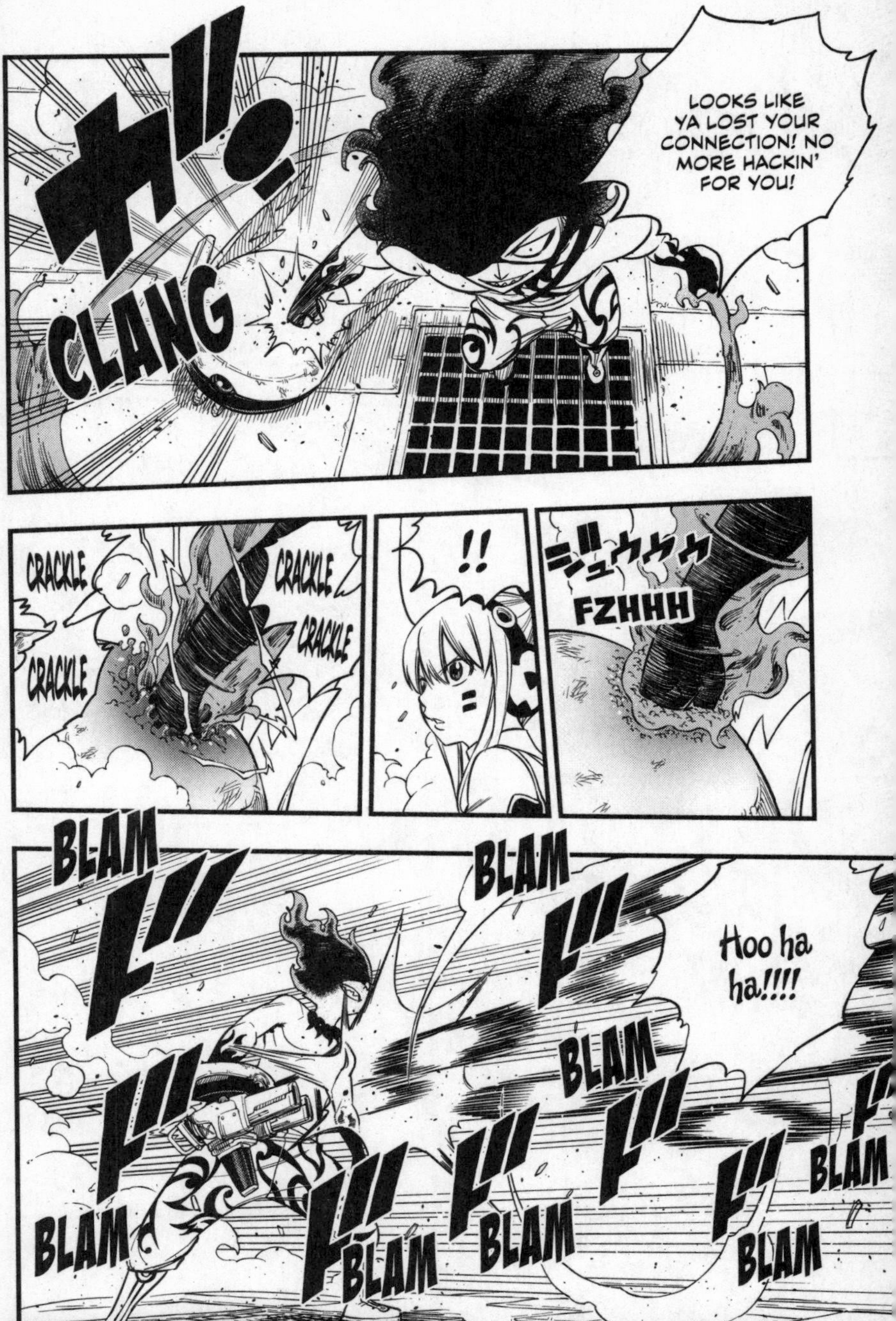
LOOKS LIKE YA LOST YOUR CONNECTION! NO MORE HACKIN' FOR YOU!
ガッ
CLANG
FZHHH
!!
CRACKLE
CRACKLE
CRACKLE
CRACKLE
Hoo ha ha!!!!
BLAM
BLAM
BLAM
BLAM
BLAM
BLAM
BLAM
BLAM
BLAM
BLAM

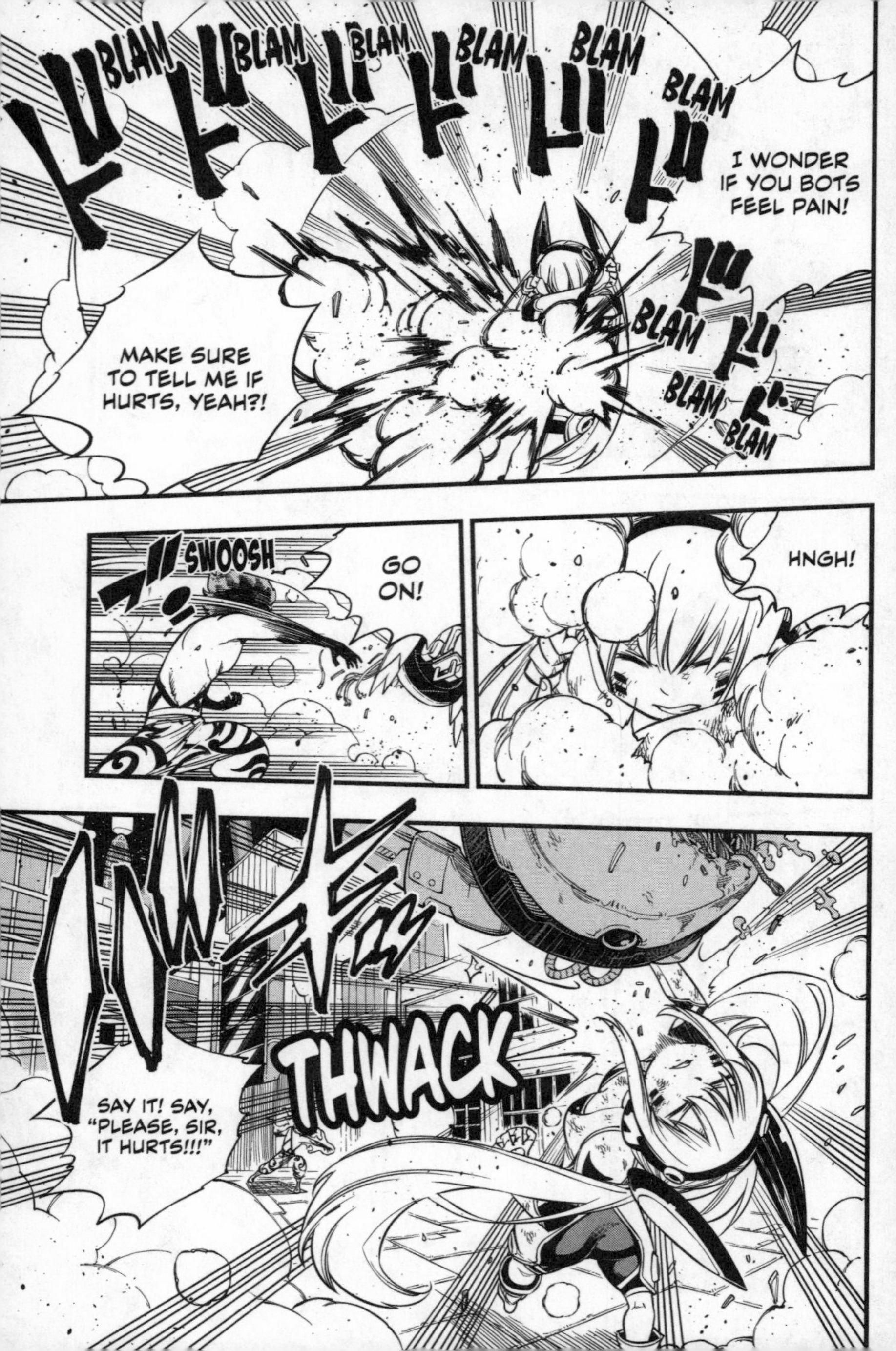
BLAM
BLAM
BLAM
BLAM
BLAM
BLAM
I WONDER IF YOU BOTS FEEL PAIN!
BLAM
BLAM
BLAM
MAKE SURE TO TELL ME IF HURTS, YEAH?!
HNGH!
GO ON!
SWOOSH
THWACK
SAY IT! SAY, "PLEASE, SIR, IT HURTS!!!"

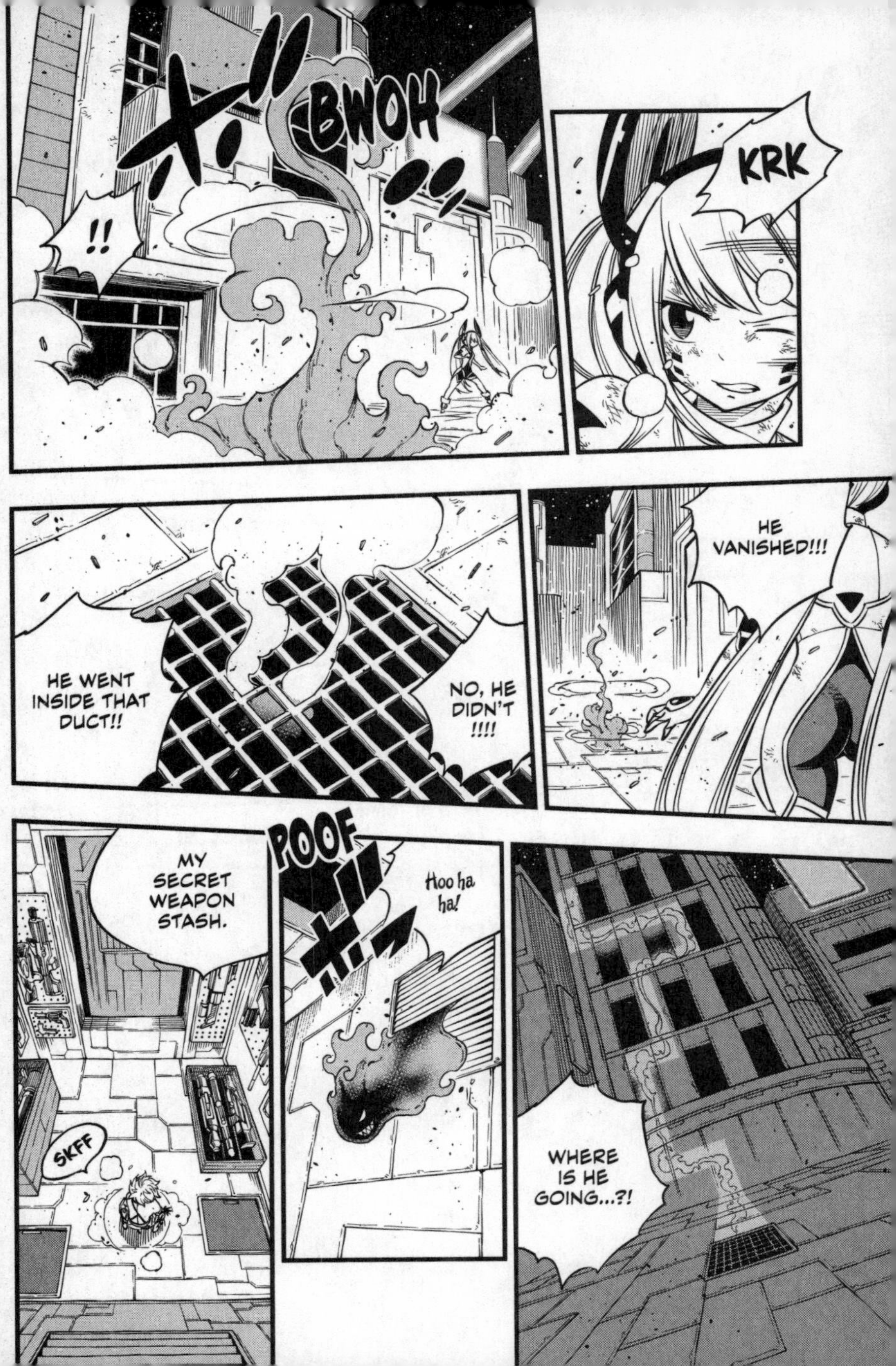
KRK
BWOH
!!
HE VANISHED!!!
HE WENT INSIDE THAT DUCT!!
NO, HE DIDN'T !!!!
WHERE IS HE GOING...?!
POOF
Hoo ha ha!
MY SECRET WEAPON STASH.
SKFF

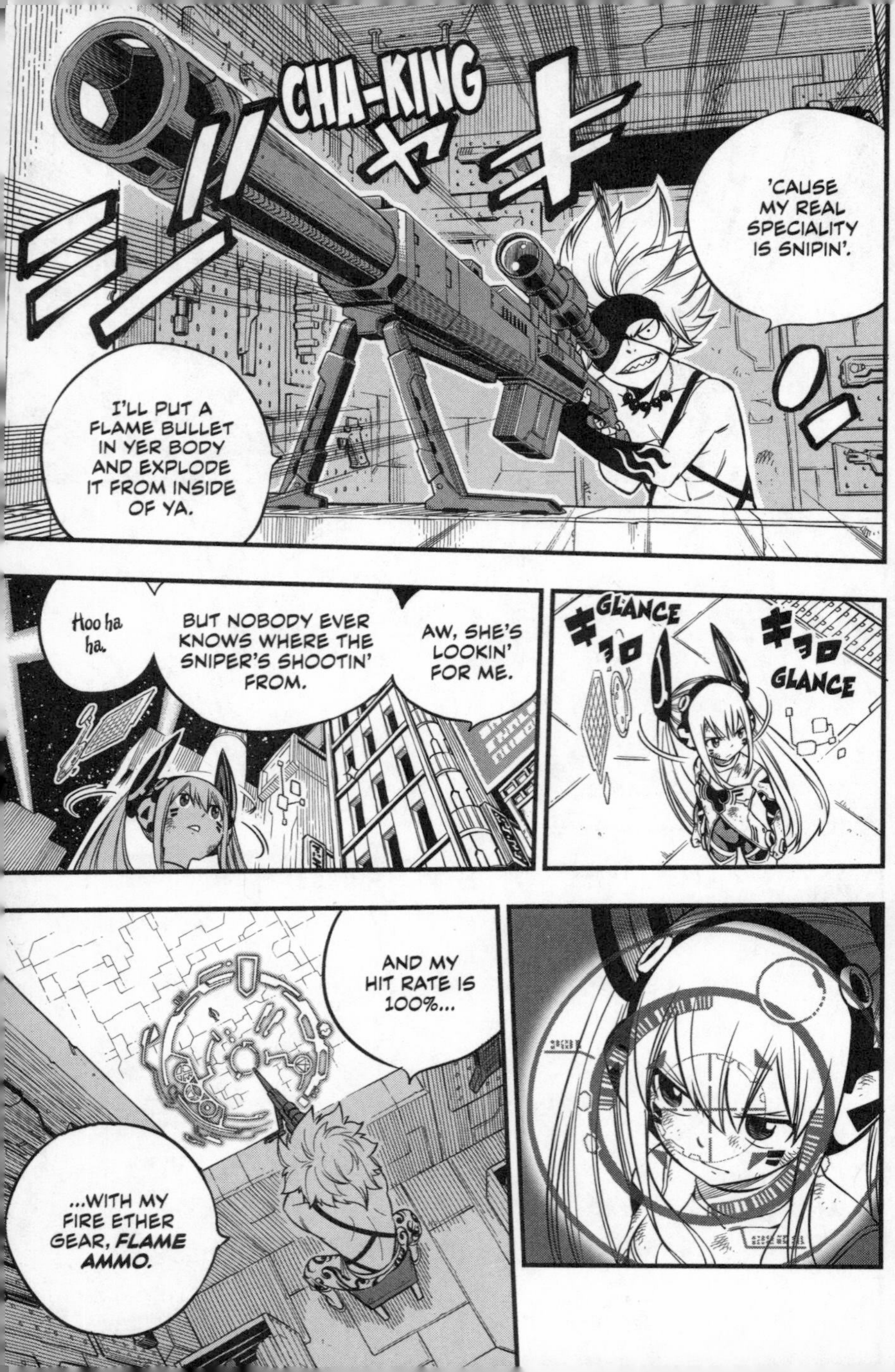
CHA-KING
'CAUSE MY REAL SPECIALITY IS SNIPIN'.
I'LL PUT A FLAME BULLET IN YER BODY AND EXPLODE IT FROM INSIDE OF YA.
GLANCE
GLANCE
AW, SHE'S LOOKIN' FOR ME.
BUT NOBODY EVER KNOWS WHERE THE SNIPER'S SHOOTIN' FROM.
Hoo ha ha.
AND MY HIT RATE IS 100%...
...WITH MY FIRE ETHER GEAR, *FLAME AMMO.*

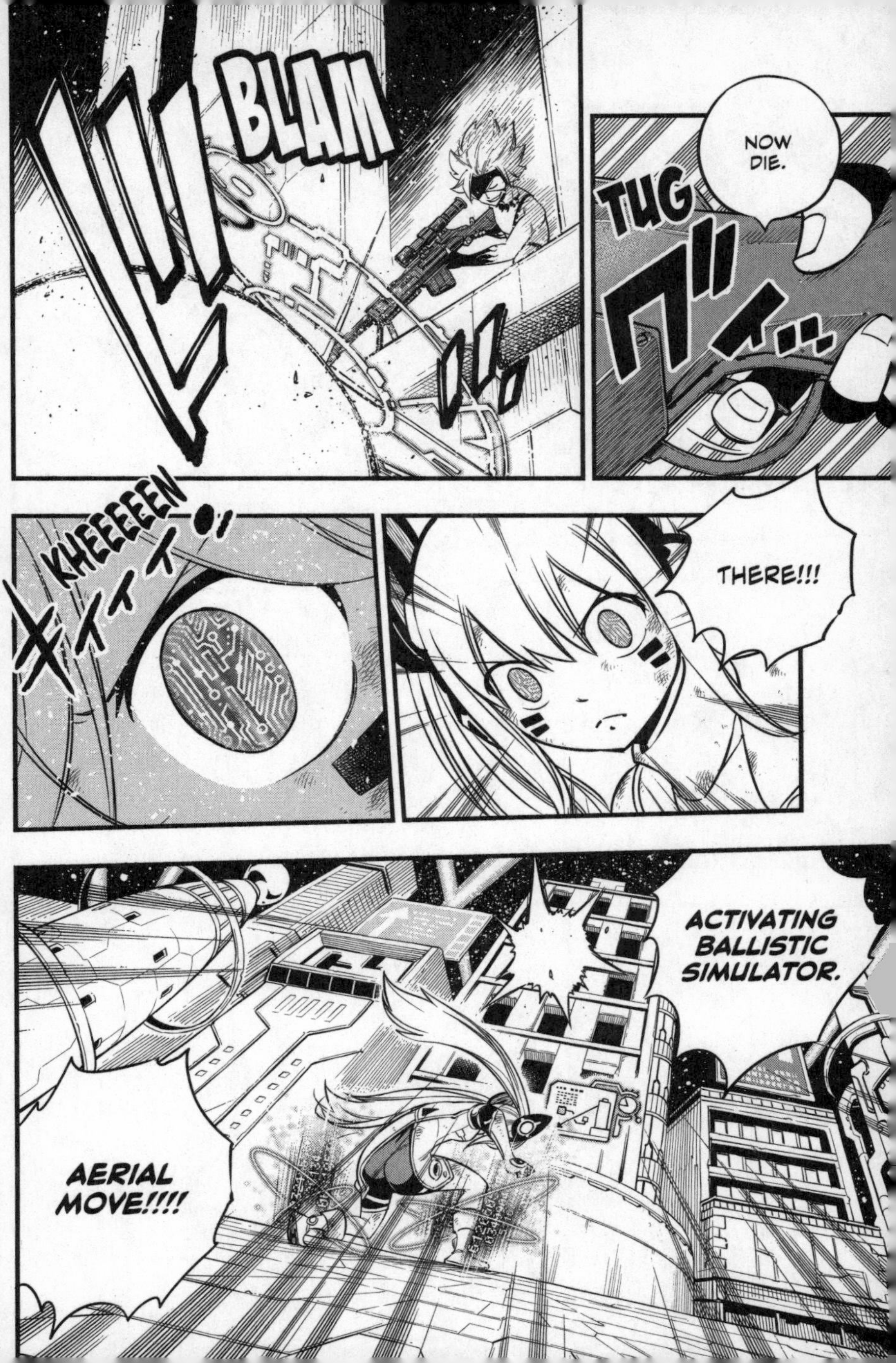
NOW DIE.
TUG
BLAM
THERE!!!
KHEEEEEN
ACTIVATING BALLISTIC SIMULATOR.
AERIAL MOVE!!!!

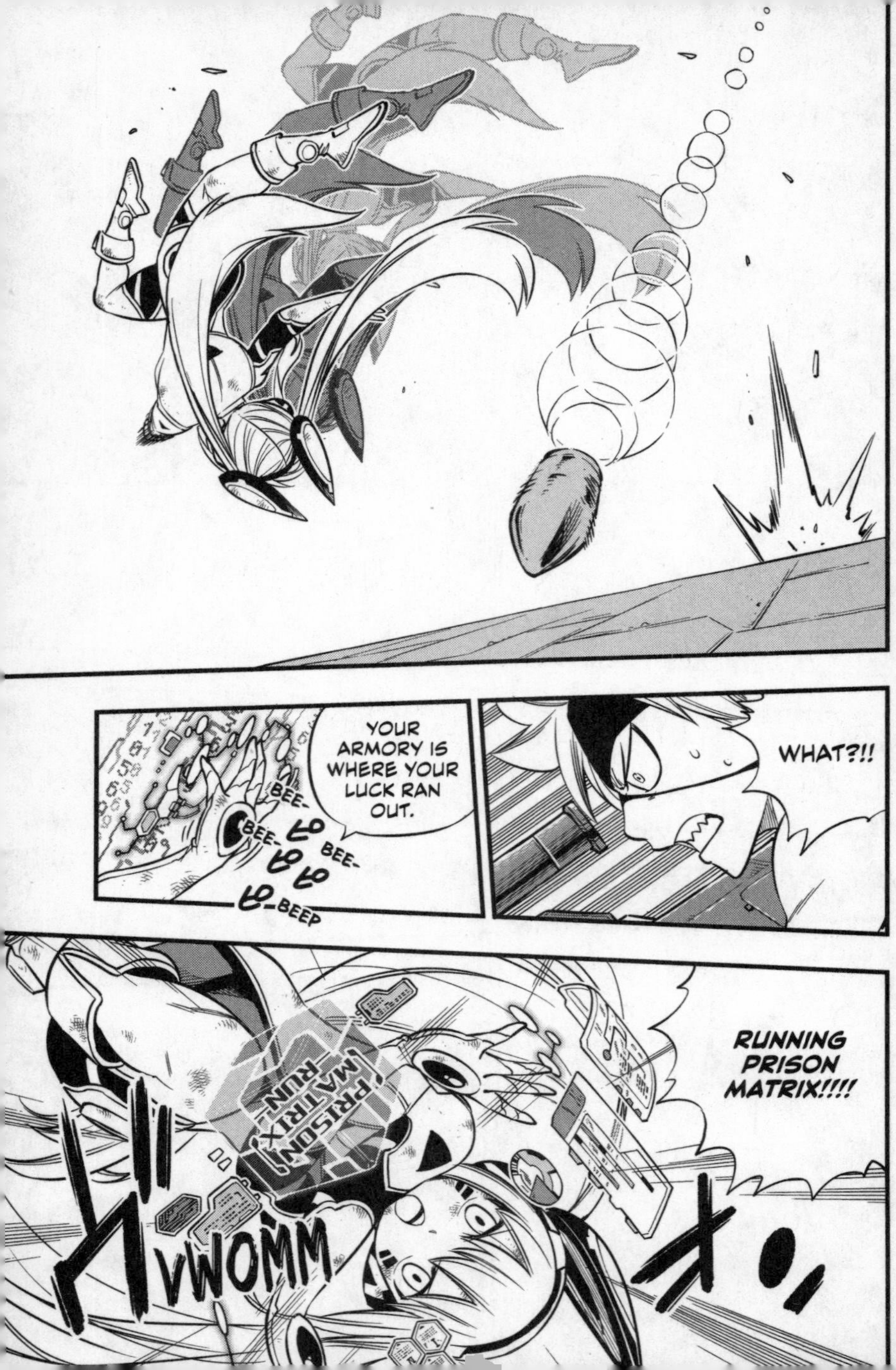
WHAT?!!
YOUR ARMORY IS WHERE YOUR LUCK RAN OUT.
BEE-
BEE-
BEE-
BEEP
RUNNING PRISON MATRIX!!!!
PRISON MATRIX RUN
VWOMM

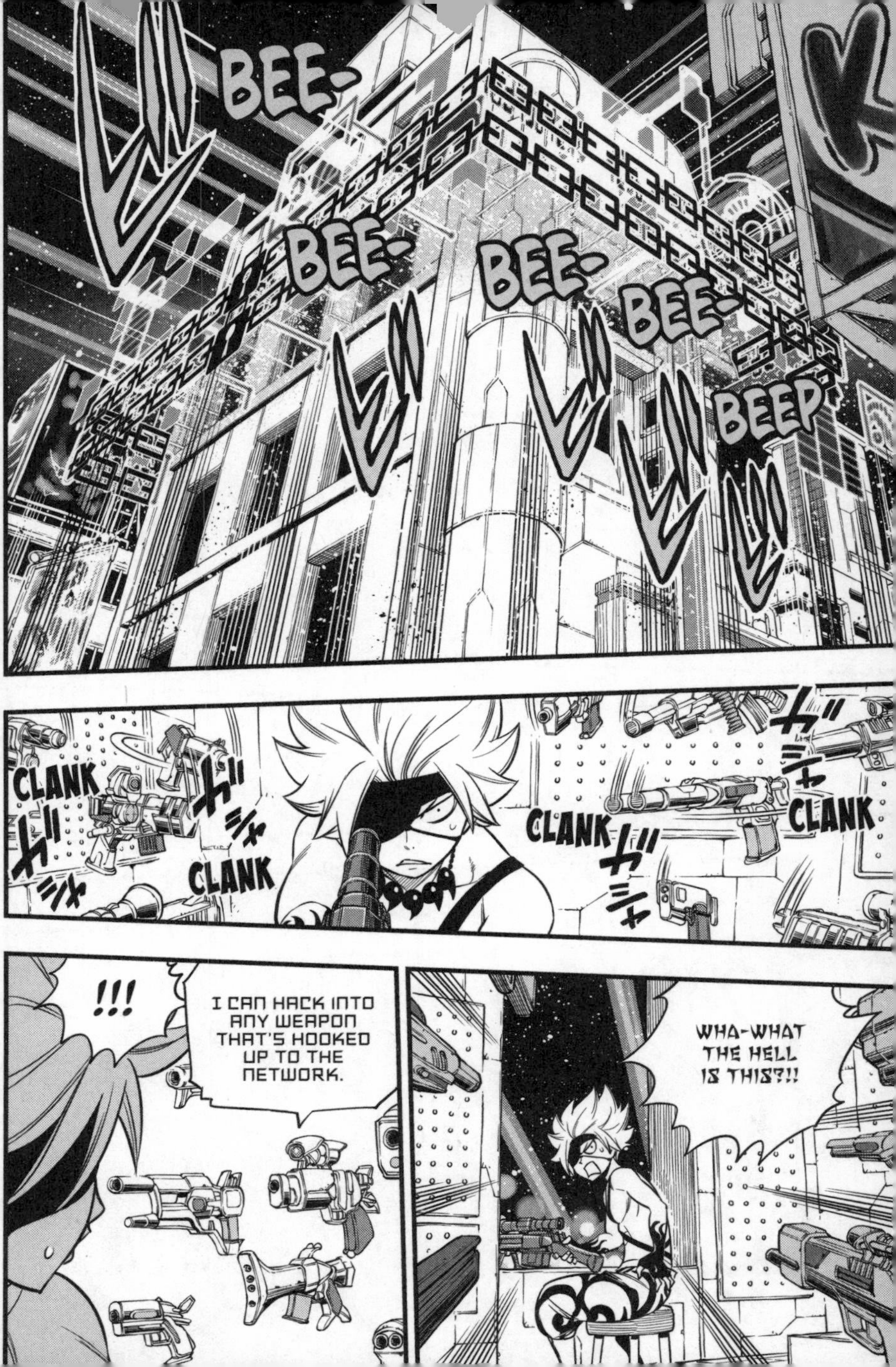
BEE-
BEE-
BEE-
BEE-
BEEP
CLANK
CLANK
CLANK
CLANK
WHA-WHAT THE HELL IS THIS?!!
!!!
I CAN HACK INTO ANY WEAPON THAT'S HOOKED UP TO THE NETWORK.

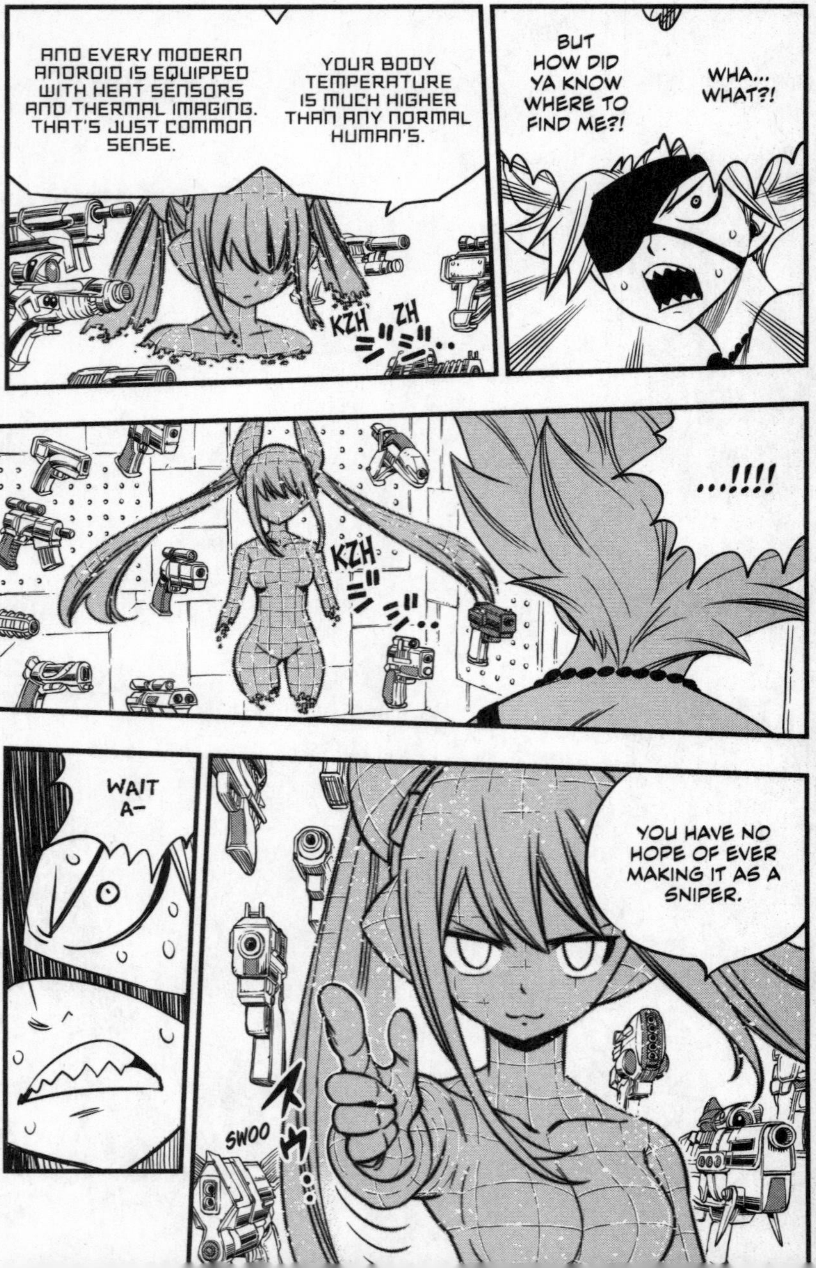
WHA... WHAT?!
BUT HOW DID YA KNOW WHERE TO FIND ME?!
YOUR BODY TEMPERATURE IS MUCH HIGHER THAN ANY NORMAL HUMAN'S.
AND EVERY MODERN ANDROID IS EQUIPPED WITH HEAT SENSORS AND THERMAL IMAGING. THAT'S JUST COMMON SENSE.
KZH ZH
...!!!!
KZH
YOU HAVE NO HOPE OF EVER MAKING IT AS A SNIPER.
SWOO
WAIT A-

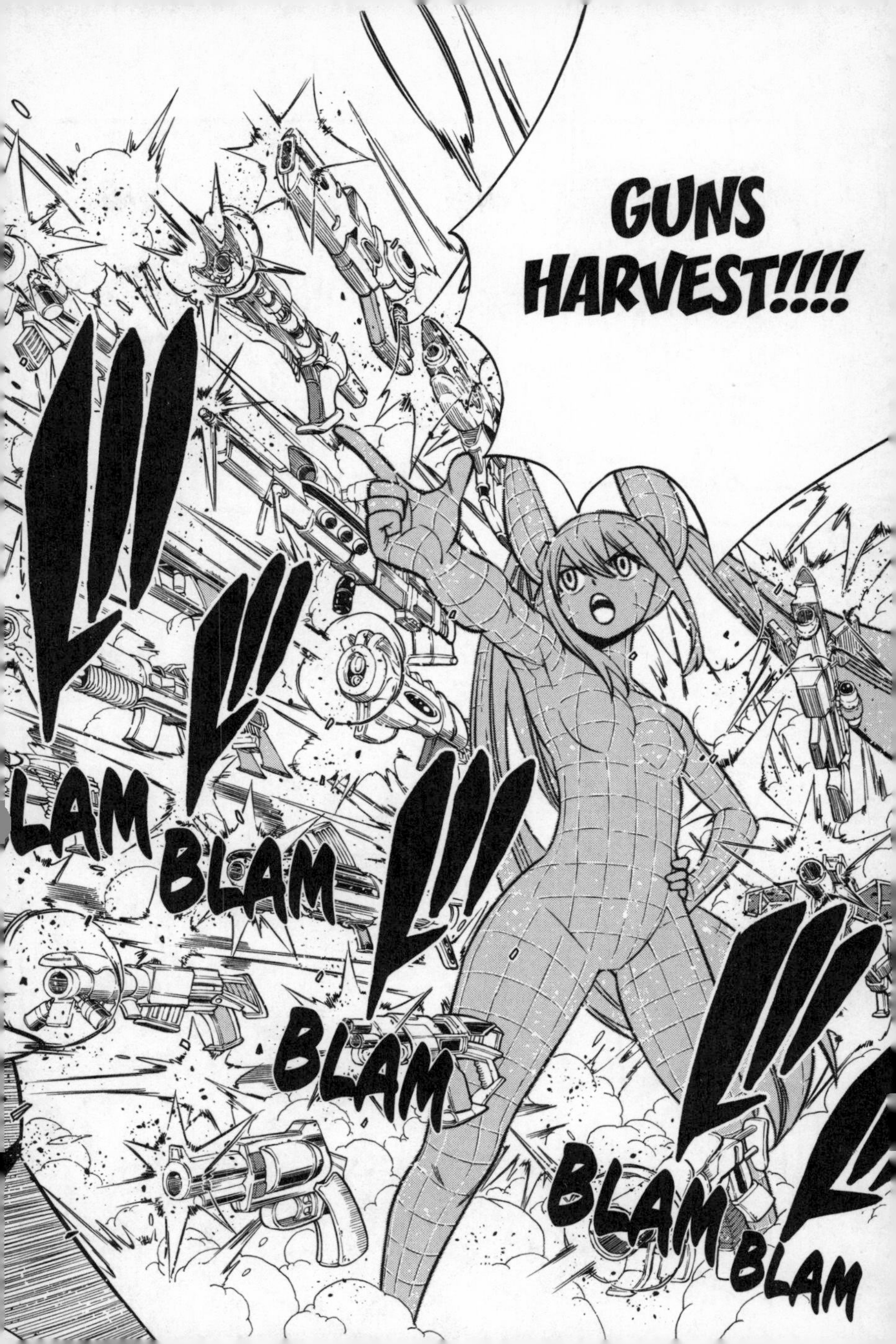
GUNS HARVEST!!!!
BLAM
BLAM
BLAM
BLAM
LAM

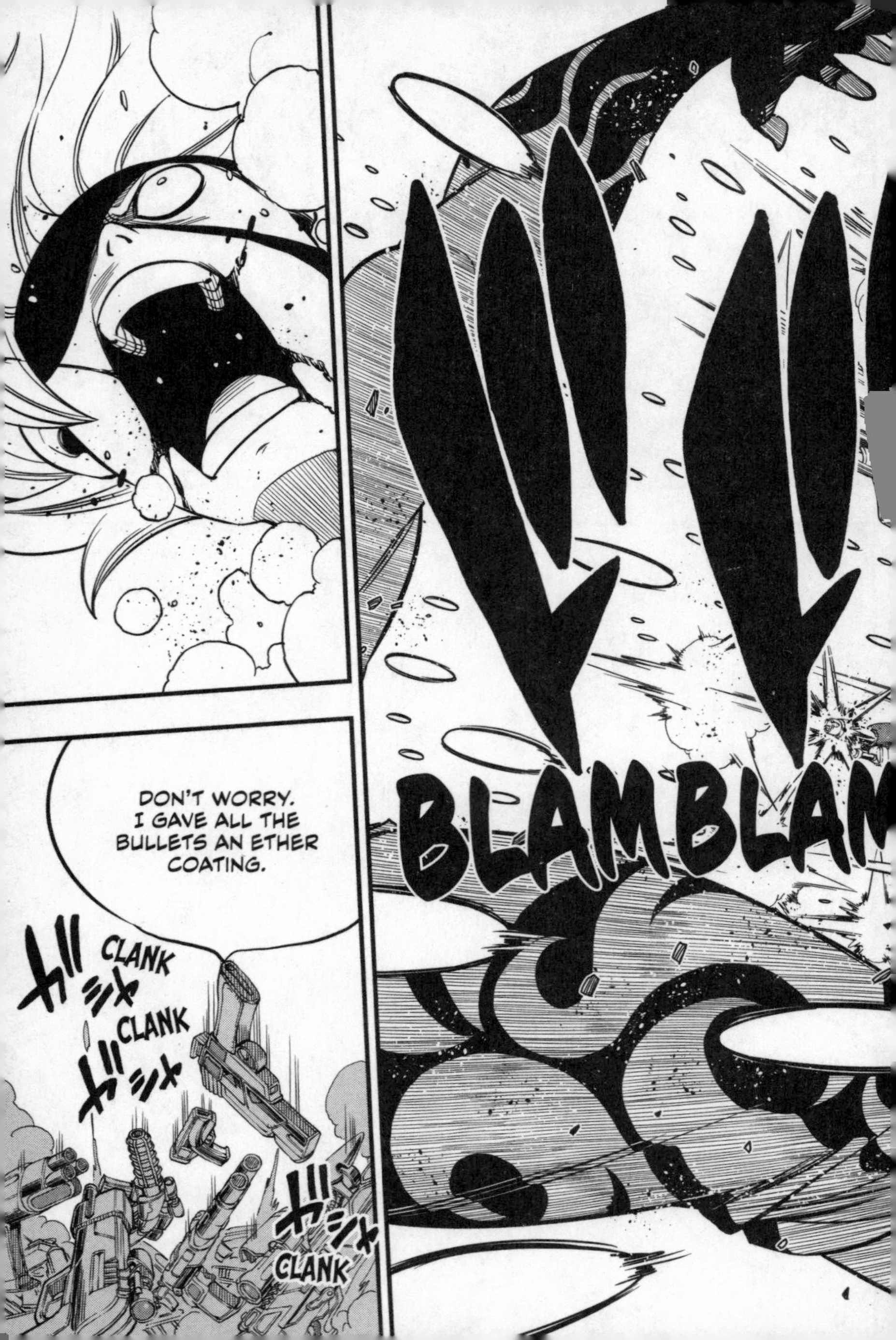
BLAMBLAM
DON'T WORRY. I GAVE ALL THE BULLETS AN ETHER COATING.
CLANK
CLANK
CLANK

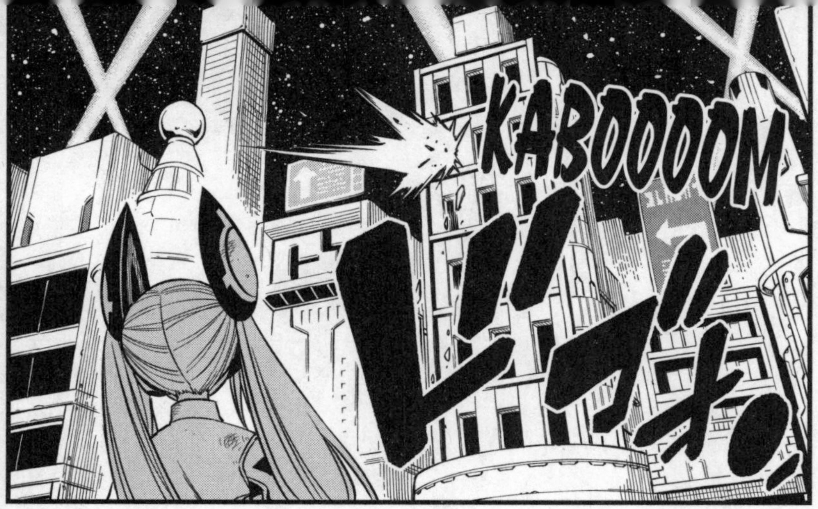
KABOOOOM

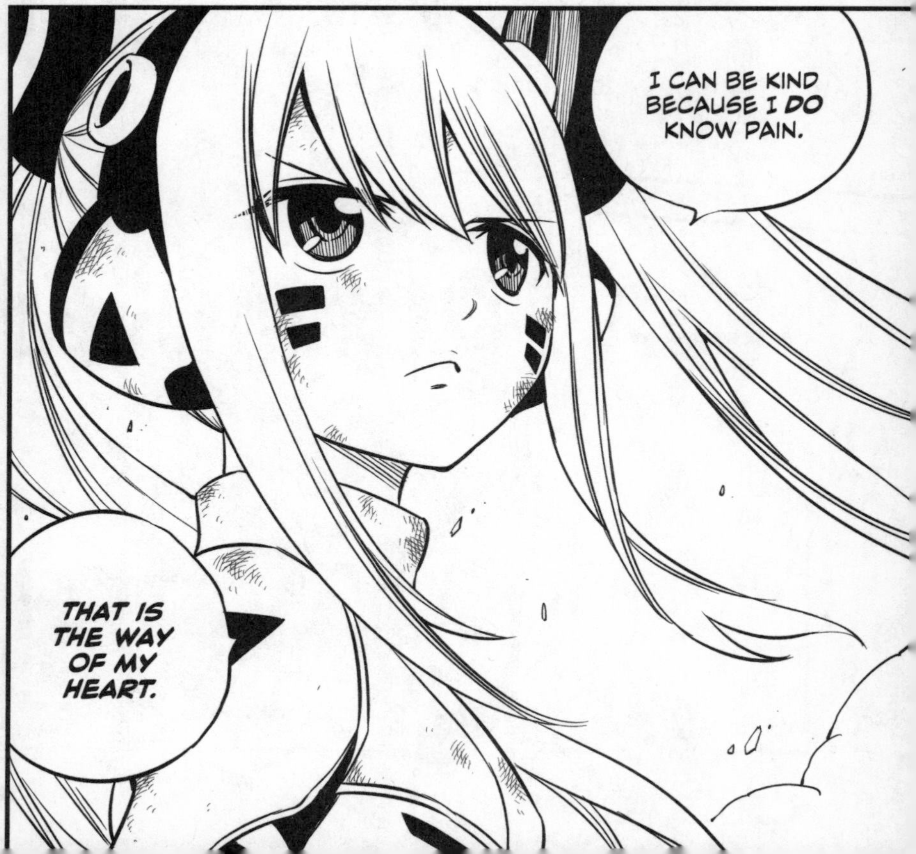
I CAN BE KIND BECAUSE I *DO* KNOW PAIN.
THAT IS THE WAY OF MY HEART.

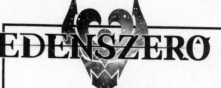

EDENS ZERO

Edens Zero
In-Depth Character File 4

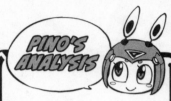

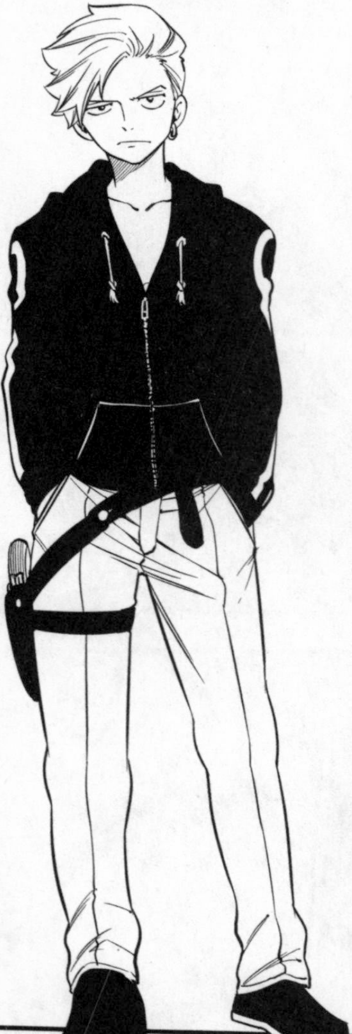

PINO'S ANALYSIS

Name: Weisz Steiner

Powers: Ether Gear

(Machina Maker)

Likes: Money, bunny girls

Dislikes: Studying

Attack: ☆☆☆

Defense: ☆☆☆☆☆

Marksmanship: ☆☆☆☆

Ether Power: ☆☆☆

Intelligence: ☆☆

Thievery: ☆☆☆

Memo

A master of modification we met on the planet Norma of 50 years ago. He uses his Ether Gear to modify all kinds of machines. At first, I thought he was scary, but he turned out to be nice, and even fixed my broken leg. He puts on mechanical armor to fight as the superhero-like persona, Arsenal.

CHAPTER 90: SISTER VS. DAICHI

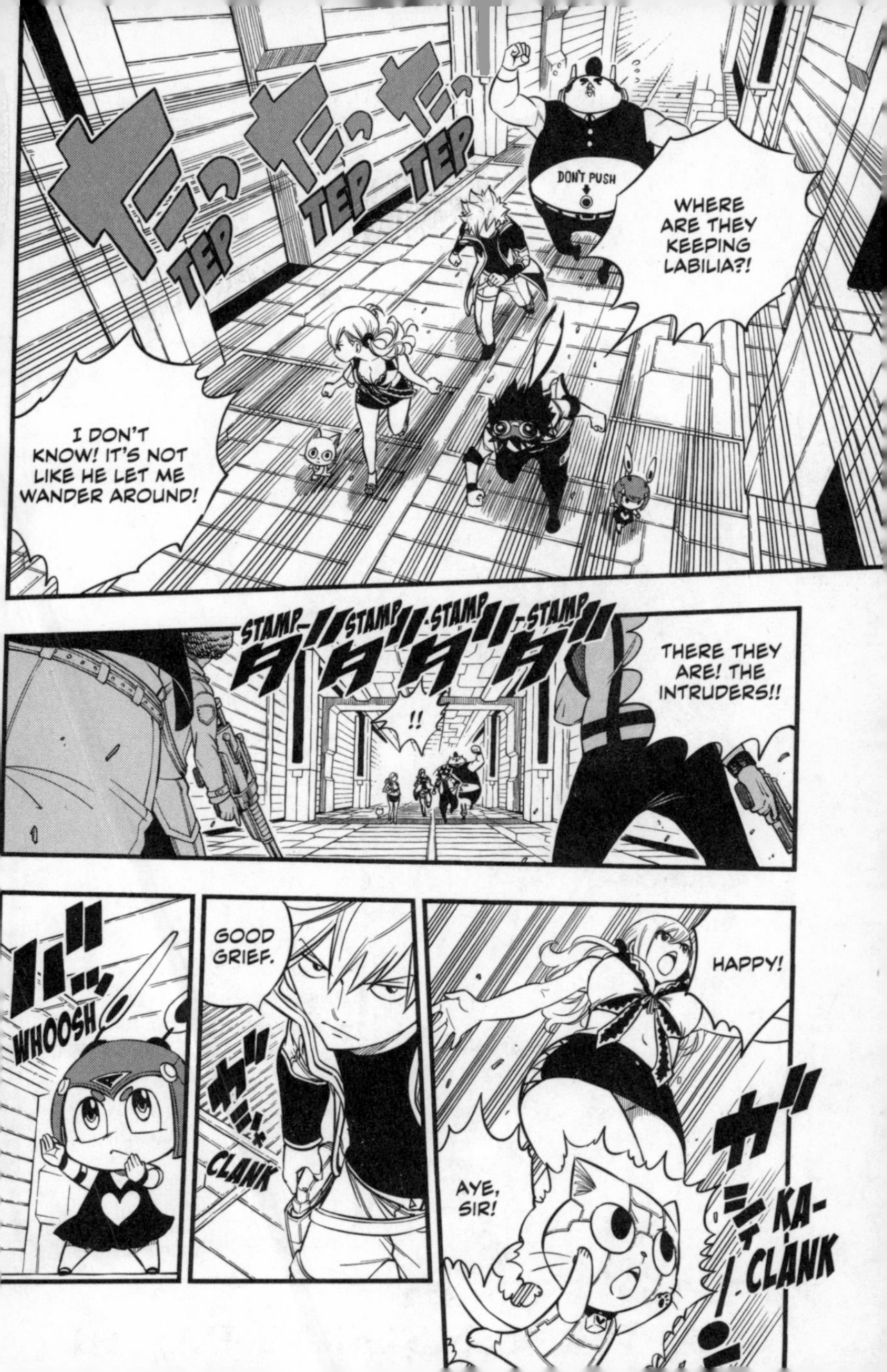
DON'T PUSH
WHERE ARE THEY KEEPING LABILIA?!
TEP TEP TEP
I DON'T KNOW! IT'S NOT LIKE HE LET ME WANDER AROUND!
THERE THEY ARE! THE INTRUDERS!!
STAMP STAMP STAMP STAMP
!!
HAPPY!
KA-CLANK
AYE, SIR!
GOOD GRIEF.
CLANK
WHOOSH

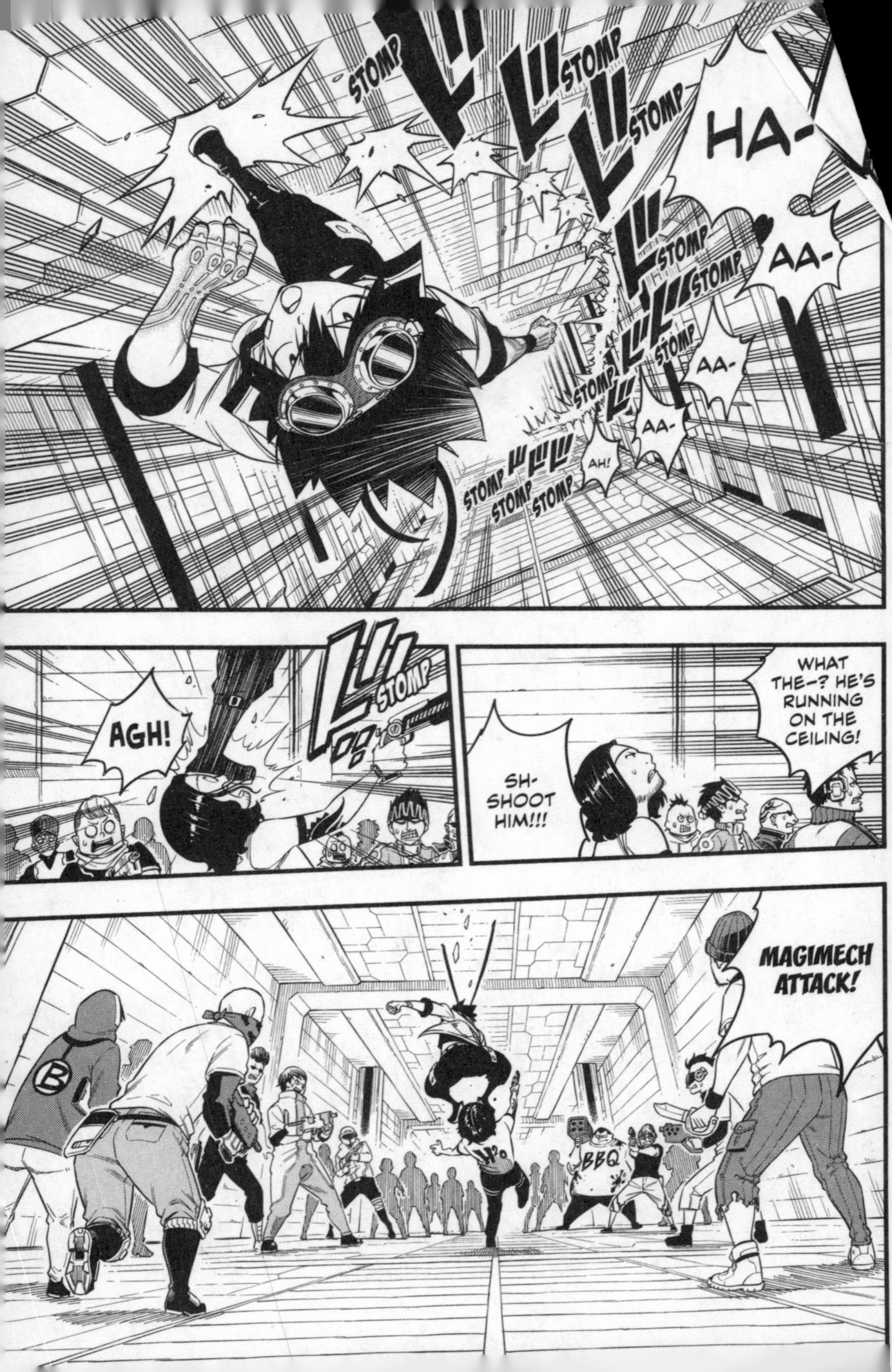

HA-
STOMP
STOMP
STOMP
AA-
STOMP
STOMP
STOMP
STOMP
AA-
AA-
AH!
STOMP
STOMP
STOMP
WHAT THE–? HE'S RUNNING ON THE CEILING!
SH- SHOOT HIM!!!
STOMP
AGH!
MAGIMECH ATTACK!
BBQ

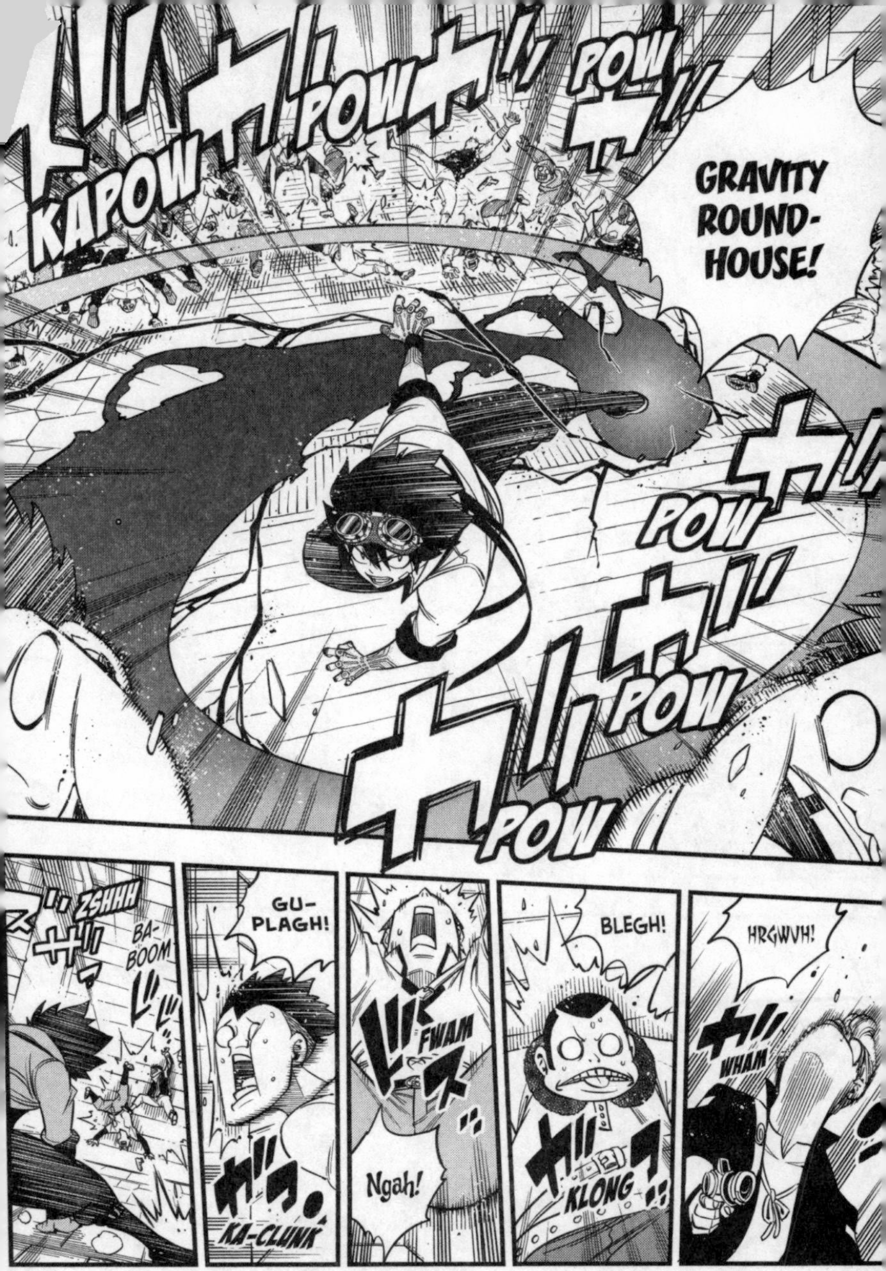
POW
POW
KAPOW
GRAVITY ROUND-HOUSE!
POW
POW
POW
HRGWUH!
WHAM
BLEGH!
KLONG
FWAM
Ngah!
GU-PLAGH!
KA-CLUNK
ZSHHH
BA-BOOM

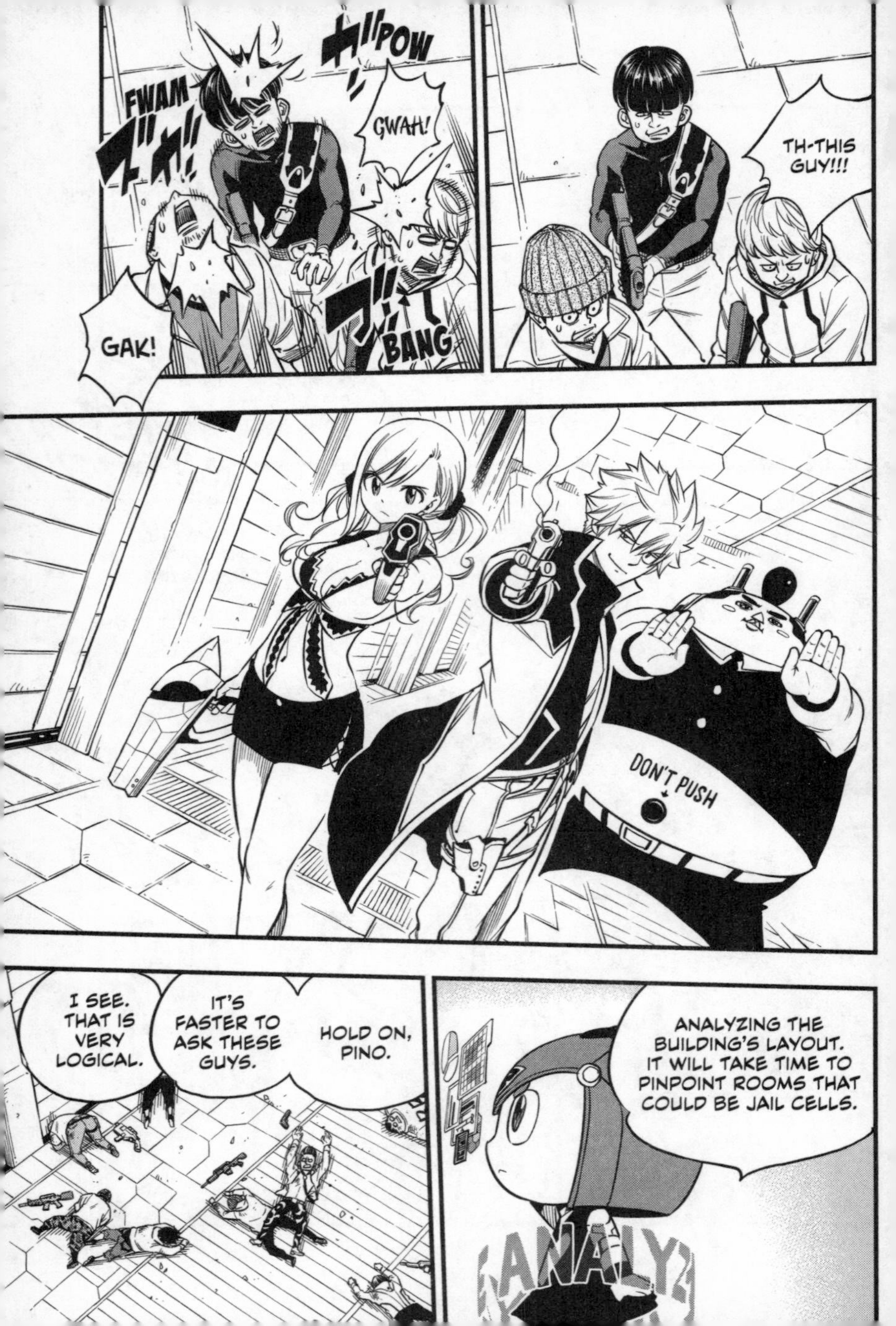
TH-THIS GUY!!!
POW
GWAH!
FWAM
BANG
GAK!
DON'T PUSH
ANALYZING THE BUILDING'S LAYOUT. IT WILL TAKE TIME TO PINPOINT ROOMS THAT COULD BE JAIL CELLS.
HOLD ON, PINO.
IT'S FASTER TO ASK THESE GUYS.
I SEE. THAT IS VERY LOGICAL.

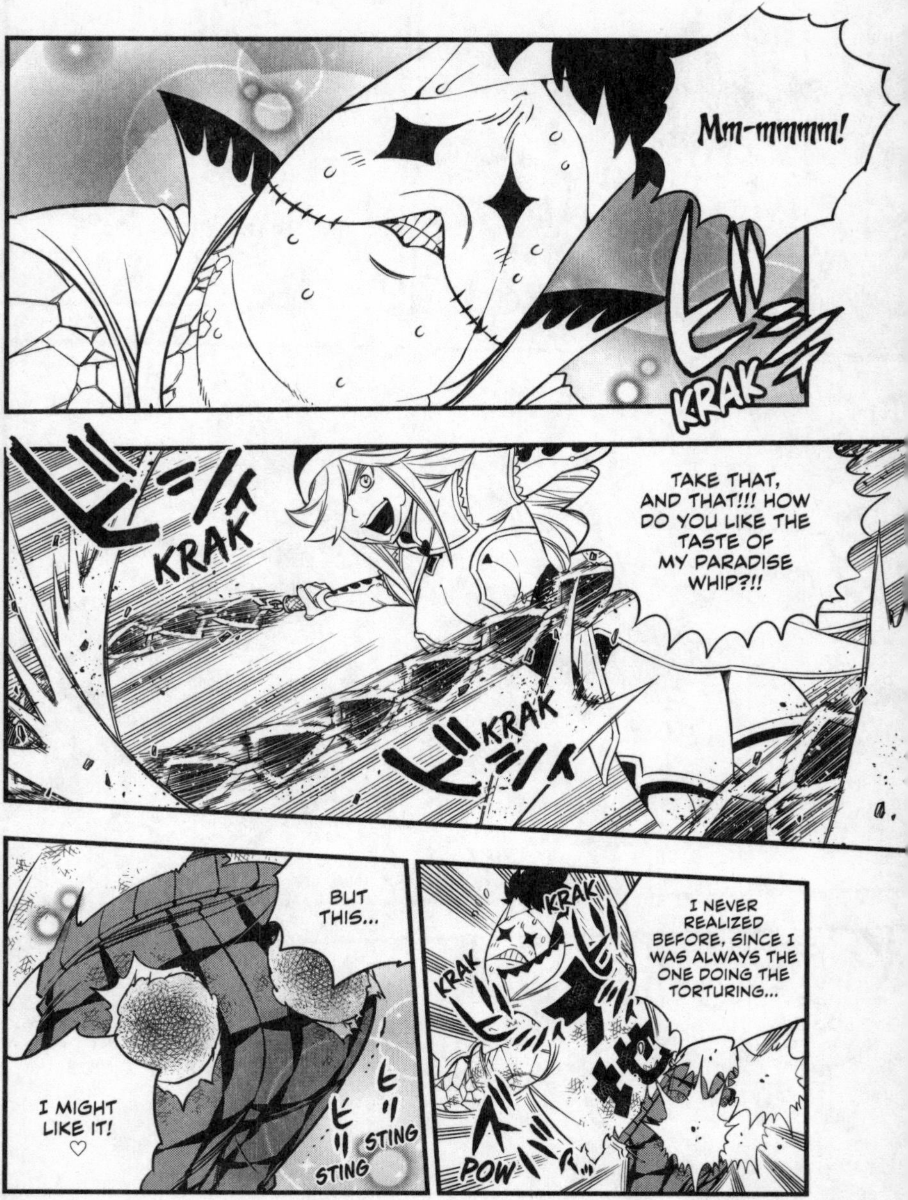
Mm-mmmm!
KRAK
TAKE THAT, AND THAT!!! HOW DO YOU LIKE THE TASTE OF MY PARADISE WHIP?!!
KRAK
KRAK
I NEVER REALIZED BEFORE, SINCE I WAS ALWAYS THE ONE DOING THE TORTURING...
KRAK
KRAK
POW
BUT THIS...
STING
STING
I MIGHT LIKE IT! ♡

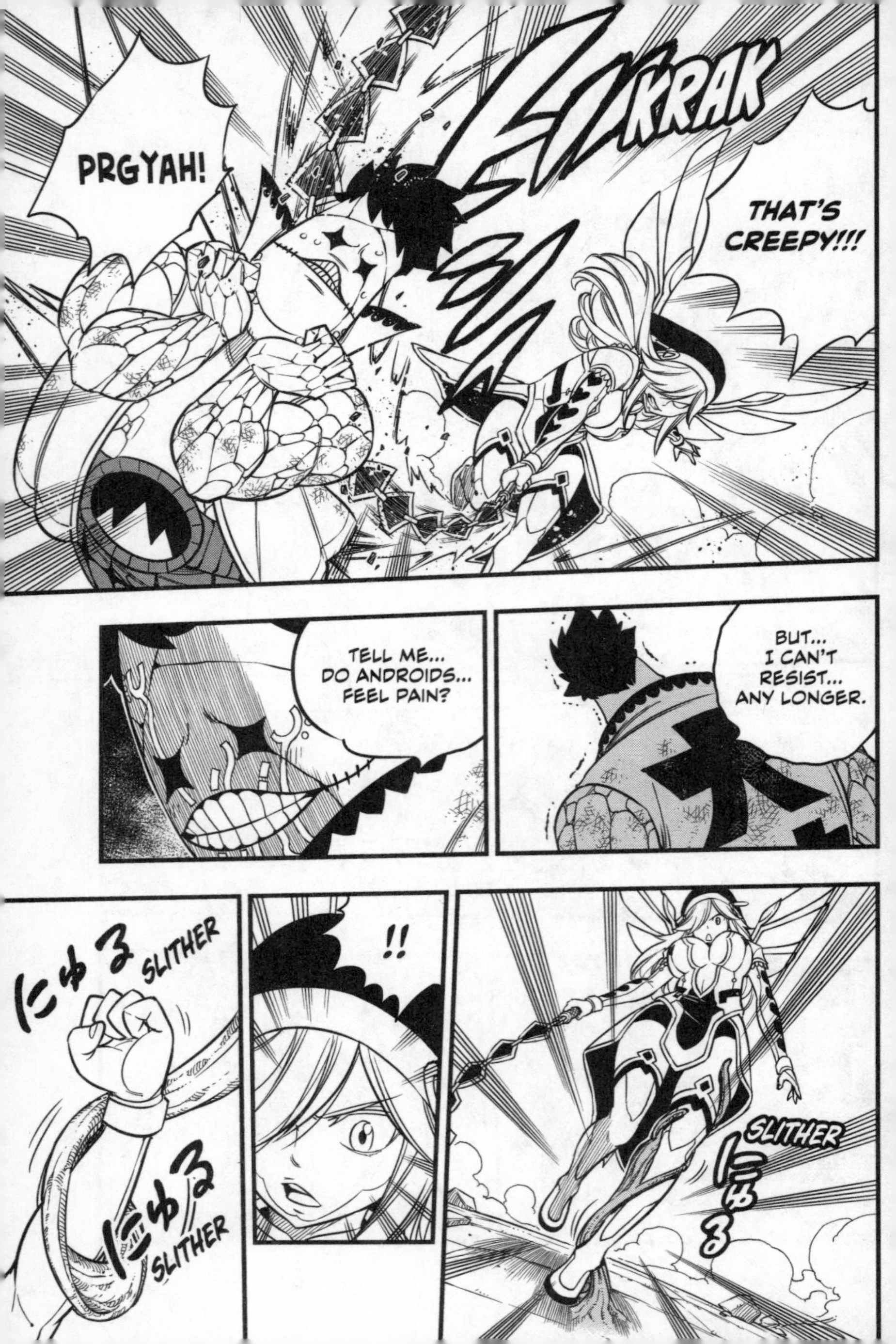
KRAK
THAT'S CREEPY!!!
PRGYAH!
BUT... I CAN'T RESIST... ANY LONGER.
TELL ME... DO ANDROIDS... FEEL PAIN?
SLITHER
にゅる
!!
にゅる
SLITHER
にゅる
SLITHER

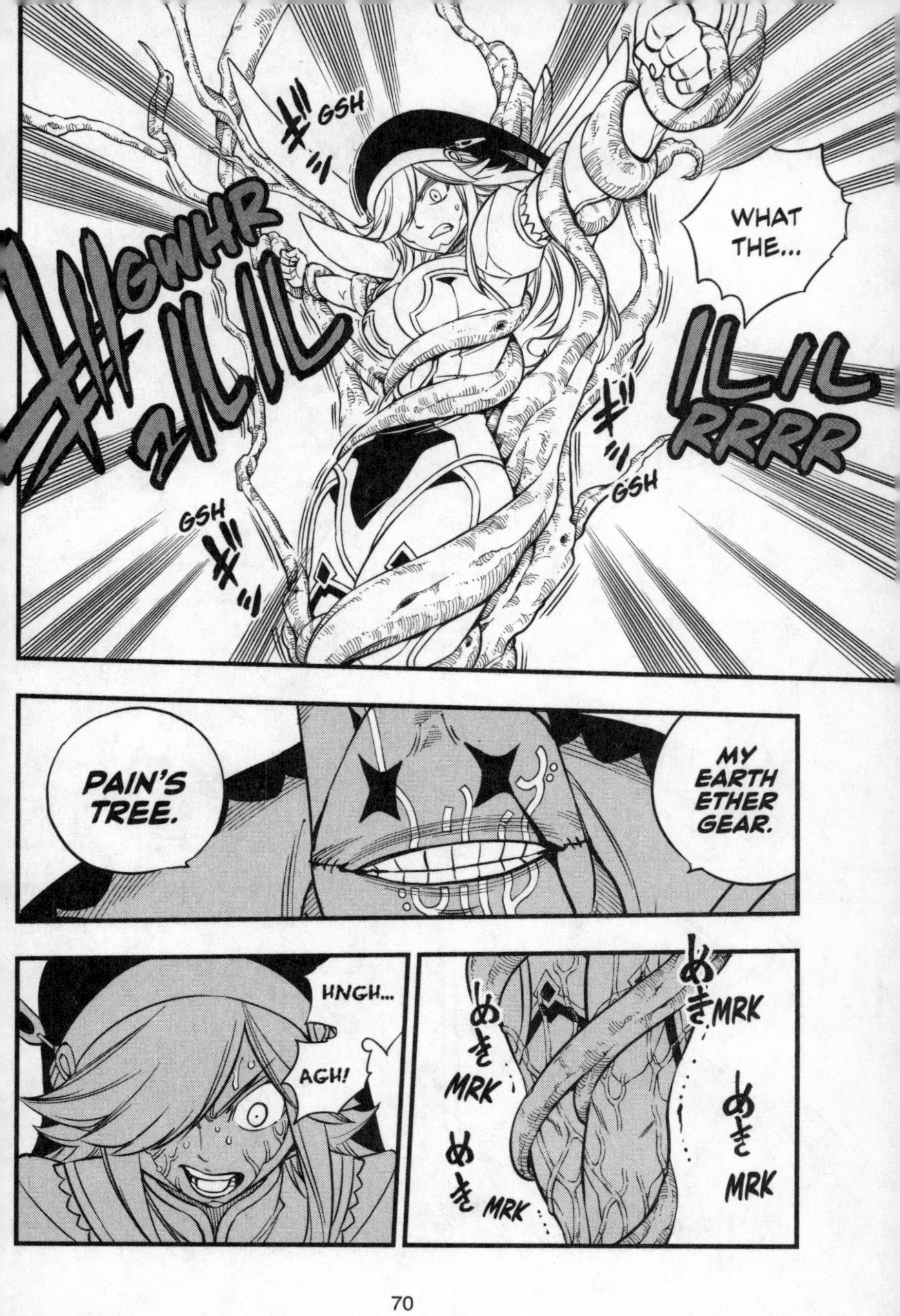
WHAT THE...
ギッ GSH
ルル RRRR
ギッ GSH
ズルル GWHR
ギッ GSH
MY EARTH ETHER GEAR.
PAIN'S TREE.
めき MRK
めき MRK
めき MRK
めき MRK
HNGH...
AGH!

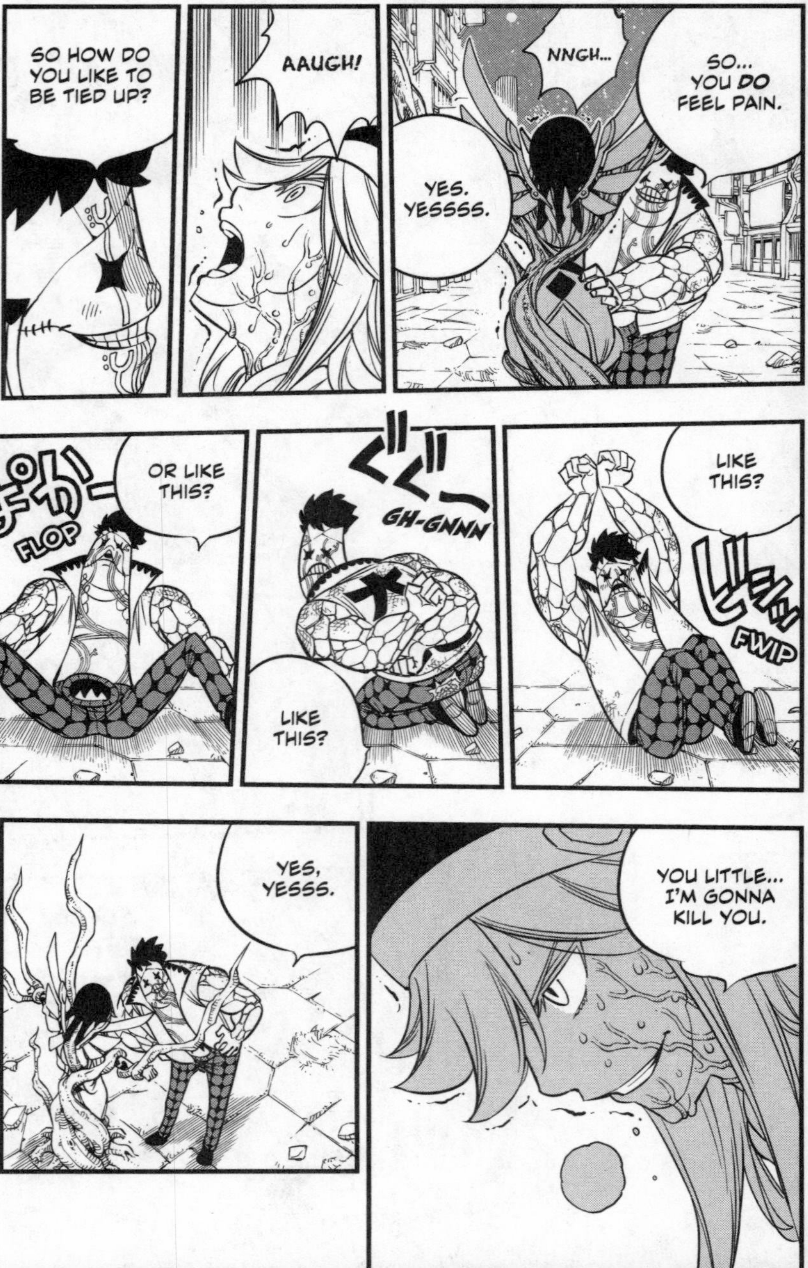
SO... YOU DO FEEL PAIN.
NNGH...
YES. YESSSS.
AAUGH!
SO HOW DO YOU LIKE TO BE TIED UP?
LIKE THIS?
FWIP
GH-GNNN
LIKE THIS?
OR LIKE THIS?
FLOP
YOU LITTLE... I'M GONNA KILL YOU.
YES, YESSS.

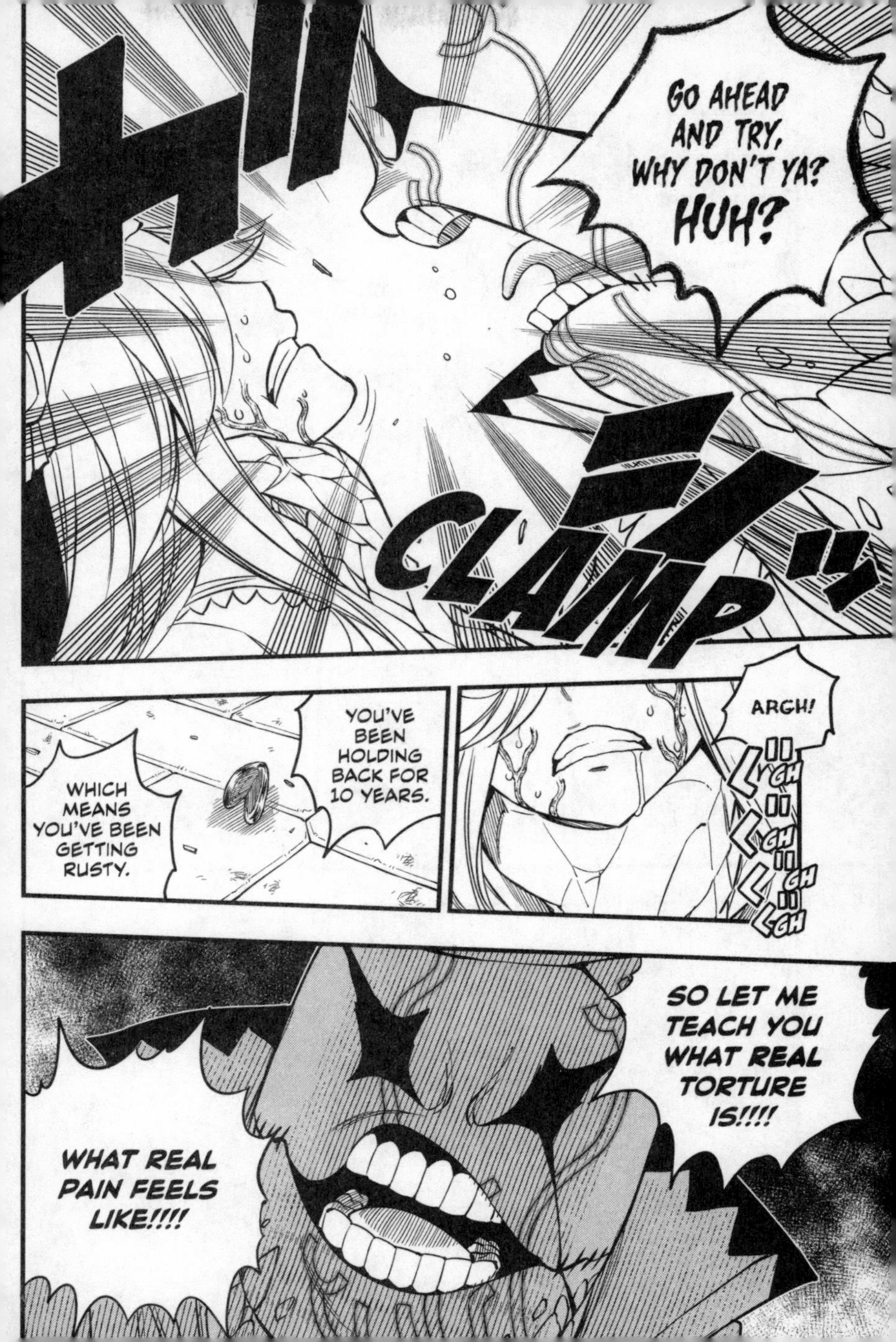
GO AHEAD AND TRY, WHY DON'T YA? HUH?
CLAMP
ARGH!
LGH!! LGH!! LGH!! LGH
YOU'VE BEEN HOLDING BACK FOR 10 YEARS.
WHICH MEANS YOU'VE BEEN GETTING RUSTY.
SO LET ME TEACH YOU WHAT REAL TORTURE IS!!!!
WHAT REAL PAIN FEELS LIKE!!!!

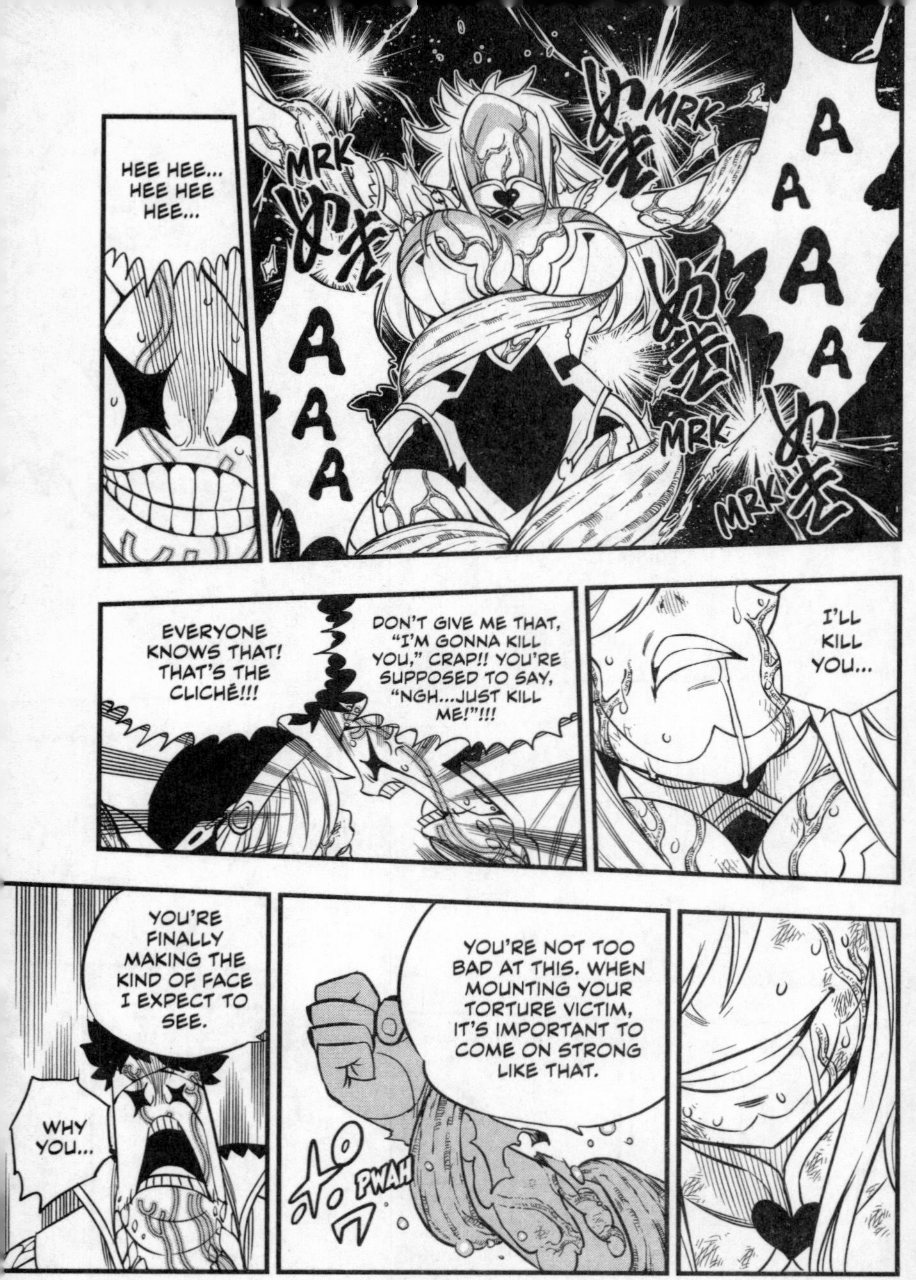
AAAAAA
MRK
MRK
AAAA
MRK
MRK
HEE HEE... HEE HEE HEE...
I'LL KILL YOU...
DON'T GIVE ME THAT, "I'M GONNA KILL YOU," CRAP!! YOU'RE SUPPOSED TO SAY, "NGH...JUST KILL ME!"!!!
EVERYONE KNOWS THAT! THAT'S THE CLICHÉ!!!
YOU'RE NOT TOO BAD AT THIS. WHEN MOUNTING YOUR TORTURE VICTIM, IT'S IMPORTANT TO COME ON STRONG LIKE THAT.
PWAH
YOU'RE FINALLY MAKING THE KIND OF FACE I EXPECT TO SEE.
WHY YOU...

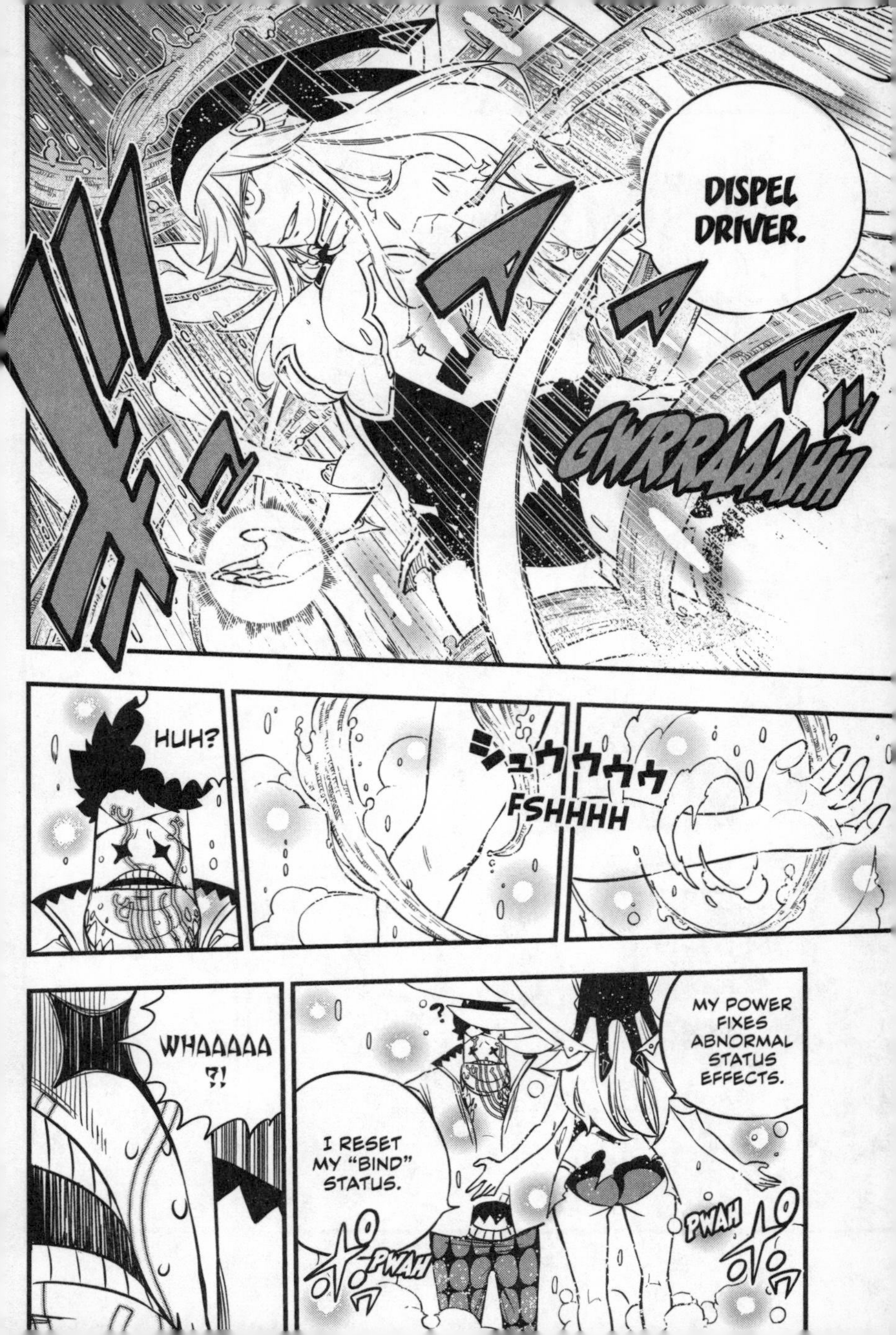
DISPEL DRIVER.
GWRRAAAHH
シュウウウウ
FSHHHH
HUH?
MY POWER FIXES ABNORMAL STATUS EFFECTS.
I RESET MY "BIND" STATUS.
PWAH
PWAH
WHAAAAA?!

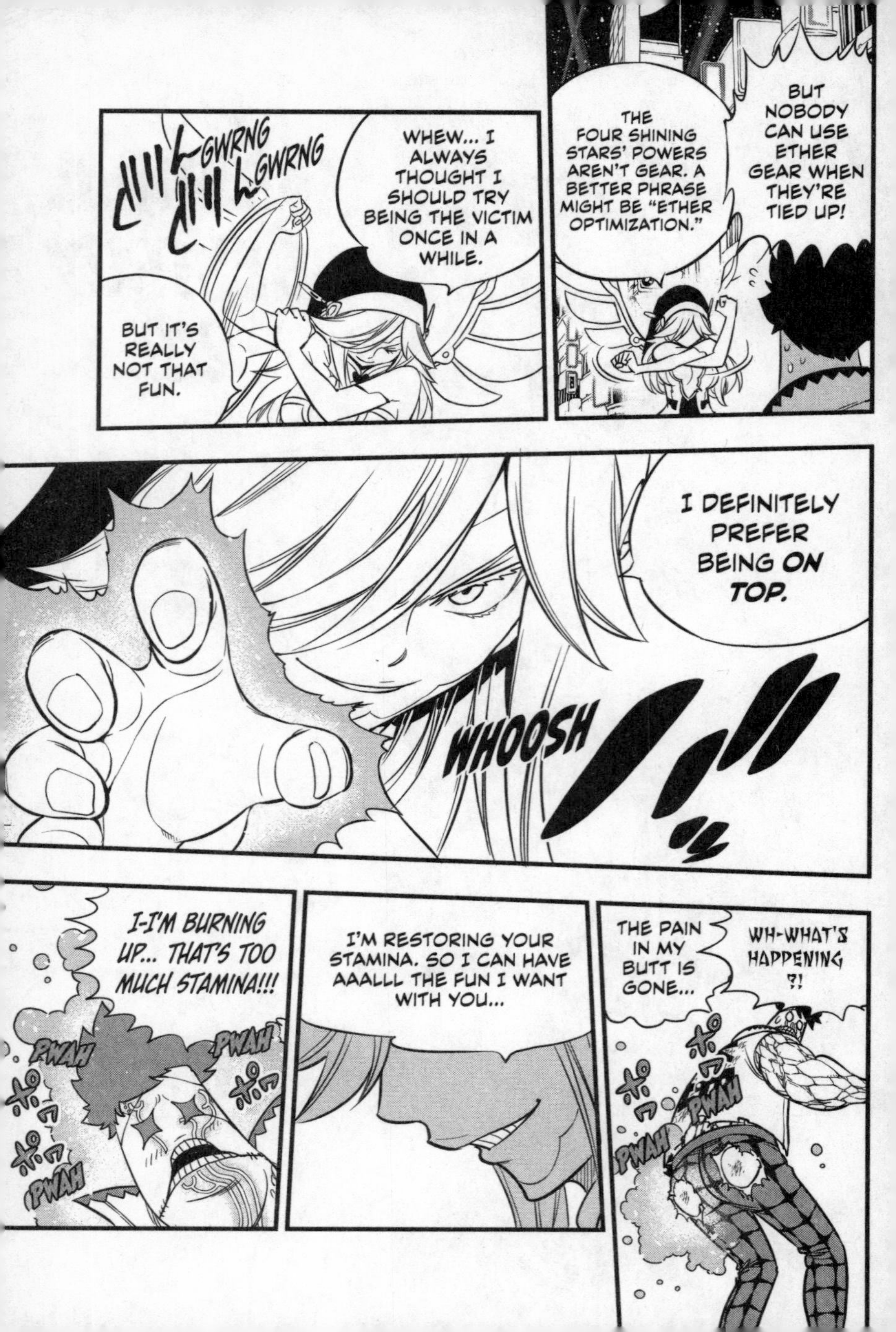
BUT NOBODY CAN USE ETHER GEAR WHEN THEY'RE TIED UP!
THE FOUR SHINING STARS' POWERS AREN'T GEAR. A BETTER PHRASE MIGHT BE "ETHER OPTIMIZATION."
GWRNG GWRNG
WHEW... I ALWAYS THOUGHT I SHOULD TRY BEING THE VICTIM ONCE IN A WHILE.
BUT IT'S REALLY NOT THAT FUN.
I DEFINITELY PREFER BEING ON TOP.
WHOOSH
WH-WHAT'S HAPPENING?!
THE PAIN IN MY BUTT IS GONE...
PWAH
PWAH
I'M RESTORING YOUR STAMINA. SO I CAN HAVE AAALLL THE FUN I WANT WITH YOU...
I-I'M BURNING UP... THAT'S TOO MUCH STAMINA!!!
PWAH
PWAH
PWAH

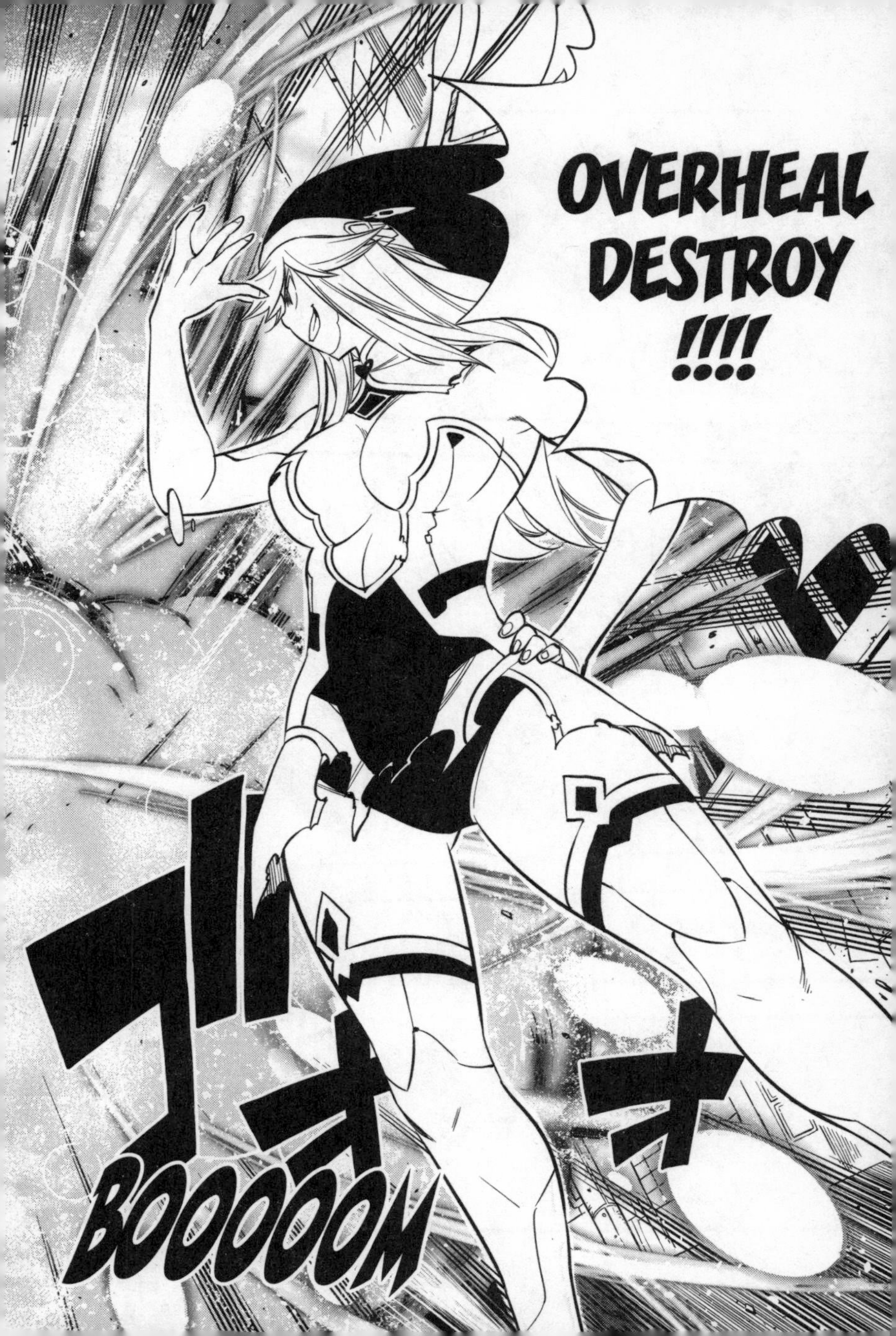
OVERHEAL DESTROY !!!!
BOOOOOM

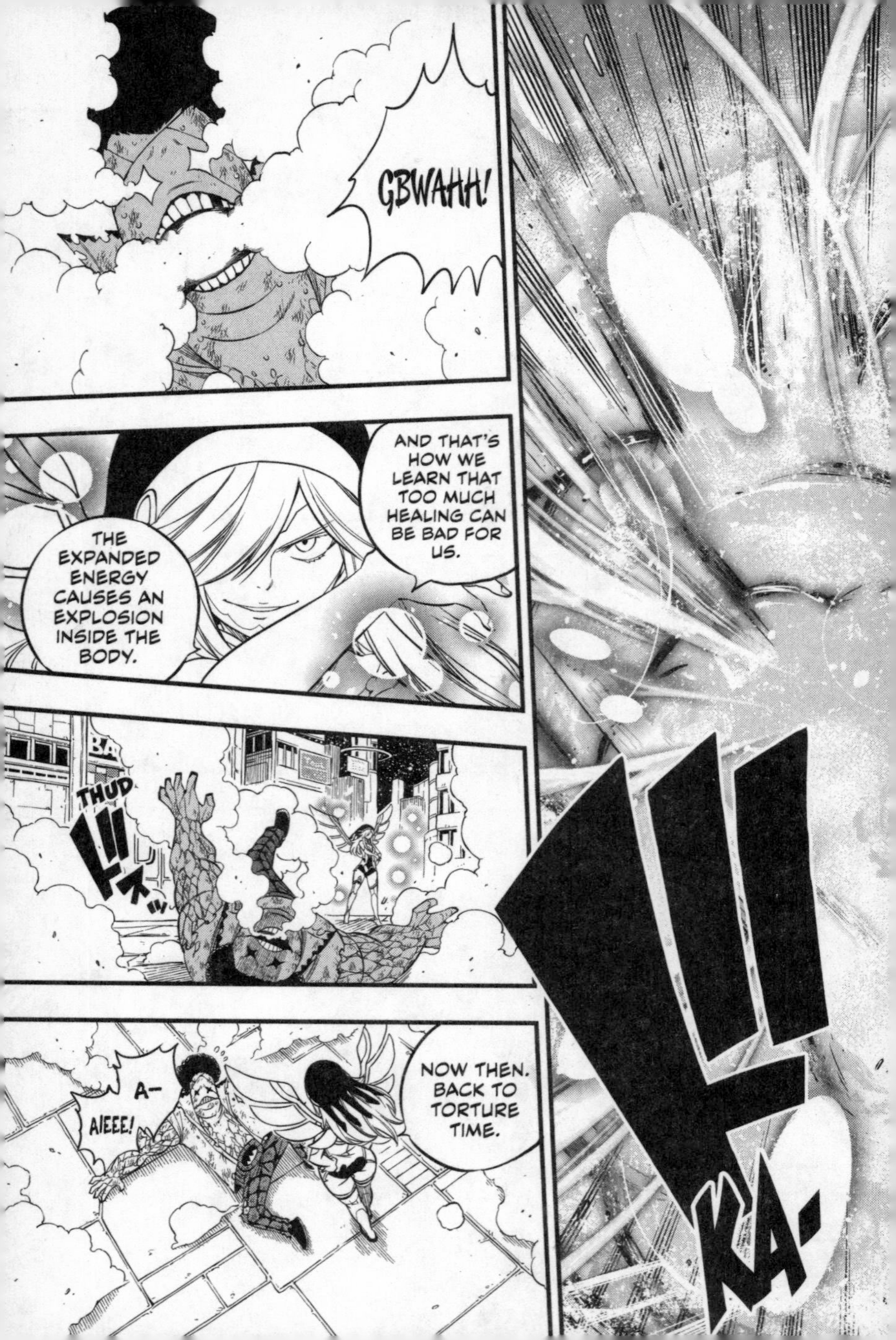
KA-
GBWAHH!
AND THAT'S HOW WE LEARN THAT TOO MUCH HEALING CAN BE BAD FOR US.
THE EXPANDED ENERGY CAUSES AN EXPLOSION INSIDE THE BODY.
THUD
NOW THEN. BACK TO TORTURE TIME.
A-
AIEEE!

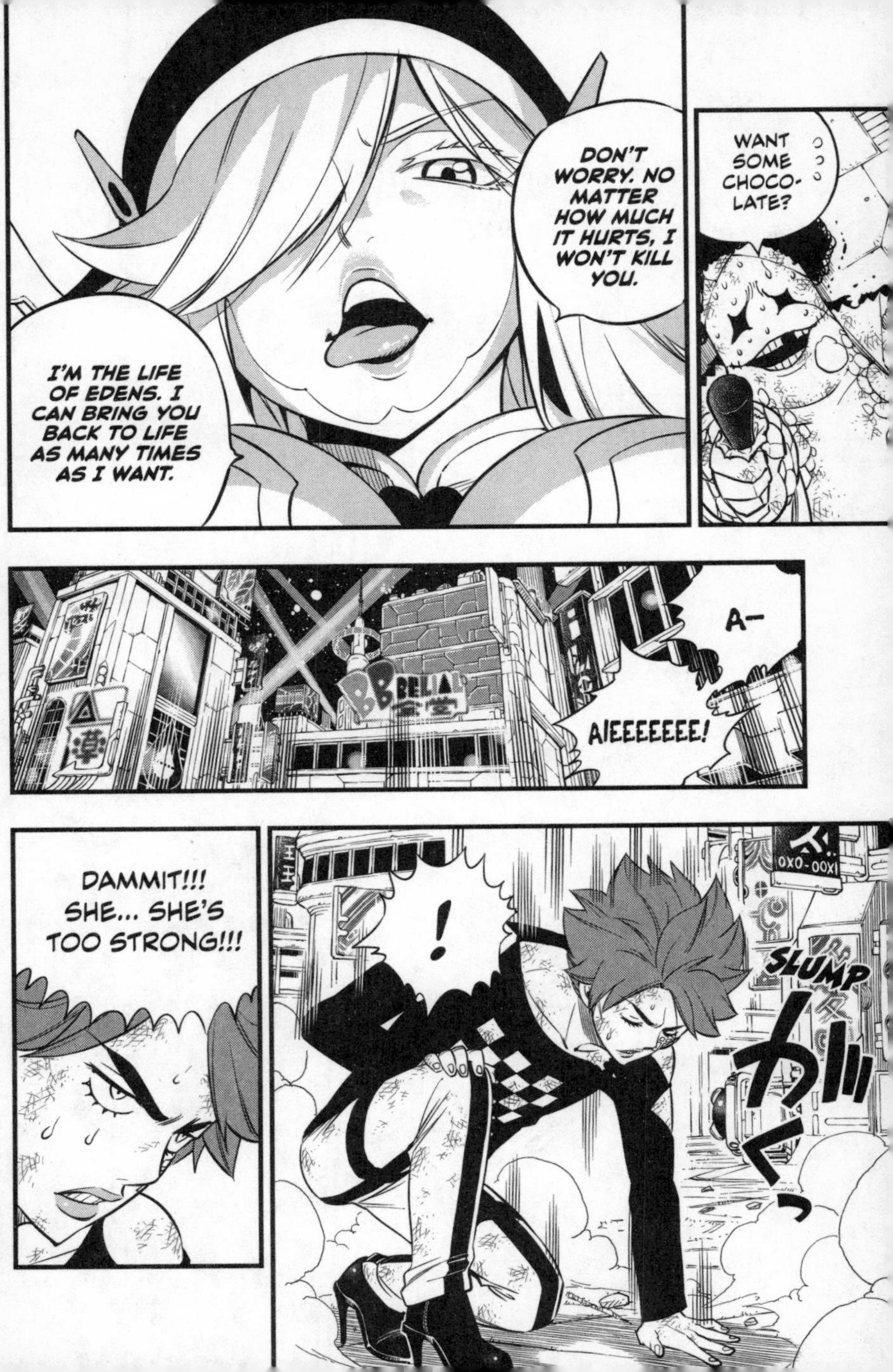
WANT SOME CHOCOLATE?
DON'T WORRY. NO MATTER HOW MUCH IT HURTS, I WON'T KILL YOU.
I'M THE LIFE OF EDENS. I CAN BRING YOU BACK TO LIFE AS MANY TIMES AS I WANT.
A—
AIEEEEEEE!
!
SLUMP
DAMMIT!!! SHE... SHE'S TOO STRONG!!!

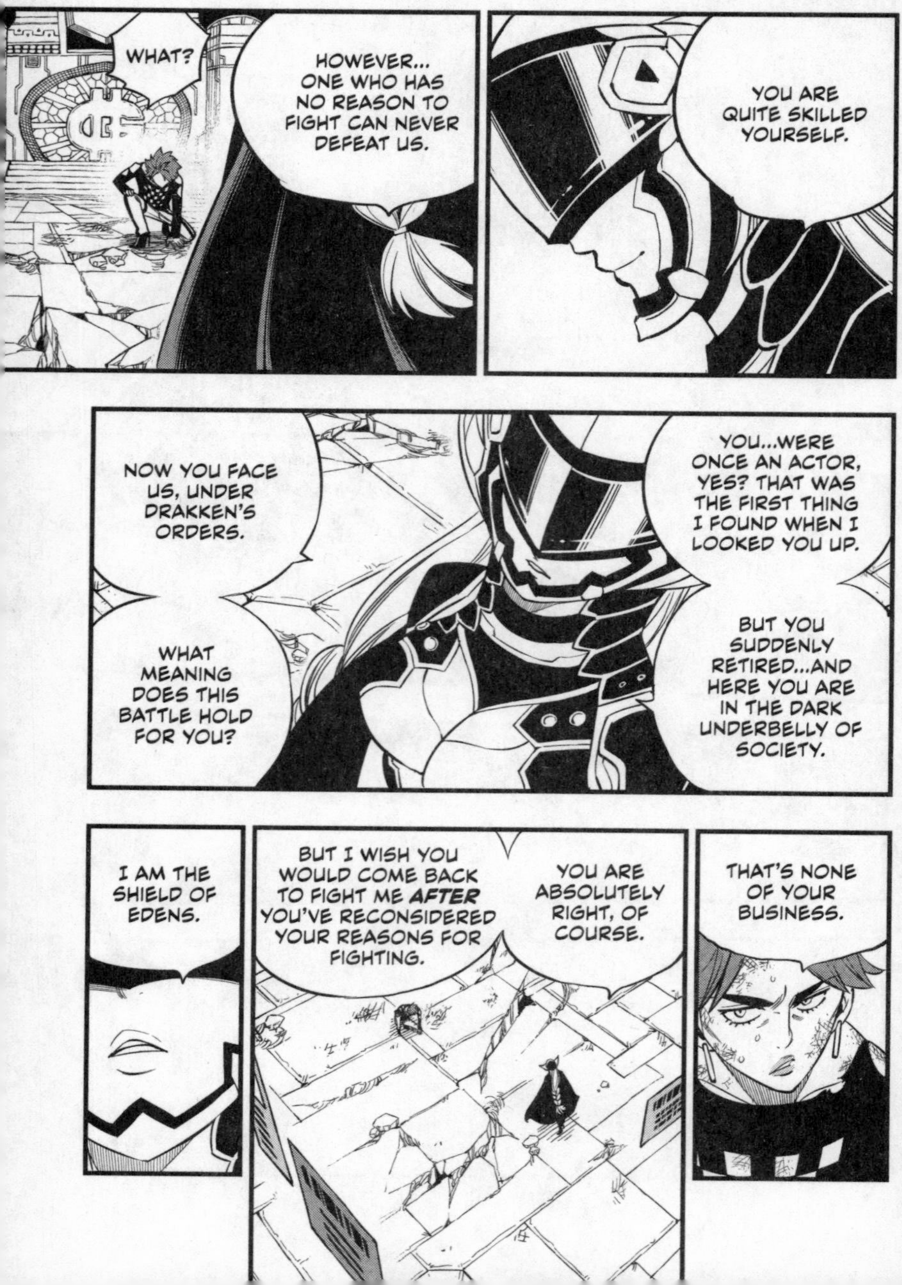
YOU ARE QUITE SKILLED YOURSELF.
HOWEVER... ONE WHO HAS NO REASON TO FIGHT CAN NEVER DEFEAT US.
WHAT?
YOU...WERE ONCE AN ACTOR, YES? THAT WAS THE FIRST THING I FOUND WHEN I LOOKED YOU UP.
BUT YOU SUDDENLY RETIRED...AND HERE YOU ARE IN THE DARK UNDERBELLY OF SOCIETY.
NOW YOU FACE US, UNDER DRAKKEN'S ORDERS.
WHAT MEANING DOES THIS BATTLE HOLD FOR YOU?
THAT'S NONE OF YOUR BUSINESS.
YOU ARE ABSOLUTELY RIGHT, OF COURSE.
BUT I WISH YOU WOULD COME BACK TO FIGHT ME *AFTER* YOU'VE RECONSIDERED YOUR REASONS FOR FIGHTING.
I AM THE SHIELD OF EDENS.

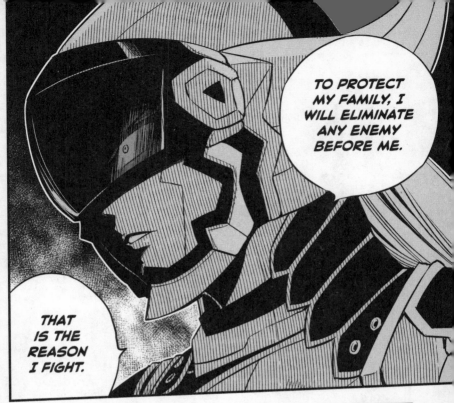

TO PROTECT MY FAMILY, I WILL ELIMINATE ANY ENEMY BEFORE ME.

THAT IS THE REASON I FIGHT.

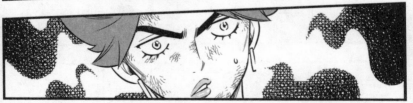

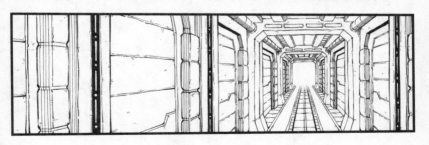

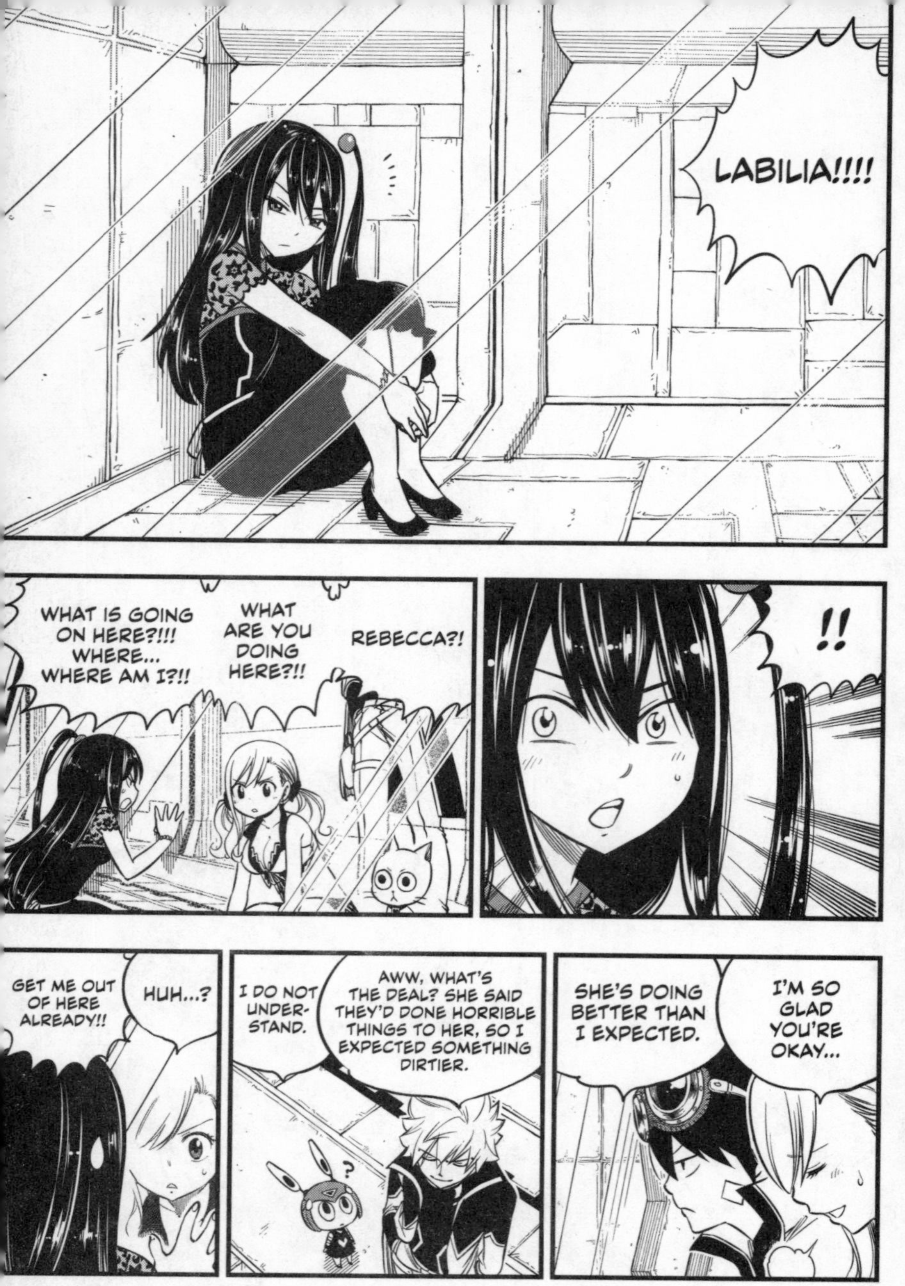
LABILIA!!!!
!!
REBECCA?!
WHAT ARE YOU DOING HERE?!!
WHAT IS GOING ON HERE?!!! WHERE... WHERE AM I?!!
I'M SO GLAD YOU'RE OKAY...
SHE'S DOING BETTER THAN I EXPECTED.
AWW, WHAT'S THE DEAL? SHE SAID THEY'D DONE HORRIBLE THINGS TO HER, SO I EXPECTED SOMETHING DIRTIER.
I DO NOT UNDER-STAND.
HUH...?
GET ME OUT OF HERE ALREADY!!

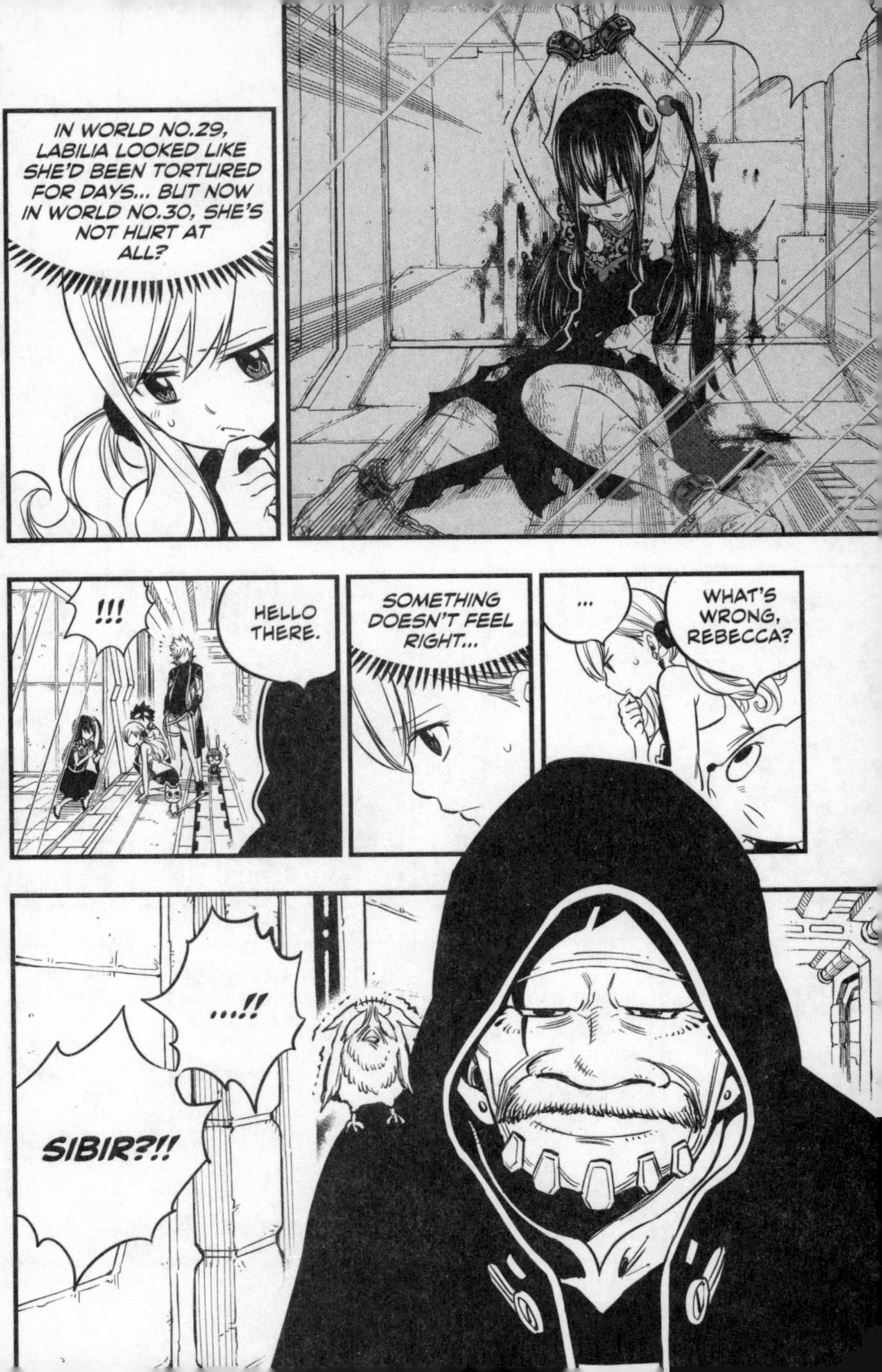
IN WORLD NO.29, LABILIA LOOKED LIKE SHE'D BEEN TORTURED FOR DAYS... BUT NOW IN WORLD NO.30, SHE'S NOT HURT AT ALL?
WHAT'S WRONG, REBECCA?
...
SOMETHING DOESN'T FEEL RIGHT...
HELLO THERE.
!!!
...!!
SIBIR?!!

CHAPTER 91: HOMURA VS. SYLPH

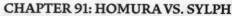

EDENS ZERO

Edens Zero
In-Depth Character File 5

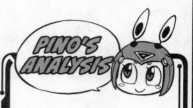

PINO'S ANALYSIS

Name: E.M. Pino

Powers: EMP

(Electro-Magnetic Pulse attack)

Likes: Master Shiki

Dislikes: Bullies

Attack:	☆
Defense:	☆
Marksmanship:	☆
Ether Power:	☆☆
Intelligence:	☆☆☆☆
Rabbit?:	☆☆☆

Memo

An anti-mech android. My EMP will short circuit every machine in range, but it shuts down Master Shiki's Ether Gear and Mr. Happy, too. My memory is damaged, so I don't know what I was made for, but I want to become human.

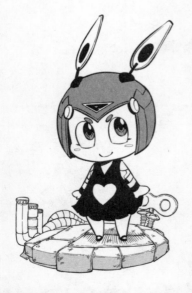

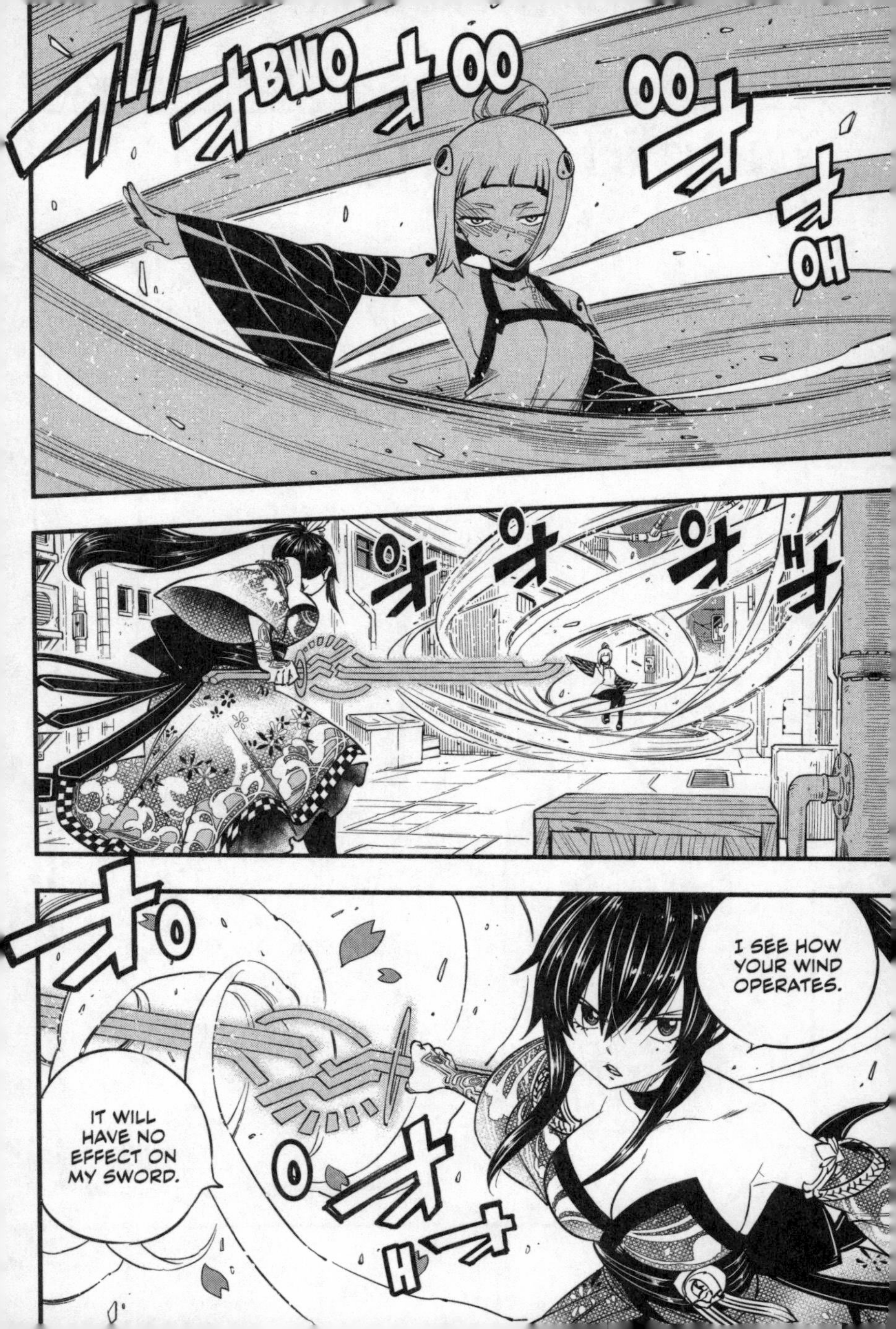
BWO
OO
OO
OH
H
H
I SEE HOW YOUR WIND OPERATES.
IT WILL HAVE NO EFFECT ON MY SWORD.
H

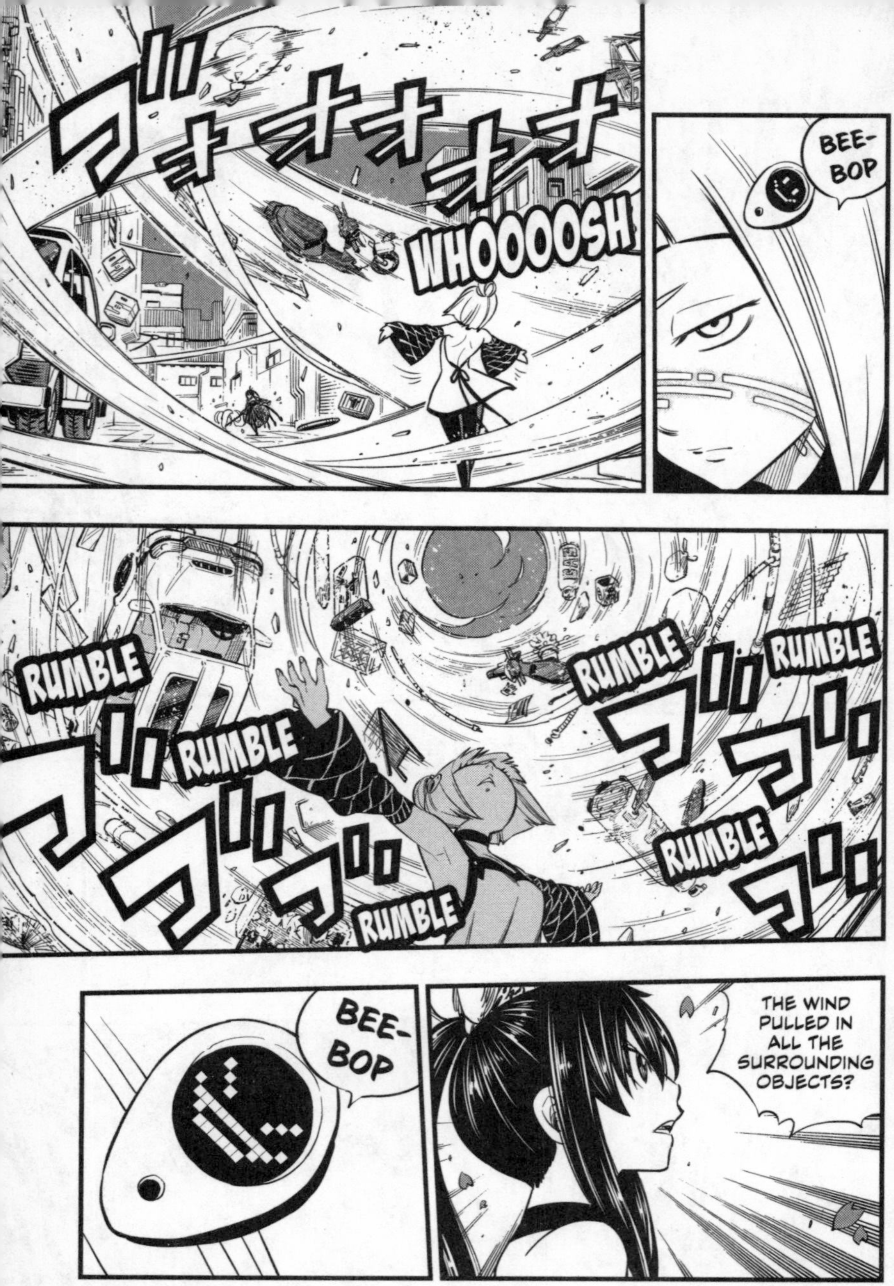
BEE-BOP
WHOOOOSH
RUMBLE
RUMBLE
RUMBLE
RUMBLE
RUMBLE
RUMBLE
THE WIND PULLED IN ALL THE SURROUNDING OBJECTS?
BEE-BOP

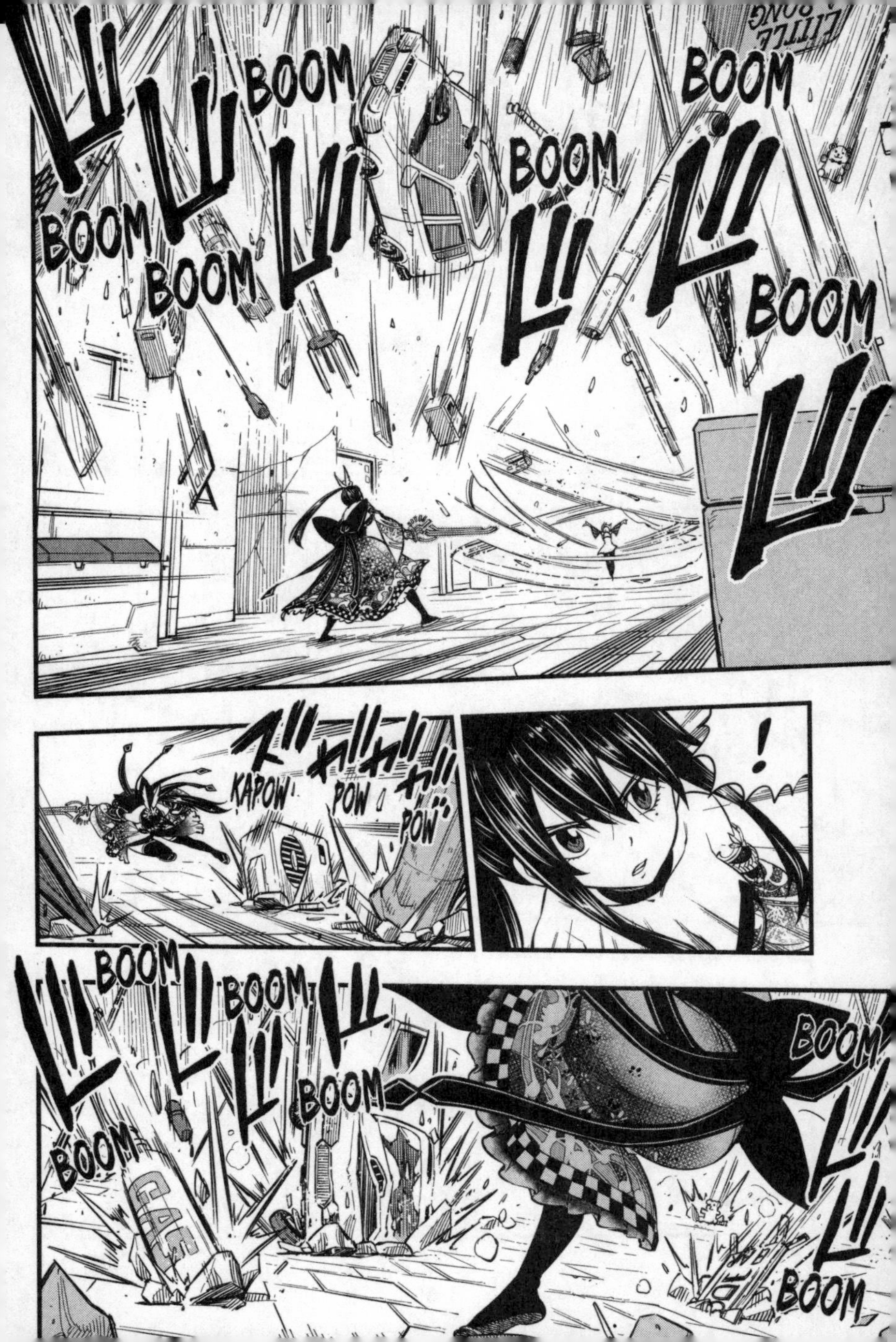
BOOM
BOOM
BOOM
BOOM
BOOM
BOOM
!
KAPOW
POW
POW
BOOM
BOOM
BOOM
BOOM
BOOM
BOOM

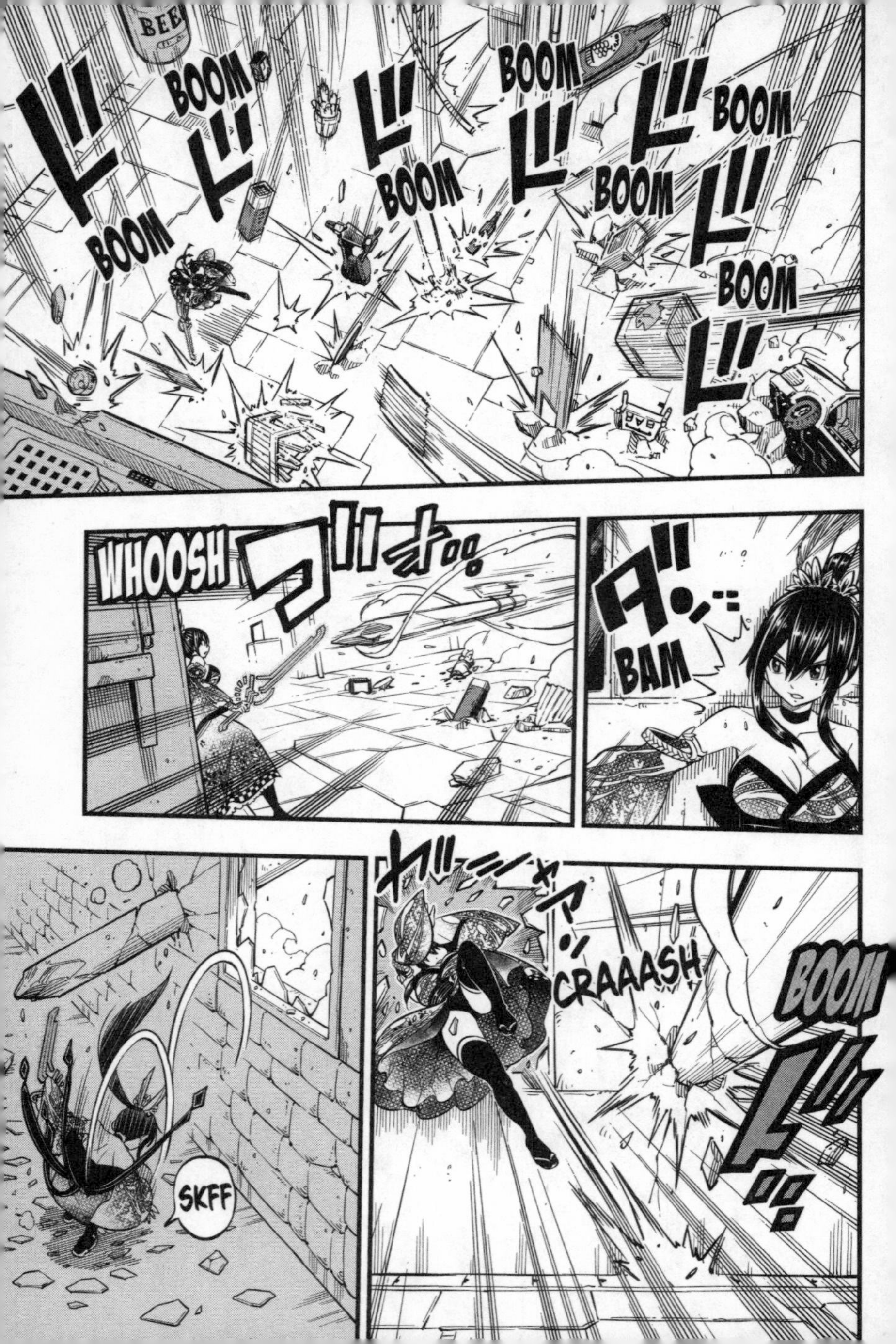
BOOM
BOOM
BOOM
BOOM
BOOM
BOOM
BOOM
BAM
WHOOSH
BOOM
CRAAASH
SKFF

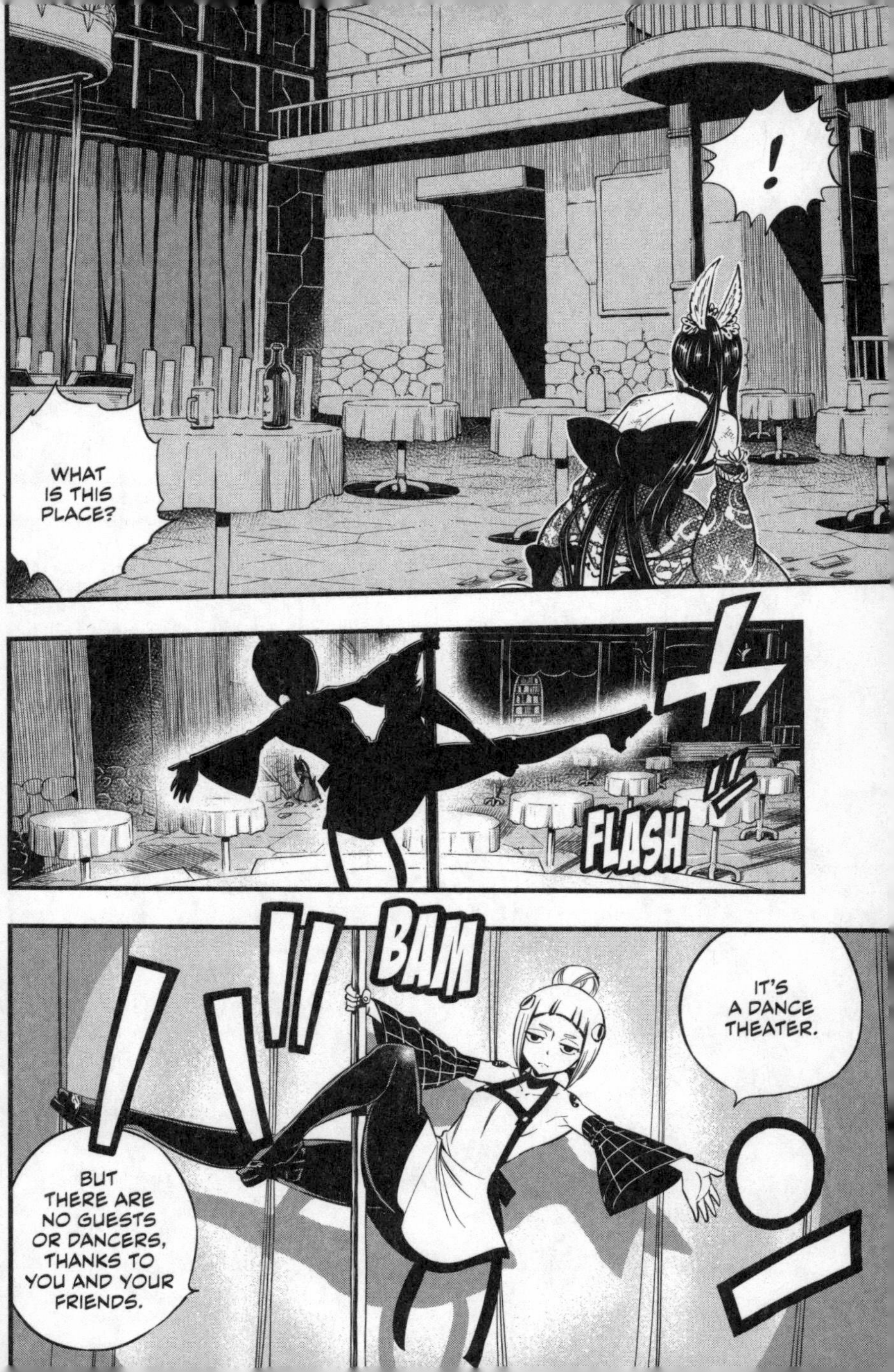
!
WHAT IS THIS PLACE?
FLASH
BAM
IT'S A DANCE THEATER.
BUT THERE ARE NO GUESTS OR DANCERS, THANKS TO YOU AND YOUR FRIENDS.

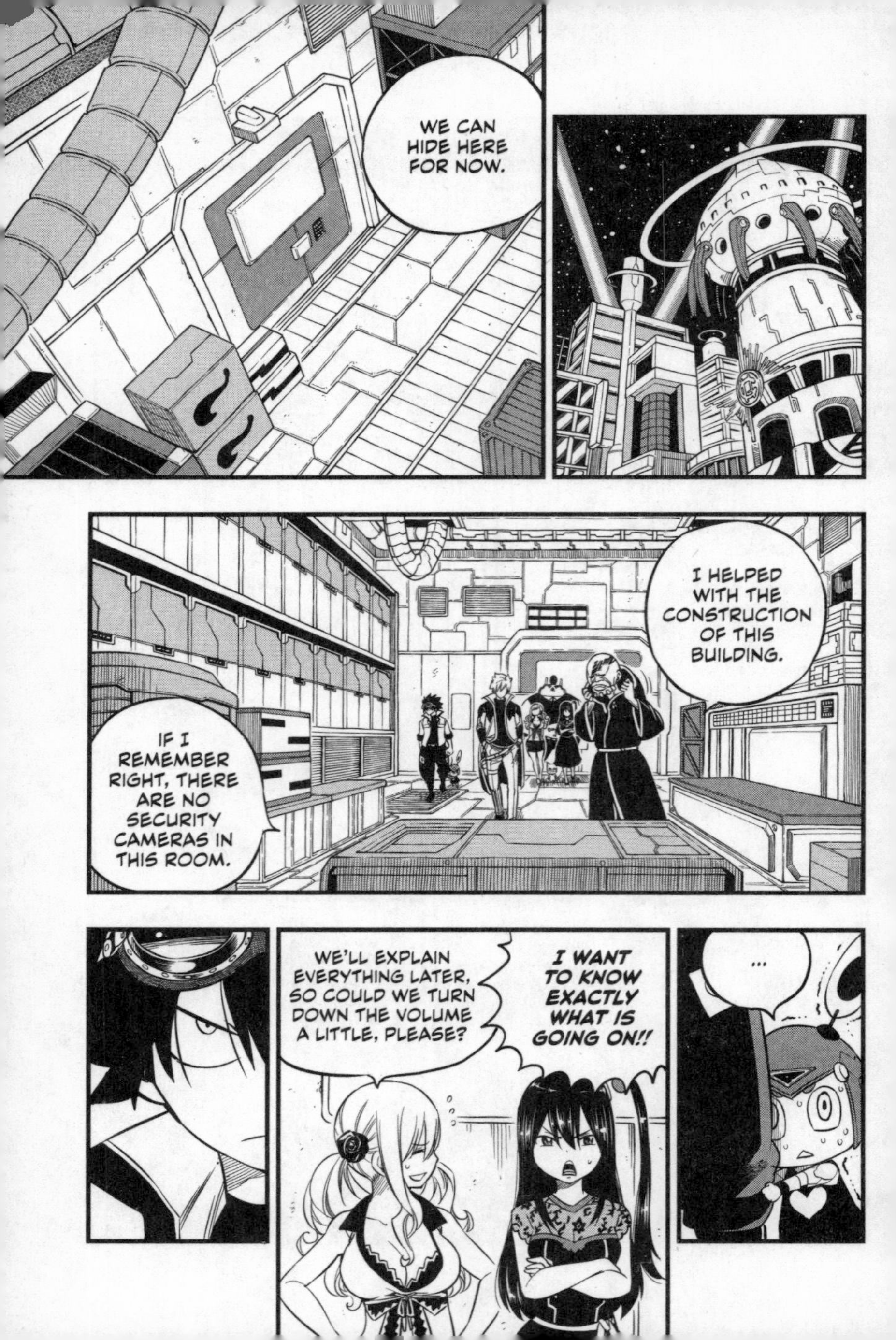
WE CAN HIDE HERE FOR NOW.
I HELPED WITH THE CONSTRUCTION OF THIS BUILDING.
IF I REMEMBER RIGHT, THERE ARE NO SECURITY CAMERAS IN THIS ROOM.
...
I WANT TO KNOW EXACTLY WHAT IS GOING ON!!
WE'LL EXPLAIN EVERYTHING LATER, SO COULD WE TURN DOWN THE VOLUME A LITTLE, PLEASE?

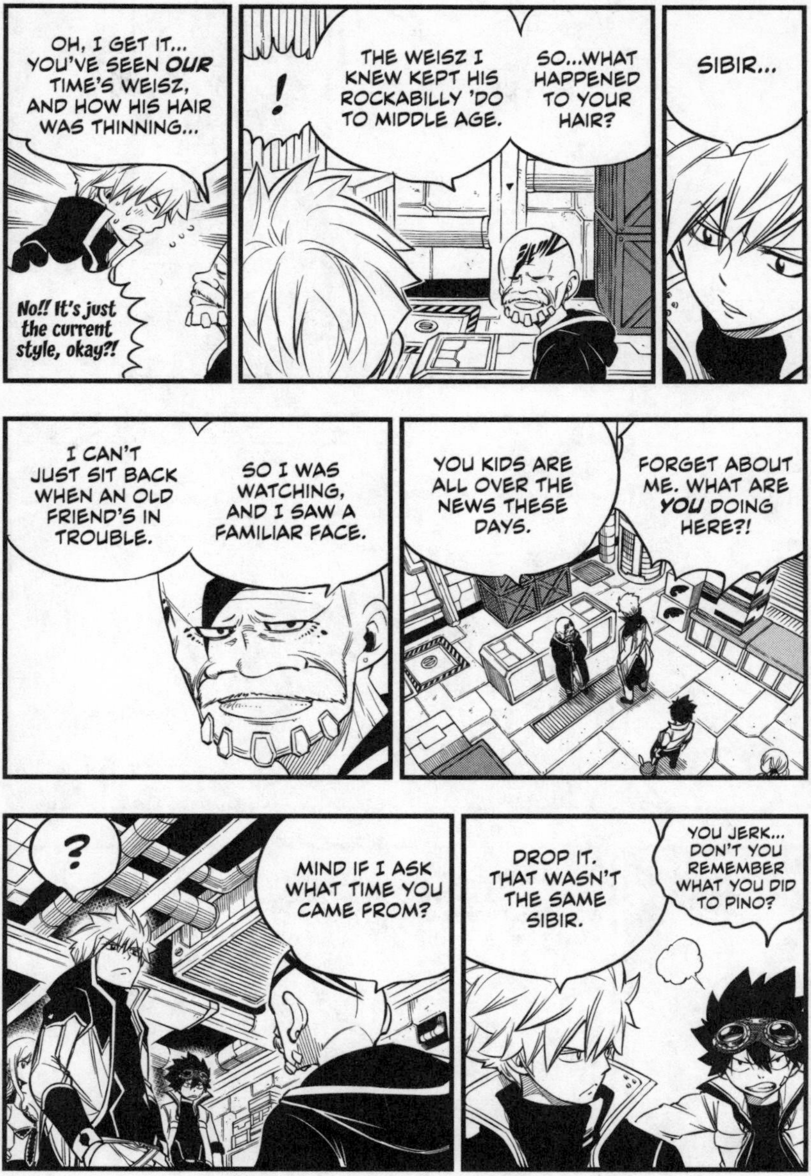

SIBIR...
SO...WHAT HAPPENED TO YOUR HAIR?
THE WEISZ I KNEW KEPT HIS ROCKABILLY 'DO TO MIDDLE AGE.
!
OH, I GET IT... YOU'VE SEEN *OUR* TIME'S WEISZ, AND HOW HIS HAIR WAS THINNING...
No!! It's just the current style, okay?!
FORGET ABOUT ME. WHAT ARE *YOU* DOING HERE?!
YOU KIDS ARE ALL OVER THE NEWS THESE DAYS.
SO I WAS WATCHING, AND I SAW A FAMILIAR FACE.
I CAN'T JUST SIT BACK WHEN AN OLD FRIEND'S IN TROUBLE.
YOU JERK... DON'T YOU REMEMBER WHAT YOU DID TO PINO?
DROP IT. THAT WASN'T THE SAME SIBIR.
MIND IF I ASK WHAT TIME YOU CAME FROM?
?

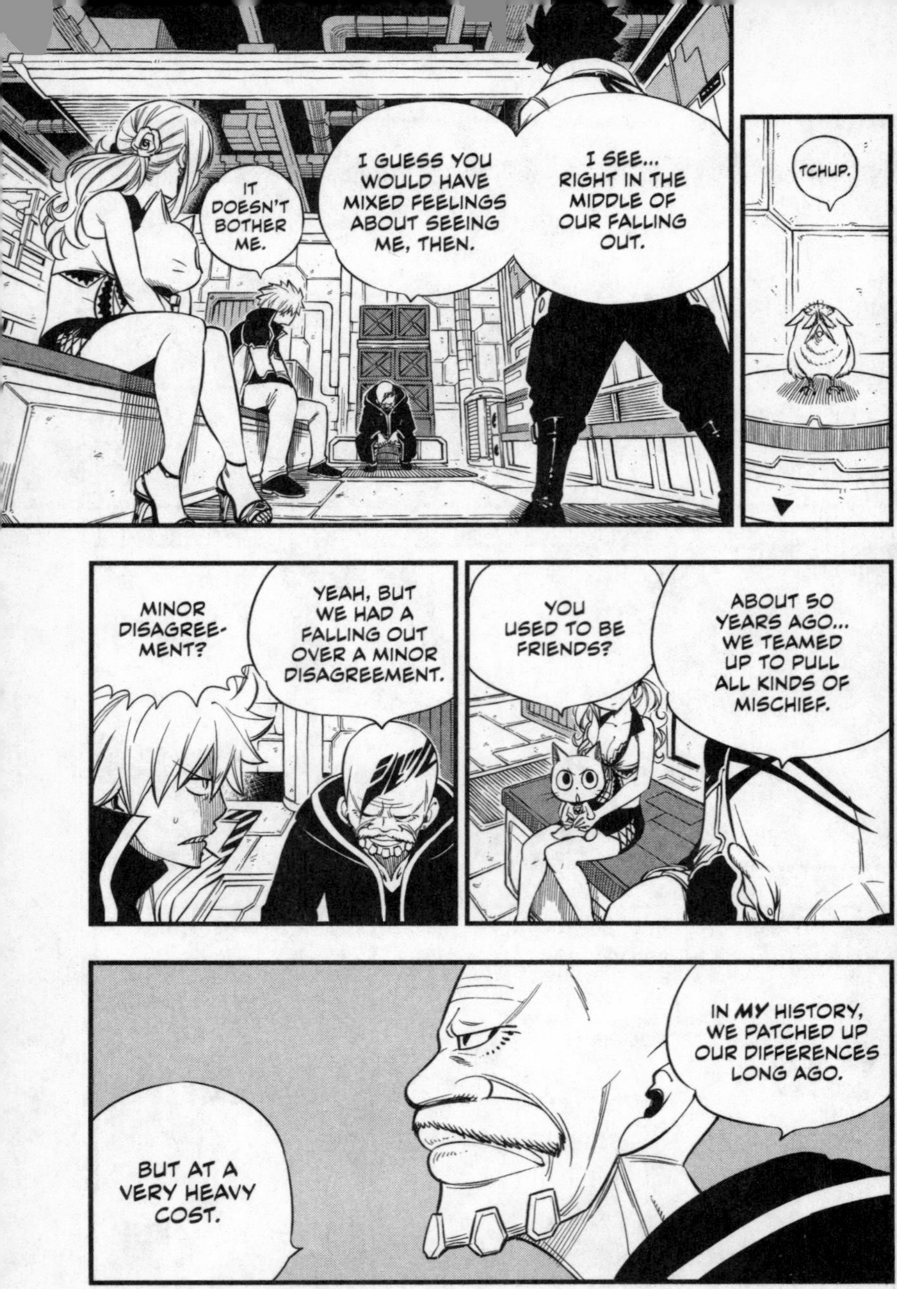
TCHUP.
I SEE... RIGHT IN THE MIDDLE OF OUR FALLING OUT.
I GUESS YOU WOULD HAVE MIXED FEELINGS ABOUT SEEING ME, THEN.
IT DOESN'T BOTHER ME.
ABOUT 50 YEARS AGO... WE TEAMED UP TO PULL ALL KINDS OF MISCHIEF.
YOU USED TO BE FRIENDS?
YEAH, BUT WE HAD A FALLING OUT OVER A MINOR DISAGREEMENT.
MINOR DISAGREE-MENT?
IN *MY* HISTORY, WE PATCHED UP OUR DIFFERENCES LONG AGO.
BUT AT A VERY HEAVY COST.

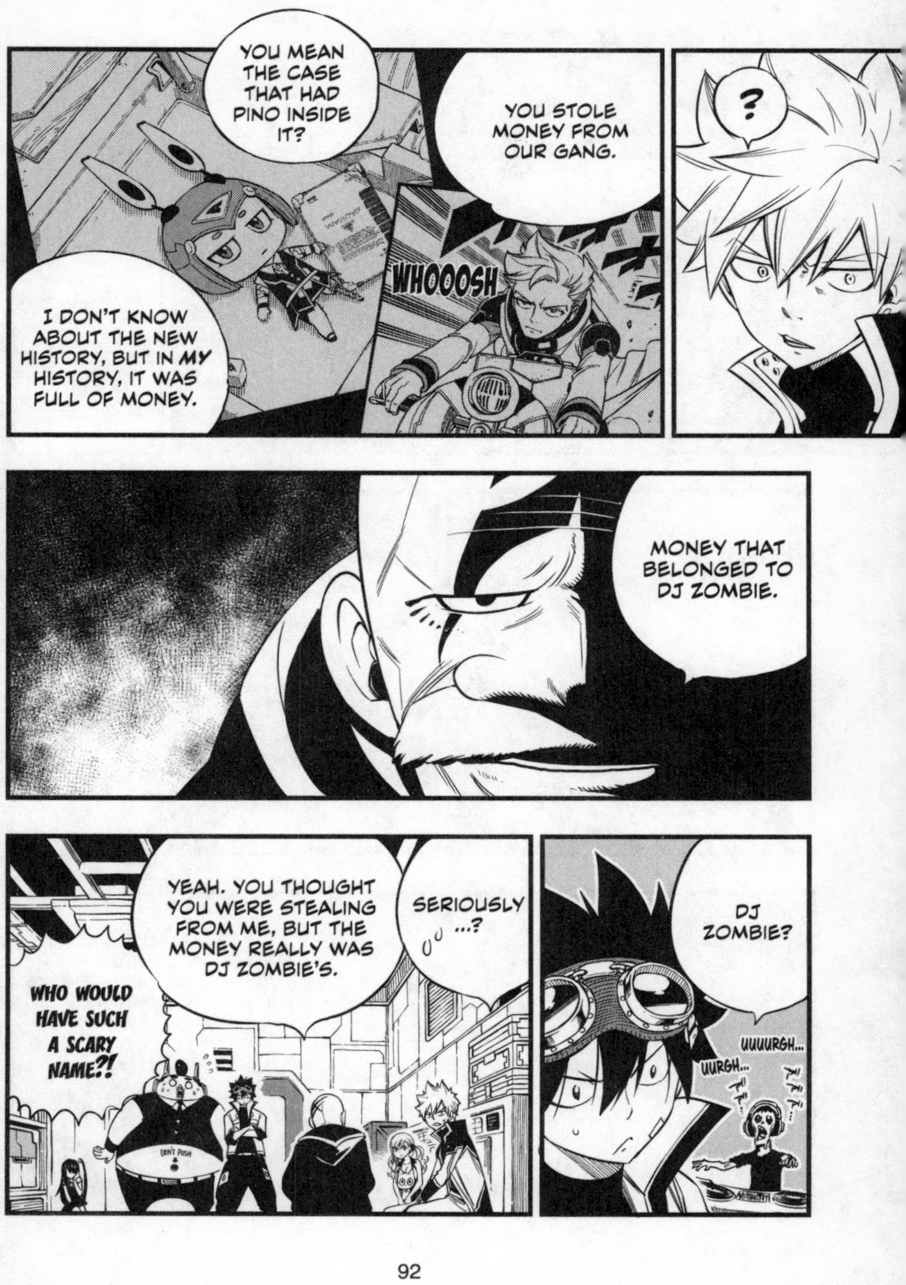
?
YOU STOLE MONEY FROM OUR GANG.
WHOOOSH
YOU MEAN THE CASE THAT HAD PINO INSIDE IT?
I DON'T KNOW ABOUT THE NEW HISTORY, BUT IN *MY* HISTORY, IT WAS FULL OF MONEY.
MONEY THAT BELONGED TO DJ ZOMBIE.
DJ ZOMBIE?
UUUURGH...
UURGH...
SERIOUSLY ...?
YEAH. YOU THOUGHT YOU WERE STEALING FROM ME, BUT THE MONEY REALLY WAS DJ ZOMBIE'S.
WHO WOULD HAVE SUCH A SCARY NAME?!
DON'T PUSH

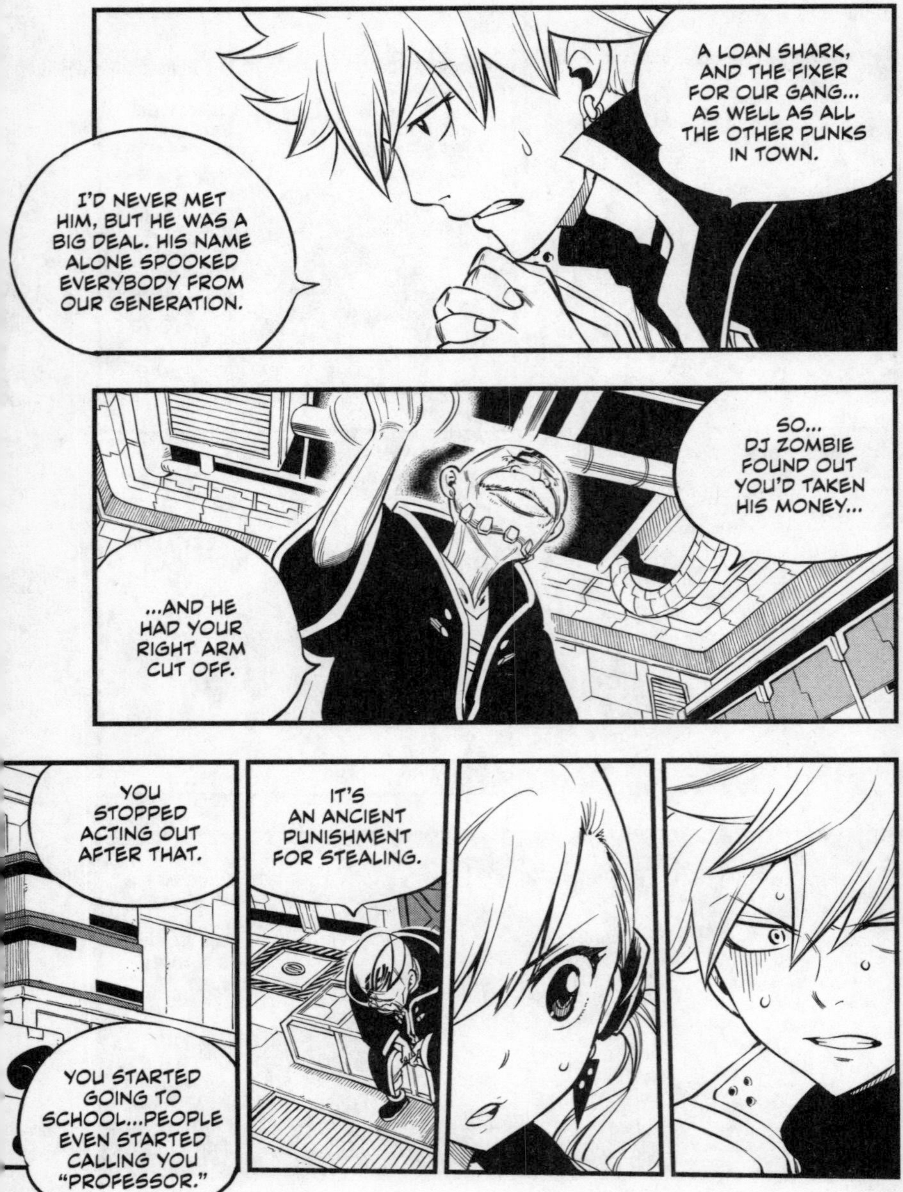
A LOAN SHARK, AND THE FIXER FOR OUR GANG... AS WELL AS ALL THE OTHER PUNKS IN TOWN.
I'D NEVER MET HIM, BUT HE WAS A BIG DEAL. HIS NAME ALONE SPOOKED EVERYBODY FROM OUR GENERATION.
SO... DJ ZOMBIE FOUND OUT YOU'D TAKEN HIS MONEY...
...AND HE HAD YOUR RIGHT ARM CUT OFF.
IT'S AN ANCIENT PUNISHMENT FOR STEALING.
YOU STOPPED ACTING OUT AFTER THAT.
YOU STARTED GOING TO SCHOOL...PEOPLE EVEN STARTED CALLING YOU "PROFESSOR."

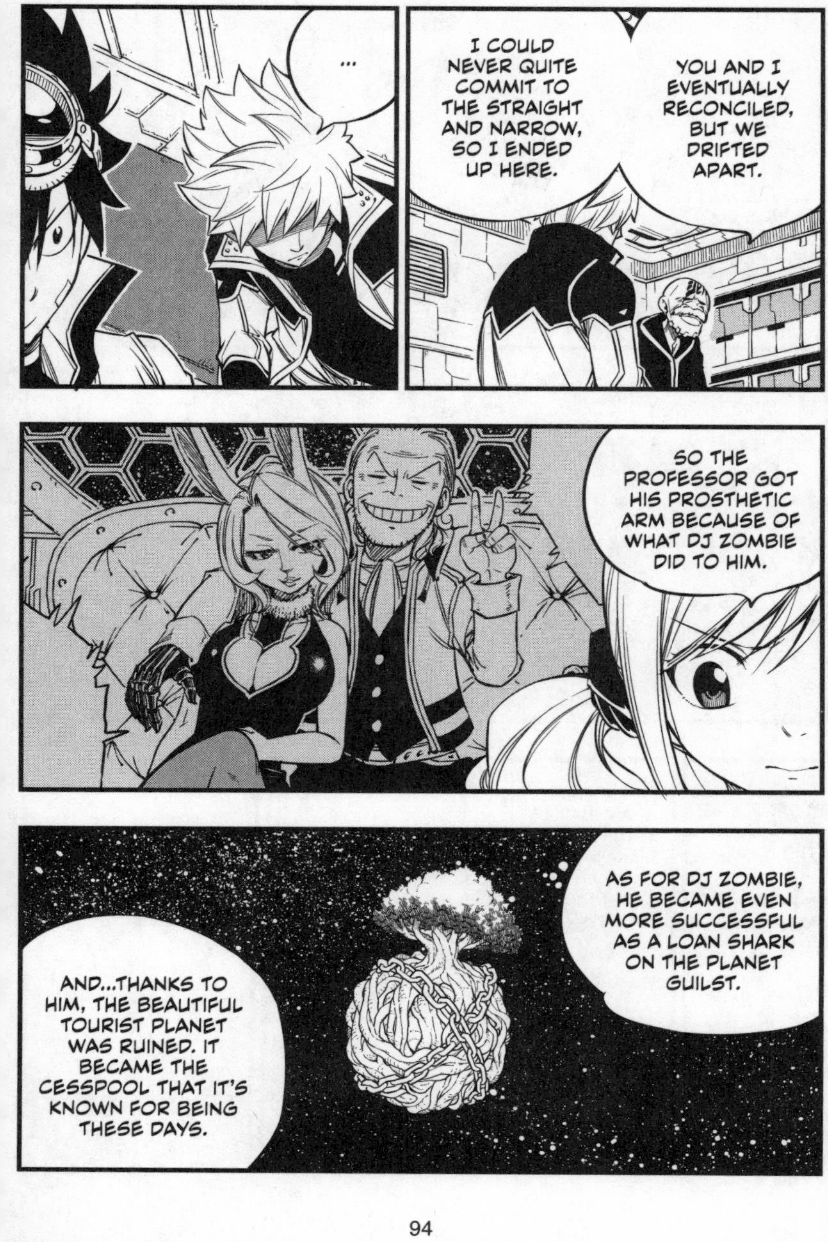
YOU AND I EVENTUALLY RECONCILED, BUT WE DRIFTED APART.
I COULD NEVER QUITE COMMIT TO THE STRAIGHT AND NARROW, SO I ENDED UP HERE.
...
SO THE PROFESSOR GOT HIS PROSTHETIC ARM BECAUSE OF WHAT DJ ZOMBIE DID TO HIM.
AS FOR DJ ZOMBIE, HE BECAME EVEN MORE SUCCESSFUL AS A LOAN SHARK ON THE PLANET GUILST.
AND...THANKS TO HIM, THE BEAUTIFUL TOURIST PLANET WAS RUINED. IT BECAME THE CESSPOOL THAT IT'S KNOWN FOR BEING THESE DAYS.

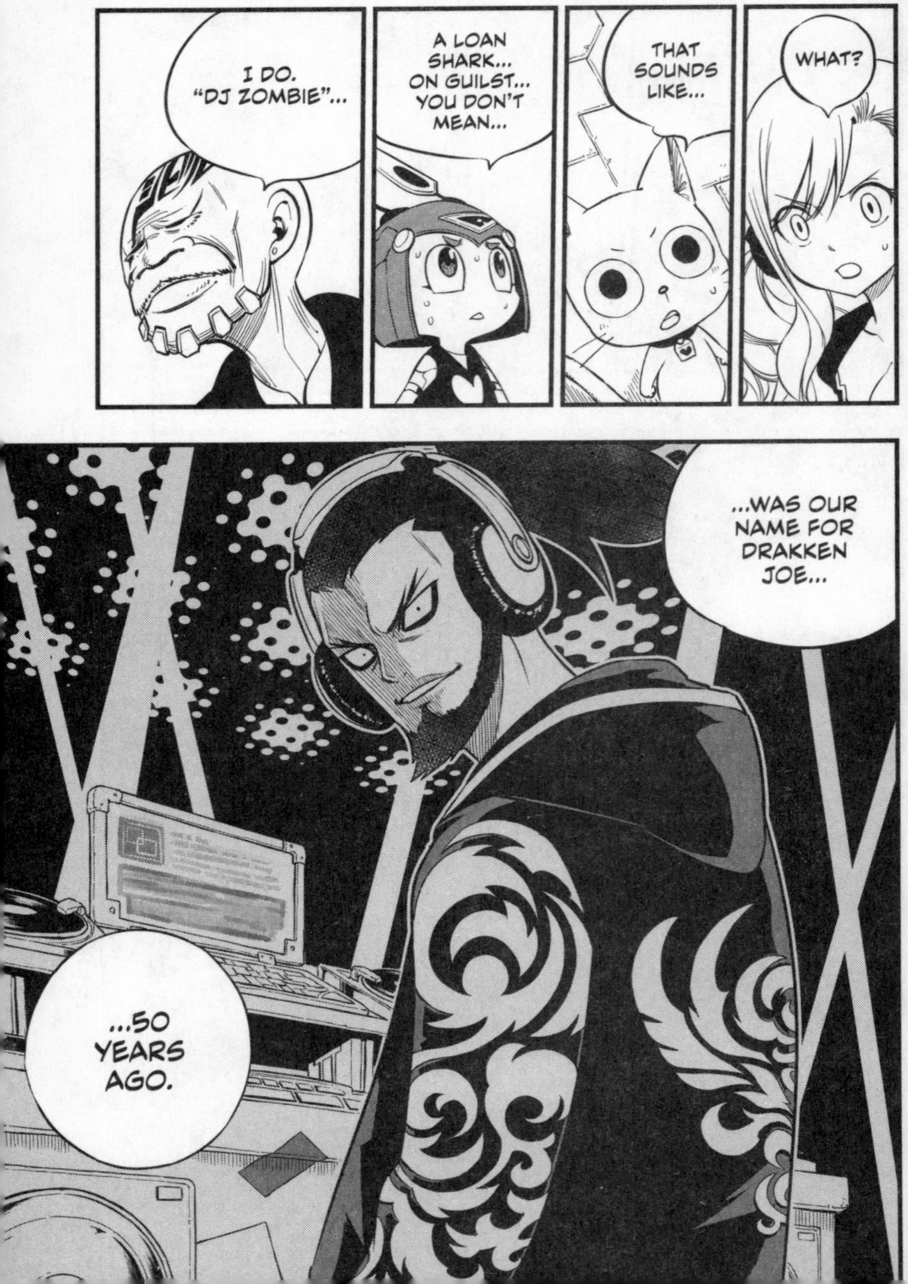
WHAT?
THAT SOUNDS LIKE...
A LOAN SHARK... ON GUILST... YOU DON'T MEAN...
I DO. "DJ ZOMBIE"...
...WAS OUR NAME FOR DRAKKEN JOE...
...50 YEARS AGO.

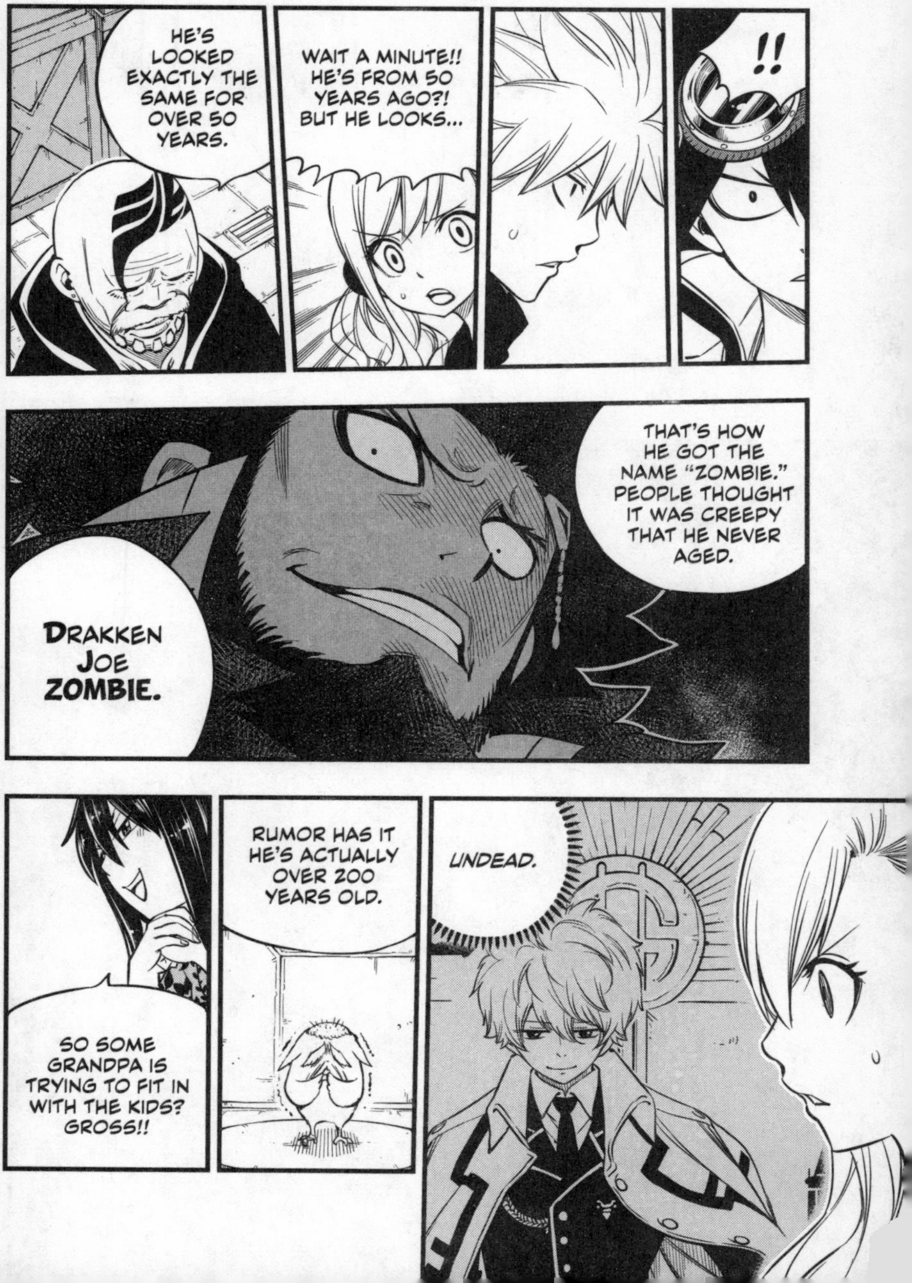
!!
WAIT A MINUTE!! HE'S FROM 50 YEARS AGO?! BUT HE LOOKS...
HE'S LOOKED EXACTLY THE SAME FOR OVER 50 YEARS.
THAT'S HOW HE GOT THE NAME "ZOMBIE." PEOPLE THOUGHT IT WAS CREEPY THAT HE NEVER AGED.
DRAKKEN JOE ZOMBIE.
UNDEAD.
RUMOR HAS IT HE'S ACTUALLY OVER 200 YEARS OLD.
SO SOME GRANDPA IS TRYING TO FIT IN WITH THE KIDS? GROSS!!

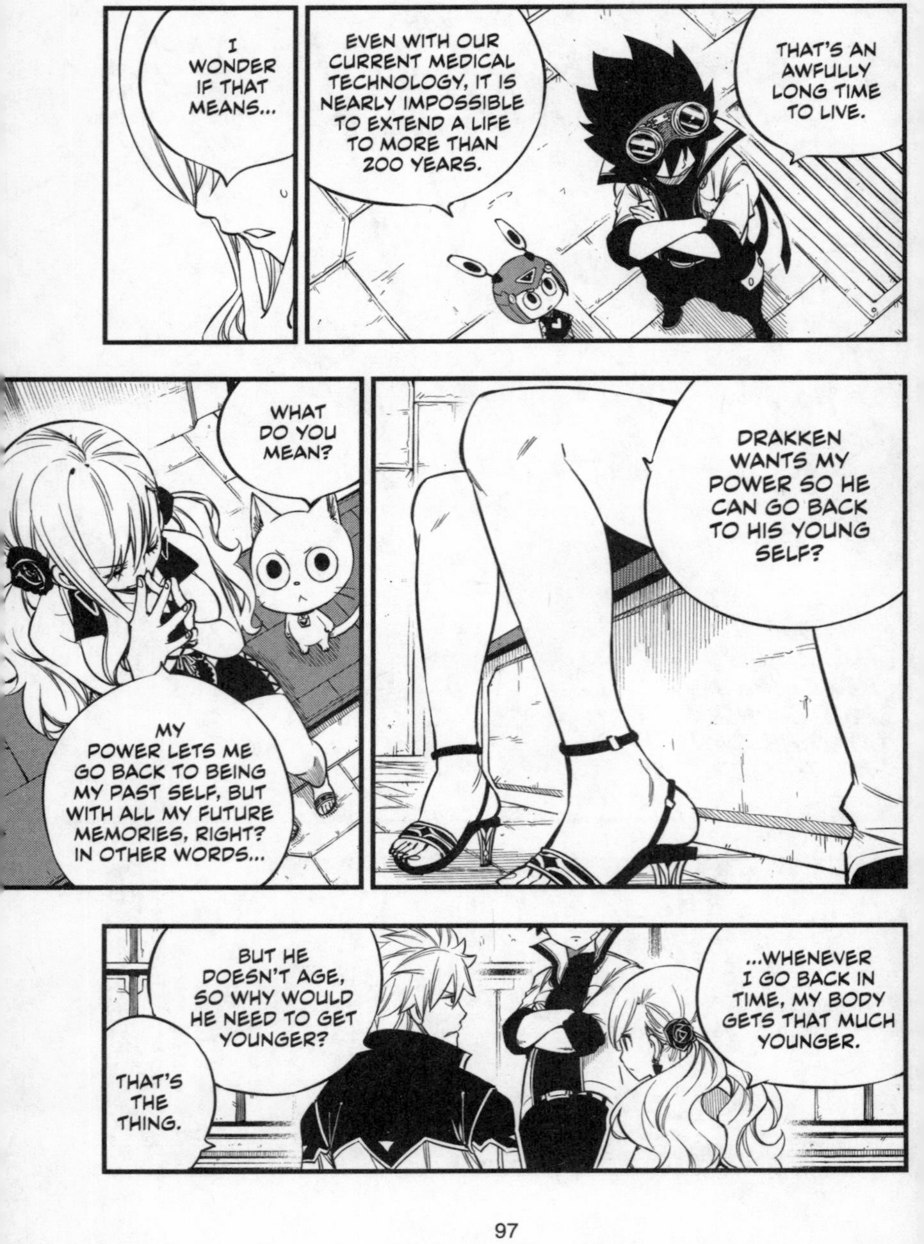

THAT'S AN AWFULLY LONG TIME TO LIVE.
EVEN WITH OUR CURRENT MEDICAL TECHNOLOGY, IT IS NEARLY IMPOSSIBLE TO EXTEND A LIFE TO MORE THAN 200 YEARS.
I WONDER IF THAT MEANS...
DRAKKEN WANTS MY POWER SO HE CAN GO BACK TO HIS YOUNG SELF?
WHAT DO YOU MEAN?
MY POWER LETS ME GO BACK TO BEING MY PAST SELF, BUT WITH ALL MY FUTURE MEMORIES, RIGHT? IN OTHER WORDS...
...WHENEVER I GO BACK IN TIME, MY BODY GETS THAT MUCH YOUNGER.
BUT HE DOESN'T AGE, SO WHY WOULD HE NEED TO GET YOUNGER?
THAT'S THE THING.

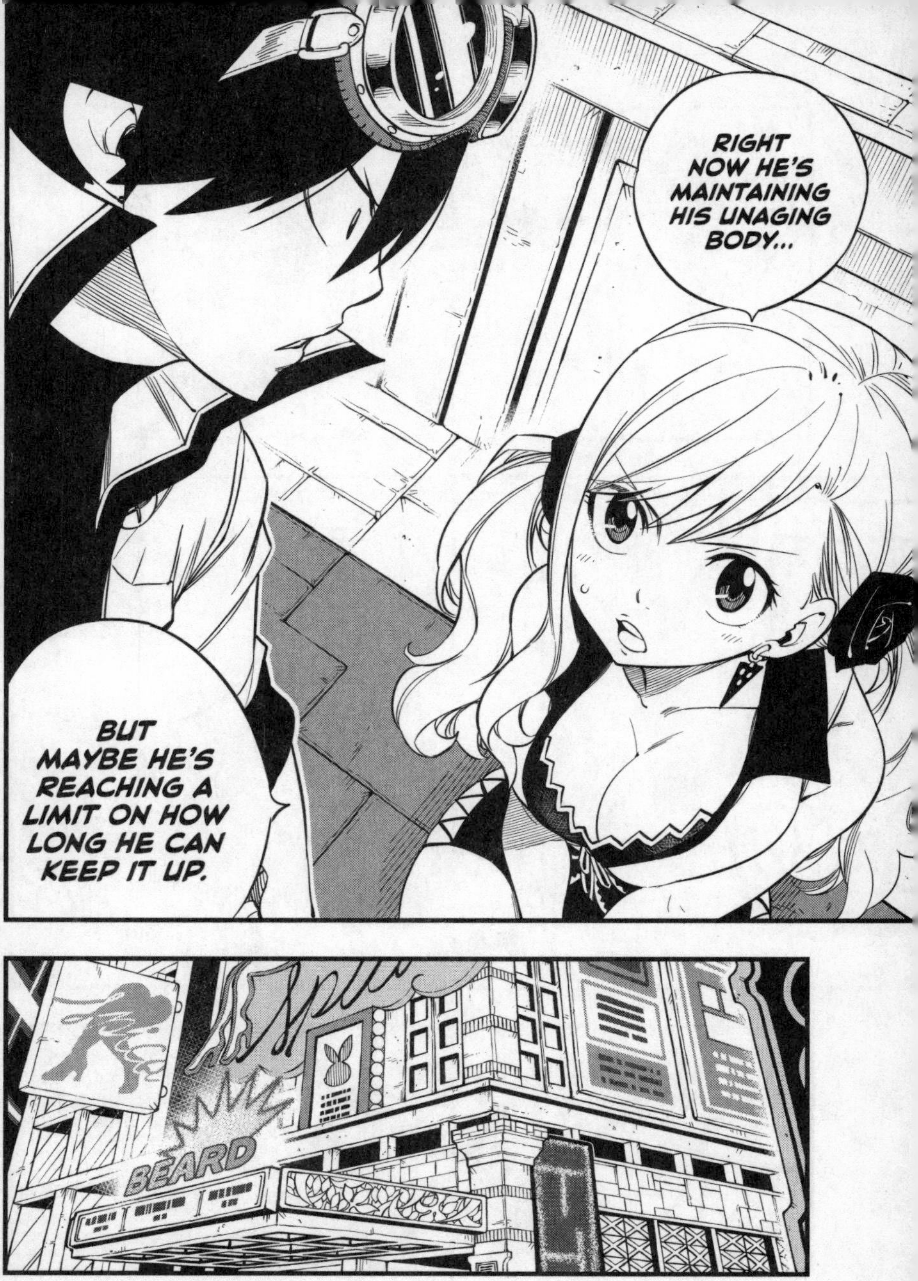
RIGHT NOW HE'S MAINTAINING HIS UNAGING BODY...
BUT MAYBE HE'S REACHING A LIMIT ON HOW LONG HE CAN KEEP IT UP.
BEARD

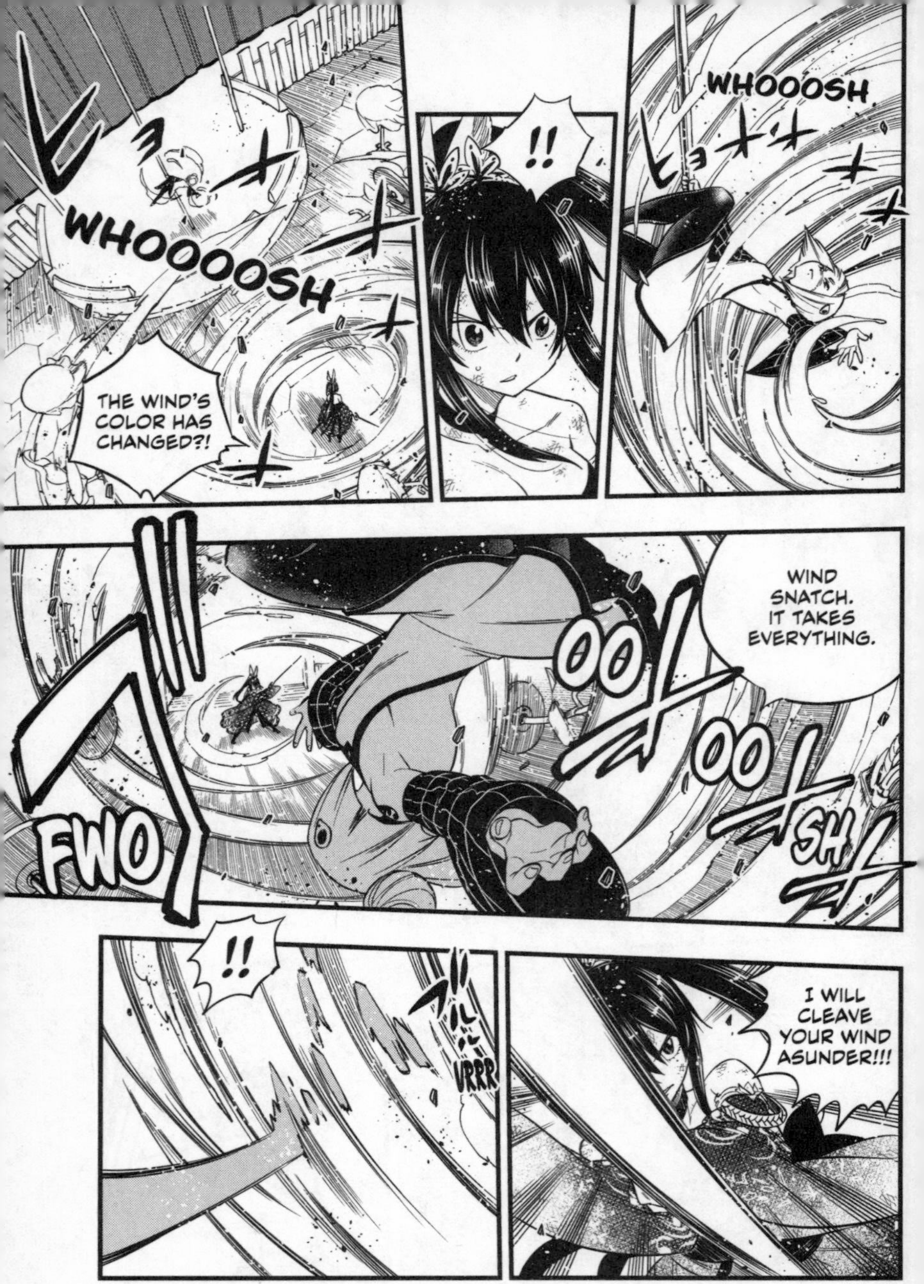
WHOOOSH
!!
WHOOOOOSH
THE WIND'S COLOR HAS CHANGED?!
WIND SNATCH. IT TAKES EVERYTHING.
OO
OO
SH
FWO
I WILL CLEAVE YOUR WIND ASUNDER!!!
VRRR
!!

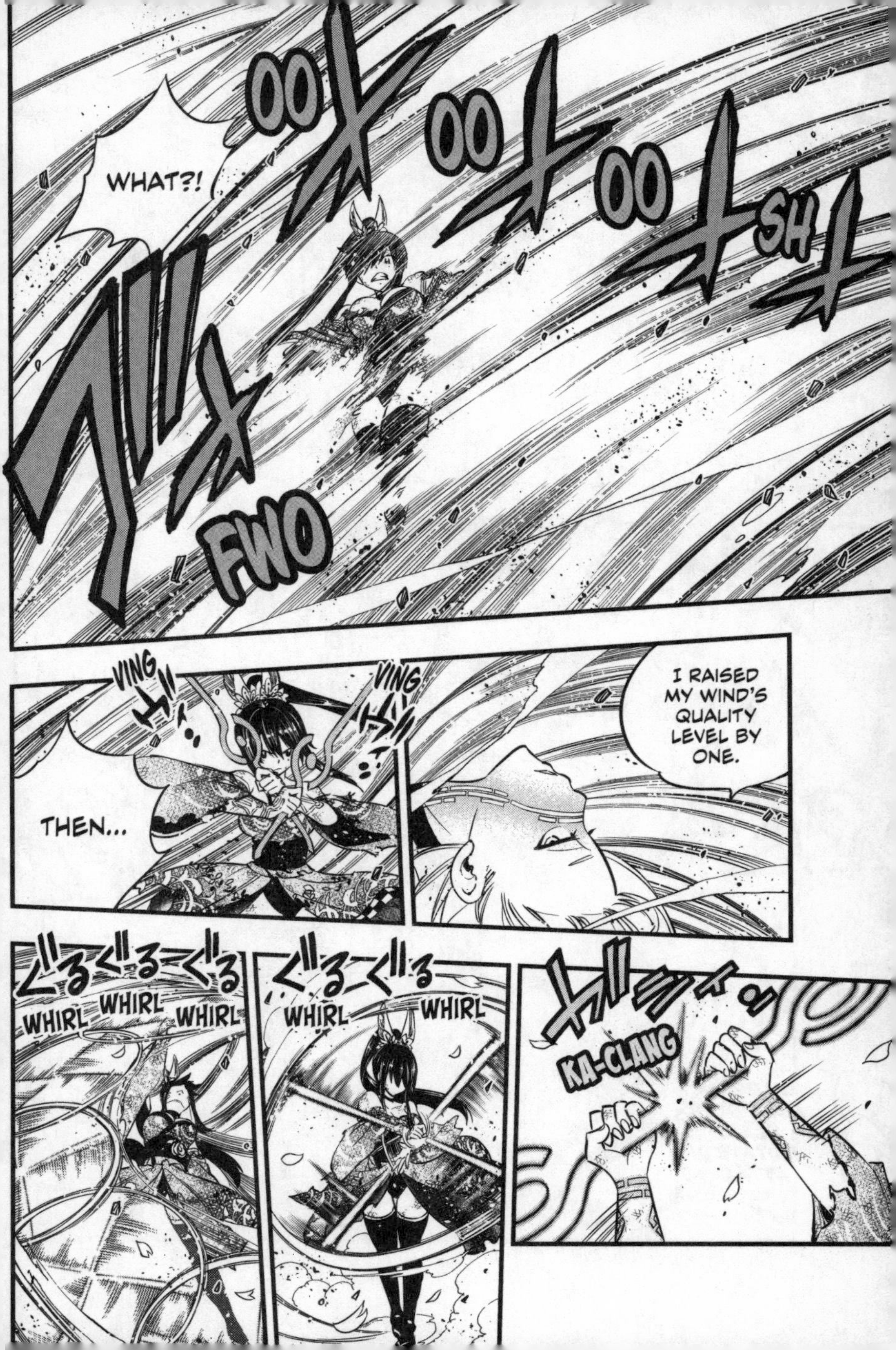
OO OO OO SH
WHAT?!
FWO
I RAISED MY WIND'S QUALITY LEVEL BY ONE.
VING
VING
THEN...
KA-CLANG
ぐるぐる
WHIRL WHIRL
ぐるぐるぐる
WHIRL WHIRL WHIRL

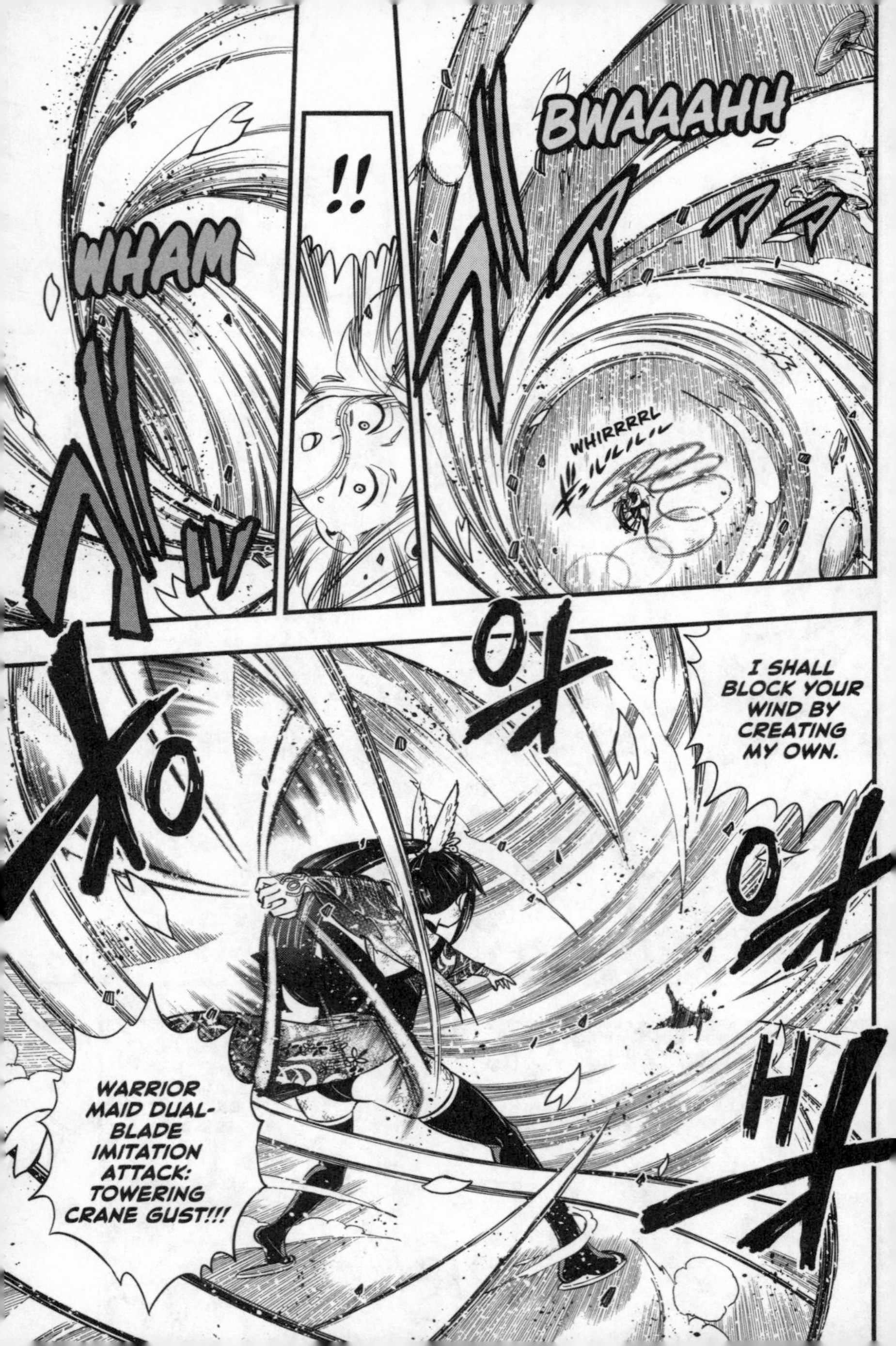
BWAAAHH
WHIRRRRL
!!
WHAM
I SHALL BLOCK YOUR WIND BY CREATING MY OWN.
WARRIOR MAID DUAL-BLADE IMITATION ATTACK: TOWERING CRANE GUST!!!

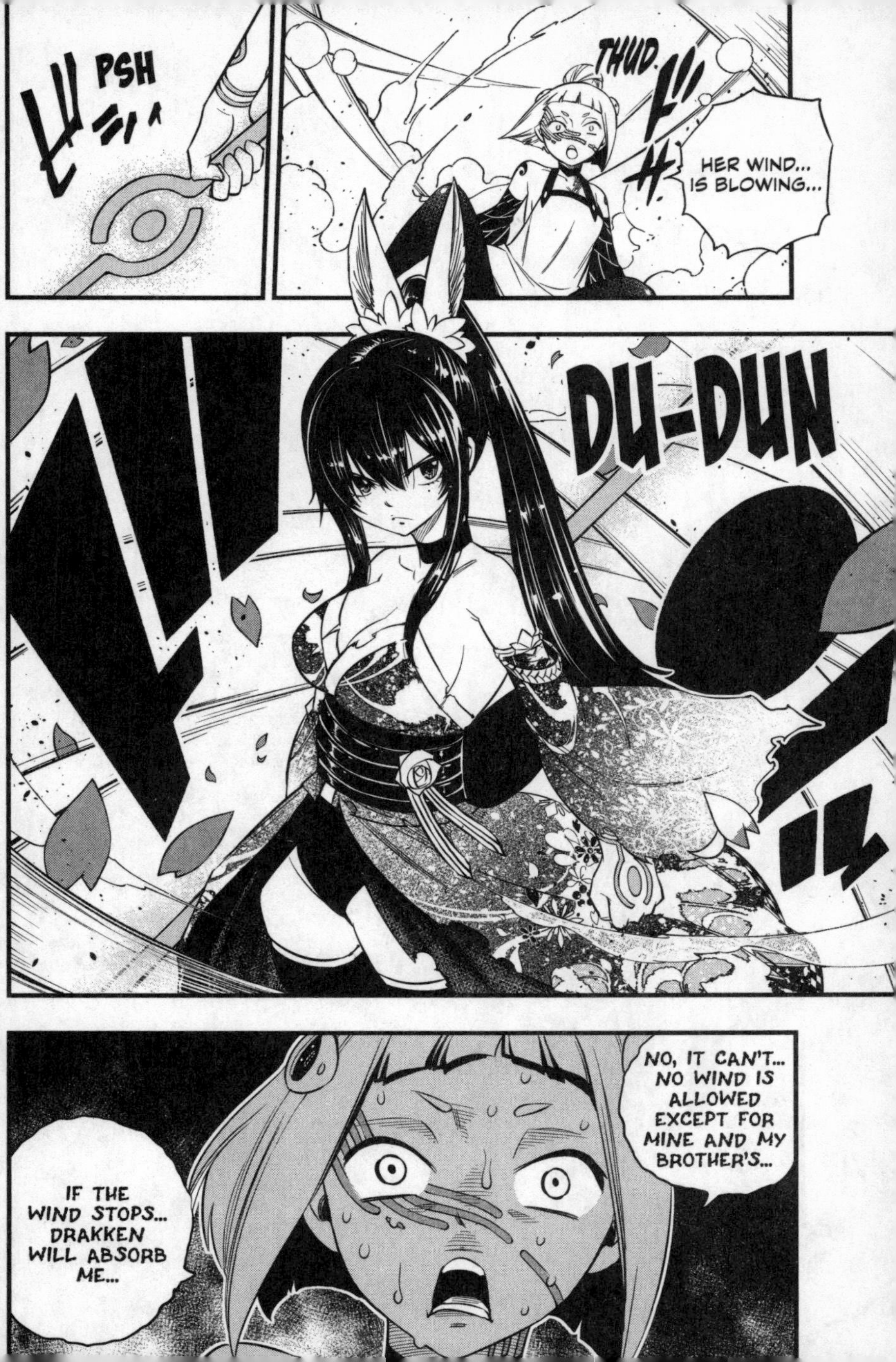
THUD
HER WIND... IS BLOWING...
PSH
DU-DUN
NO, IT CAN'T... NO WIND IS ALLOWED EXCEPT FOR MINE AND MY BROTHER'S...
IF THE WIND STOPS... DRAKKEN WILL ABSORB ME...

EDENS ZERO

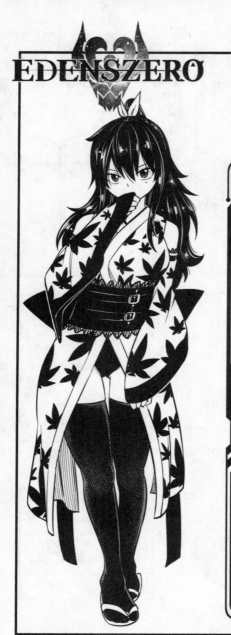

Edens Zero
In-Depth Character File 6

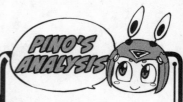

PINO'S ANALYSIS

Name: Homura Kôgetsu

Powers: Ether Gear

(Soul Blade)

Likes: Her mentor

Dislikes: Anything hot

Attack: ☆☆☆☆

Defense: ☆☆☆☆

Marksmanship: ☆

Ether Power: ☆☆☆

Intelligence: ☆☆

Yamato Fashion: ☆☆☆☆☆

Memo

A swordswoman who wields a blade made of Ether. She has a habit of automatically saying whatever is on her mind. She had been searching for her mentor Valkyrie, but has now inherited her teacher's legacy and become the second Valkyrie.

CHAPTER 92: THE SWORD OF EDENS

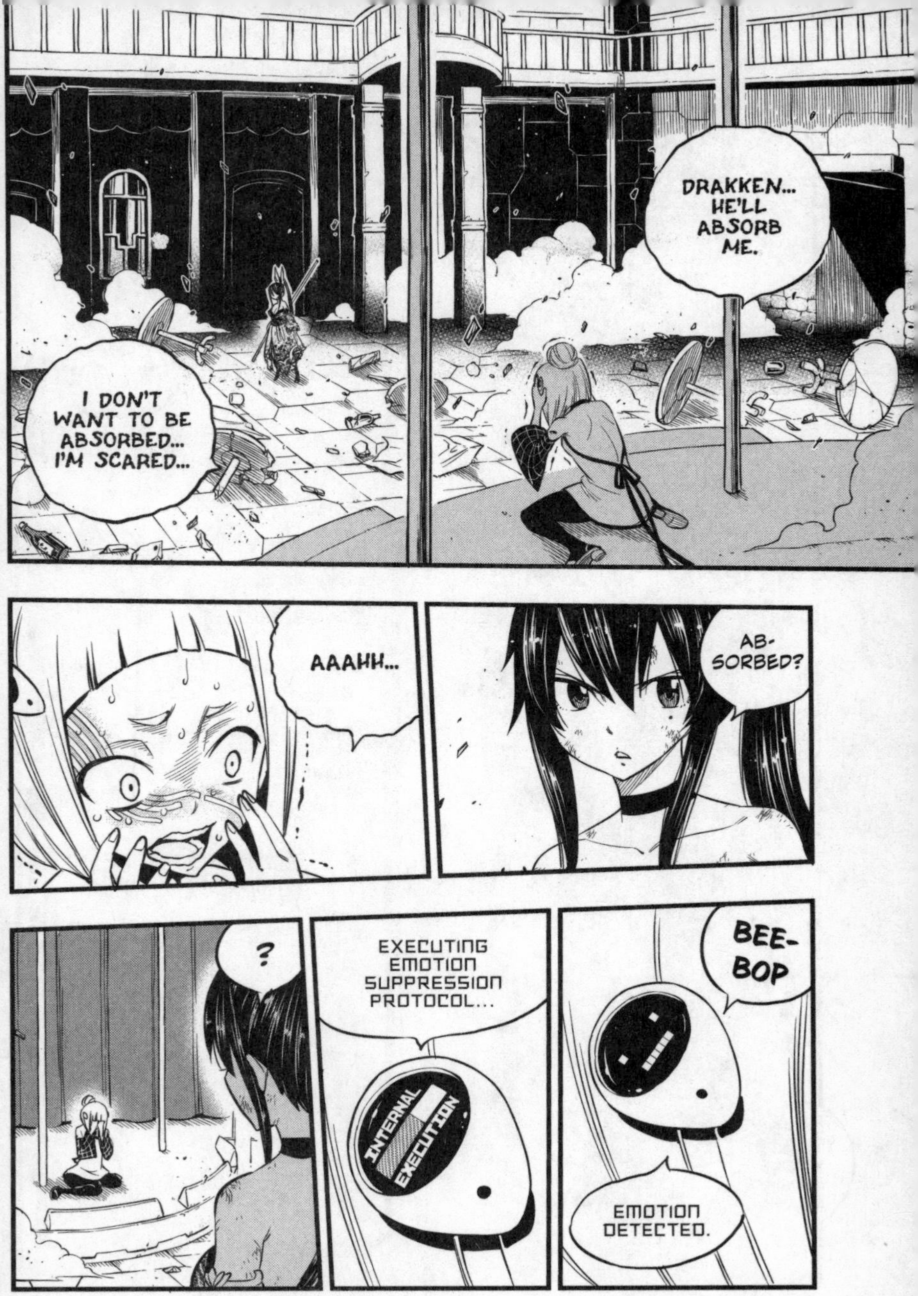

DRAKKEN... HE'LL ABSORB ME.
I DON'T WANT TO BE ABSORBED... I'M SCARED...
AB-SORBED?
AAAHH...
BEE-BOP
EMOTION DETECTED.
EXECUTING EMOTION SUPPRESSION PROTOCOL...
INTERNAL EXECUTION
?

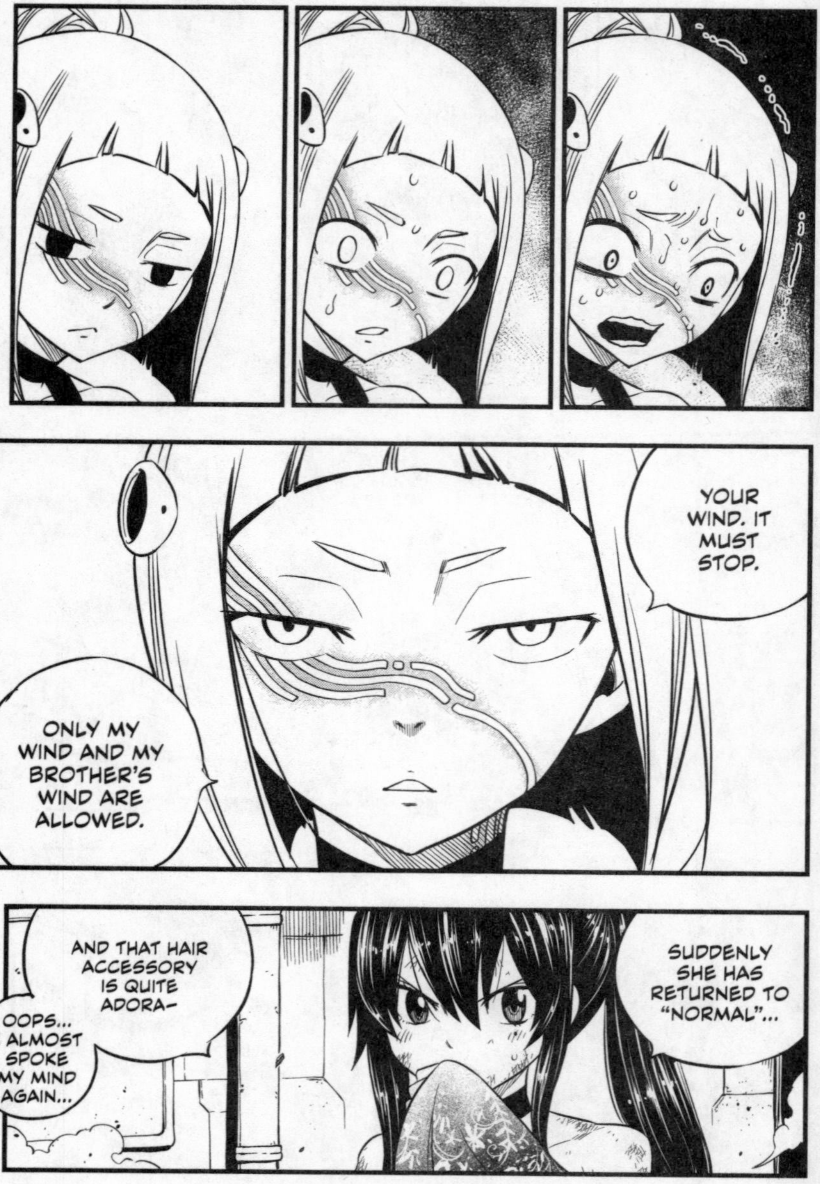
YOUR WIND. IT MUST STOP.
ONLY MY WIND AND MY BROTHER'S WIND ARE ALLOWED.
SUDDENLY SHE HAS RETURNED TO "NORMAL"...
AND THAT HAIR ACCESSORY IS QUITE ADORA-
OOPS... I ALMOST SPOKE MY MIND AGAIN...

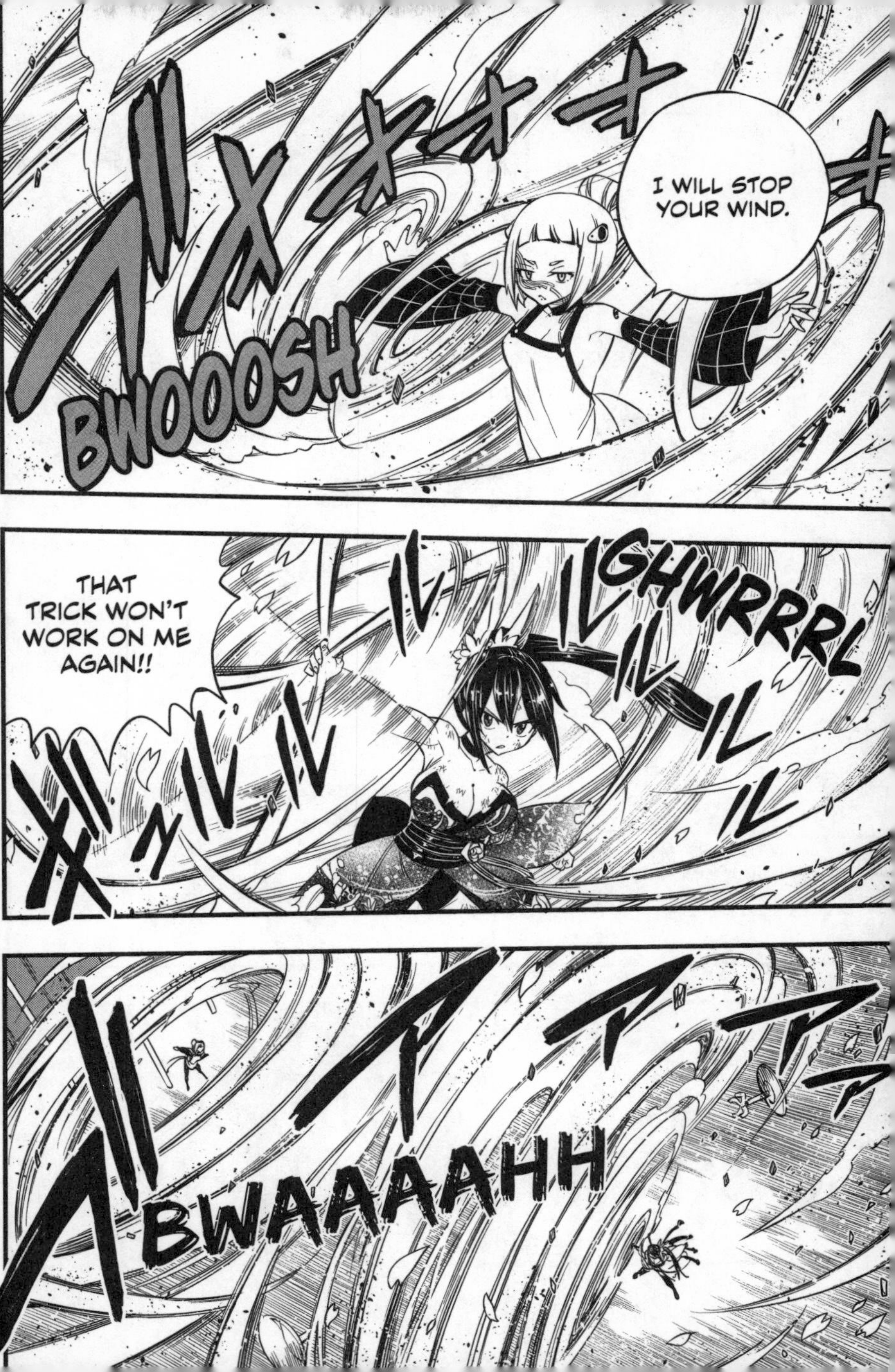
I WILL STOP YOUR WIND.
BWOOOSH
GHWRRRL
THAT TRICK WON'T WORK ON ME AGAIN!!
BWAAAAAHH

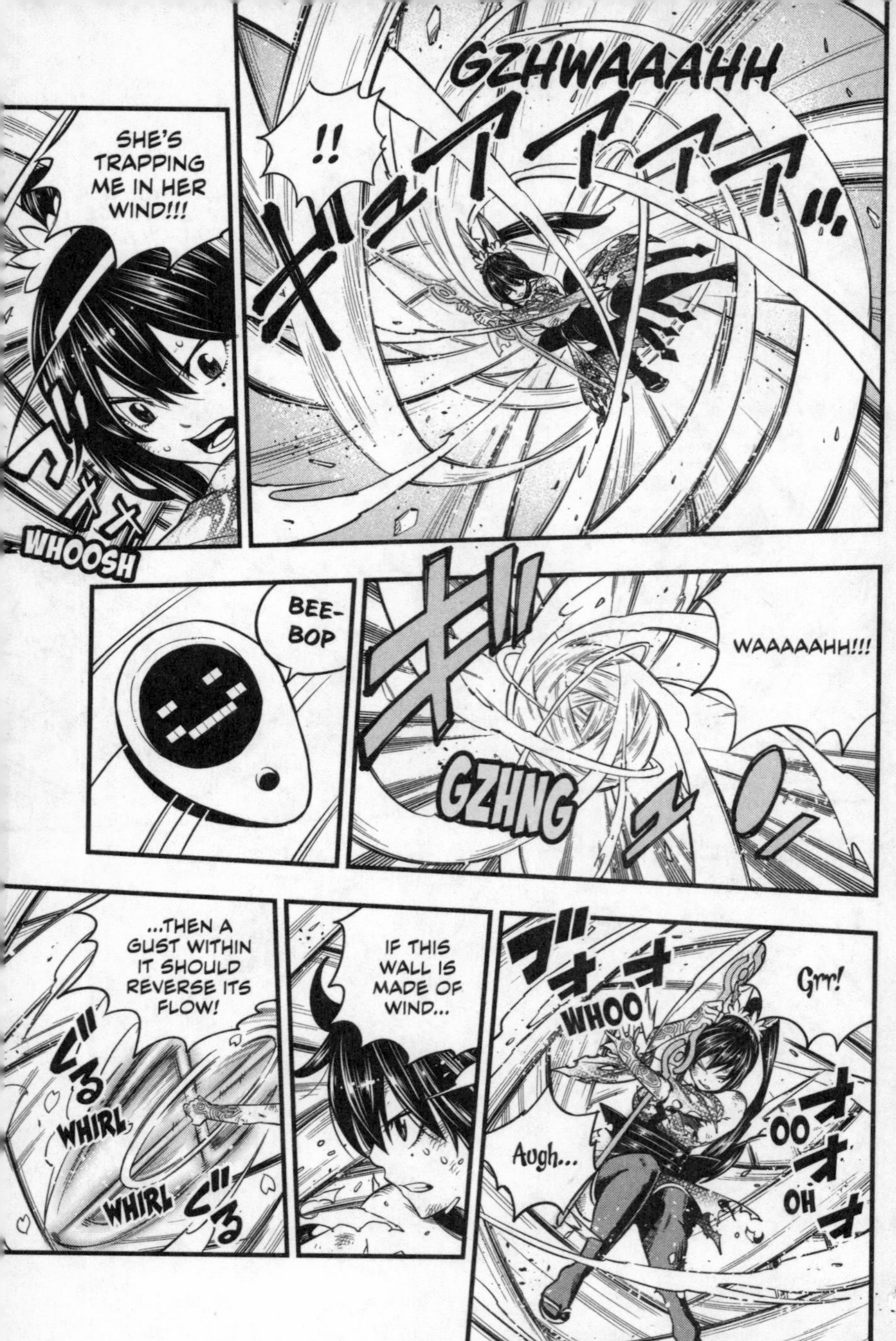
GZHWAAAHH
!!
SHE'S TRAPPING ME IN HER WIND!!!
WHOOSH
WAAAAAHH!!!
GZHNG
BEE-BOP
Grr!
WHOO
OO
OH
Augh...
IF THIS WALL IS MADE OF WIND...
...THEN A GUST WITHIN IT SHOULD REVERSE ITS FLOW!
WHIRL
WHIRL

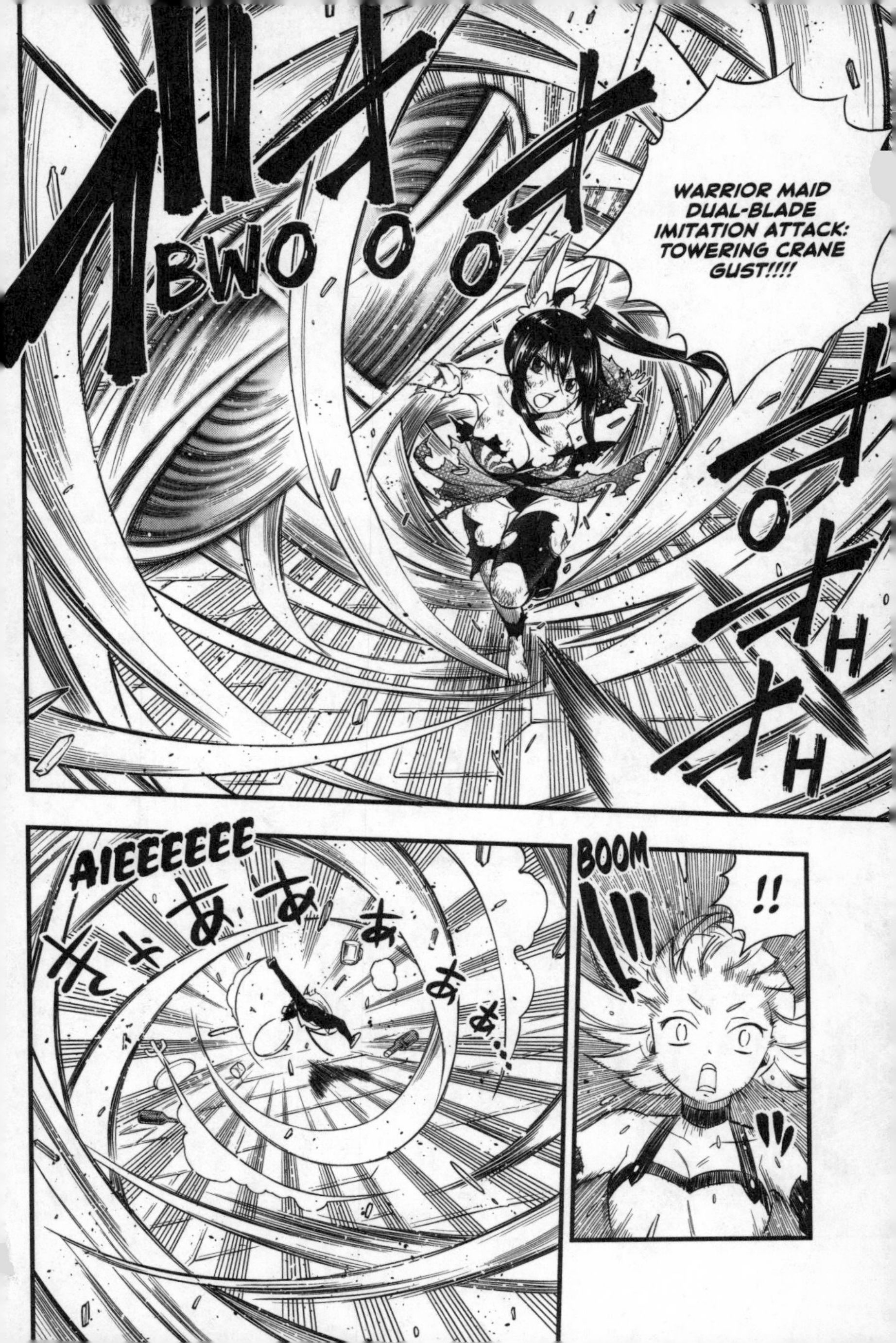
WARRIOR MAID DUAL-BLADE IMITATION ATTACK: TOWERING CRANE GUST!!!!
BWOOOO
OHH
BOOM
!!
AIEEEEEE

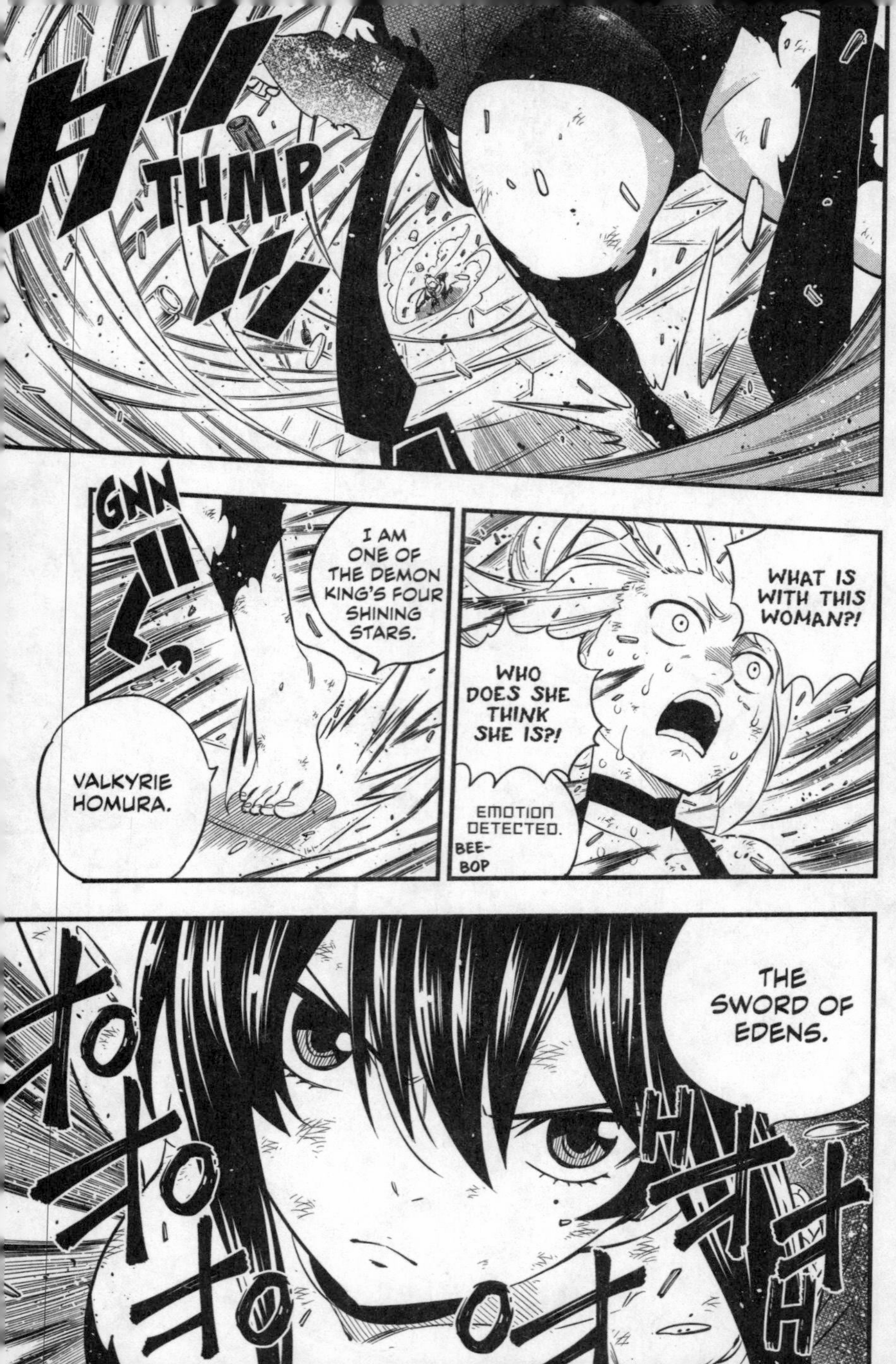
THMP
WHAT IS WITH THIS WOMAN?!
WHO DOES SHE THINK SHE IS?!
EMOTION DETECTED.
BEE-BOP
GNN
I AM ONE OF THE DEMON KING'S FOUR SHINING STARS.
VALKYRIE HOMURA.
THE SWORD OF EDENS.

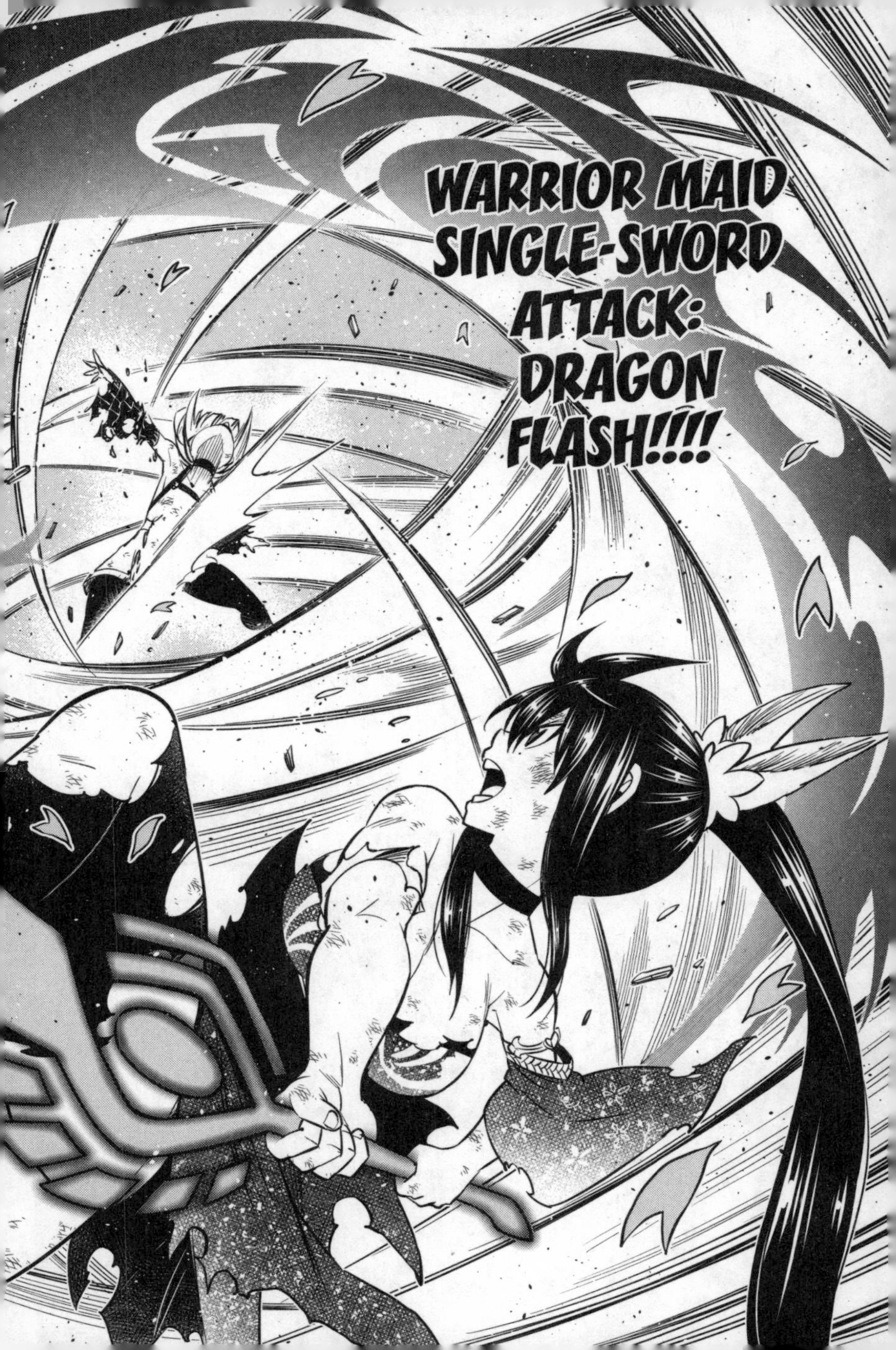
WARRIOR MAID SINGLE-SWORD ATTACK: DRAGON FLASH!!!!

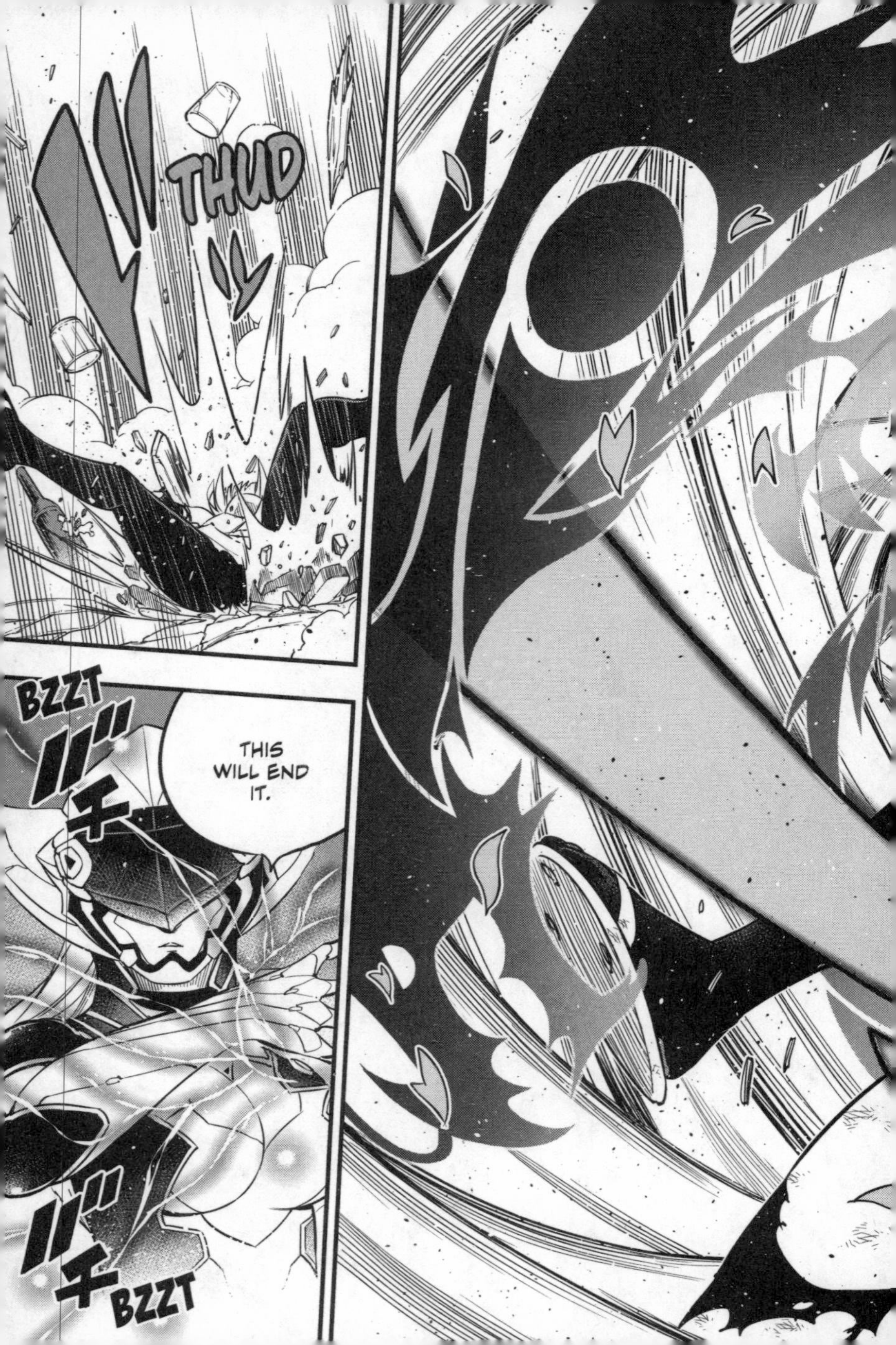
THUD
BZZT
バチ
THIS WILL END IT.
バチ
BZZT

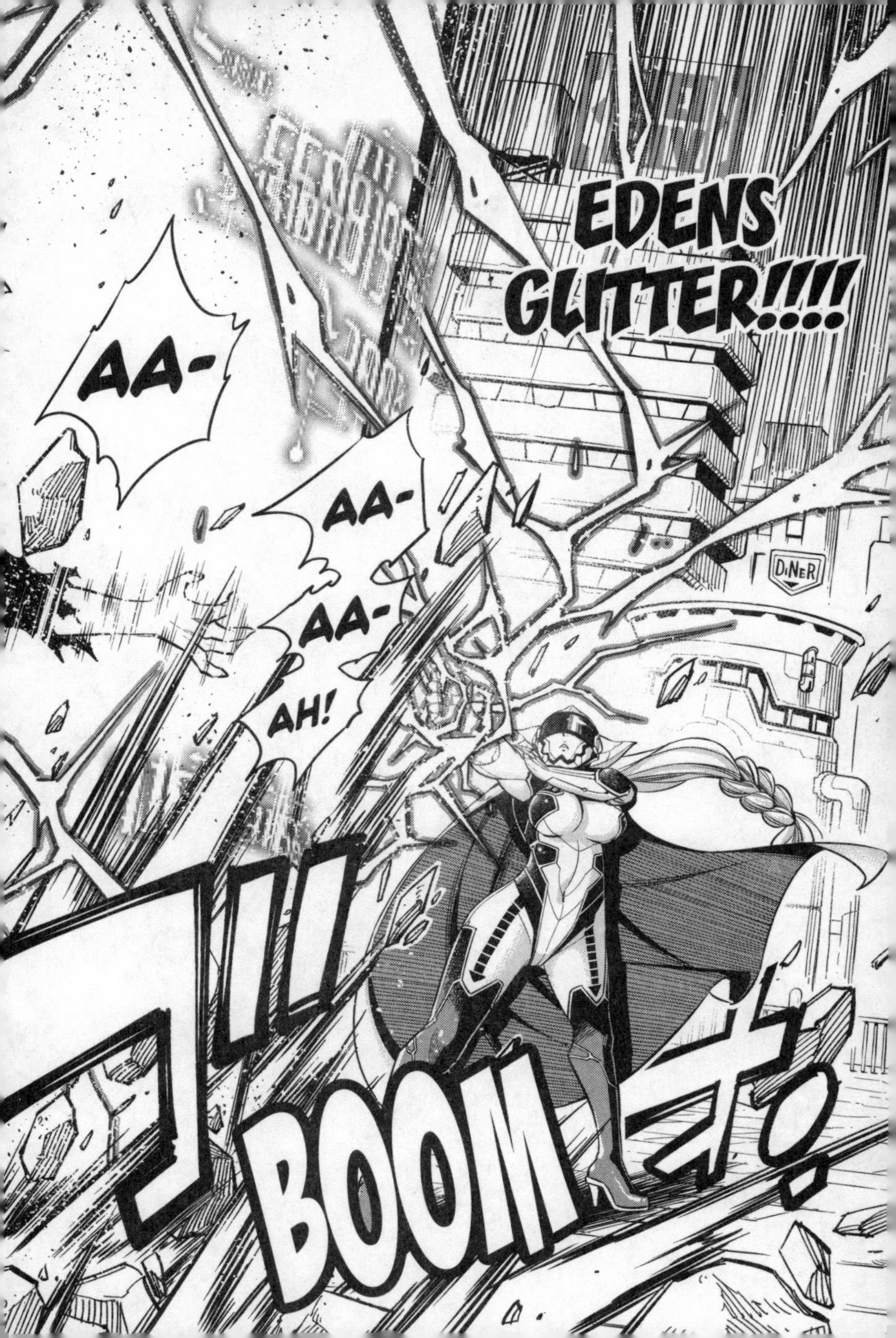
EDENS GLITTER!!!!
AA-
AA-
AA-
AH!
DiNER
BOOM

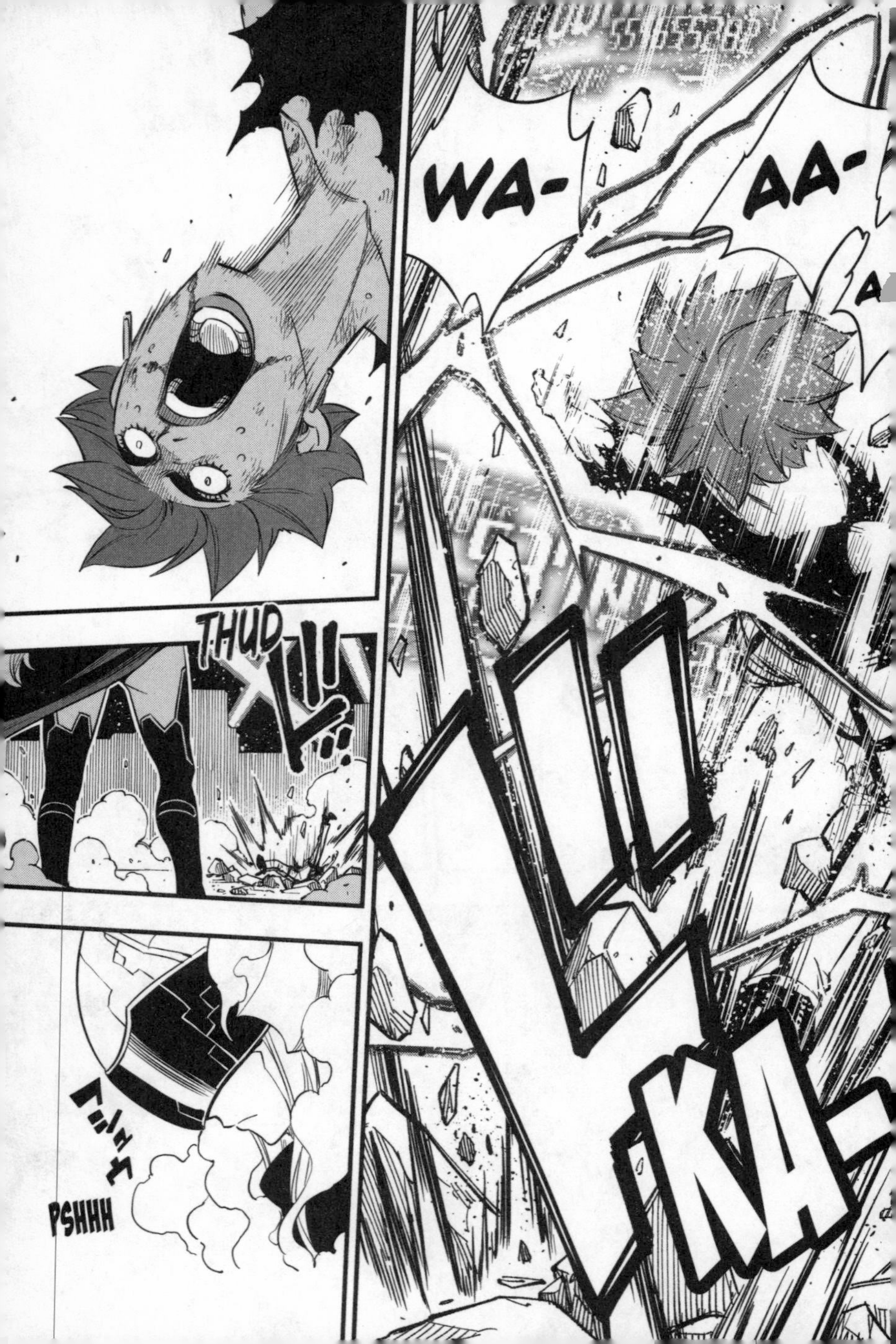
WA-
AA-
A
KA-
THUD
PSHHH

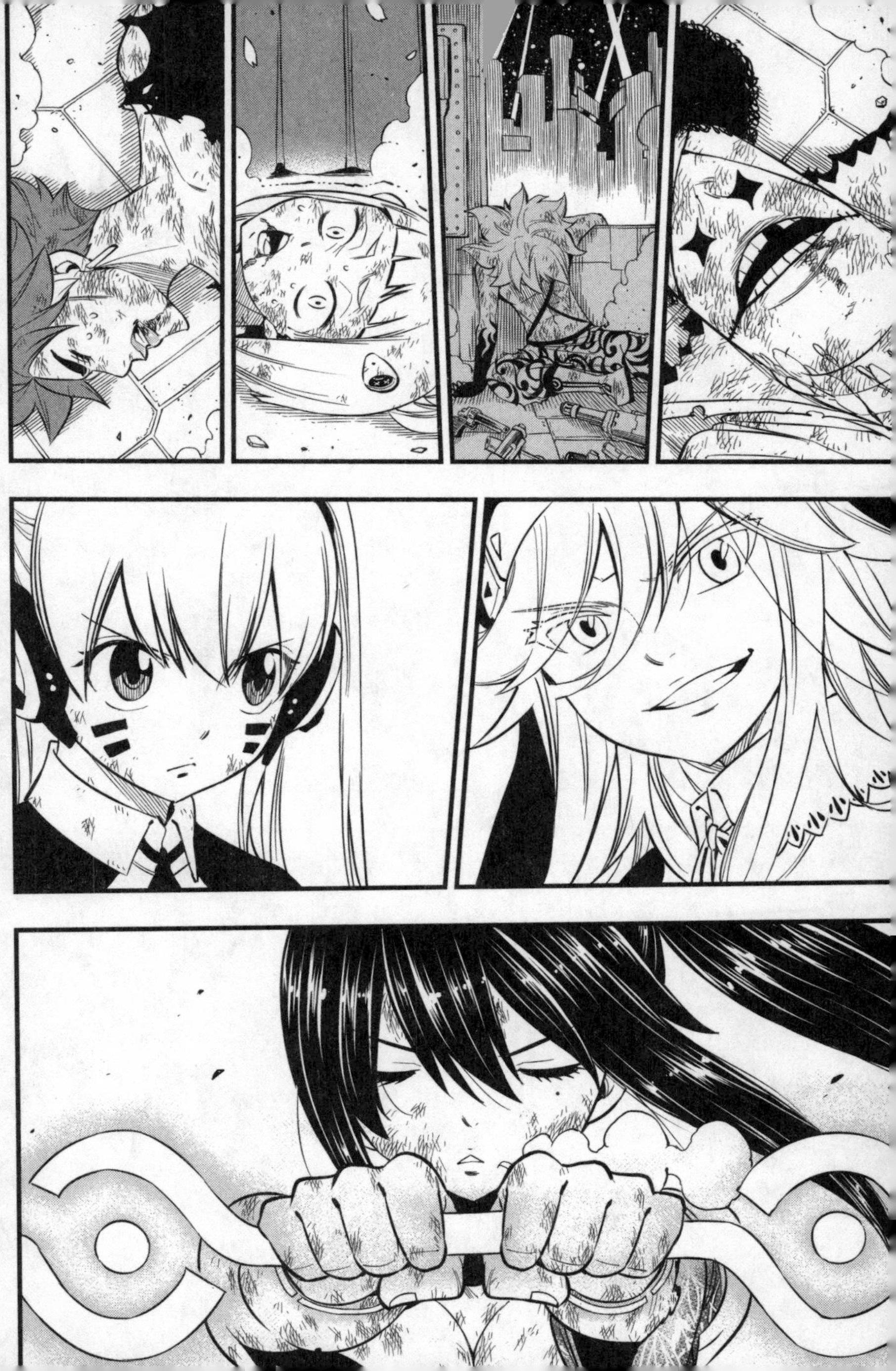

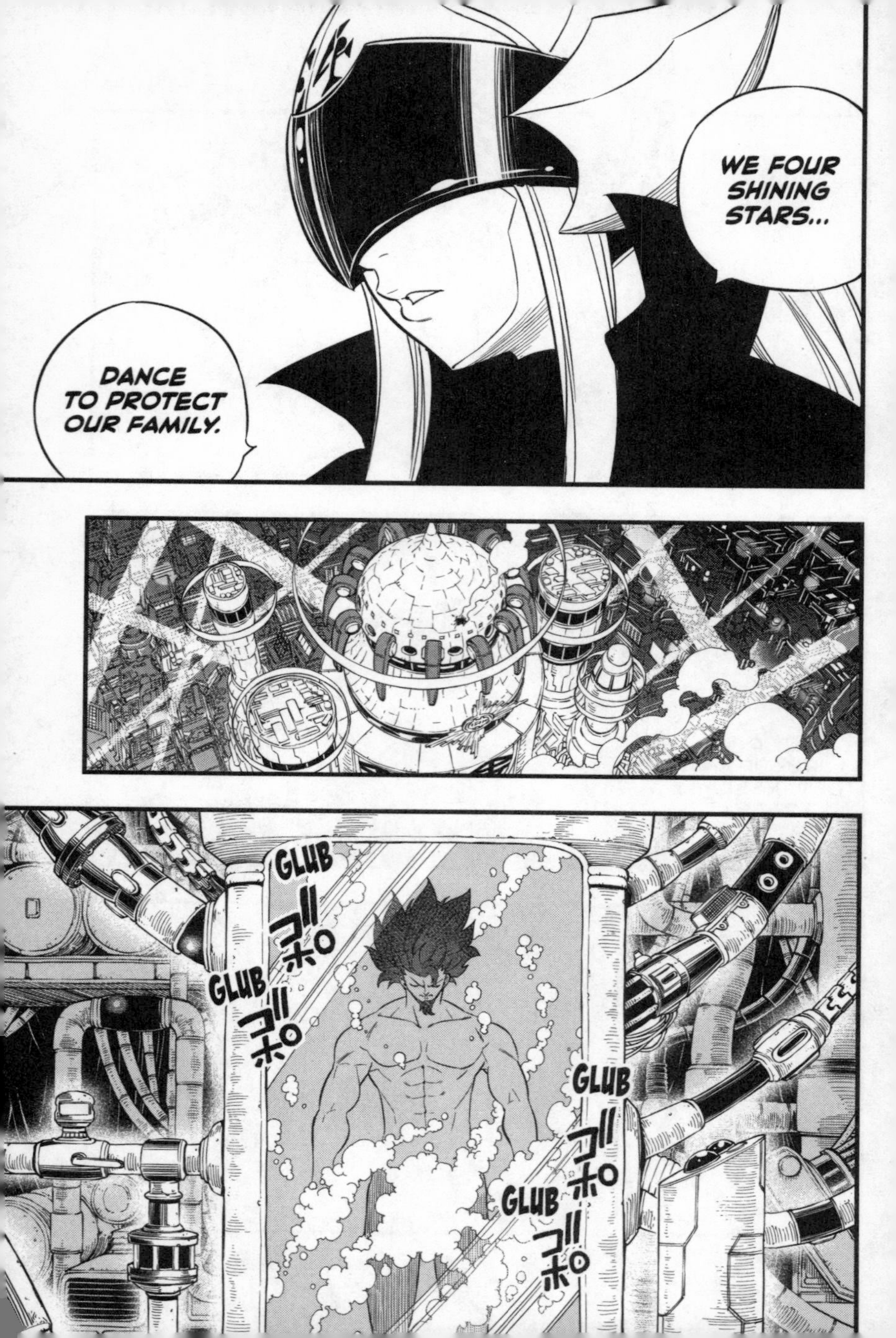
WE FOUR SHINING STARS...
DANCE TO PROTECT OUR FAMILY.
GLUB
ゴポ
GLUB
ゴポ
GLUB
ゴポ
GLUB
ゴポ

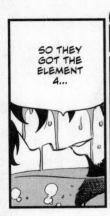

SO THEY GOT THE ELEMENT A...

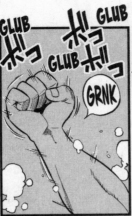

GLUB
ポコ
GLUB
ポコ
GLUB
ポコ
GRNK

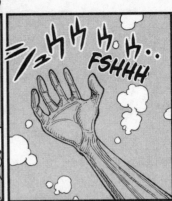

シュカカカ...
FSHHH

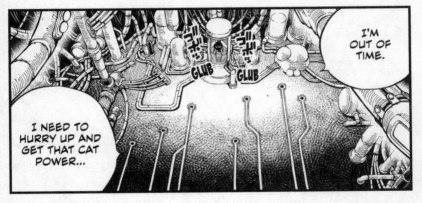

GLUB GLUB

I'M OUT OF TIME.

I NEED TO HURRY UP AND GET THAT CAT POWER...

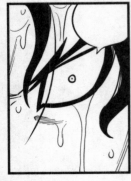

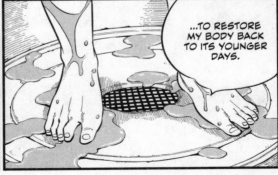

...TO RESTORE MY BODY BACK TO ITS YOUNGER DAYS.

118

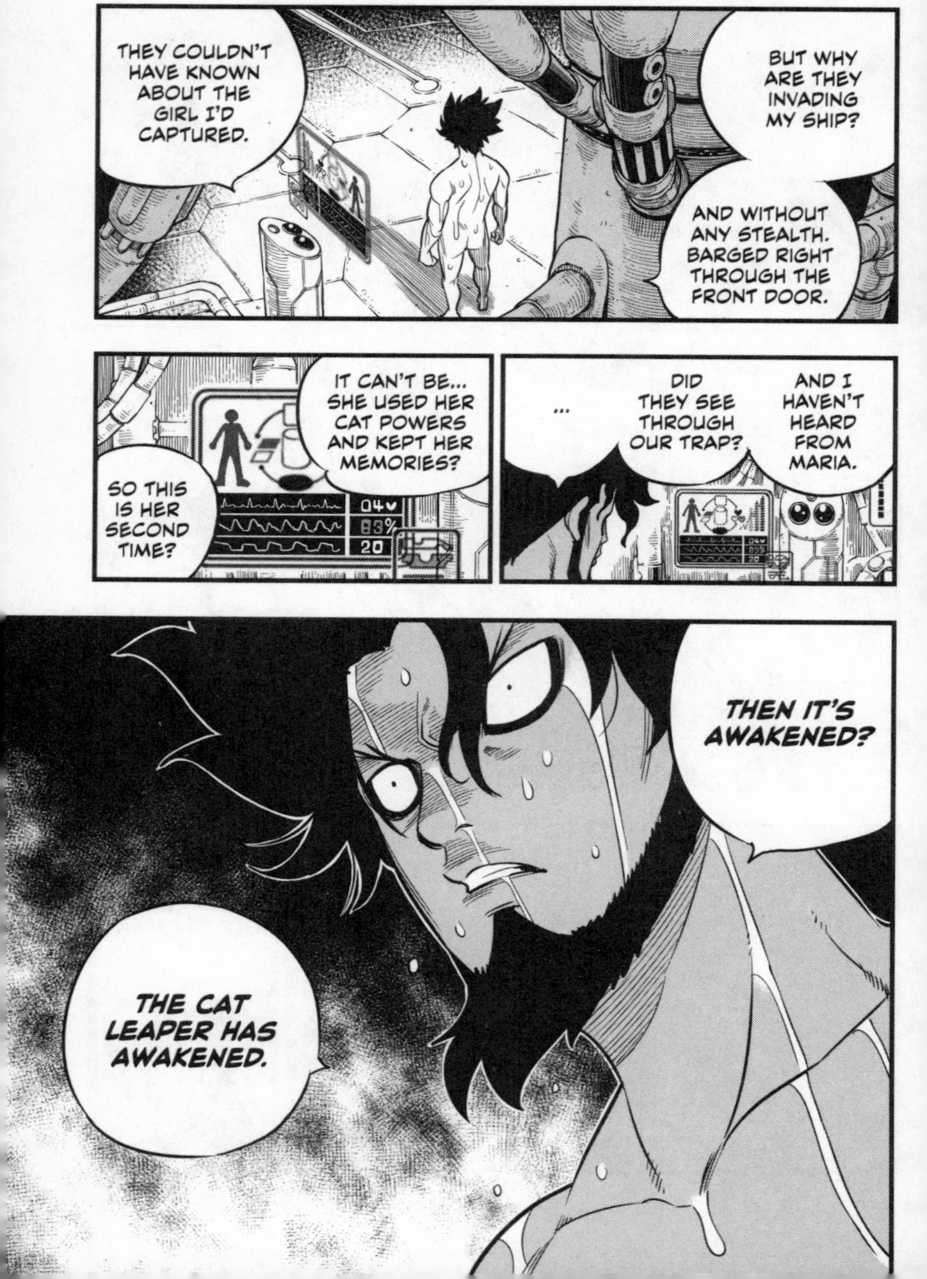
BUT WHY ARE THEY INVADING MY SHIP?
AND WITHOUT ANY STEALTH. BARGED RIGHT THROUGH THE FRONT DOOR.
THEY COULDN'T HAVE KNOWN ABOUT THE GIRL I'D CAPTURED.
AND I HAVEN'T HEARD FROM MARIA.
DID THEY SEE THROUGH OUR TRAP?
...
IT CAN'T BE... SHE USED HER CAT POWERS AND KEPT HER MEMORIES?
SO THIS IS HER SECOND TIME?
THEN IT'S AWAKENED?
THE CAT LEAPER HAS AWAKENED.

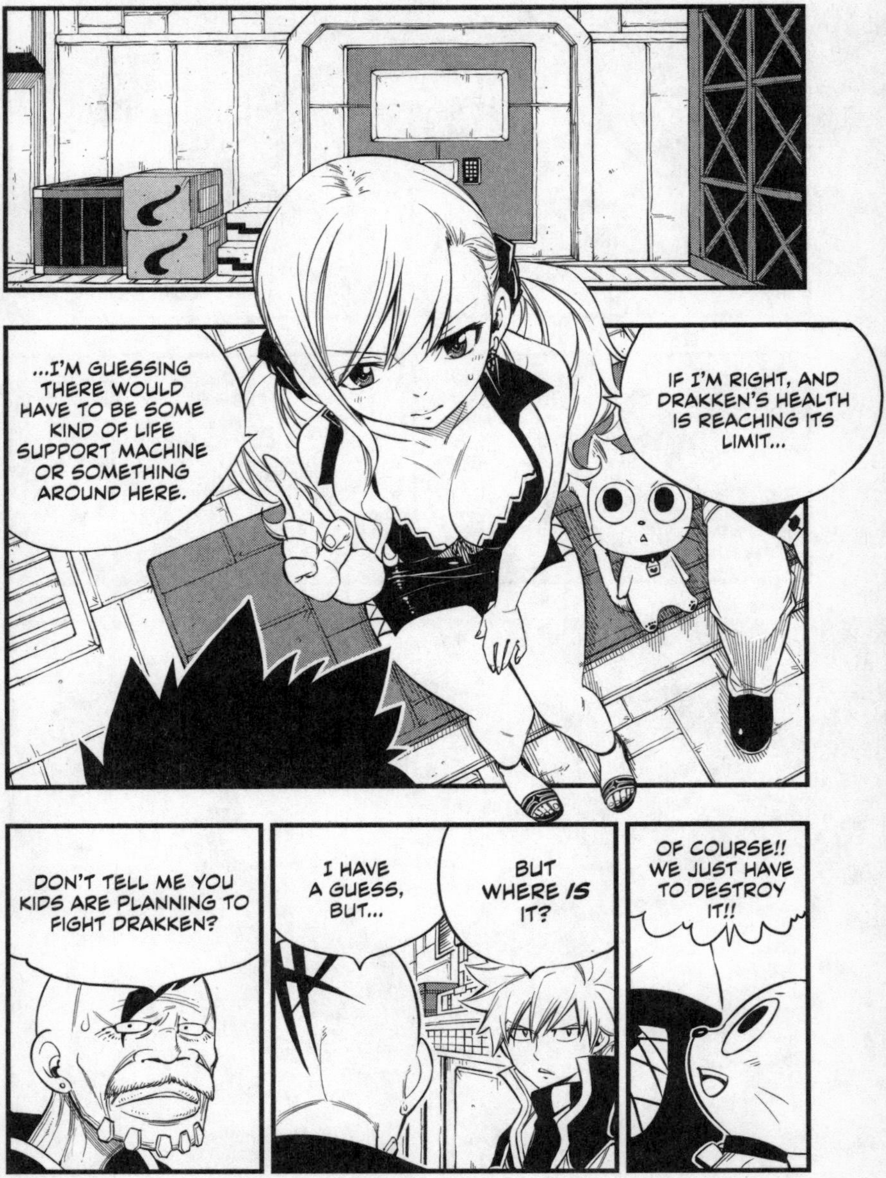
IF I'M RIGHT, AND DRAKKEN'S HEALTH IS REACHING ITS LIMIT...
...I'M GUESSING THERE WOULD HAVE TO BE SOME KIND OF LIFE SUPPORT MACHINE OR SOMETHING AROUND HERE.
OF COURSE!! WE JUST HAVE TO DESTROY IT!!
BUT WHERE *IS* IT?
I HAVE A GUESS, BUT...
DON'T TELL ME YOU KIDS ARE PLANNING TO FIGHT DRAKKEN?

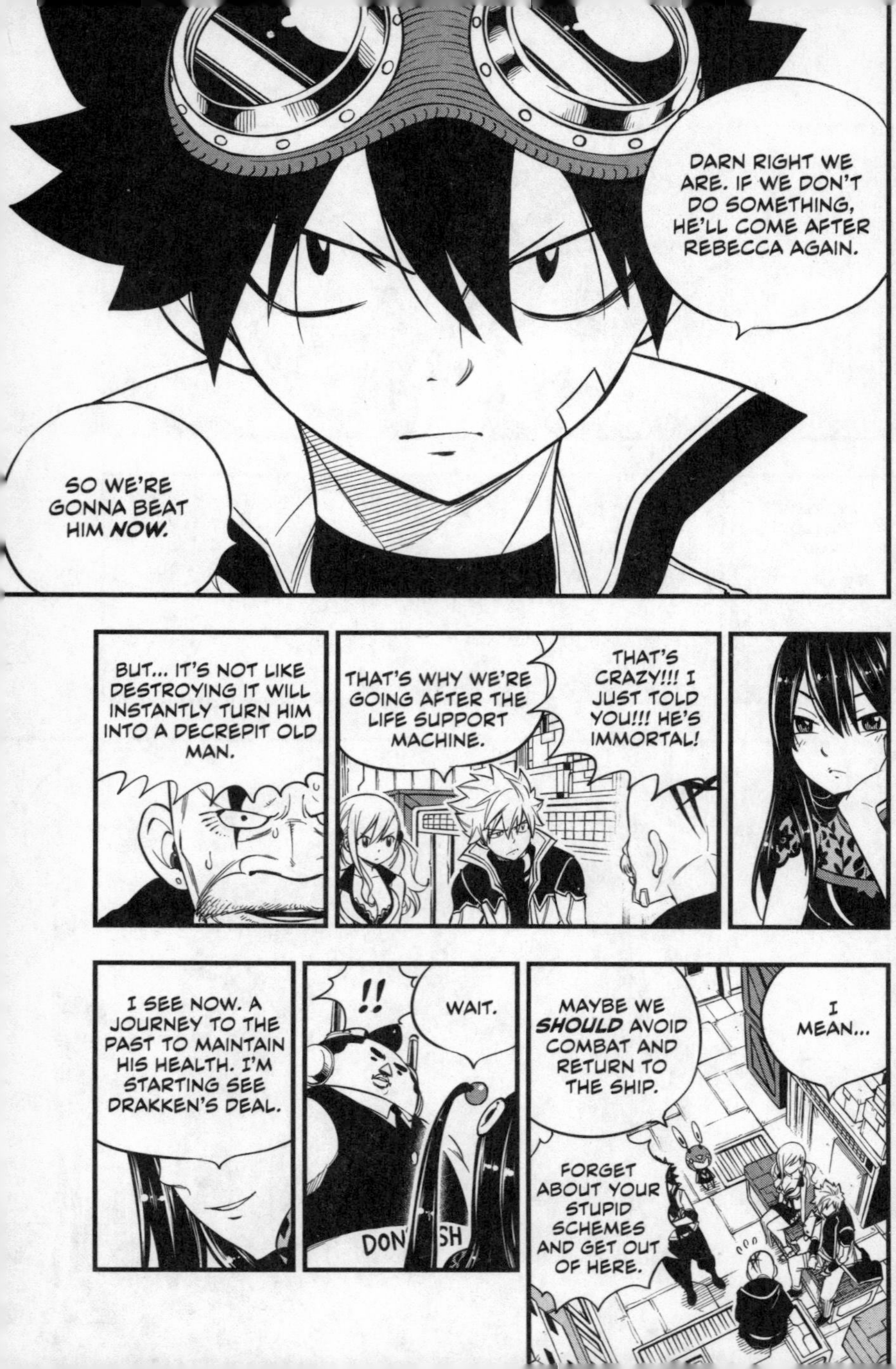
DARN RIGHT WE ARE. IF WE DON'T DO SOMETHING, HE'LL COME AFTER REBECCA AGAIN.
SO WE'RE GONNA BEAT HIM *NOW.*
THAT'S CRAZY!!! I JUST TOLD YOU!!! HE'S IMMORTAL!
THAT'S WHY WE'RE GOING AFTER THE LIFE SUPPORT MACHINE.
BUT... IT'S NOT LIKE DESTROYING IT WILL INSTANTLY TURN HIM INTO A DECREPIT OLD MAN.
I MEAN...
MAYBE WE *SHOULD* AVOID COMBAT AND RETURN TO THE SHIP.
FORGET ABOUT YOUR STUPID SCHEMES AND GET OUT OF HERE.
WAIT.
!!
DON' SH
I SEE NOW. A JOURNEY TO THE PAST TO MAINTAIN HIS HEALTH. I'M STARTING SEE DRAKKEN'S DEAL.

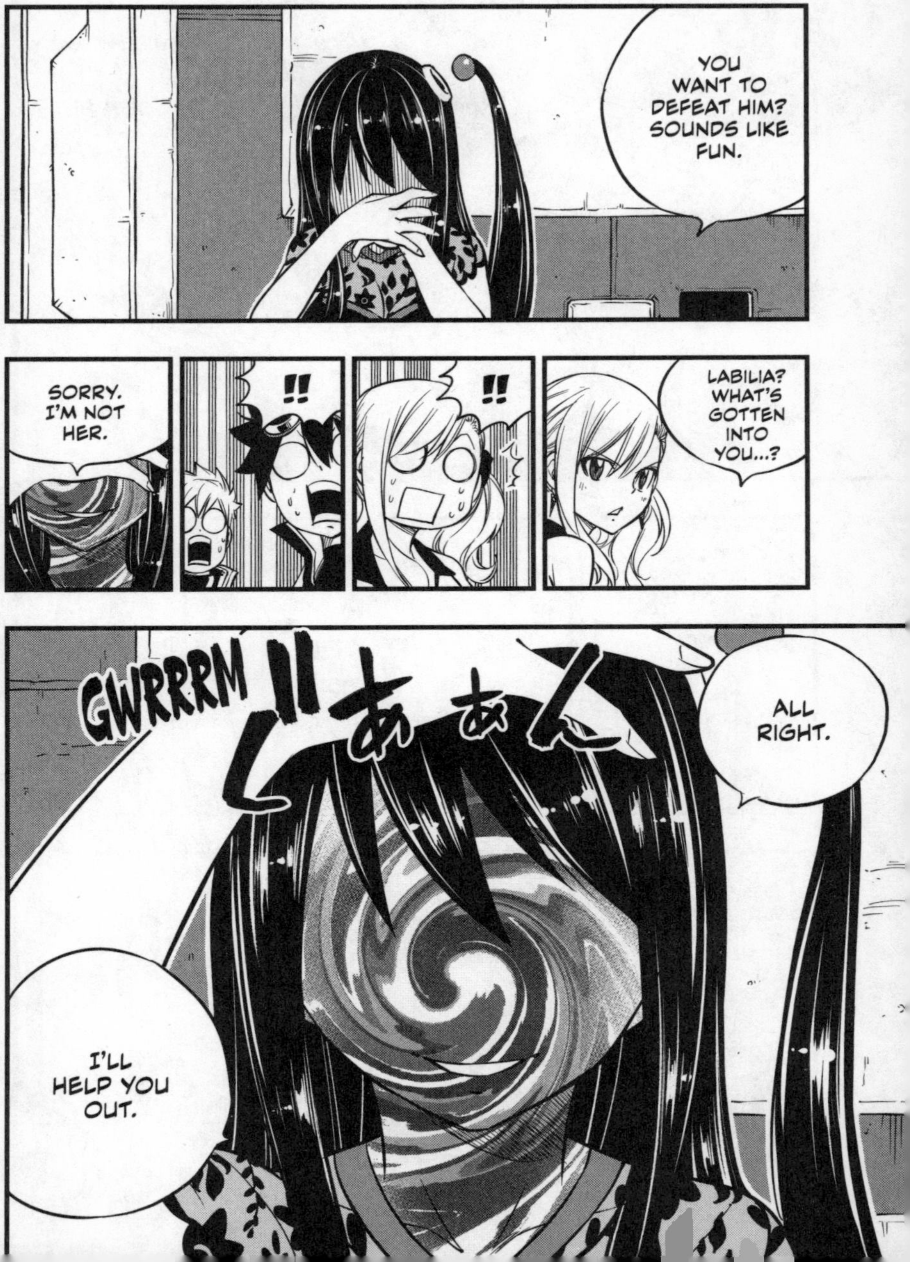
YOU WANT TO DEFEAT HIM? SOUNDS LIKE FUN.
LABILIA? WHAT'S GOTTEN INTO YOU...?
!!
!!
SORRY. I'M NOT HER.
ALL RIGHT.
GWRRRM
ぐああん
I'LL HELP YOU OUT.

EDENSZERO

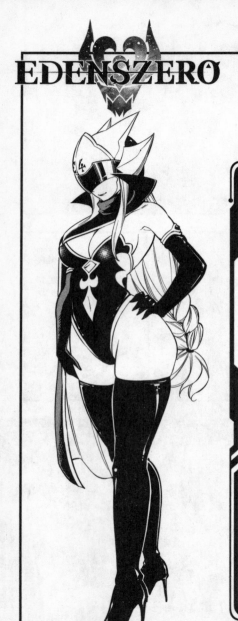

**Edens Zero
In-Depth Character File 7**

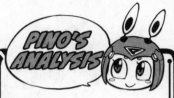

PINO'S ANALYSIS

Name: Witch Regret

Powers: Shield Ether

Element: Ether

Likes: Edens Zero

Dislikes: Intruders

Attack: ☆☆☆☆

Defense: ☆☆☆☆☆

Marksmanship: ☆☆☆

Ether Power: ☆☆☆☆☆

Intelligence: ☆☆☆☆

Dog Impersonation: ☆

Memo

One of the Demon King's Four Shining Stars, a sorceress-type android also known as the Shield of Edens. She normally keeps her face covered and is very kind and gentle, but when someone threatens the *Edens Zero*, she can be cold and ruthless.

CHAPTER 93: THE EXECUTION SITE

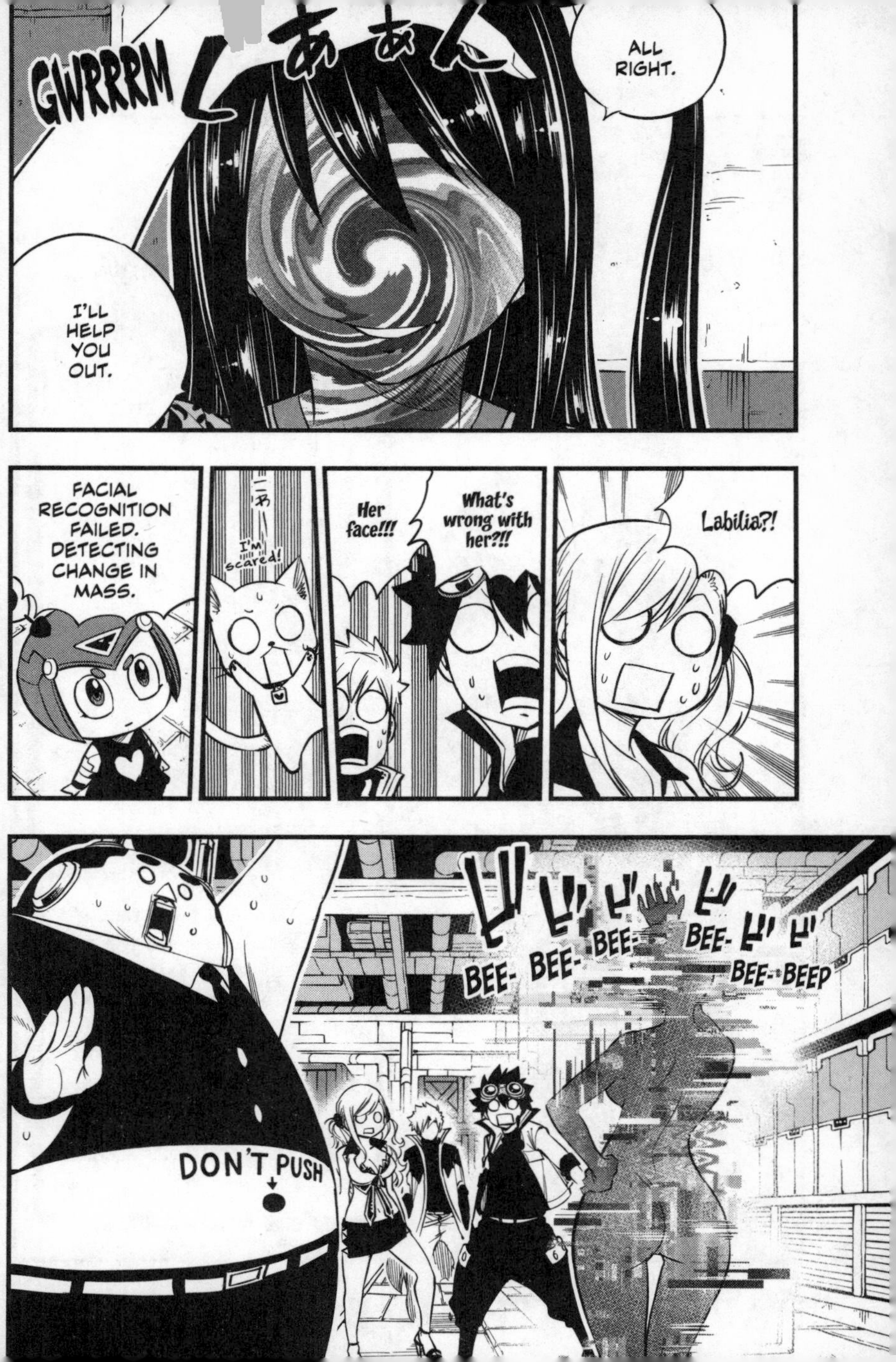
ALL RIGHT.
GWRRRM
I'LL HELP YOU OUT.
Labilia?!
What's wrong with her?!!
Her face!!!
I'm scared!
FACIAL RECOGNITION FAILED. DETECTING CHANGE IN MASS.
BEE- BEE- BEE- BEE- BEE-BEEP
DON'T PUSH

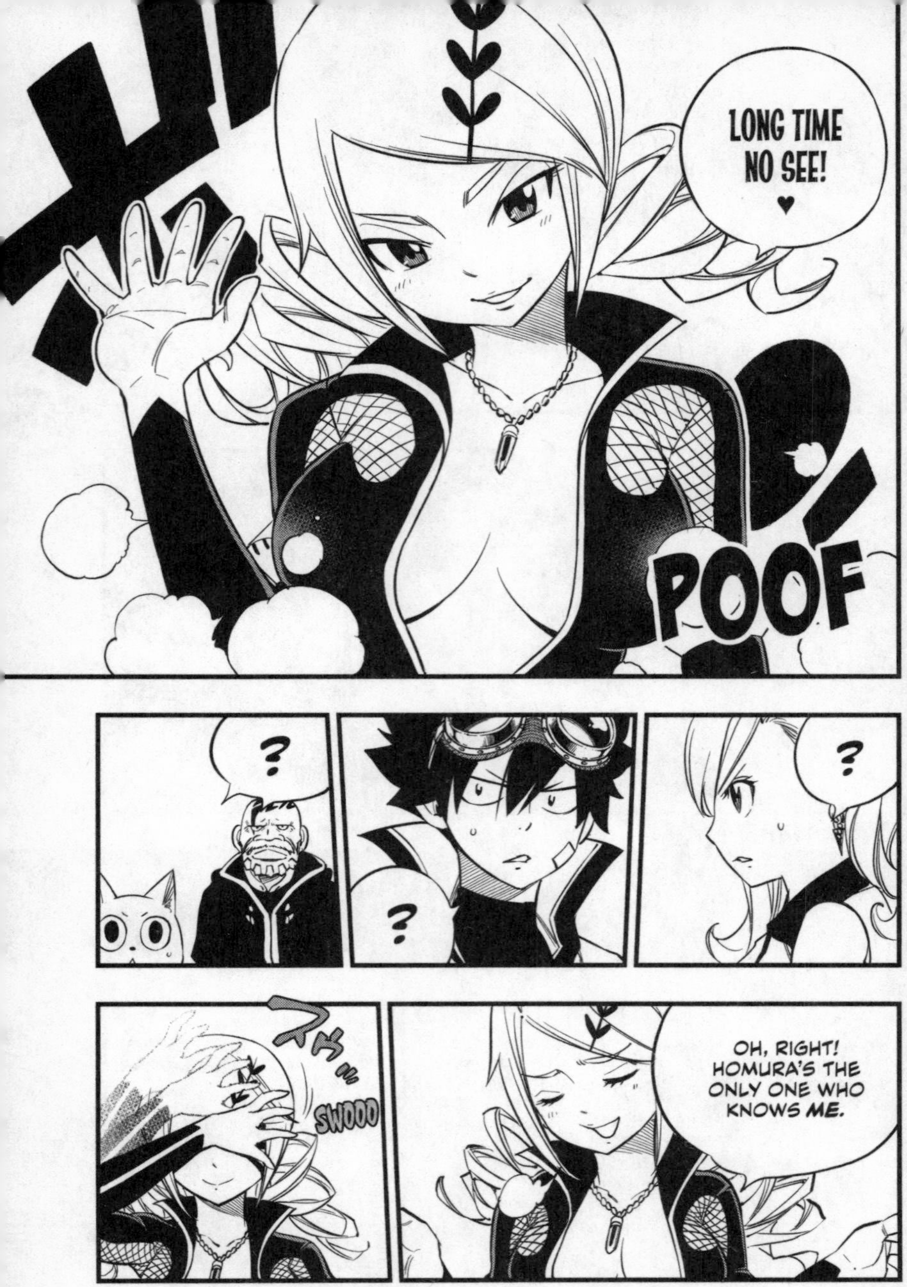
LONG TIME NO SEE! ♥
POOF
?
?
?
?
OH, RIGHT! HOMURA'S THE ONLY ONE WHO KNOWS *ME.*
SWOOO

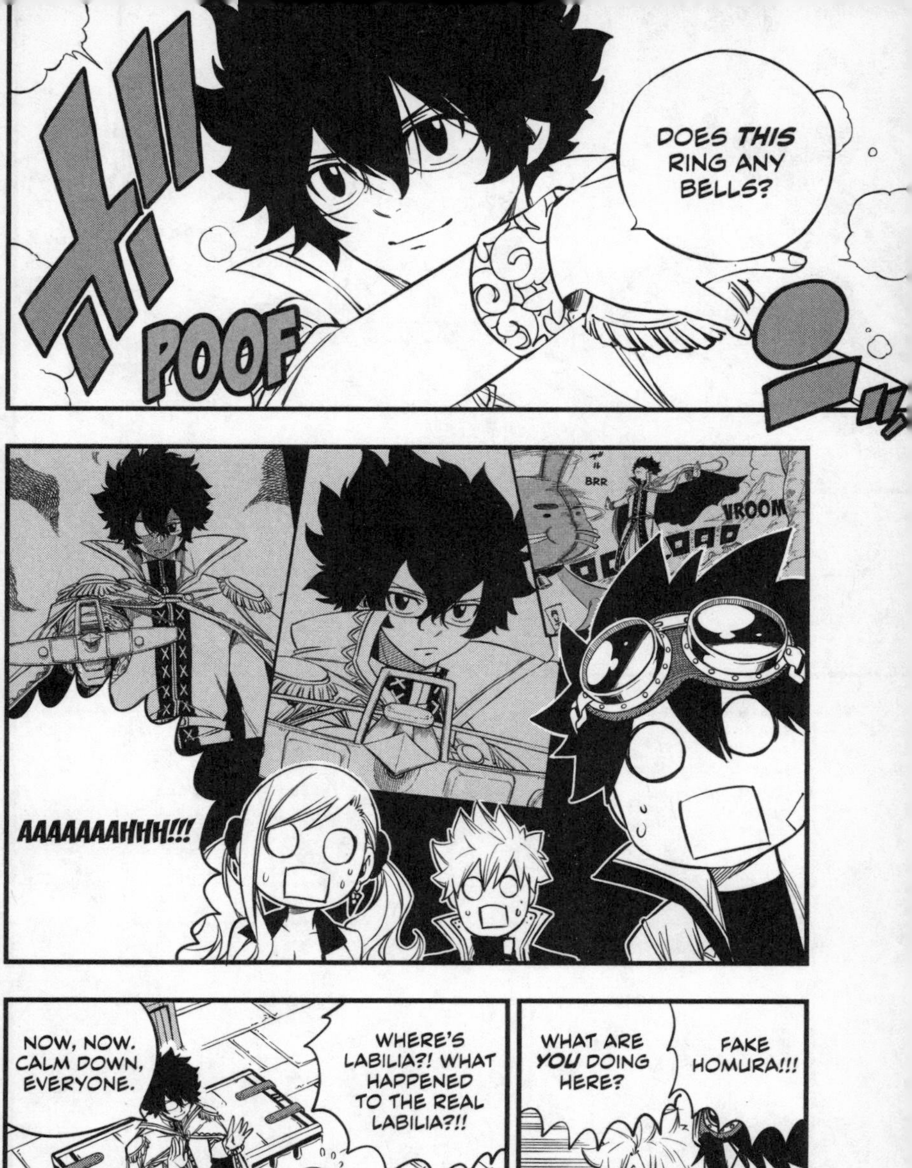
DOES THIS RING ANY BELLS?
POOF
BRR
VROOM
AAAAAAAHHH!!!
FAKE HOMURA!!!
WHAT ARE YOU DOING HERE?
WHERE'S LABILIA?! WHAT HAPPENED TO THE REAL LABILIA?!!
NOW, NOW. CALM DOWN, EVERYONE.

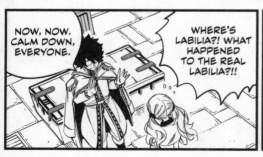

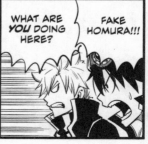

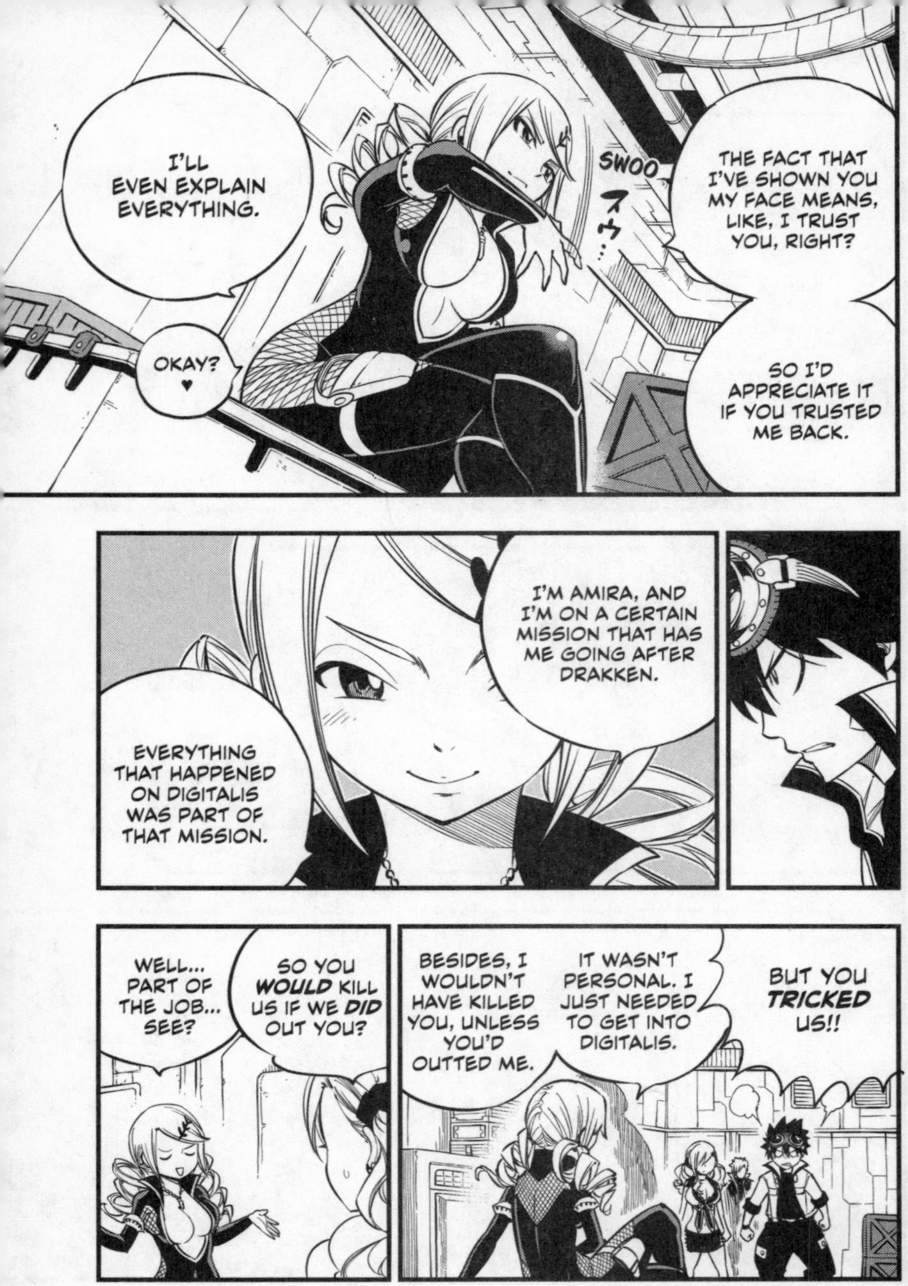
THE FACT THAT I'VE SHOWN YOU MY FACE MEANS, LIKE, I TRUST YOU, RIGHT?
SWOO
スウ…
SO I'D APPRECIATE IT IF YOU TRUSTED ME BACK.
I'LL EVEN EXPLAIN EVERYTHING.
OKAY? ♥
I'M AMIRA, AND I'M ON A CERTAIN MISSION THAT HAS ME GOING AFTER DRAKKEN.
EVERYTHING THAT HAPPENED ON DIGITALIS WAS PART OF THAT MISSION.
BUT YOU TRICKED US!!
IT WASN'T PERSONAL. I JUST NEEDED TO GET INTO DIGITALIS.
BESIDES, I WOULDN'T HAVE KILLED YOU, UNLESS YOU'D OUTTED ME.
SO YOU WOULD KILL US IF WE DID OUT YOU?
WELL... PART OF THE JOB... SEE?

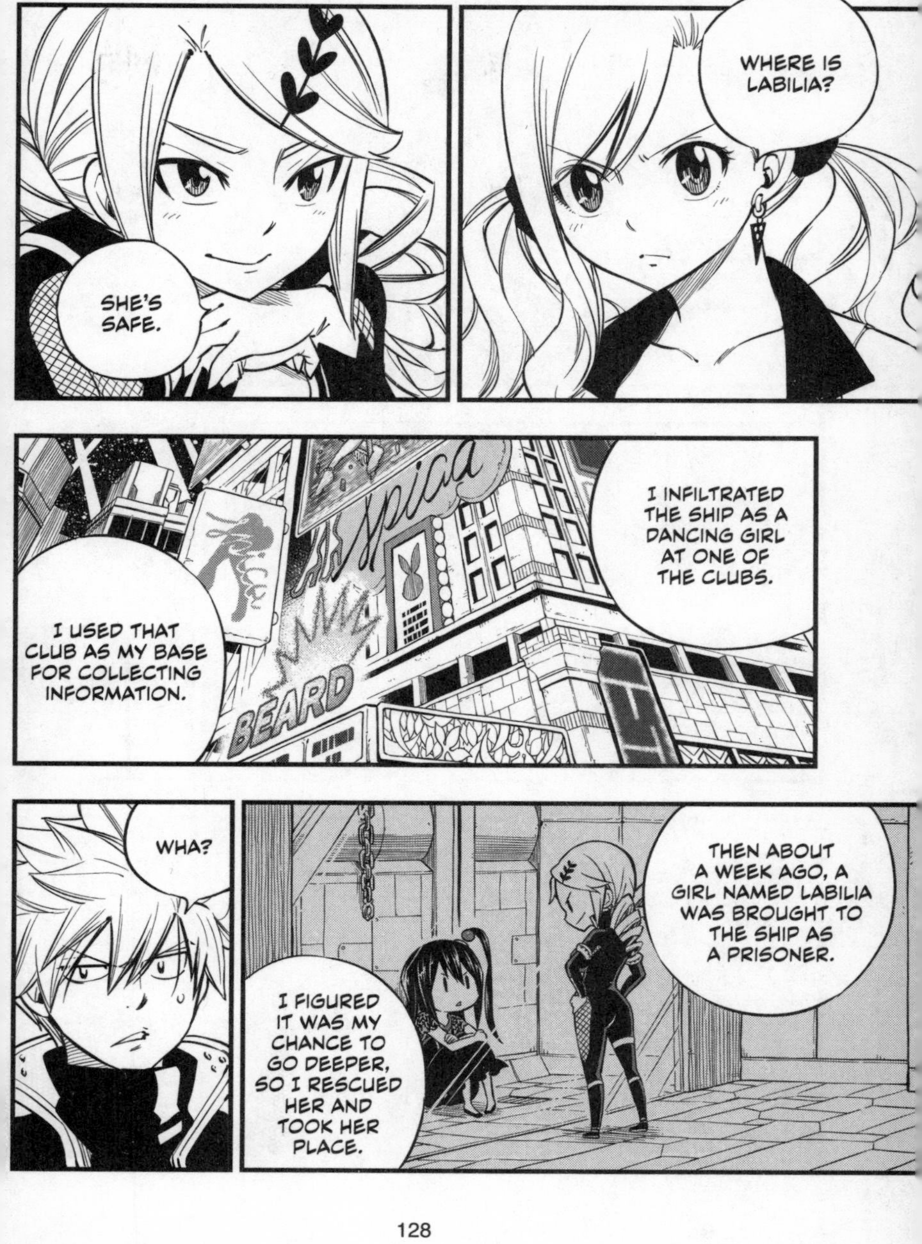
WHERE IS LABILIA?
SHE'S SAFE.
I INFILTRATED THE SHIP AS A DANCING GIRL AT ONE OF THE CLUBS.
I USED THAT CLUB AS MY BASE FOR COLLECTING INFORMATION.
BEARD
THEN ABOUT A WEEK AGO, A GIRL NAMED LABILIA WAS BROUGHT TO THE SHIP AS A PRISONER.
I FIGURED IT WAS MY CHANCE TO GO DEEPER, SO I RESCUED HER AND TOOK HER PLACE.
WHA?

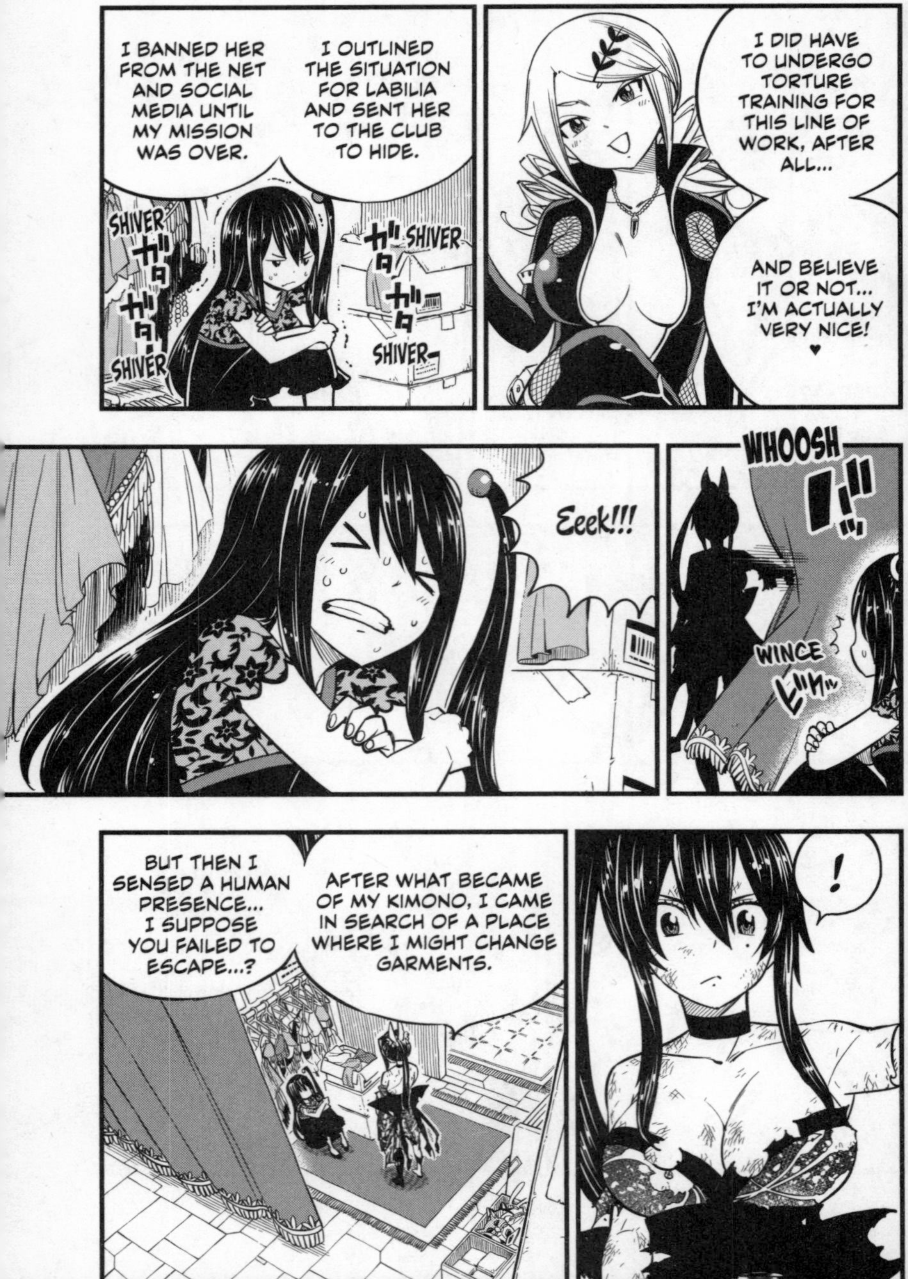
I DID HAVE TO UNDERGO TORTURE TRAINING FOR THIS LINE OF WORK, AFTER ALL...
AND BELIEVE IT OR NOT... I'M ACTUALLY VERY NICE! ♥
I OUTLINED THE SITUATION FOR LABILIA AND SENT HER TO THE CLUB TO HIDE.
I BANNED HER FROM THE NET AND SOCIAL MEDIA UNTIL MY MISSION WAS OVER.
SHIVER ガタ SHIVER
ガタガタ SHIVER
SHIVER ガタガタ SHIVER
WHOOSH
WINCE ビクッ
Eeek!!!
!
AFTER WHAT BECAME OF MY KIMONO, I CAME IN SEARCH OF A PLACE WHERE I MIGHT CHANGE GARMENTS.
BUT THEN I SENSED A HUMAN PRESENCE... I SUPPOSE YOU FAILED TO ESCAPE...?

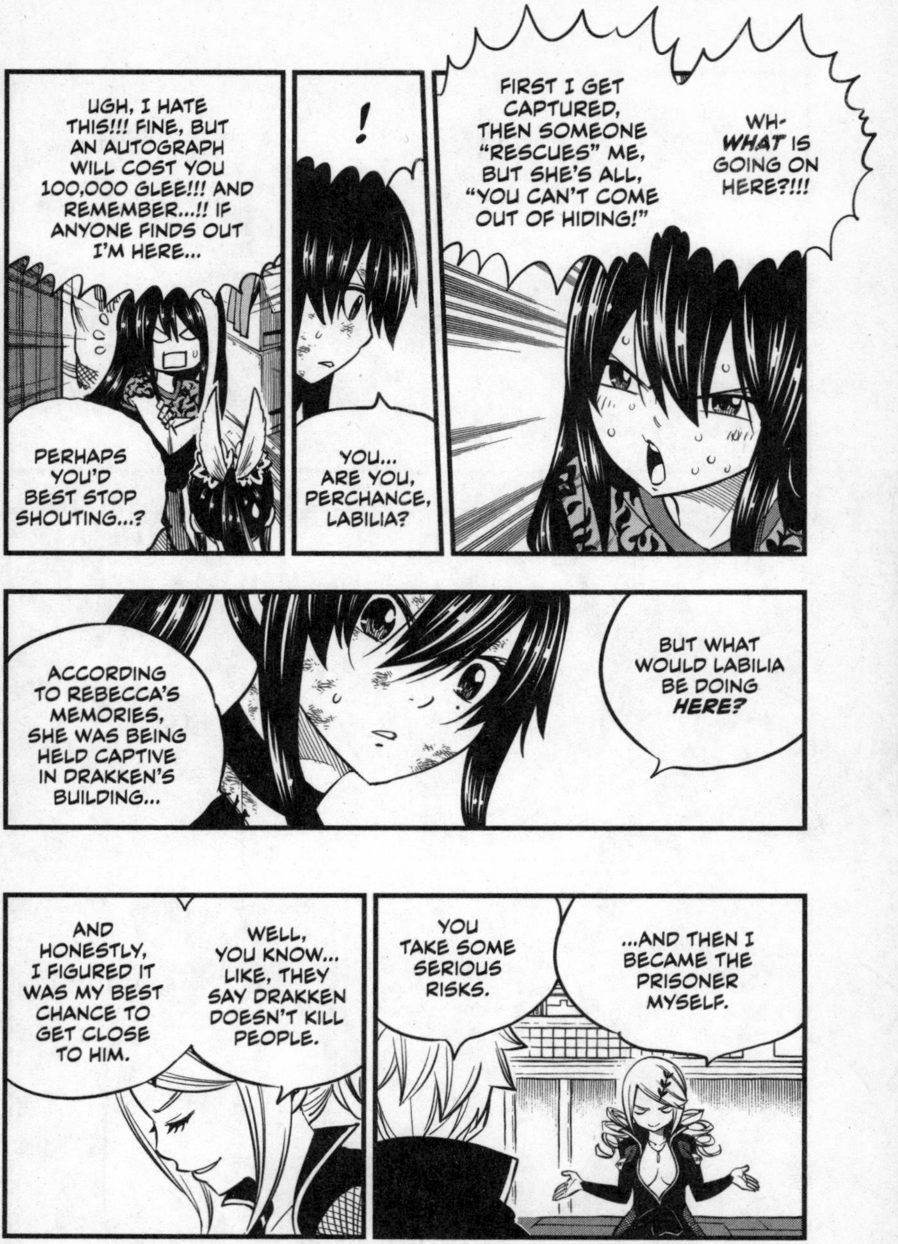
WH- WHAT IS GOING ON HERE?!!!
FIRST I GET CAPTURED, THEN SOMEONE "RESCUES" ME, BUT SHE'S ALL, "YOU CAN'T COME OUT OF HIDING!"
!
YOU... ARE YOU, PERCHANCE, LABILIA?
UGH, I HATE THIS!!! FINE, BUT AN AUTOGRAPH WILL COST YOU 100,000 GLEE!!! AND REMEMBER...!! IF ANYONE FINDS OUT I'M HERE...
PERHAPS YOU'D BEST STOP SHOUTING...?
BUT WHAT WOULD LABILIA BE DOING HERE?
ACCORDING TO REBECCA'S MEMORIES, SHE WAS BEING HELD CAPTIVE IN DRAKKEN'S BUILDING...
...AND THEN I BECAME THE PRISONER MYSELF.
YOU TAKE SOME SERIOUS RISKS.
WELL, YOU KNOW... LIKE, THEY SAY DRAKKEN DOESN'T KILL PEOPLE.
AND HONESTLY, I FIGURED IT WAS MY BEST CHANCE TO GET CLOSE TO HIM.

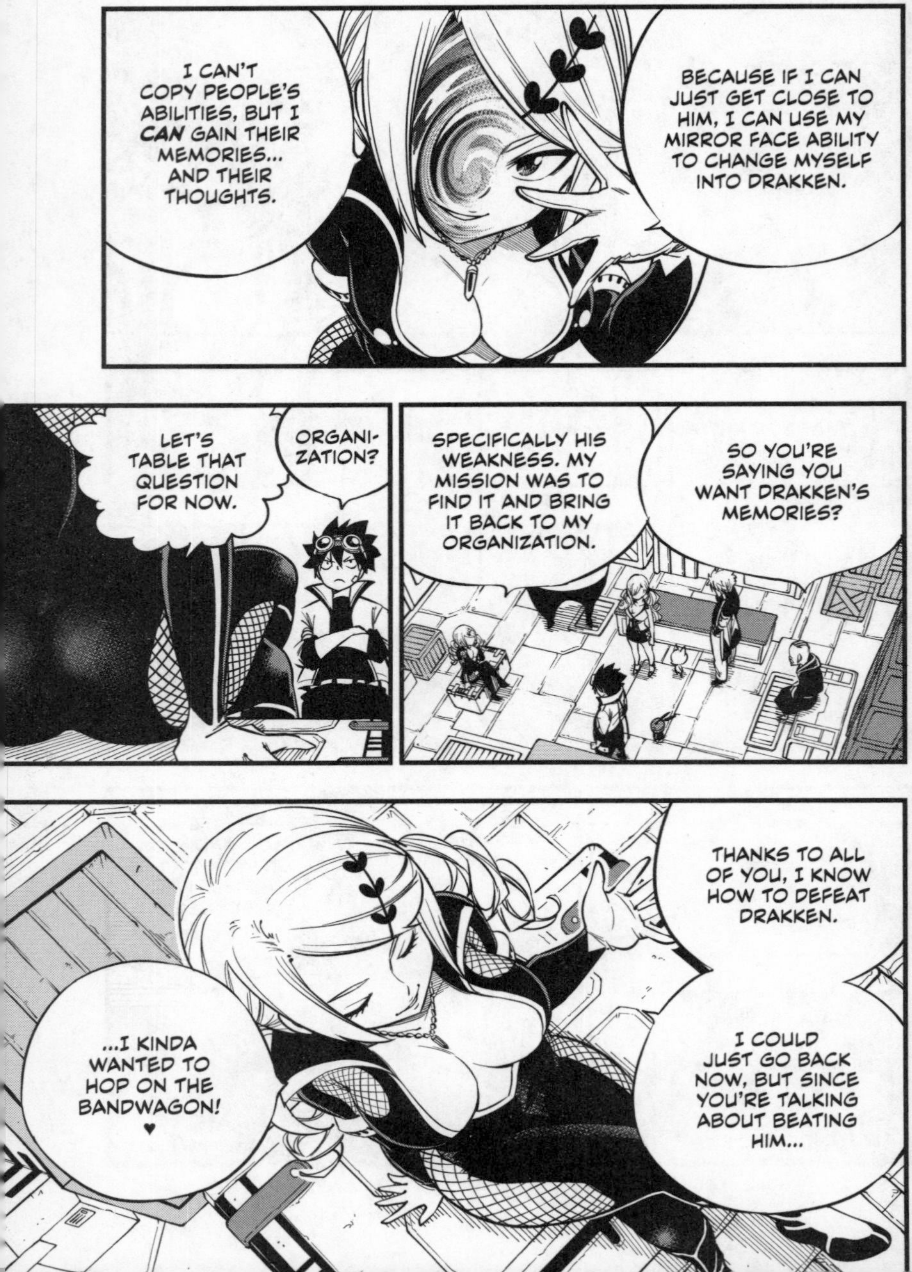
BECAUSE IF I CAN JUST GET CLOSE TO HIM, I CAN USE MY MIRROR FACE ABILITY TO CHANGE MYSELF INTO DRAKKEN.
I CAN'T COPY PEOPLE'S ABILITIES, BUT I *CAN* GAIN THEIR MEMORIES... AND THEIR THOUGHTS.
SO YOU'RE SAYING YOU WANT DRAKKEN'S MEMORIES?
SPECIFICALLY HIS WEAKNESS. MY MISSION WAS TO FIND IT AND BRING IT BACK TO MY ORGANIZATION.
ORGANIZATION?
LET'S TABLE THAT QUESTION FOR NOW.
THANKS TO ALL OF YOU, I KNOW HOW TO DEFEAT DRAKKEN.
I COULD JUST GO BACK NOW, BUT SINCE YOU'RE TALKING ABOUT BEATING HIM...
...I KINDA WANTED TO HOP ON THE BANDWAGON! ♥

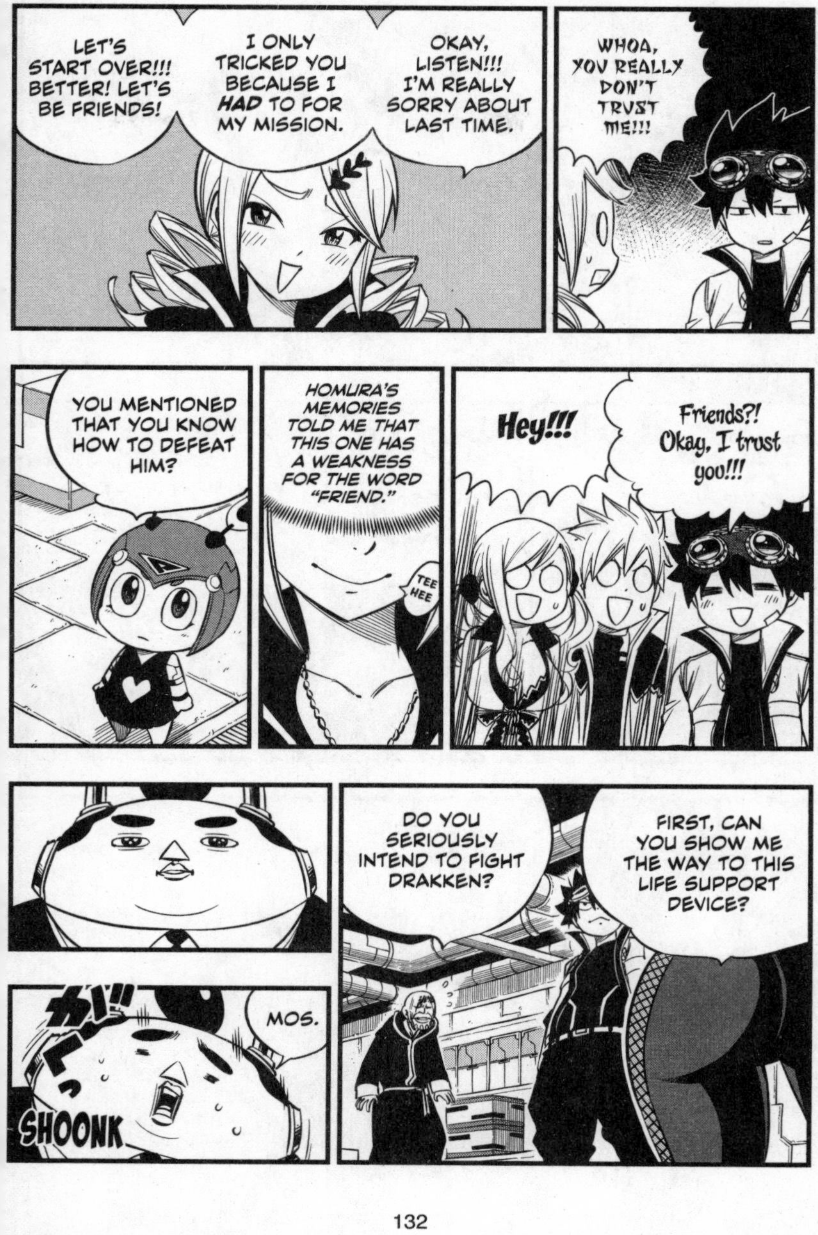
WHOA, YOU REALLY DON'T TRUST ME!!!
OKAY, LISTEN!!! I'M REALLY SORRY ABOUT LAST TIME.
I ONLY TRICKED YOU BECAUSE I *HAD* TO FOR MY MISSION.
LET'S START OVER!!! BETTER! LET'S BE FRIENDS!
Friends?! Okay, I trust you!!!
Hey!!!
HOMURA'S MEMORIES TOLD ME THAT THIS ONE HAS A WEAKNESS FOR THE WORD "FRIEND."
TEE HEE
YOU MENTIONED THAT YOU KNOW HOW TO DEFEAT HIM?
FIRST, CAN YOU SHOW ME THE WAY TO THIS LIFE SUPPORT DEVICE?
DO YOU SERIOUSLY INTEND TO FIGHT DRAKKEN?
MOS.
SHOONK

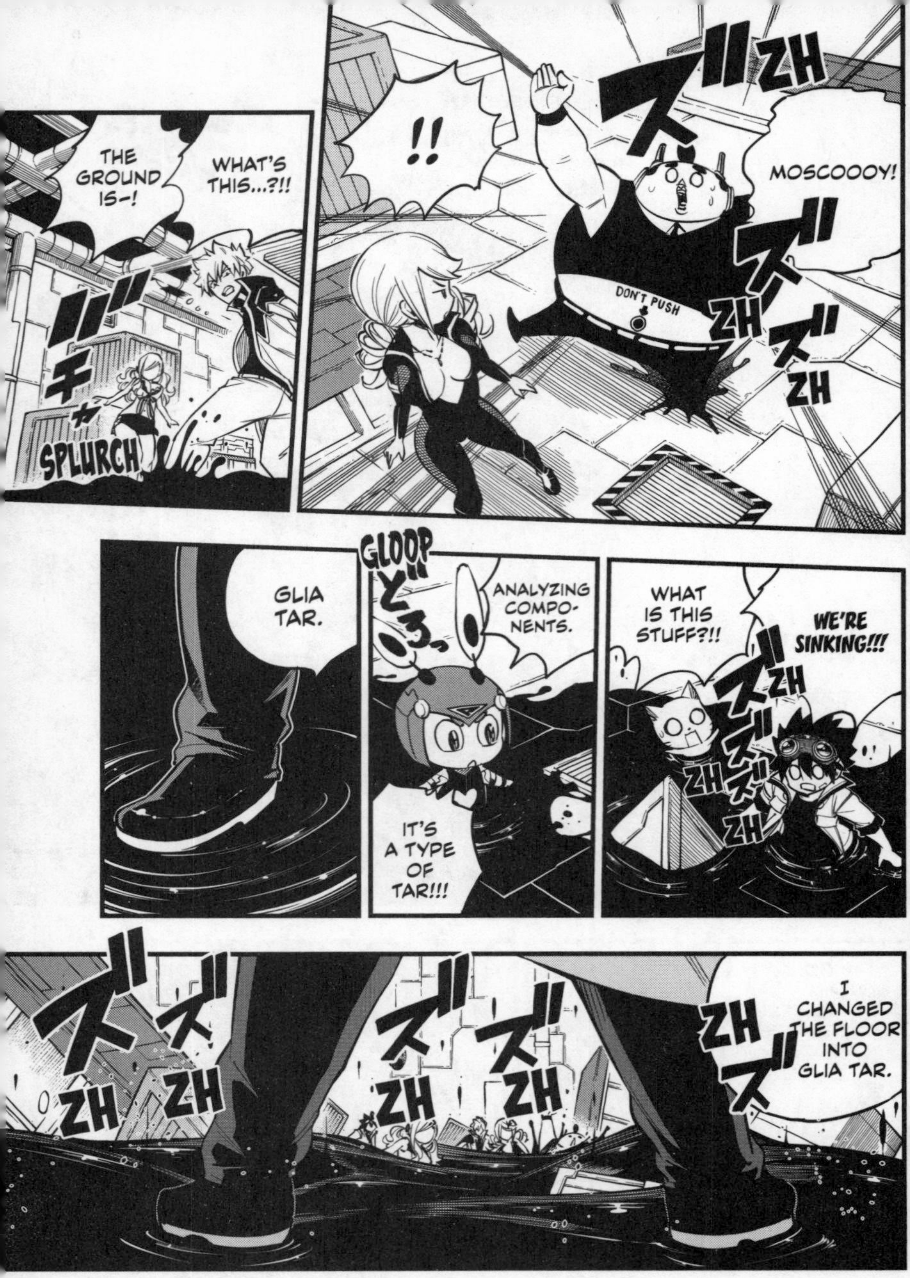
!!
ZH
MOSCOOOY!
DON'T PUSH
ZH
ZH
WHAT'S THIS...?!!
THE GROUND IS-!
SPLURCH
WHAT IS THIS STUFF?!!
WE'RE SINKING!!!
ZH
ZH
ZH
GLOOP
ANALYZING COMPONENTS.
IT'S A TYPE OF TAR!!!
GLIA TAR.
I CHANGED THE FLOOR INTO GLIA TAR.
ZH
ZH
ZH
ZH
ZH

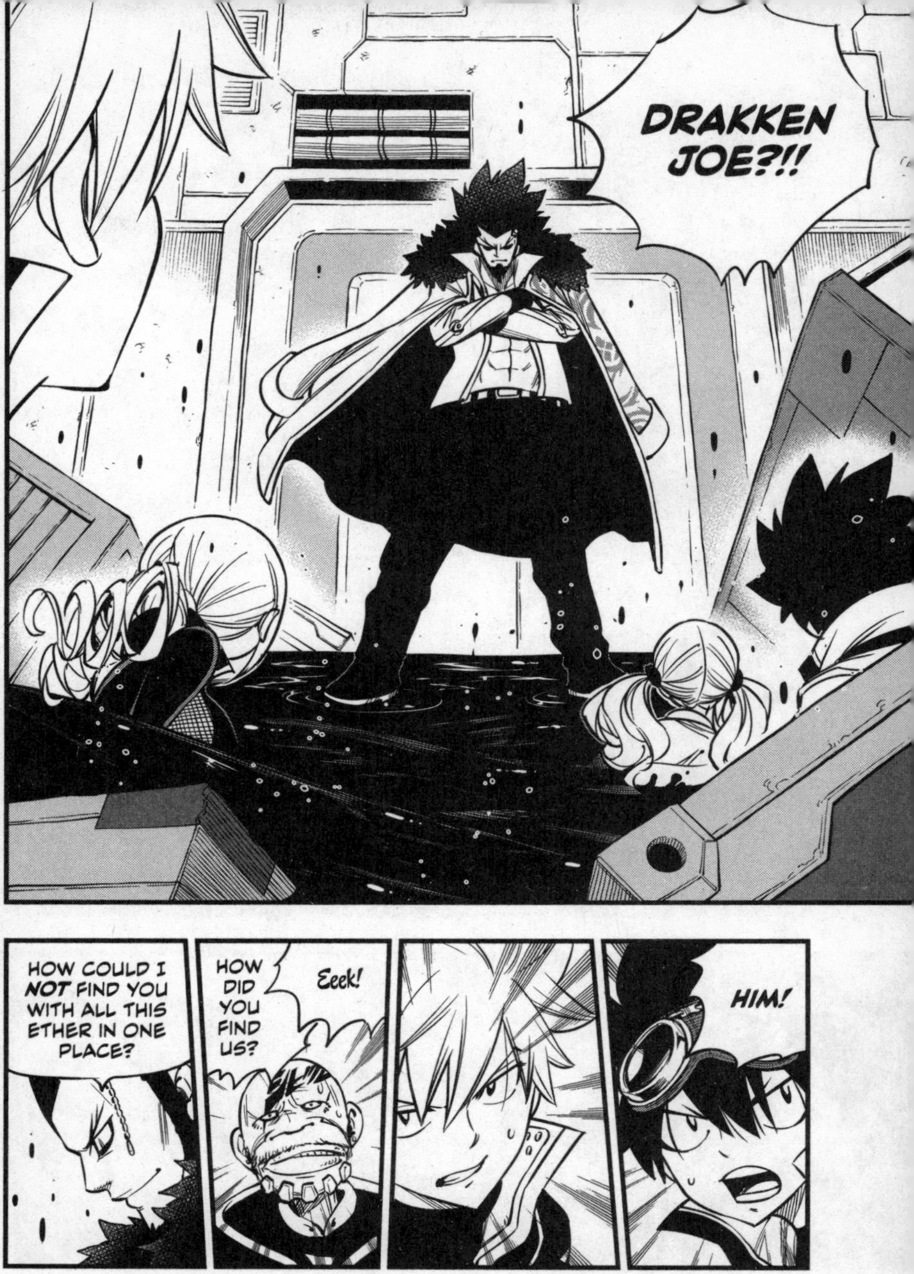
DRAKKEN JOE?!!
HIM!
Eeek!
HOW DID YOU FIND US?
HOW COULD I **NOT** FIND YOU WITH ALL THIS ETHER IN ONE PLACE?

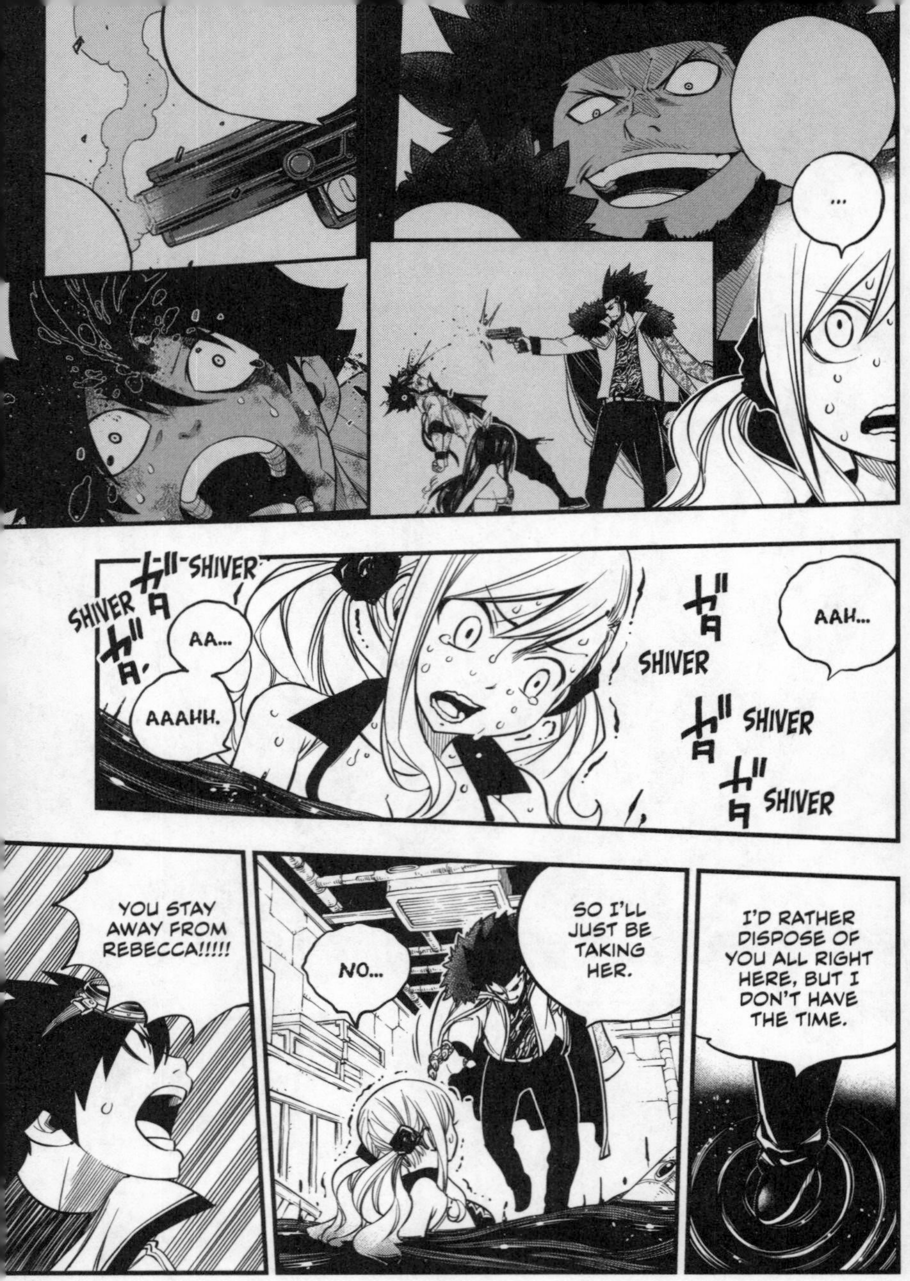
...
AAH...
ガタ SHIVER
ガタ SHIVER
ガタ SHIVER
ガタ SHIVER
ガタ SHIVER
AA...
AAAHH.
I'D RATHER DISPOSE OF YOU ALL RIGHT HERE, BUT I DON'T HAVE THE TIME.
SO I'LL JUST BE TAKING HER.
NO...
YOU STAY AWAY FROM REBECCA!!!!!

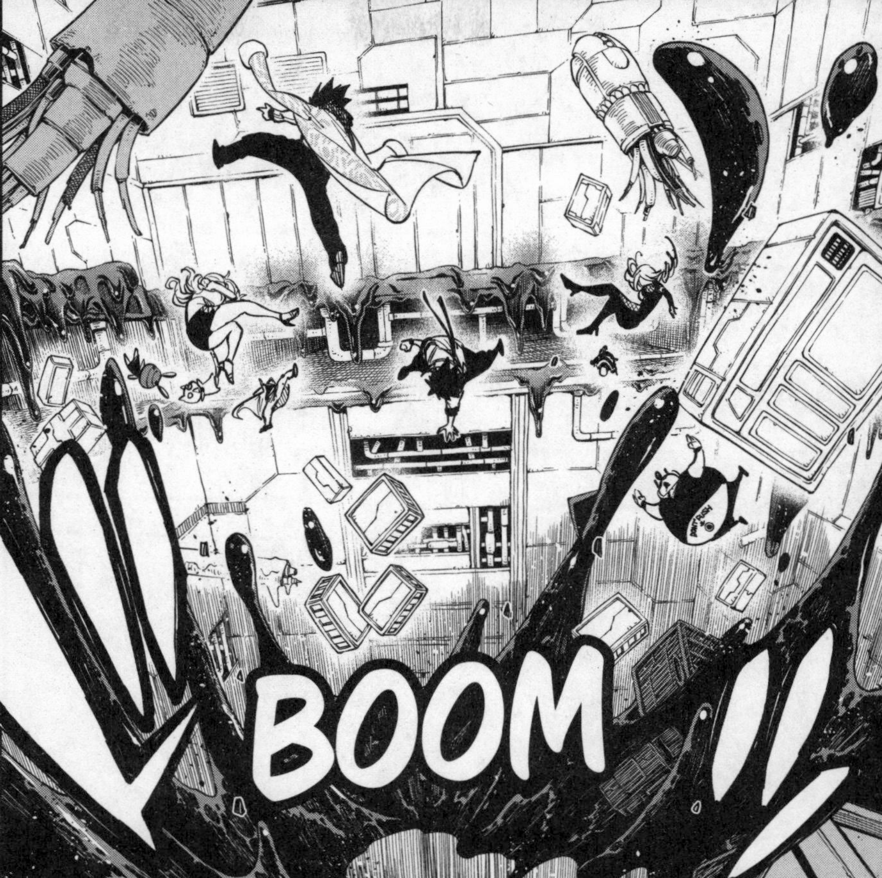
BOOM

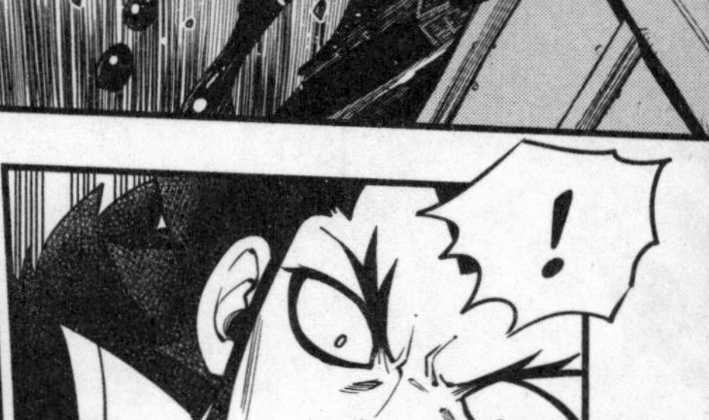
!

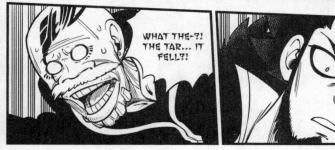

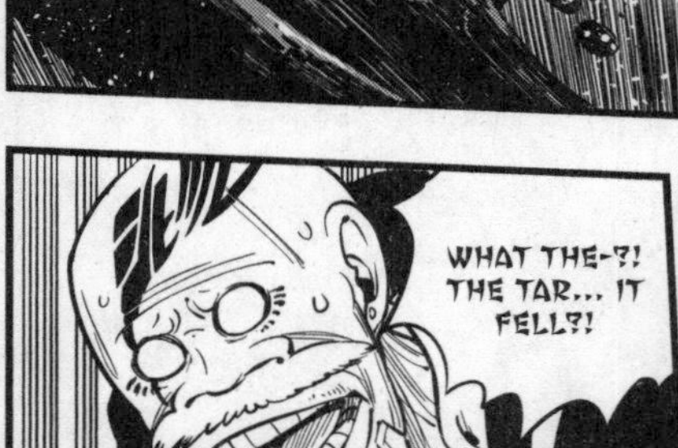
WHAT THE-?! THE TAR... IT FELL?!

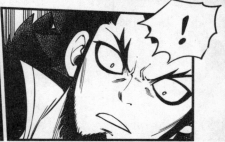

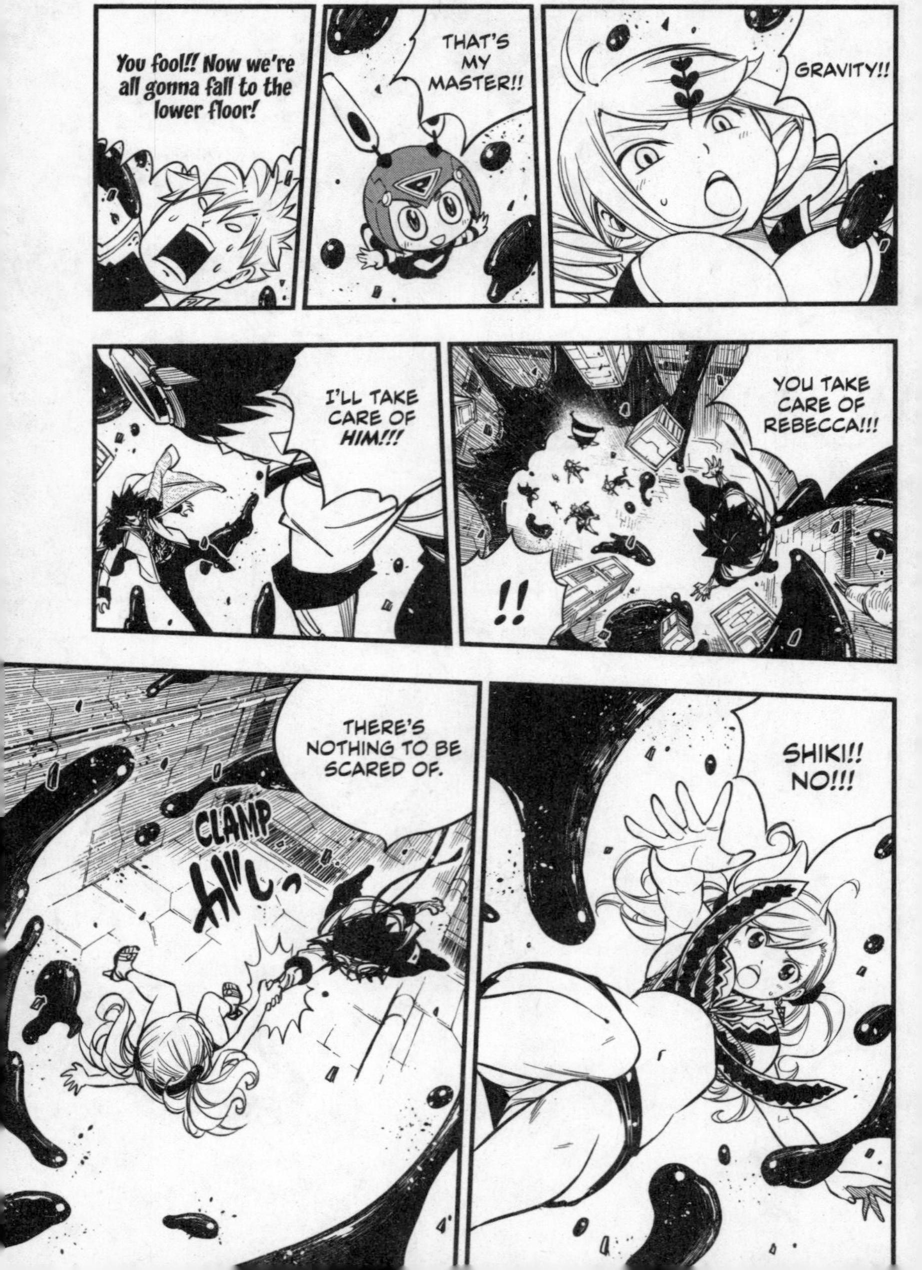
GRAVITY!!
THAT'S MY MASTER!!
You fool!! Now we're all gonna fall to the lower floor!
YOU TAKE CARE OF REBECCA!!!
!!
I'LL TAKE CARE OF HIM!!!
SHIKI!!! NO!!!
THERE'S NOTHING TO BE SCARED OF.
CLAMP

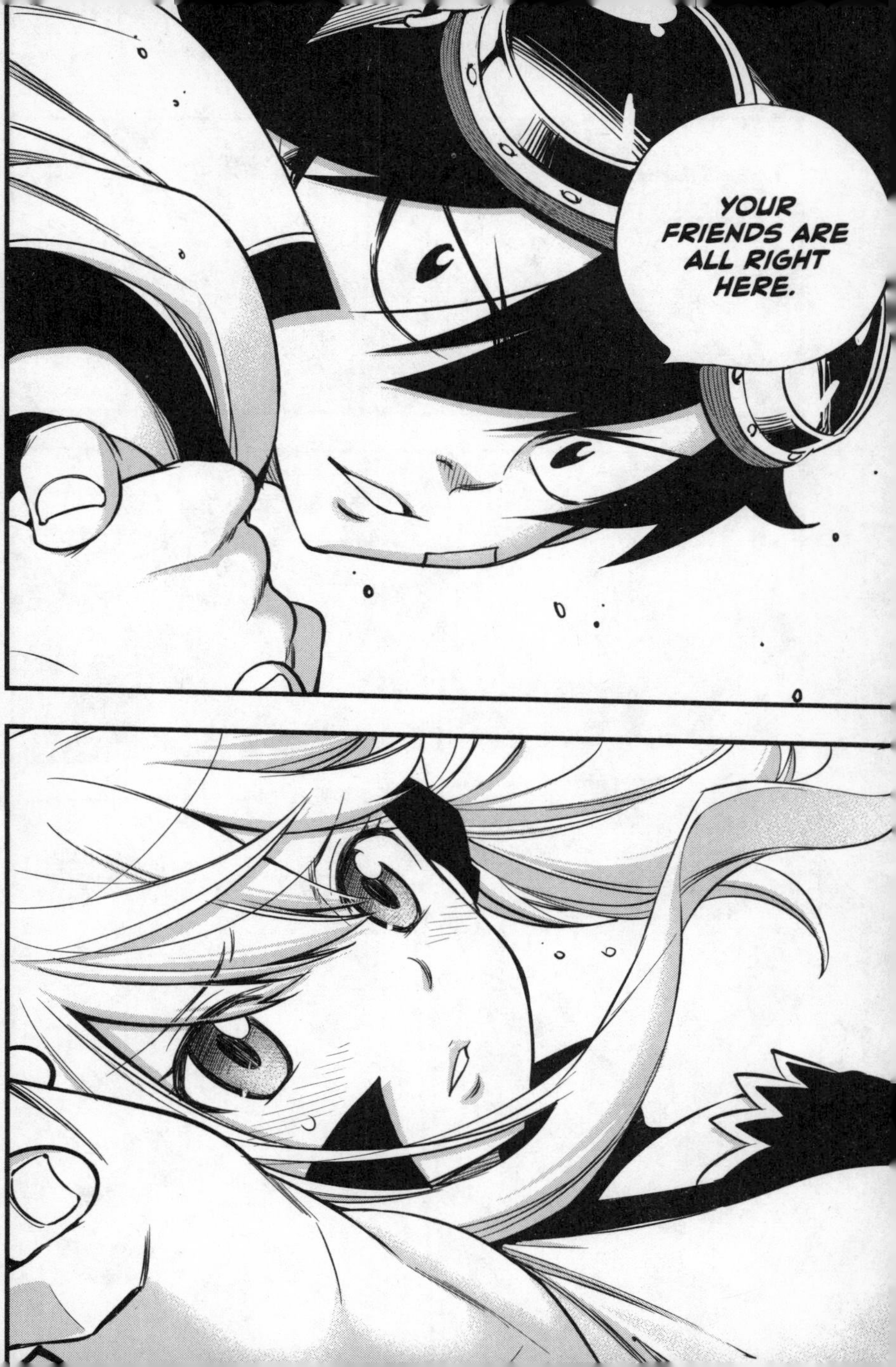
YOUR FRIENDS ARE ALL RIGHT HERE.

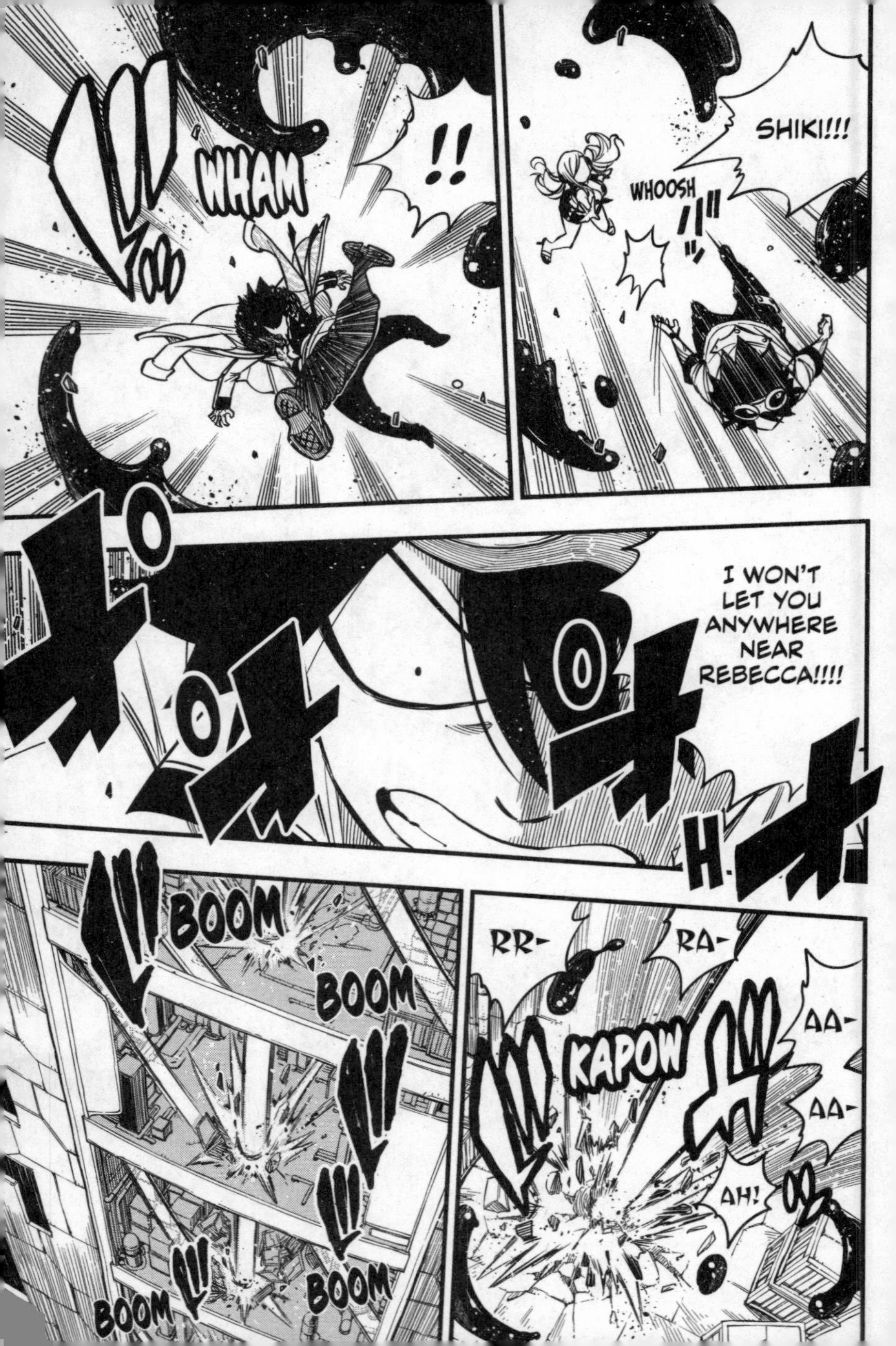
SHIKI!!!
WHOOSH
!!
WHAM
I WON'T LET YOU ANYWHERE NEAR REBECCA!!!!
RR-
RA-
AA-
AA-
KAPOW
AH!
BOOM
BOOM
BOOM
BOOM

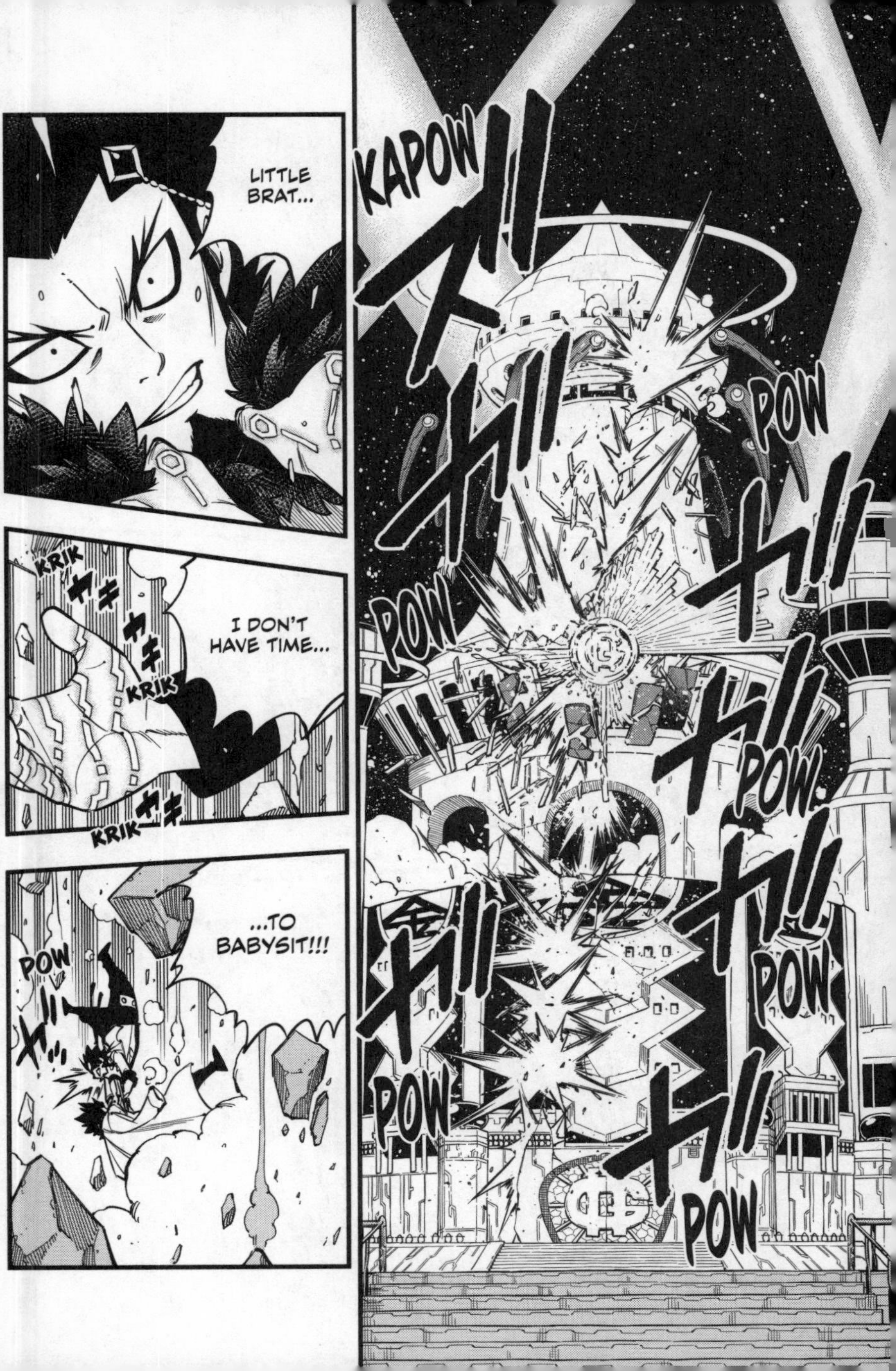
KAPOW
POW
POW
POW
POW
POW
POW
LITTLE BRAT...
KRIK
KRIK
I DON'T HAVE TIME...
KRIK
...TO BABYSIT!!!
POW

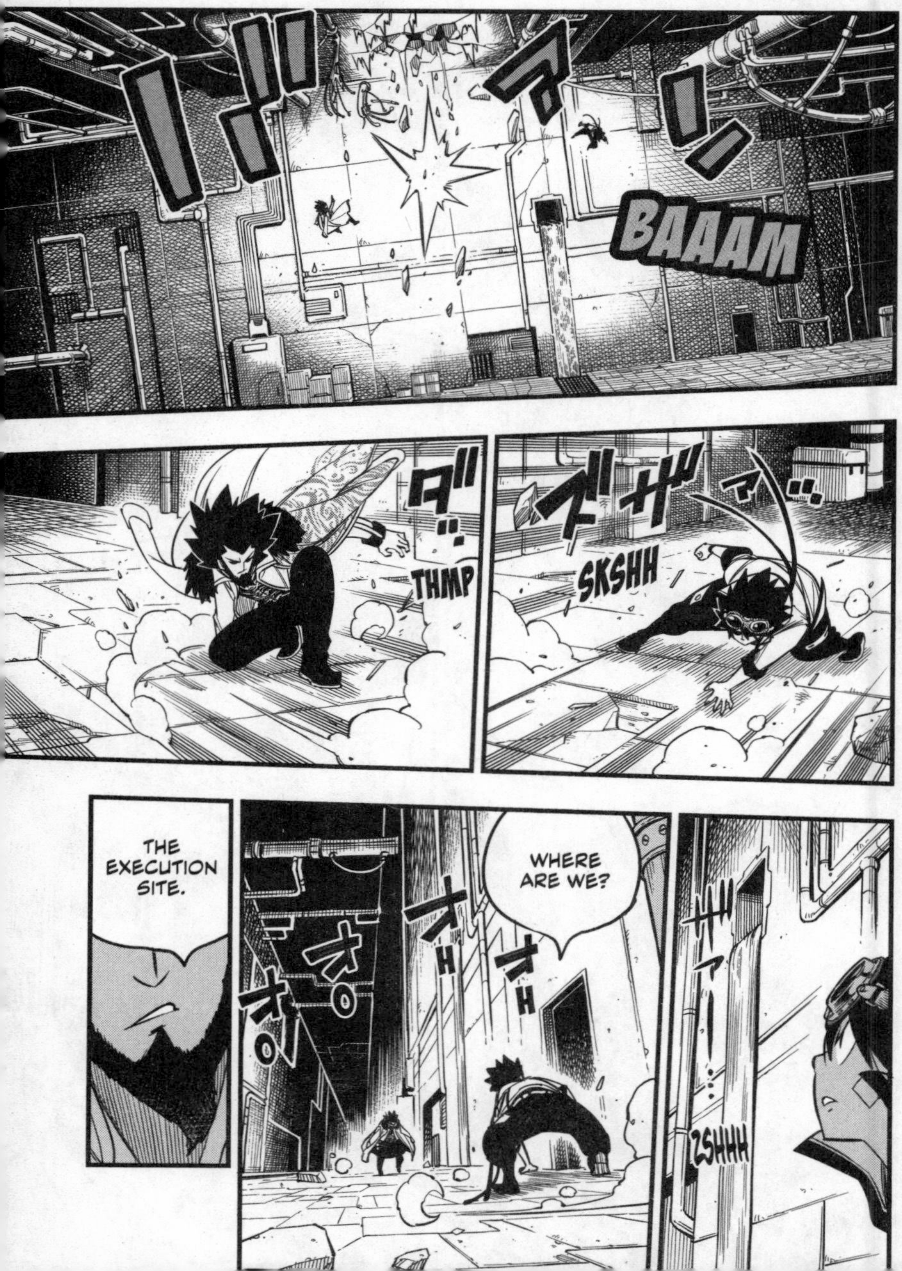
BAAAM
SKSHH
THMP
ZSHHH
WHERE ARE WE?
THE EXECUTION SITE.

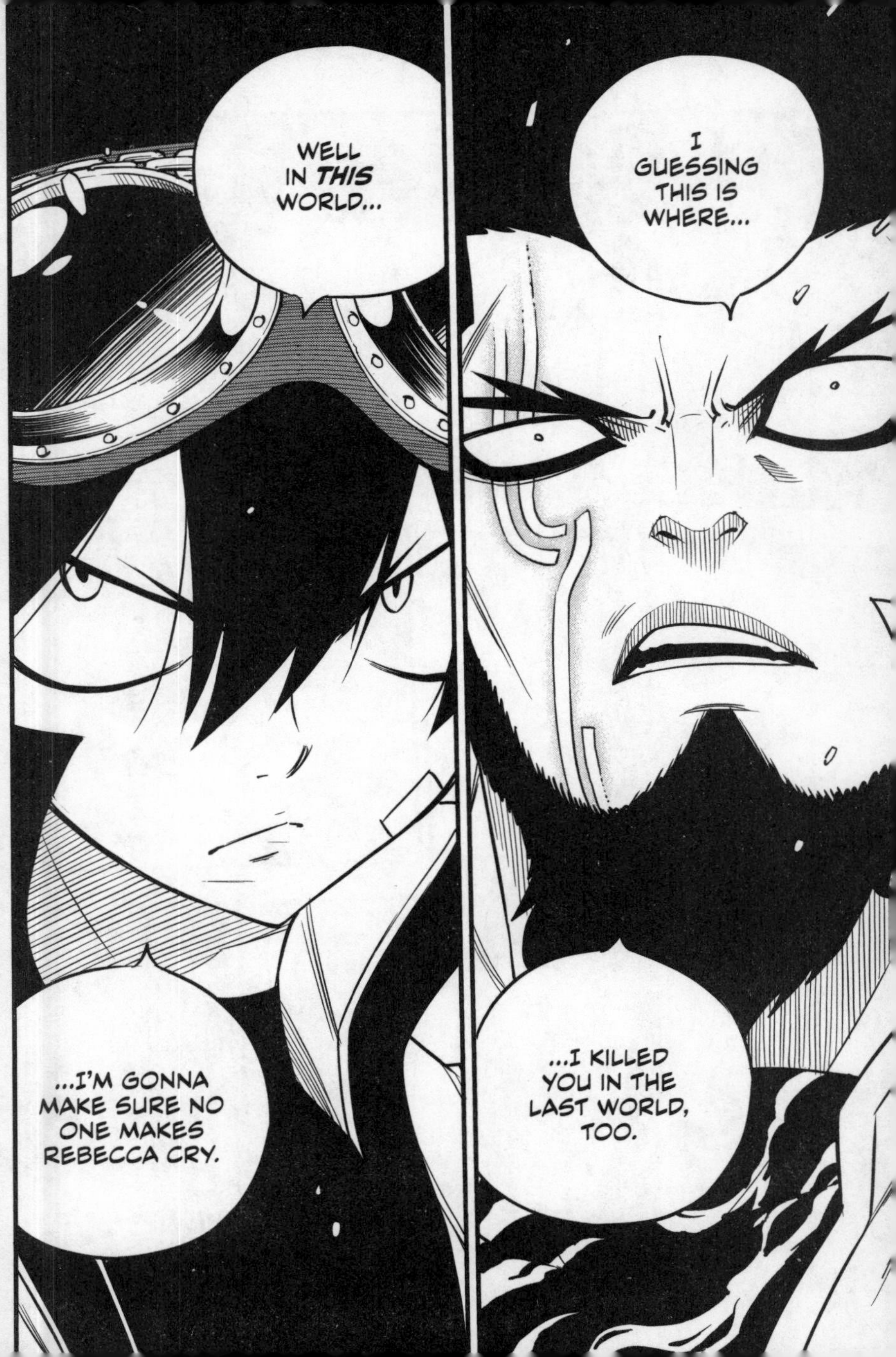
I GUESSING THIS IS WHERE...
...I KILLED YOU IN THE LAST WORLD, TOO.
WELL IN *THIS* WORLD...
...I'M GONNA MAKE SURE NO ONE MAKES REBECCA CRY.

EDENSZERO

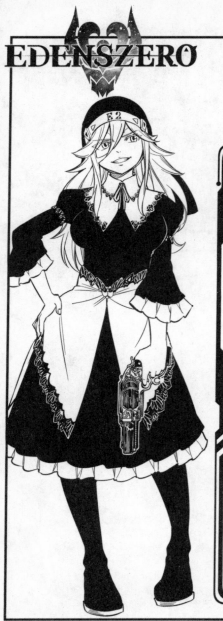

Edens Zero
In-Depth Character File 8

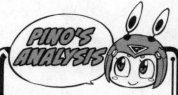

PINO'S ANALYSIS

Name: Sister Ivry

Powers: Healing Ether

(Heal Atomizer)

Likes: Torture

Dislikes: Things that can't be healed

Attack: ☆☆

Defense: ☆☆☆

Marksmanship: ☆☆☆

Ether Power: ☆☆☆☆

Intelligence: ☆☆

Healing: ☆☆☆☆☆

Memo

She may be a scary lady with
a foul mouth, but she's also a
healer-model android who fixes
everyone's wounds and injuries.
She is one of the Demon King's
Four Shining Stars, and is always
(according to her) showing
affection to Mr. Mosco. Her
phone's lock screen is a picture
of Miss Rebecca.

CHAPTER 94: SHIKI VS. DRAKKEN

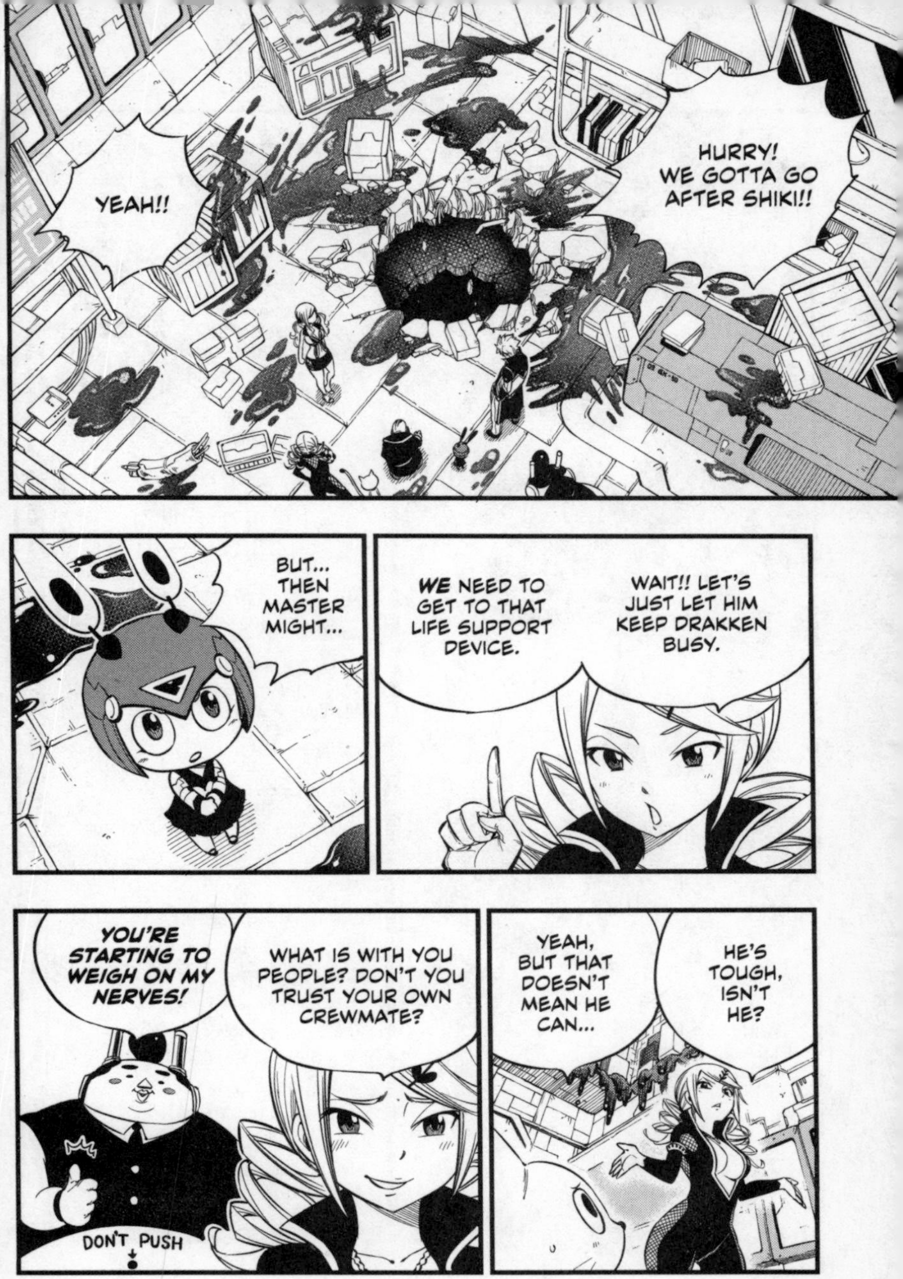
HURRY! WE GOTTA GO AFTER SHIKI!!
YEAH!!
WAIT!! LET'S JUST LET HIM KEEP DRAKKEN BUSY.
WE NEED TO GET TO THAT LIFE SUPPORT DEVICE.
BUT... THEN MASTER MIGHT...
HE'S TOUGH, ISN'T HE?
YEAH, BUT THAT DOESN'T MEAN HE CAN...
WHAT IS WITH YOU PEOPLE? DON'T YOU TRUST YOUR OWN CREWMATE?
YOU'RE STARTING TO WEIGH ON MY NERVES!
DON'T PUSH

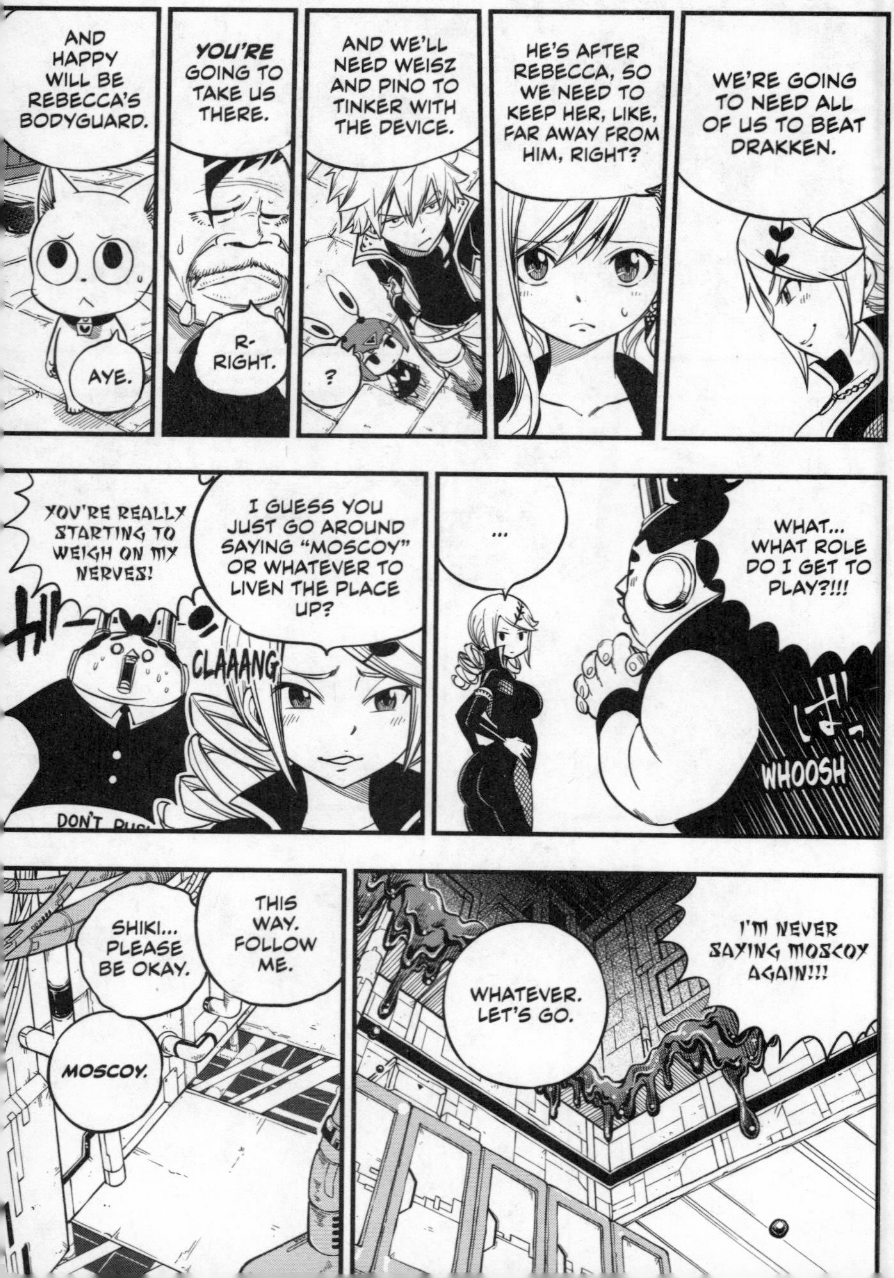
WE'RE GOING TO NEED ALL OF US TO BEAT DRAKKEN.
HE'S AFTER REBECCA, SO WE NEED TO KEEP HER, LIKE, FAR AWAY FROM HIM, RIGHT?
AND WE'LL NEED WEISZ AND PINO TO TINKER WITH THE DEVICE.
?
YOU'RE GOING TO TAKE US THERE.
R-RIGHT.
AND HAPPY WILL BE REBECCA'S BODYGUARD.
AYE.
WHAT... WHAT ROLE DO I GET TO PLAY?!!!
WHOOSH
...
I GUESS YOU JUST GO AROUND SAYING "MOSCOY" OR WHATEVER TO LIVEN THE PLACE UP?
CLAAANG
YOU'RE REALLY STARTING TO WEIGH ON MY NERVES!
I'M NEVER SAYING MOSCOY AGAIN!!!
WHATEVER. LET'S GO.
THIS WAY. FOLLOW ME.
SHIKI... PLEASE BE OKAY.
MOSCOY.

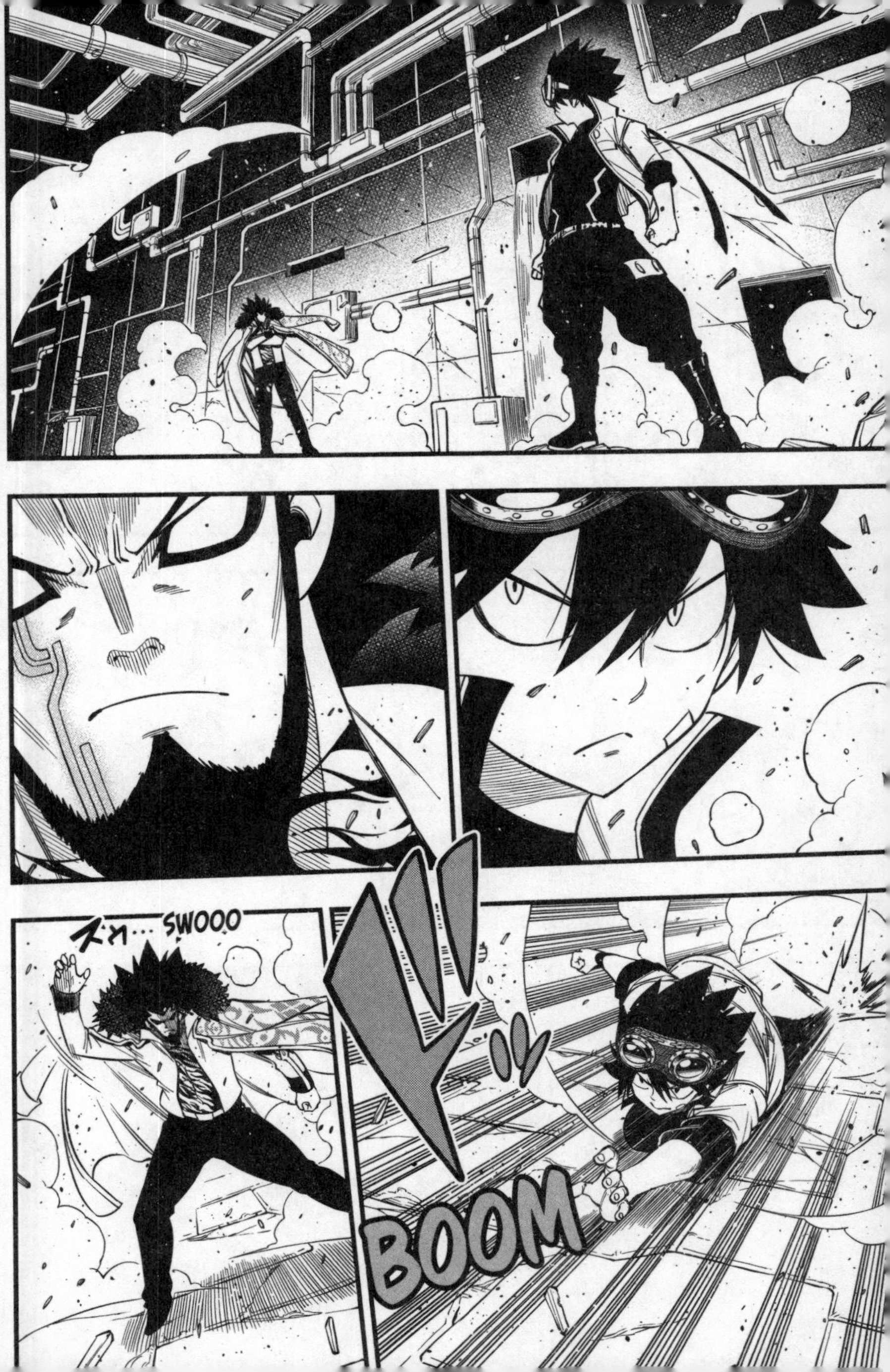
BOOM
ズッ… SWOOO

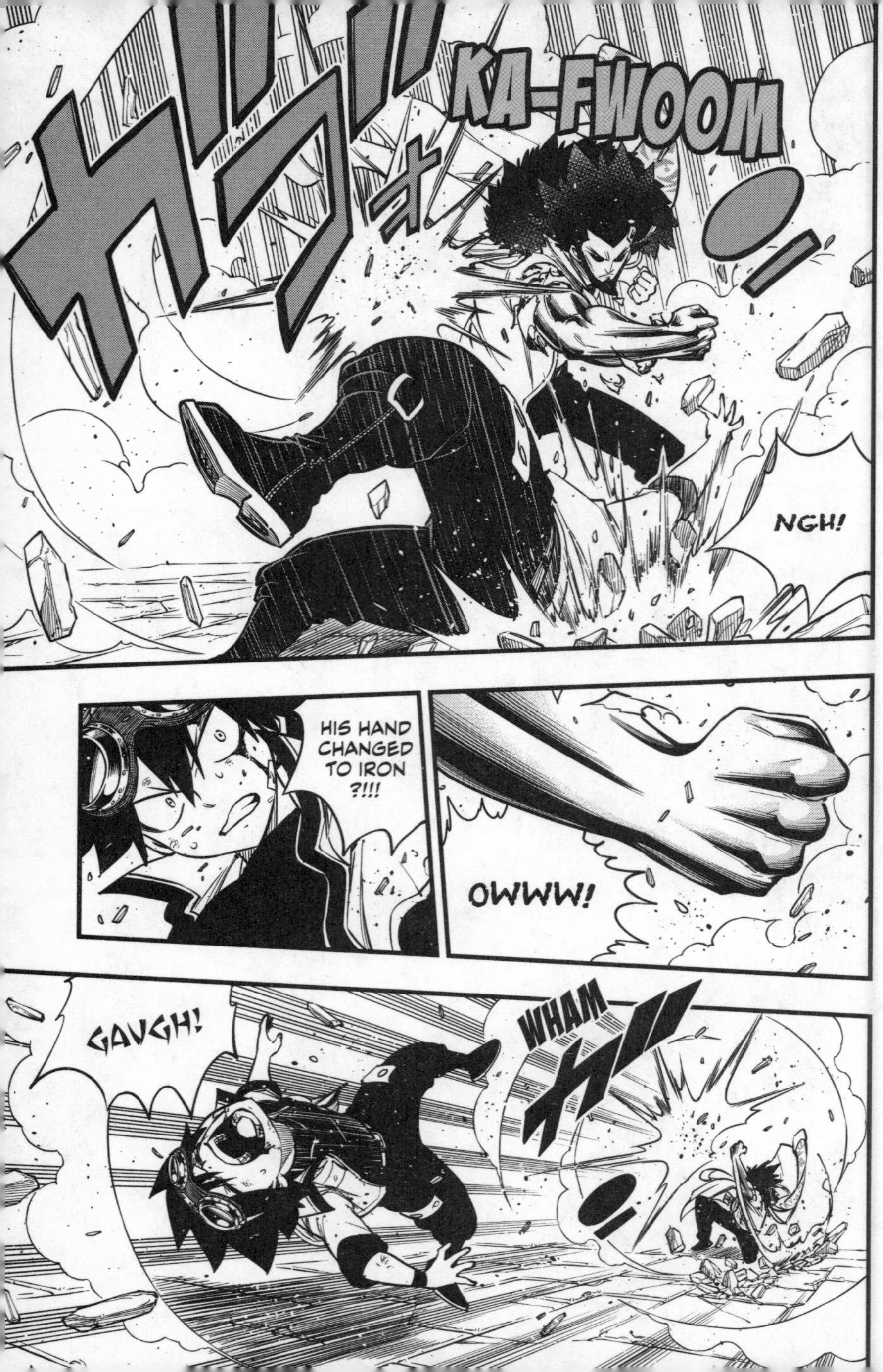
KA-FWOOM
NGH!
OWWW!
HIS HAND CHANGED TO IRON ?!!!
WHAM
GAUGH!

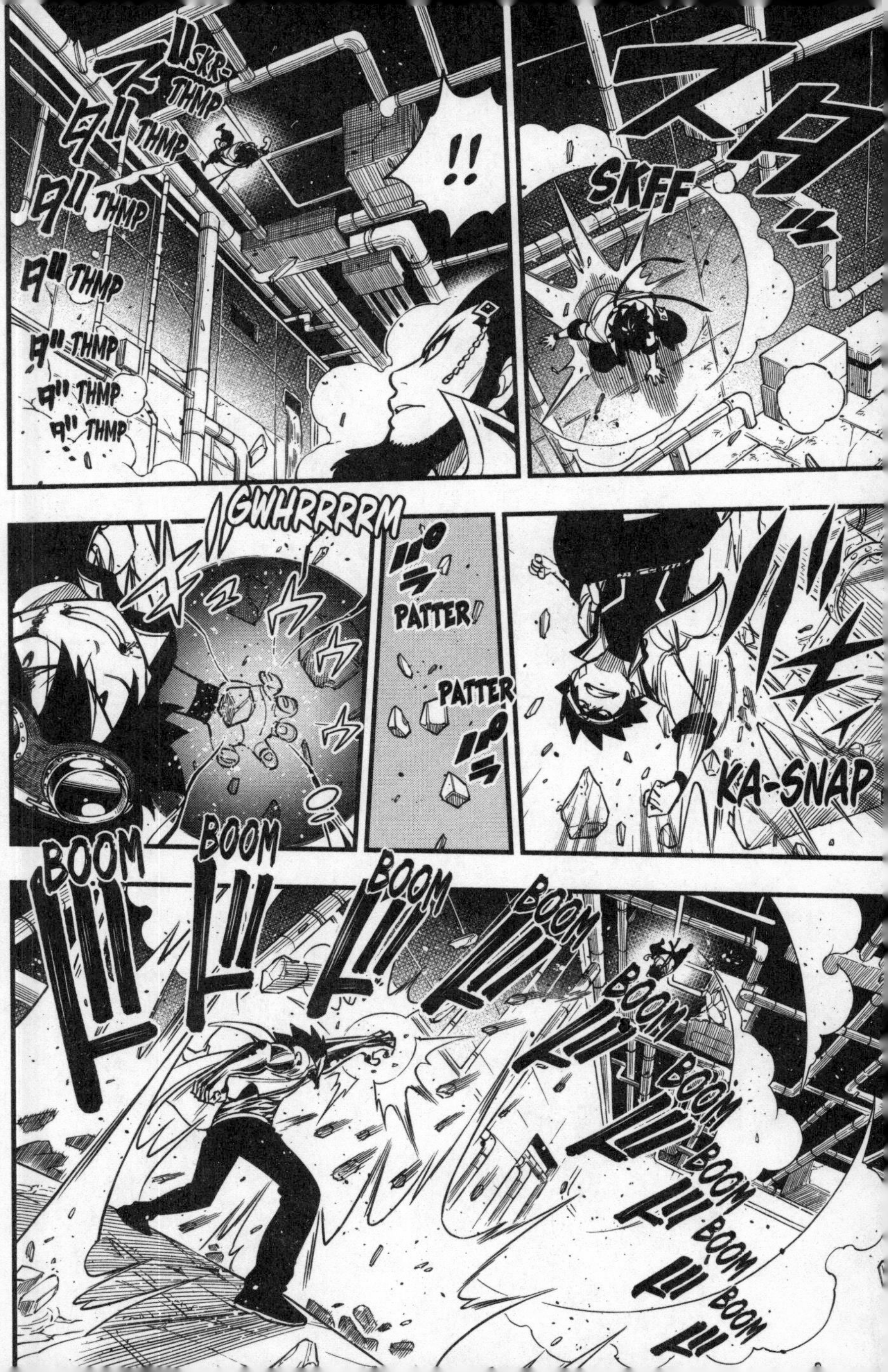

SKFF
SKR-
THMP
THMP
THMP
THMP
THMP
THMP
THMP
!!
KA-SNAP
PATTER
PATTER
GWHRRRRM
BOOM
BOOM
BOOM
BOOM
BOOM
BOOM
BOOM
BOOM
BOOM

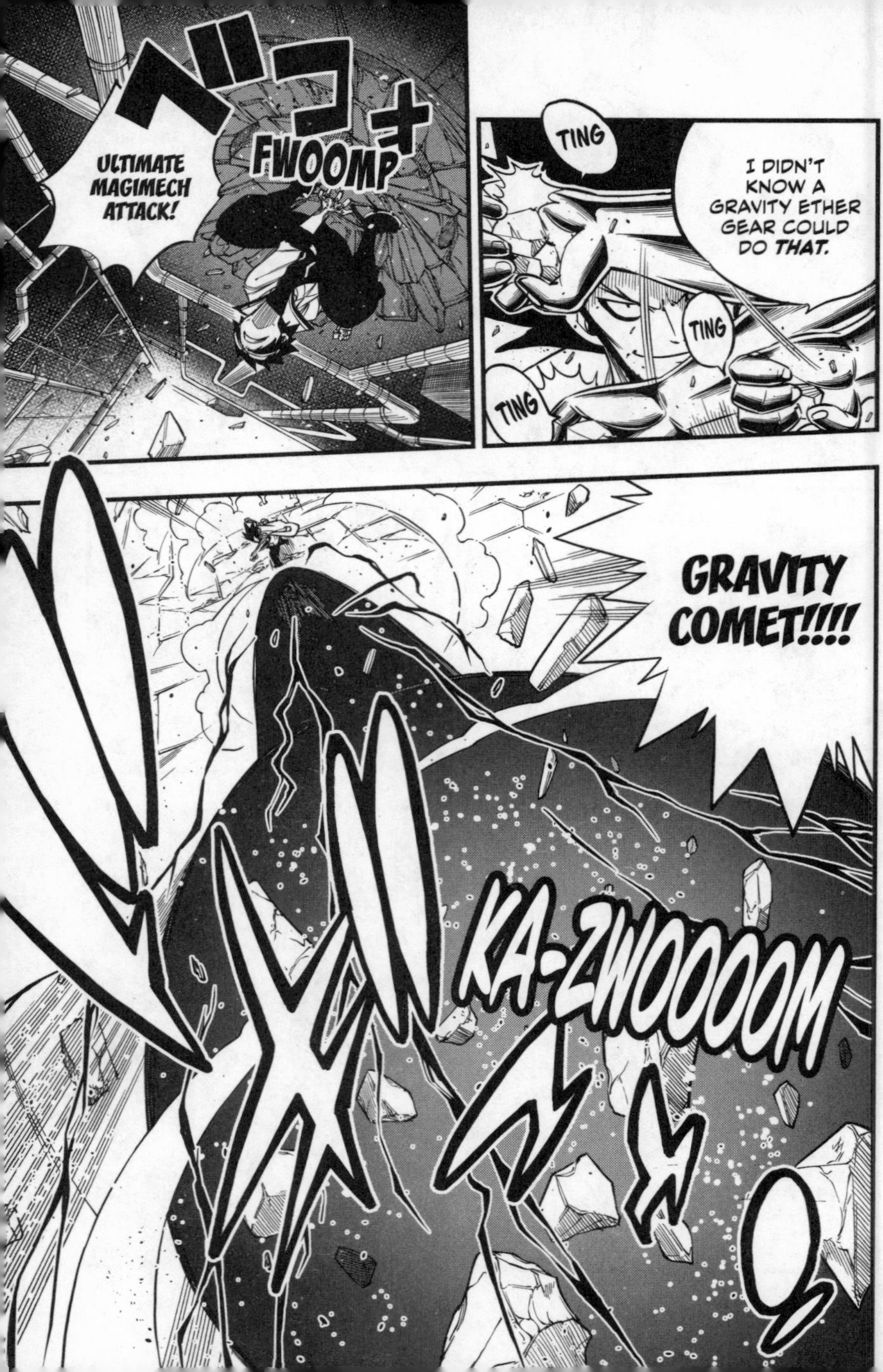
TING
I DIDN'T KNOW A GRAVITY ETHER GEAR COULD DO *THAT.*
TING
TING
FWOOMP
ULTIMATE MAGIMECH ATTACK!
GRAVITY COMET!!!!
KA-ZWOOOOM

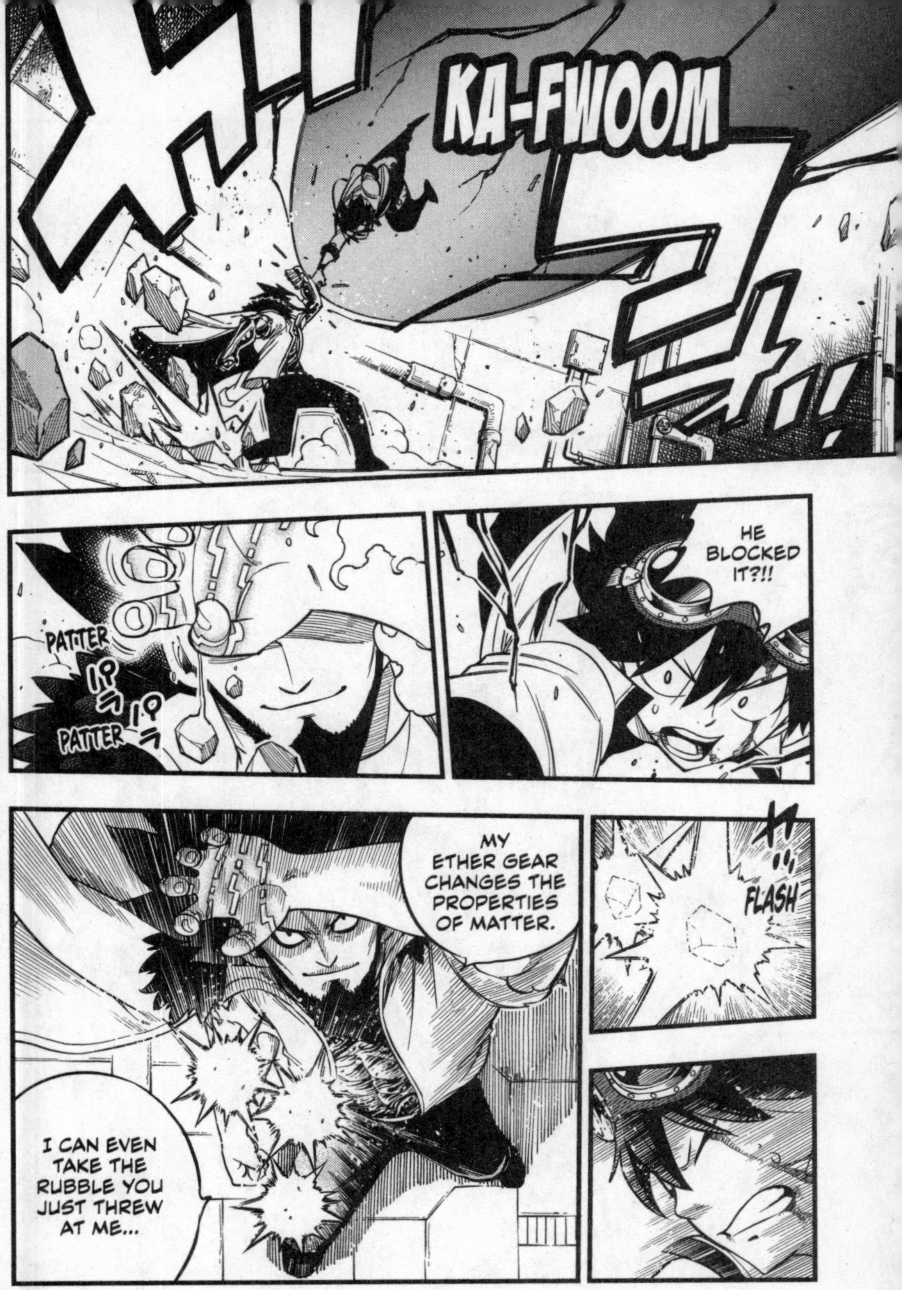
KA-FWOOM
HE BLOCKED IT?!!
PATTER
PATTER
FLASH
MY ETHER GEAR CHANGES THE PROPERTIES OF MATTER.
I CAN EVEN TAKE THE RUBBLE YOU JUST THREW AT ME...

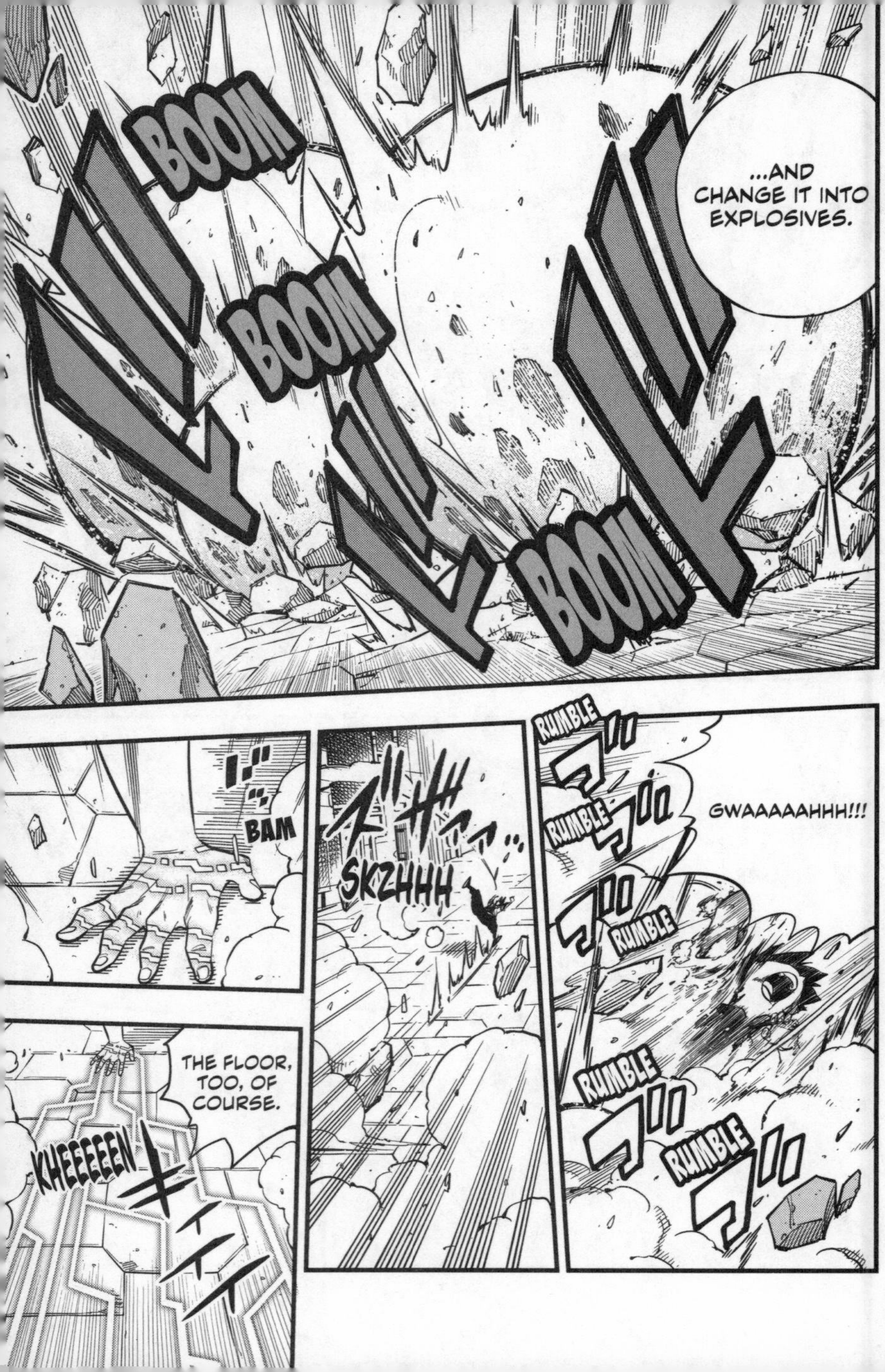
...AND CHANGE IT INTO EXPLOSIVES.
BOOM
BOOM
BOOM
GWAAAAAHHH!!!
RUMBLE
RUMBLE
RUMBLE
RUMBLE
RUMBLE
SKZHHH
BAM
THE FLOOR, TOO, OF COURSE.
KHEEEEEEN

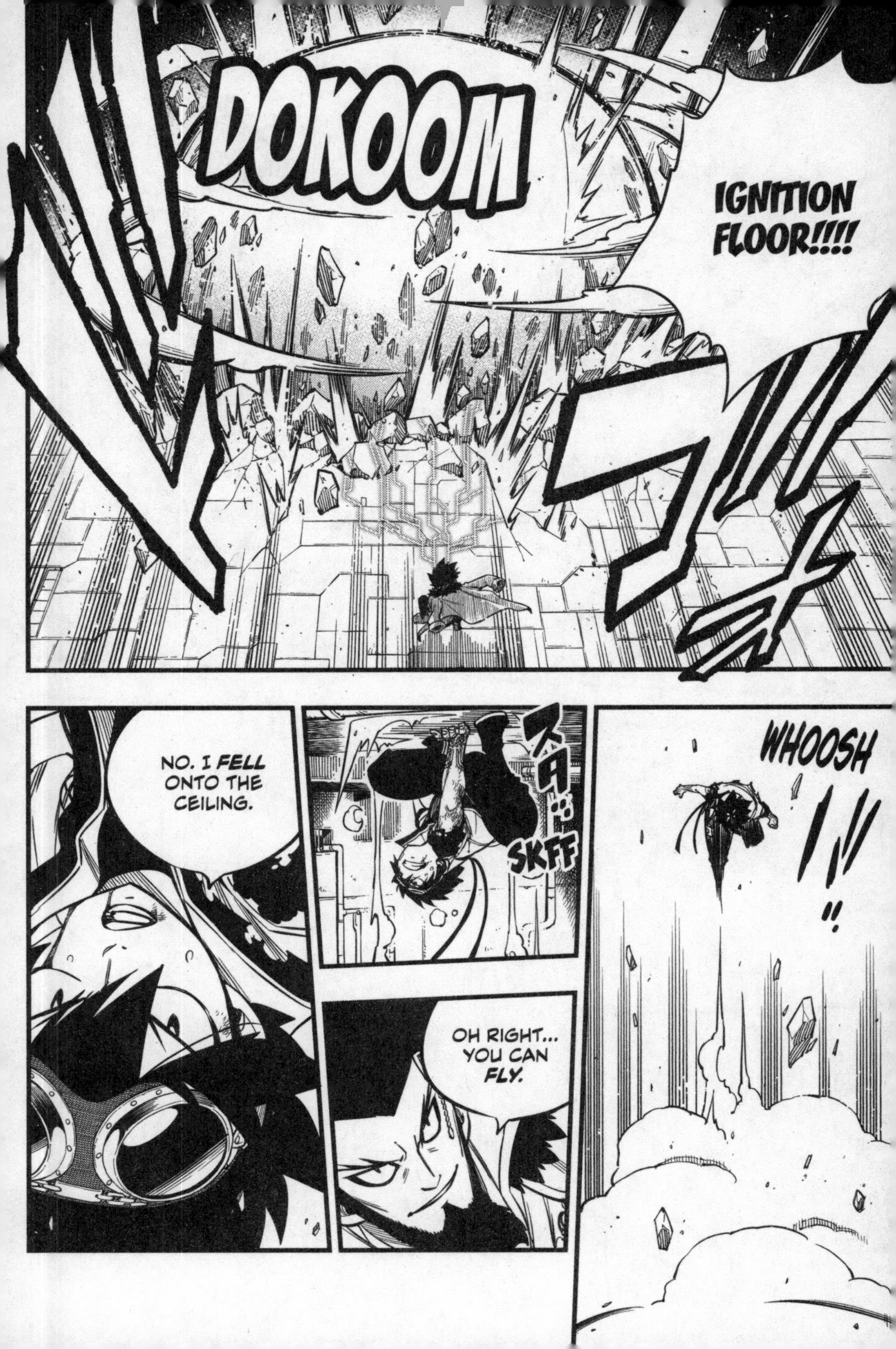
IGNITION FLOOR!!!!
DOKOOM
WHOOSH
SKFF
OH RIGHT... YOU CAN *FLY*.
NO. I *FELL* ONTO THE CEILING.

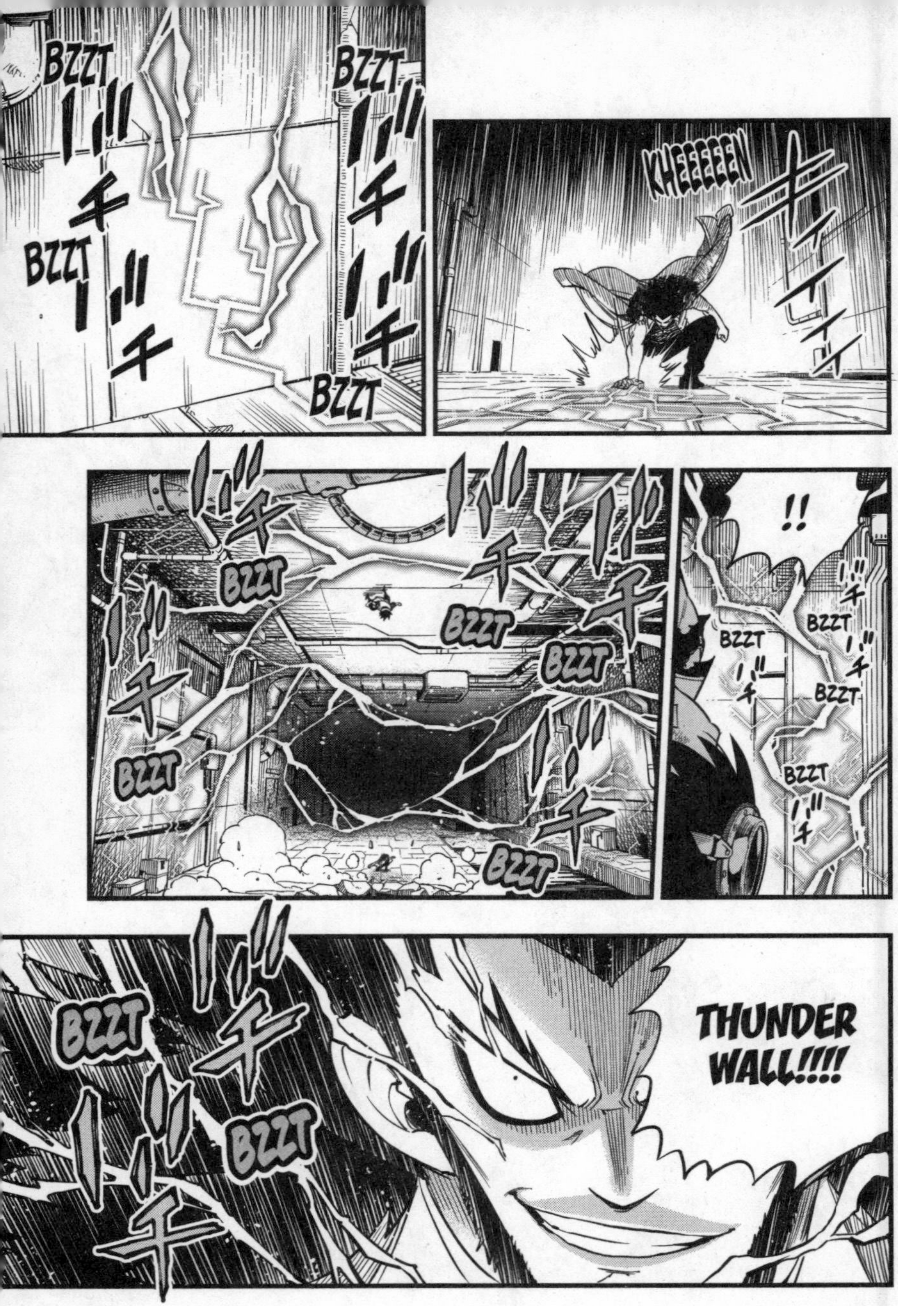
KHEEEEEN
BZZT
BZZT
BZZT
BZZT
!!
BZZT
BZZT
BZZT
BZZT
BZZT
BZZT
BZZT
BZZT
BZZT
BZZT
THUNDER WALL!!!!
BZZT
BZZT

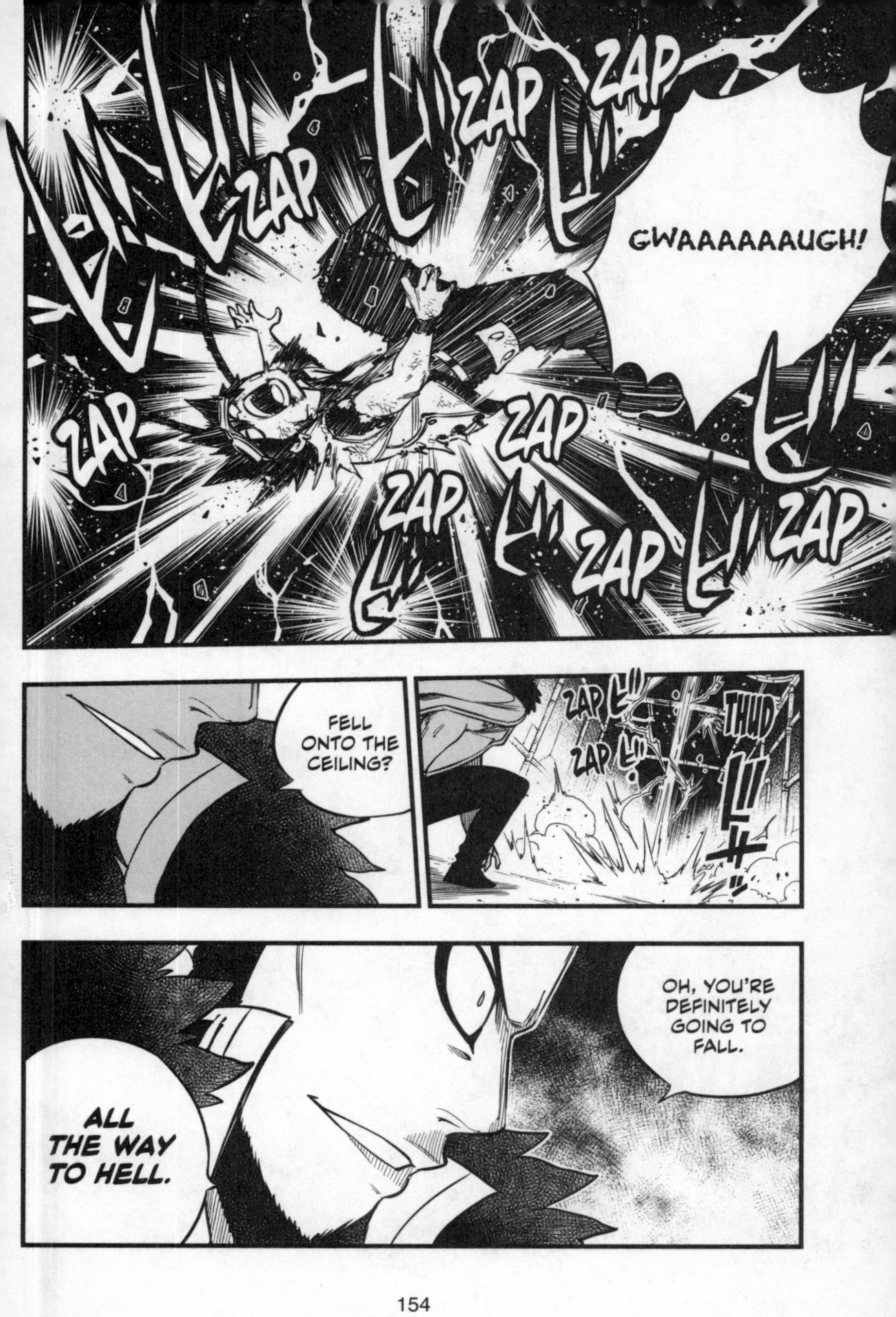
GWAAAAAAUGH!
ZAP
ZAP
ZAP
ZAP
ZAP
ZAP
ZAP
ZAP
ZAP
ZAP
THUD
FELL ONTO THE CEILING?
OH, YOU'RE DEFINITELY GOING TO FALL.
ALL THE WAY TO HELL.

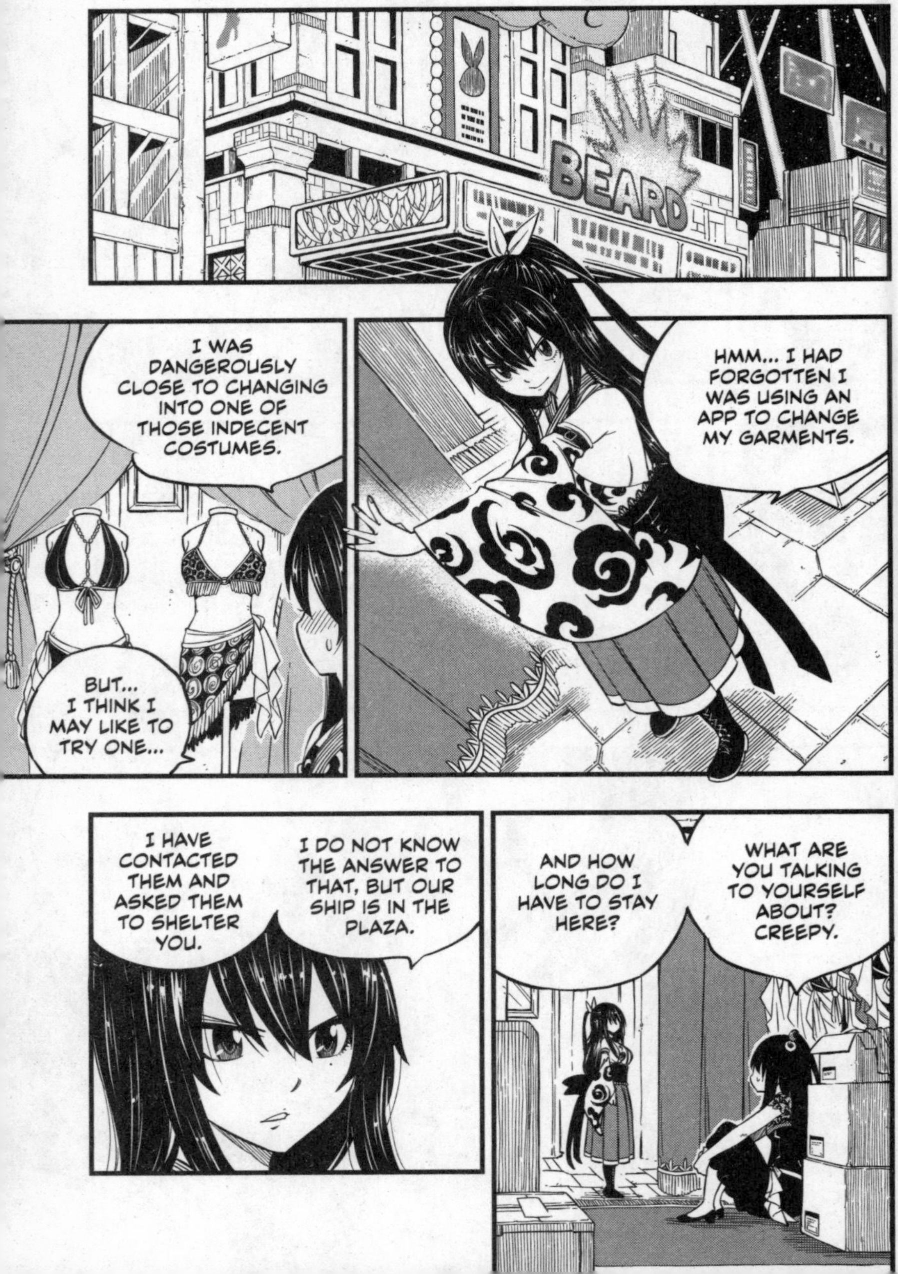
BEARD
HMM... I HAD FORGOTTEN I WAS USING AN APP TO CHANGE MY GARMENTS.
I WAS DANGEROUSLY CLOSE TO CHANGING INTO ONE OF THOSE INDECENT COSTUMES.
BUT... I THINK I MAY LIKE TO TRY ONE...
WHAT ARE YOU TALKING TO YOURSELF ABOUT? CREEPY.
AND HOW LONG DO I HAVE TO STAY HERE?
I DO NOT KNOW THE ANSWER TO THAT, BUT OUR SHIP IS IN THE PLAZA.
I HAVE CONTACTED THEM AND ASKED THEM TO SHELTER YOU.

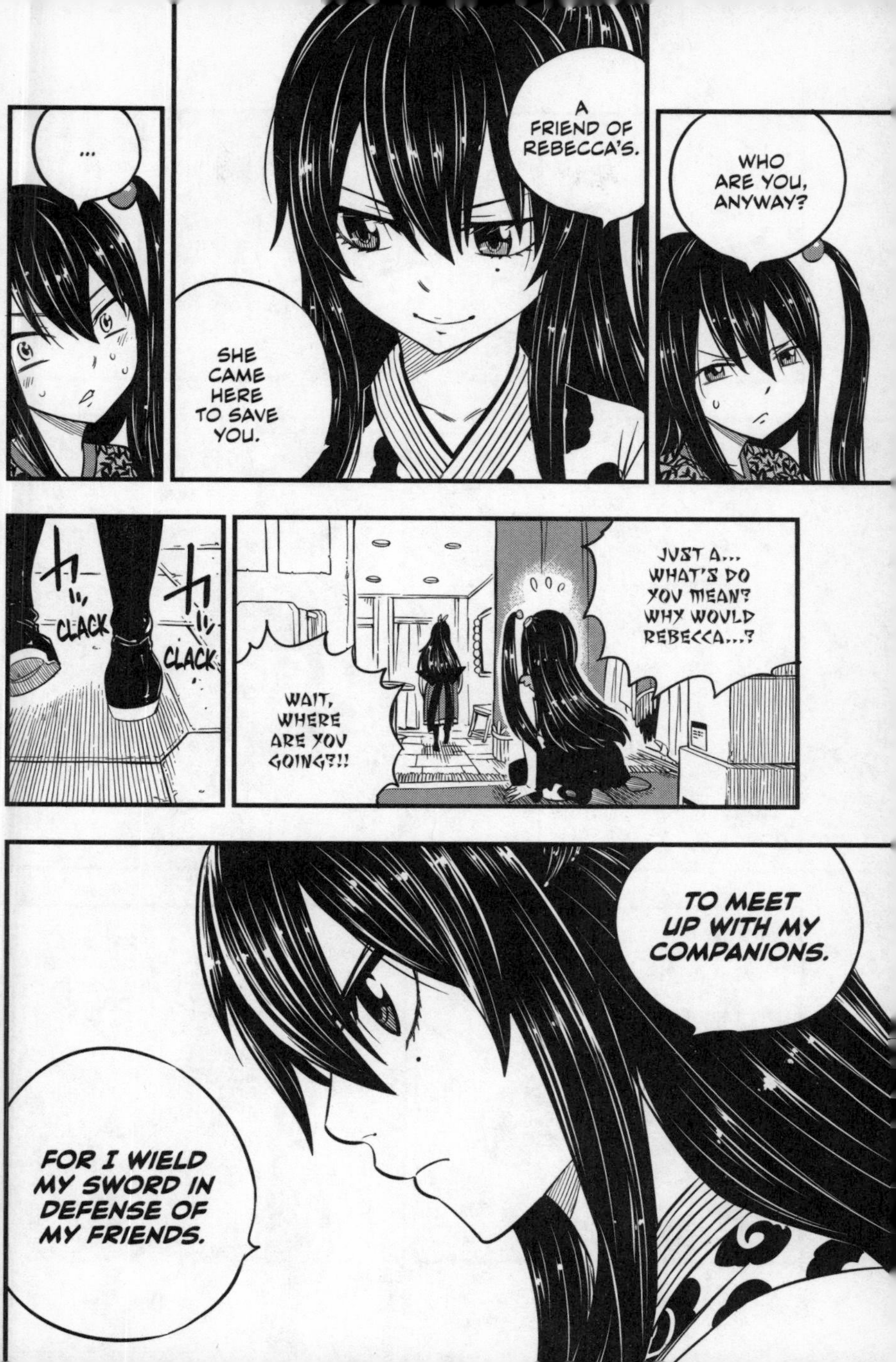
WHO ARE YOU, ANYWAY?
A FRIEND OF REBECCA'S.
SHE CAME HERE TO SAVE YOU.
...
JUST A... WHAT'S DO YOU MEAN? WHY WOULD REBECCA...?
WAIT, WHERE ARE YOU GOING?!!
カ
CLACK
カ
CLACK
TO MEET UP WITH MY COMPANIONS.
FOR I WIELD MY SWORD IN DEFENSE OF MY FRIENDS.

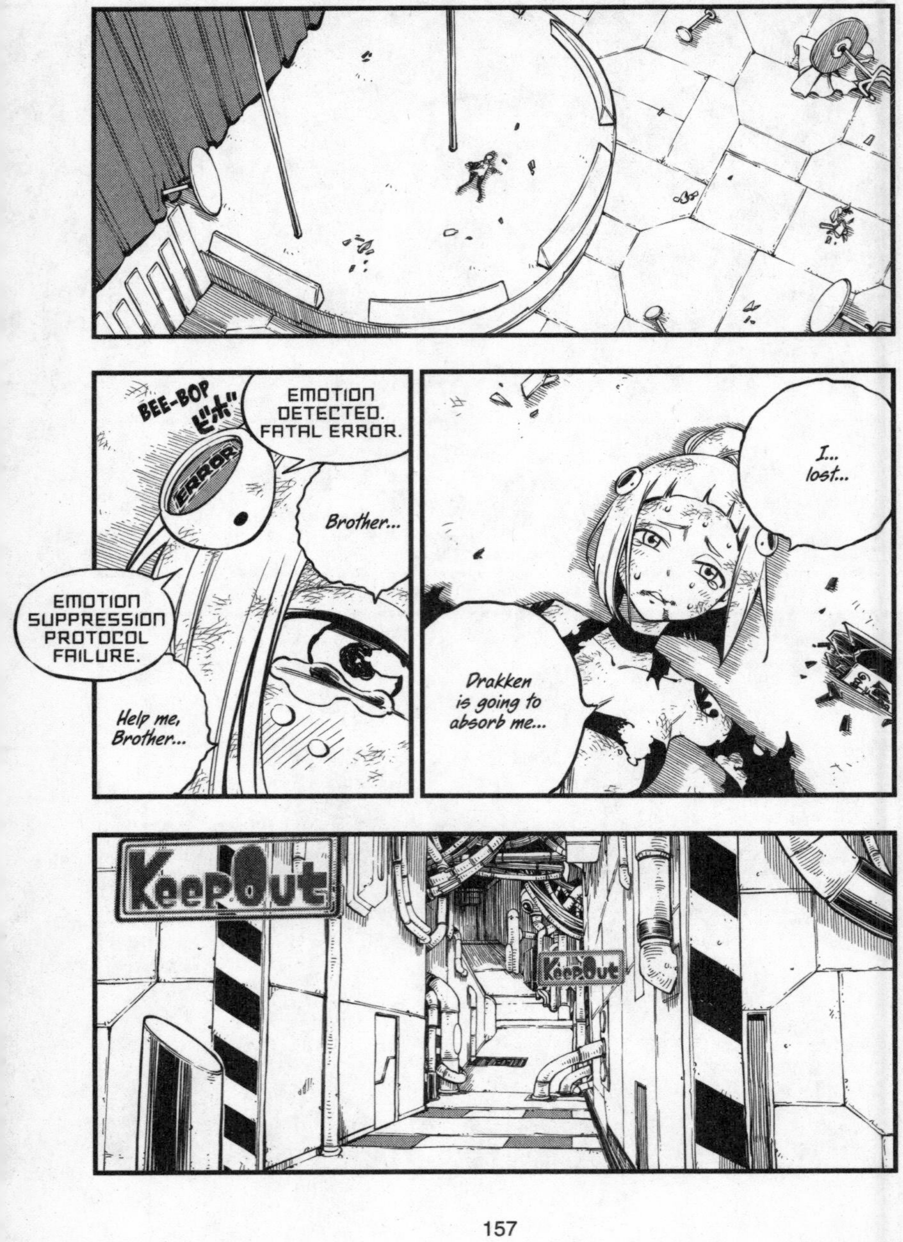

I... lost...
Drakken is going to absorb me...
EMOTION DETECTED. FATAL ERROR.
BEE-BOP
ビボ
ERROR
Brother...
EMOTION SUPPRESSION PROTOCOL FAILURE.
Help me, Brother...
KeepOut
KeepOut

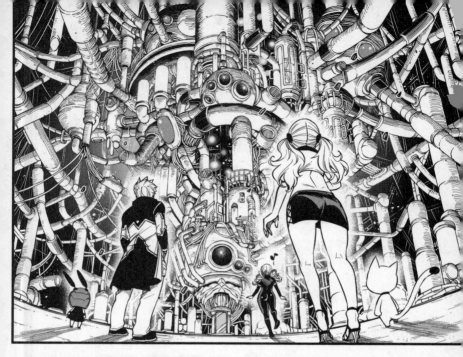

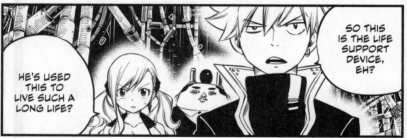

SO THIS IS THE LIFE SUPPORT DEVICE, EH?

HE'S USED THIS TO LIVE SUCH A LONG LIFE?

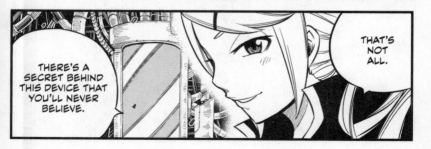

THAT'S NOT ALL.

THERE'S A SECRET BEHIND THIS DEVICE THAT YOU'LL NEVER BELIEVE.

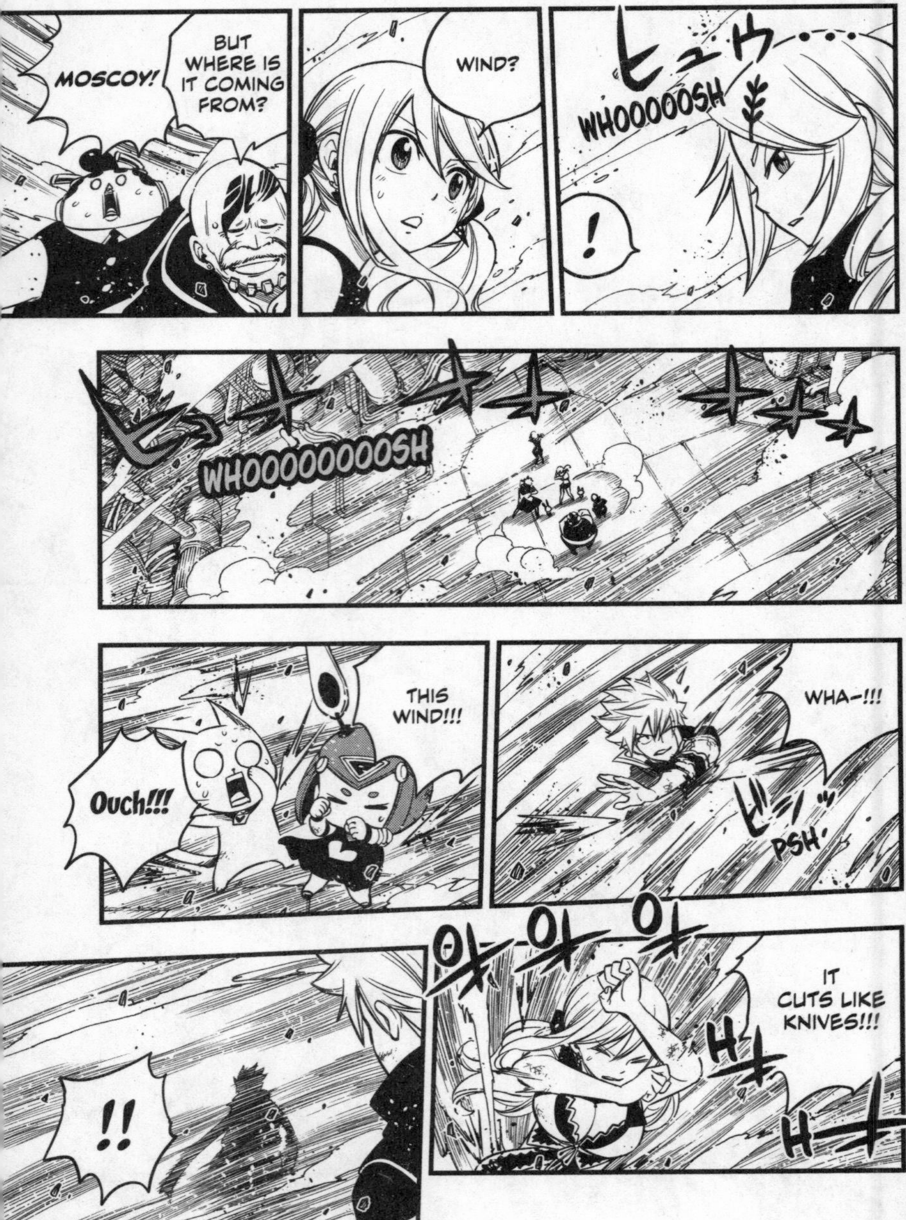

ヒュウ
WHOOOOOSH
!
WIND?
BUT WHERE IS IT COMING FROM?
MOSCOY!
WHOOOOOOOOSH
WHA-!!!
PSH
THIS WIND!!!
Ouch!!!
IT CUTS LIKE KNIVES!!!
!!

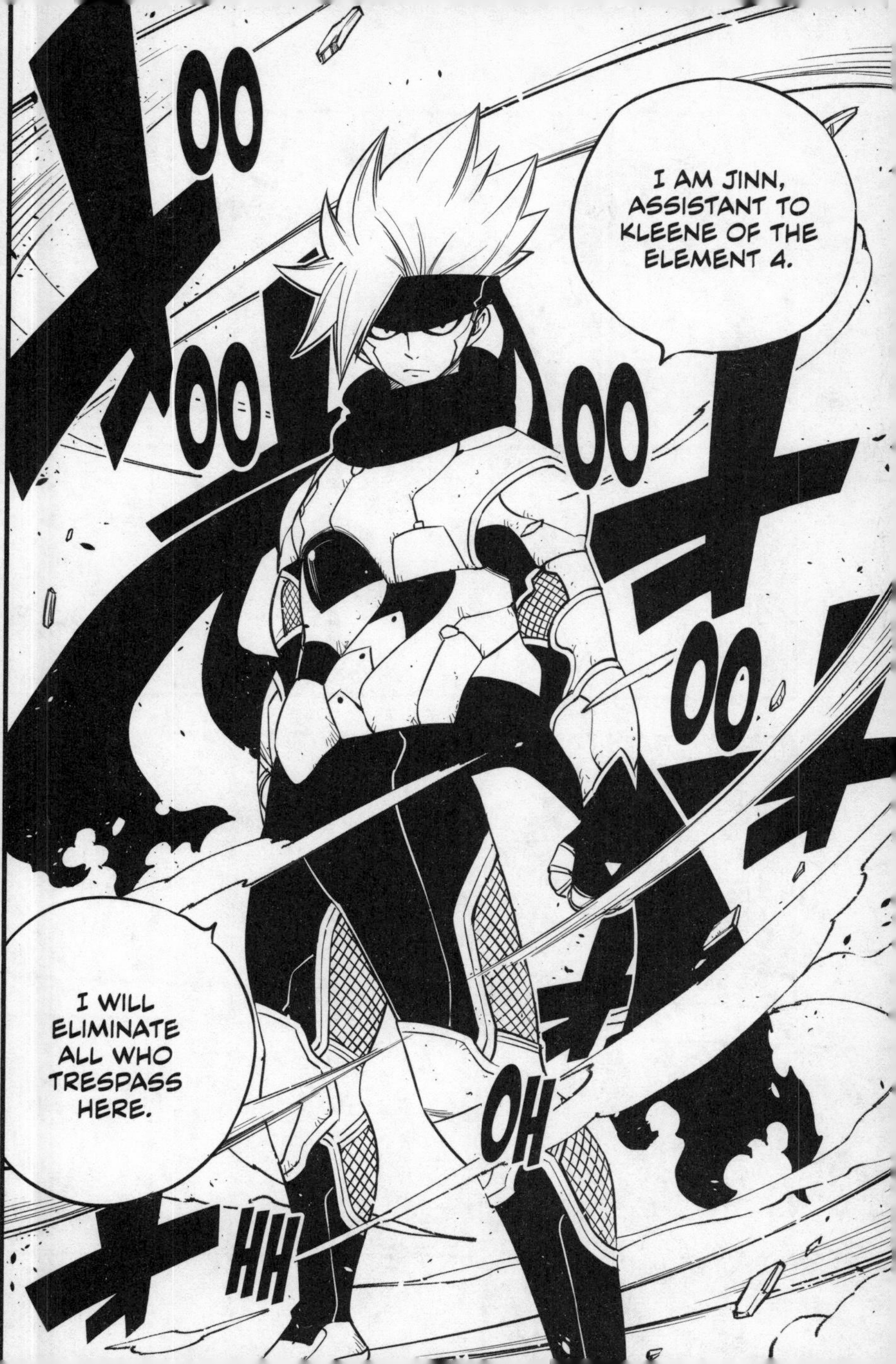
I AM JINN, ASSISTANT TO KLEENE OF THE ELEMENT 4.
I WILL ELIMINATE ALL WHO TRESPASS HERE.

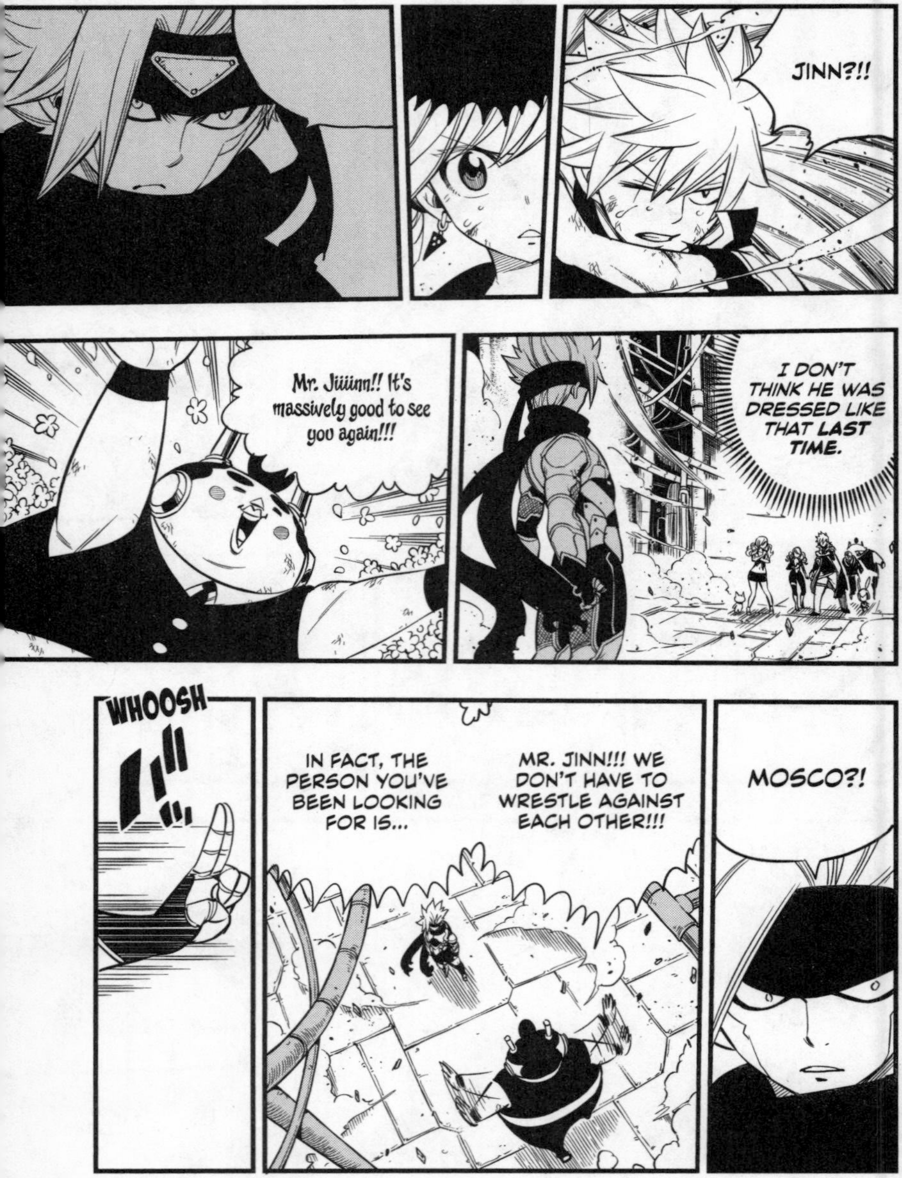
JINN?!!
I DON'T THINK HE WAS DRESSED LIKE THAT LAST TIME.
Mr. Jiiiinn!! It's massively good to see you again!!!
MOSCO?!
MR. JINN!!! WE DON'T HAVE TO WRESTLE AGAINST EACH OTHER!!!
IN FACT, THE PERSON YOU'VE BEEN LOOKING FOR IS...
WHOOSH

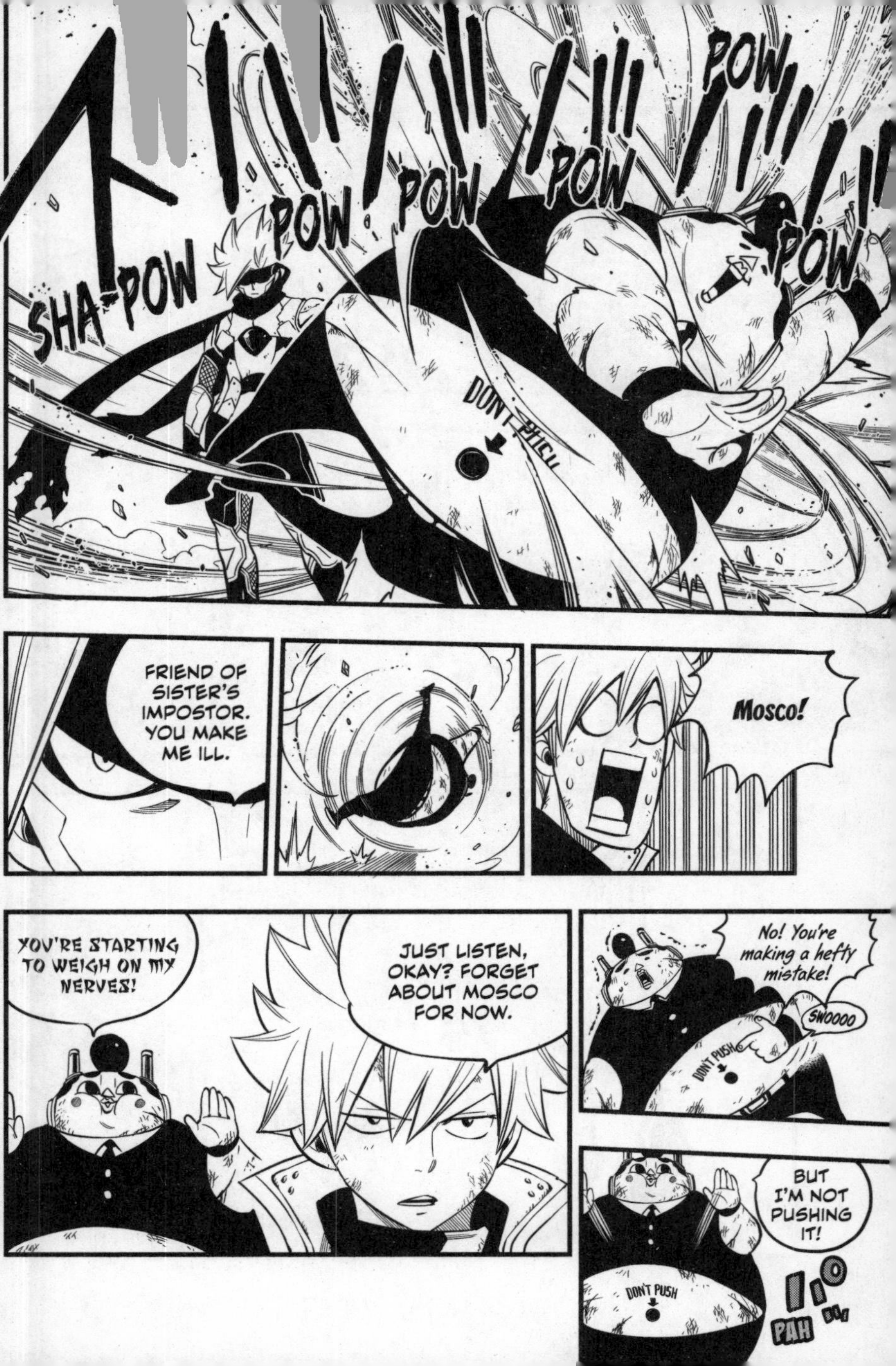
POW
POW
POW
POW
POW
SHA-POW
Mosco!
FRIEND OF SISTER'S IMPOSTOR. YOU MAKE ME ILL.
No! You're making a hefty mistake!
SWOOOO
DON'T PUSH
BUT I'M NOT PUSHING IT!
DON'T PUSH
PAH
JUST LISTEN, OKAY? FORGET ABOUT MOSCO FOR NOW.
YOU'RE STARTING TO WEIGH ON MY NERVES!

EDENS ZERO

Edens Zero
In-Depth Character File 9

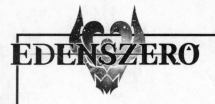

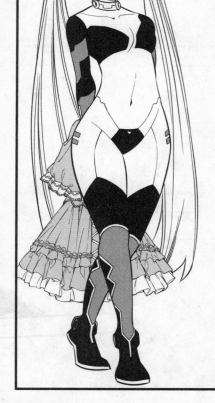

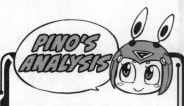

PINO'S ANALYSIS

Name: Hermit Milon

Powers: Program Hacking
(Master Code)

Likes: Clothes, video games

Dislikes: Humans...but not anymore.

Attack:	☆☆
Defense:	☆☆
Marksmanship:	☆☆☆☆
Ether Power:	☆☆☆
Intelligence:	☆☆☆☆☆
Tsundere:	☆☆☆☆

Memo

One of the Demon King's Four Shining Stars, she is the heart and Mind of Edens. She once hated humans for the cruel things they did to her, but thanks to my Master and his friends, she learned how to smile again. She loves fashion and has even made clothes for me.

CHAPTER 95: KRIS RUTHERFORD

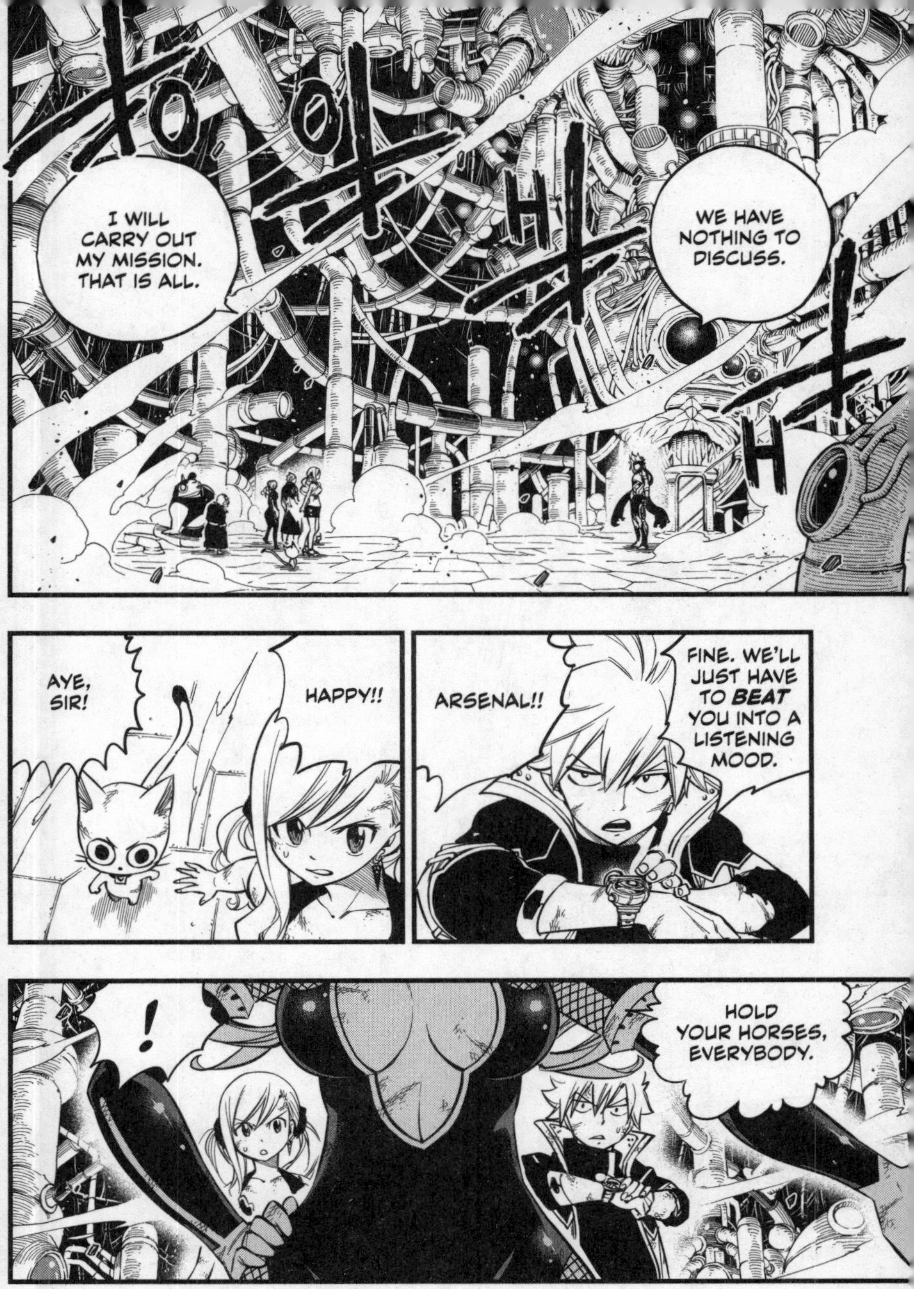
WE HAVE NOTHING TO DISCUSS.
I WILL CARRY OUT MY MISSION. THAT IS ALL.
FINE. WE'LL JUST HAVE TO **BEAT** YOU INTO A LISTENING MOOD.
ARSENAL!!
HAPPY!!
AYE, SIR!
HOLD YOUR HORSES, EVERYBODY.
!

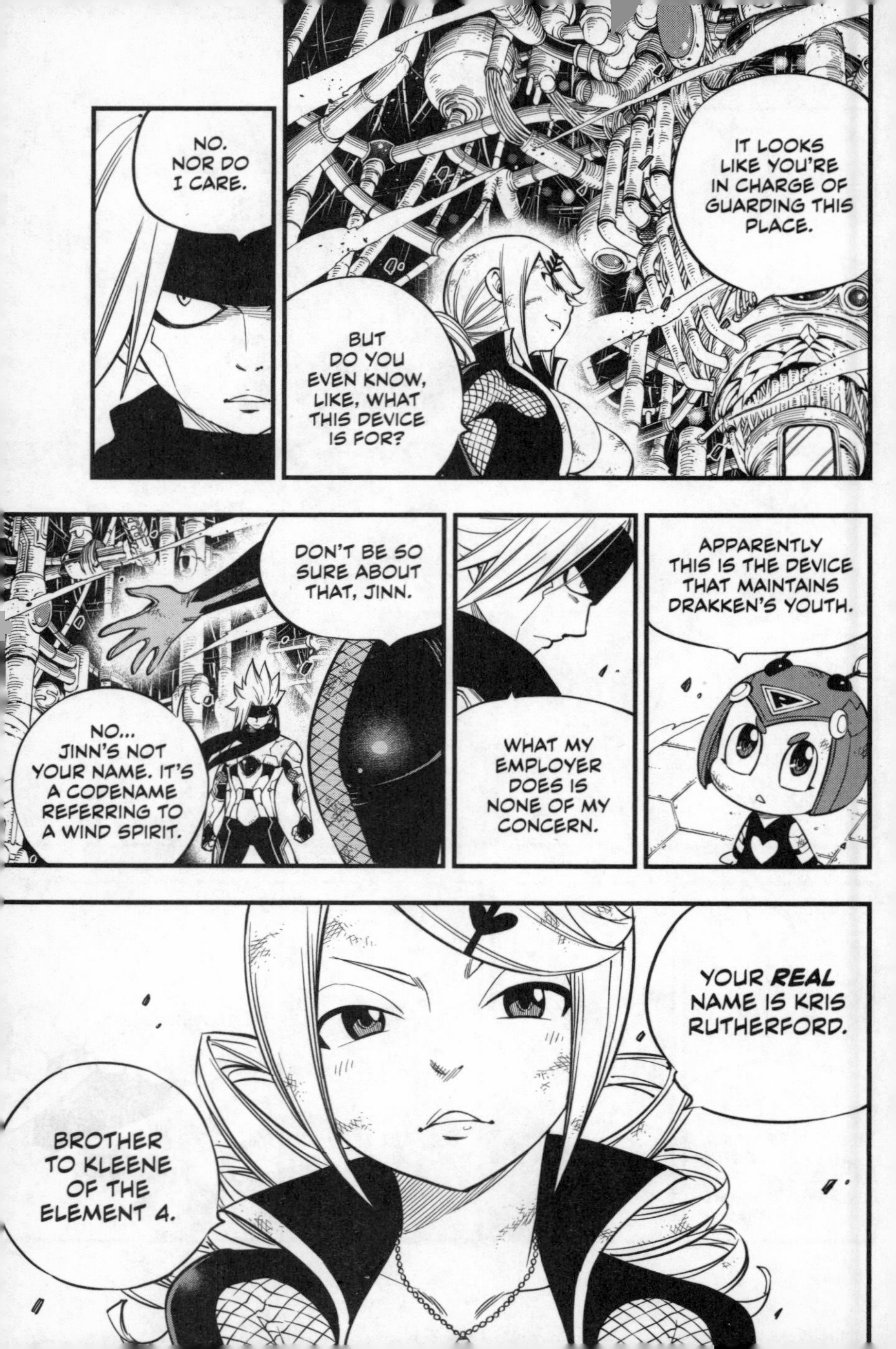
IT LOOKS LIKE YOU'RE IN CHARGE OF GUARDING THIS PLACE.
BUT DO YOU EVEN KNOW, LIKE, WHAT THIS DEVICE IS FOR?
NO. NOR DO I CARE.
APPARENTLY THIS IS THE DEVICE THAT MAINTAINS DRAKKEN'S YOUTH.
WHAT MY EMPLOYER DOES IS NONE OF MY CONCERN.
DON'T BE SO SURE ABOUT THAT, JINN.
NO... JINN'S NOT YOUR NAME. IT'S A CODENAME REFERRING TO A WIND SPIRIT.
YOUR ***REAL*** NAME IS KRIS RUTHERFORD.
BROTHER TO KLEENE OF THE ELEMENT 4.

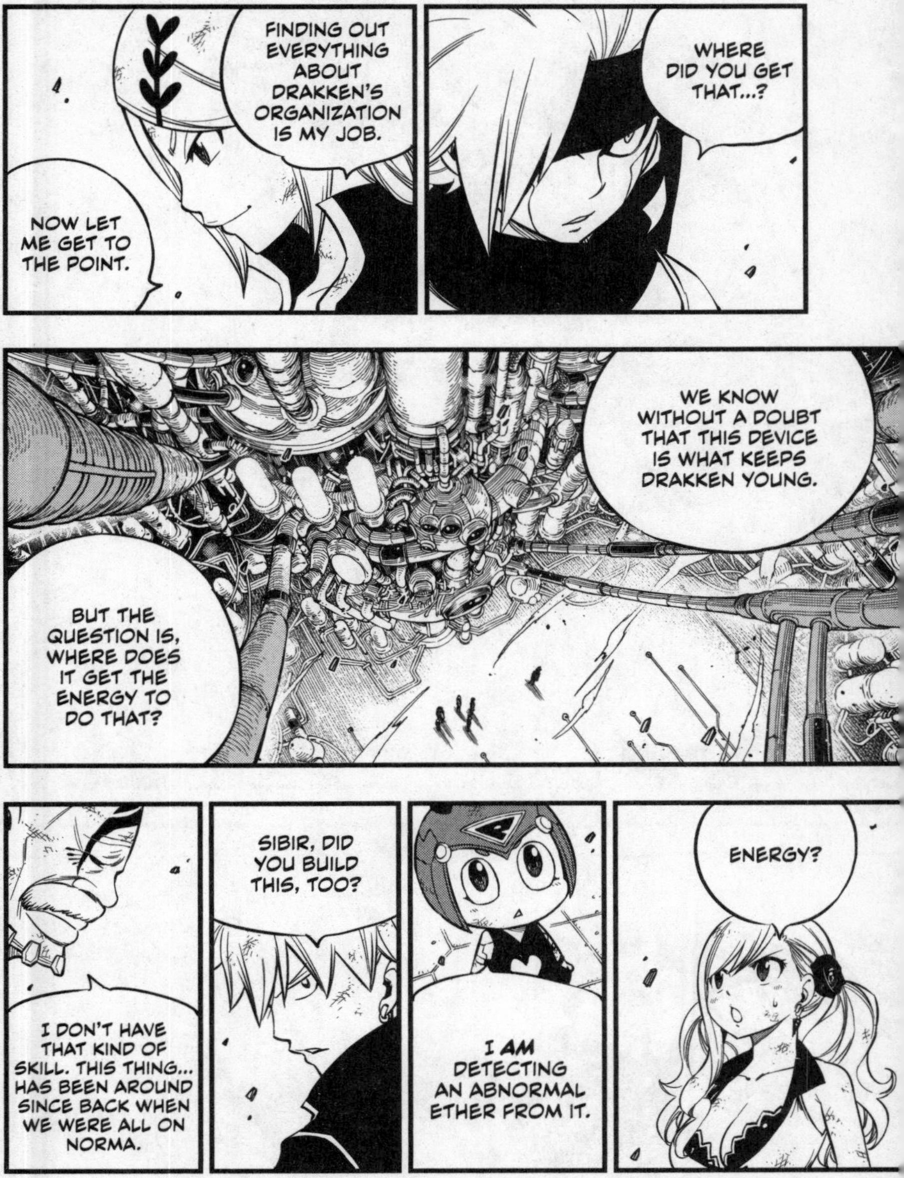
WHERE DID YOU GET THAT...?
FINDING OUT EVERYTHING ABOUT DRAKKEN'S ORGANIZATION IS MY JOB.
NOW LET ME GET TO THE POINT.
WE KNOW WITHOUT A DOUBT THAT THIS DEVICE IS WHAT KEEPS DRAKKEN YOUNG.
BUT THE QUESTION IS, WHERE DOES IT GET THE ENERGY TO DO THAT?
ENERGY?
I *AM* DETECTING AN ABNORMAL ETHER FROM IT.
SIBIR, DID YOU BUILD THIS, TOO?
I DON'T HAVE THAT KIND OF SKILL. THIS THING... HAS BEEN AROUND SINCE BACK WHEN WE WERE ALL ON NORMA.

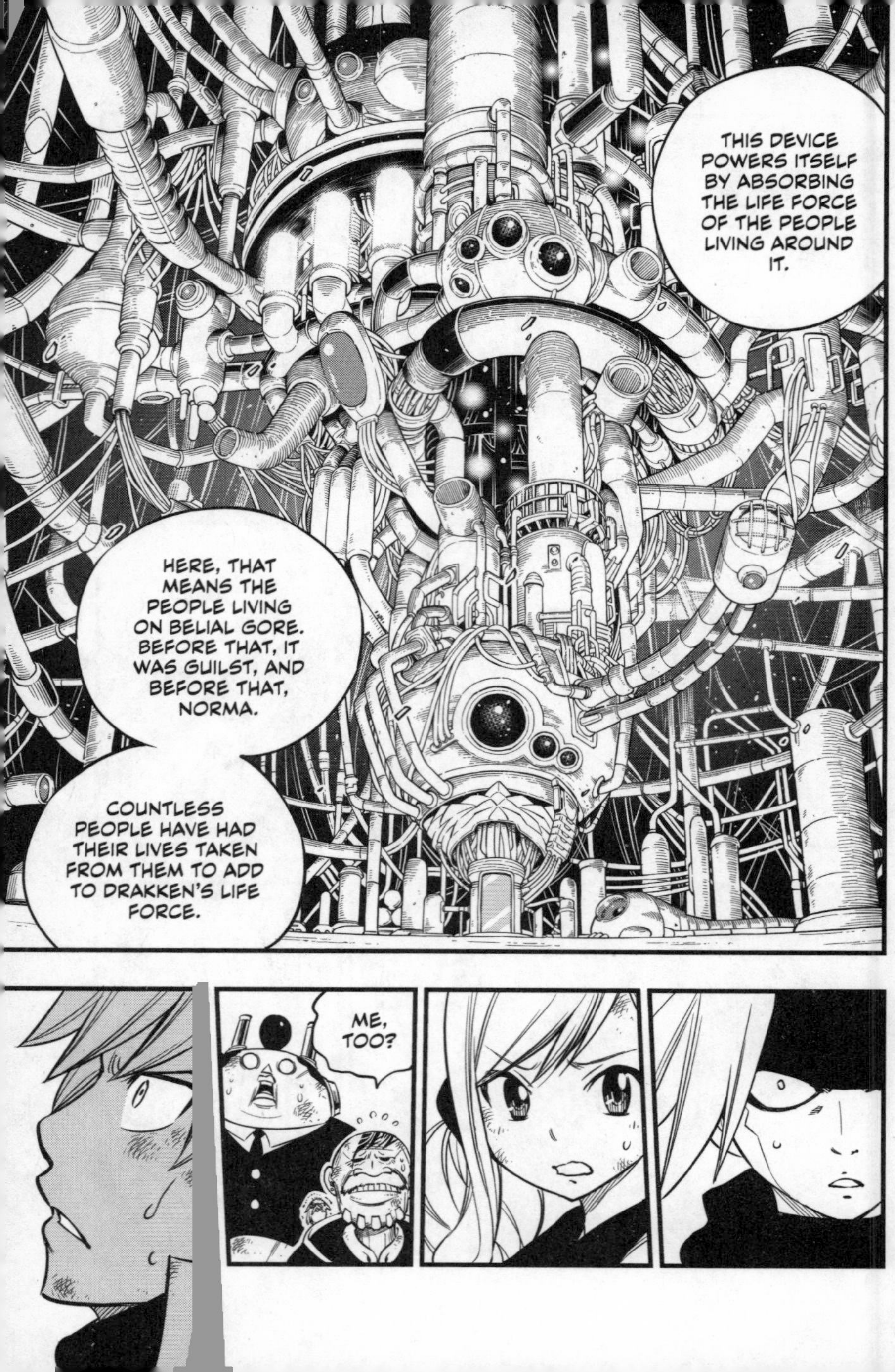
THIS DEVICE POWERS ITSELF BY ABSORBING THE LIFE FORCE OF THE PEOPLE LIVING AROUND IT.
HERE, THAT MEANS THE PEOPLE LIVING ON BELIAL GORE. BEFORE THAT, IT WAS GUILST, AND BEFORE THAT, NORMA.
COUNTLESS PEOPLE HAVE HAD THEIR LIVES TAKEN FROM THEM TO ADD TO DRAKKEN'S LIFE FORCE.
ME, TOO?

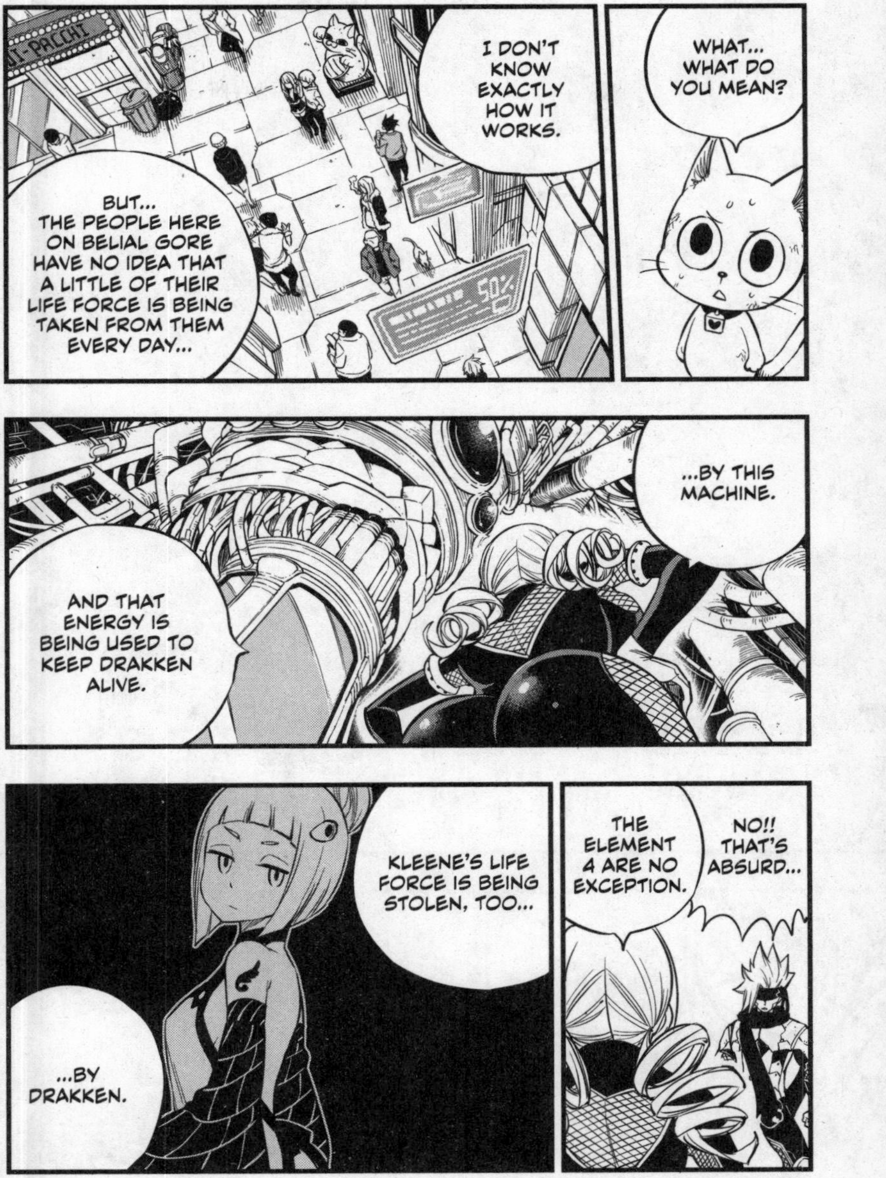
WHAT... WHAT DO YOU MEAN?
I DON'T KNOW EXACTLY HOW IT WORKS.
BUT... THE PEOPLE HERE ON BELIAL GORE HAVE NO IDEA THAT A LITTLE OF THEIR LIFE FORCE IS BEING TAKEN FROM THEM EVERY DAY...
...BY THIS MACHINE.
AND THAT ENERGY IS BEING USED TO KEEP DRAKKEN ALIVE.
NO!! THAT'S ABSURD...
THE ELEMENT 4 ARE NO EXCEPTION.
KLEENE'S LIFE FORCE IS BEING STOLEN, TOO...
...BY DRAKKEN.

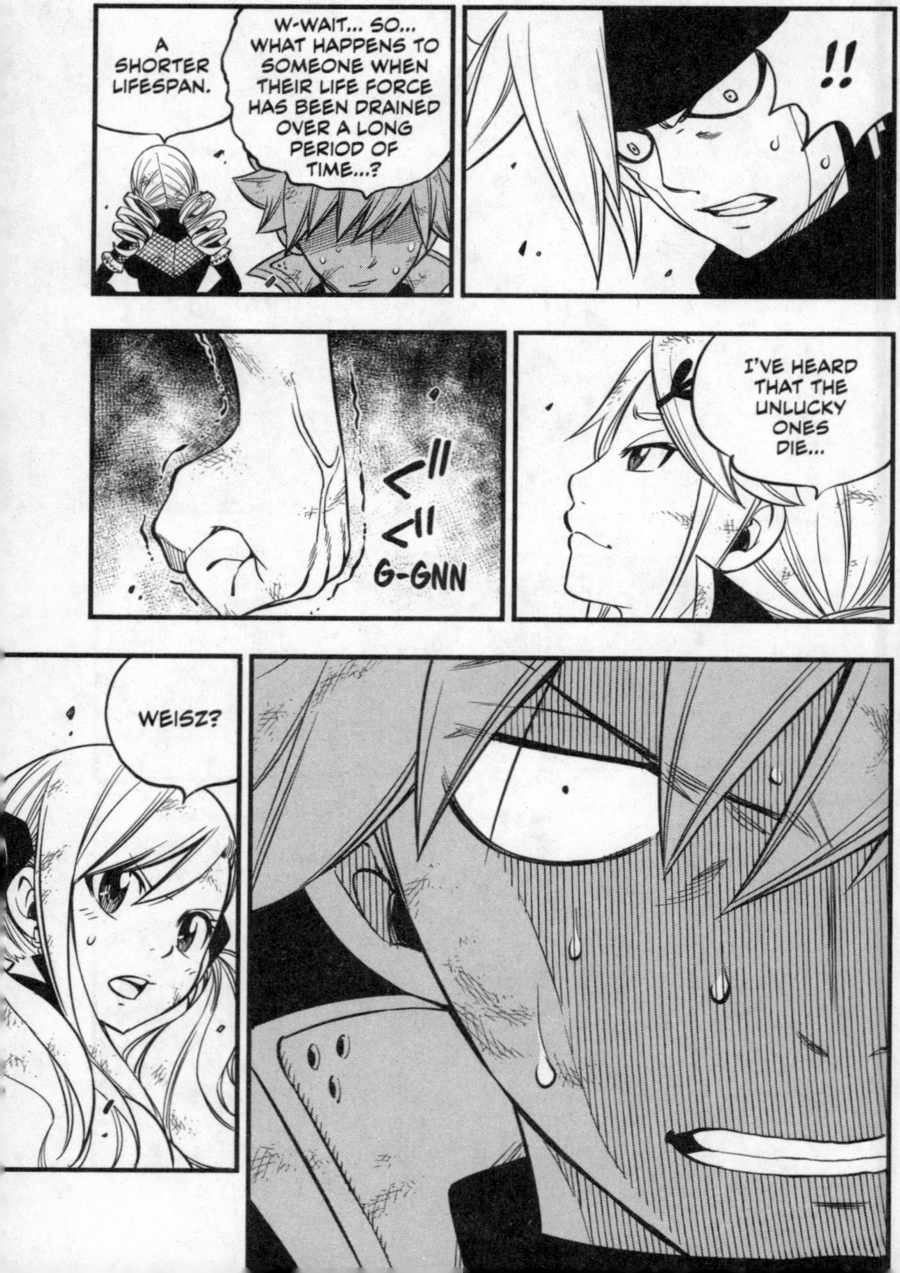
!!
W-WAIT... SO... WHAT HAPPENS TO SOMEONE WHEN THEIR LIFE FORCE HAS BEEN DRAINED OVER A LONG PERIOD OF TIME...?
A SHORTER LIFESPAN.
I'VE HEARD THAT THE UNLUCKY ONES DIE...
G-GNN
WEISZ?

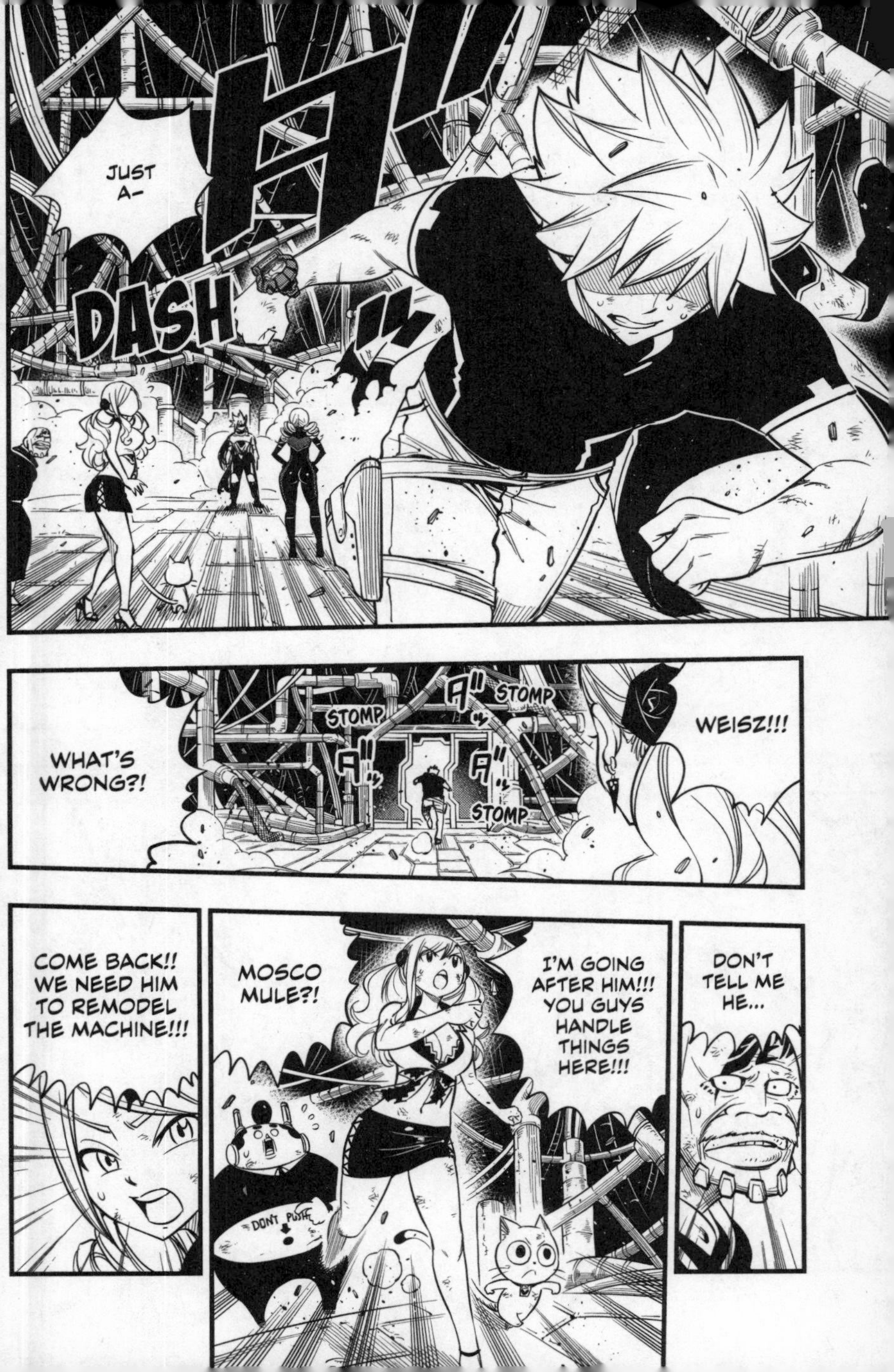
JUST A-
DASH
WEISZ!!!
STOMP
STOMP
STOMP
WHAT'S WRONG?!
DON'T TELL ME HE...
I'M GOING AFTER HIM!!! YOU GUYS HANDLE THINGS HERE!!!
MOSCO MULE?!
DON'T PUSH
COME BACK!! WE NEED HIM TO REMODEL THE MACHINE!!!

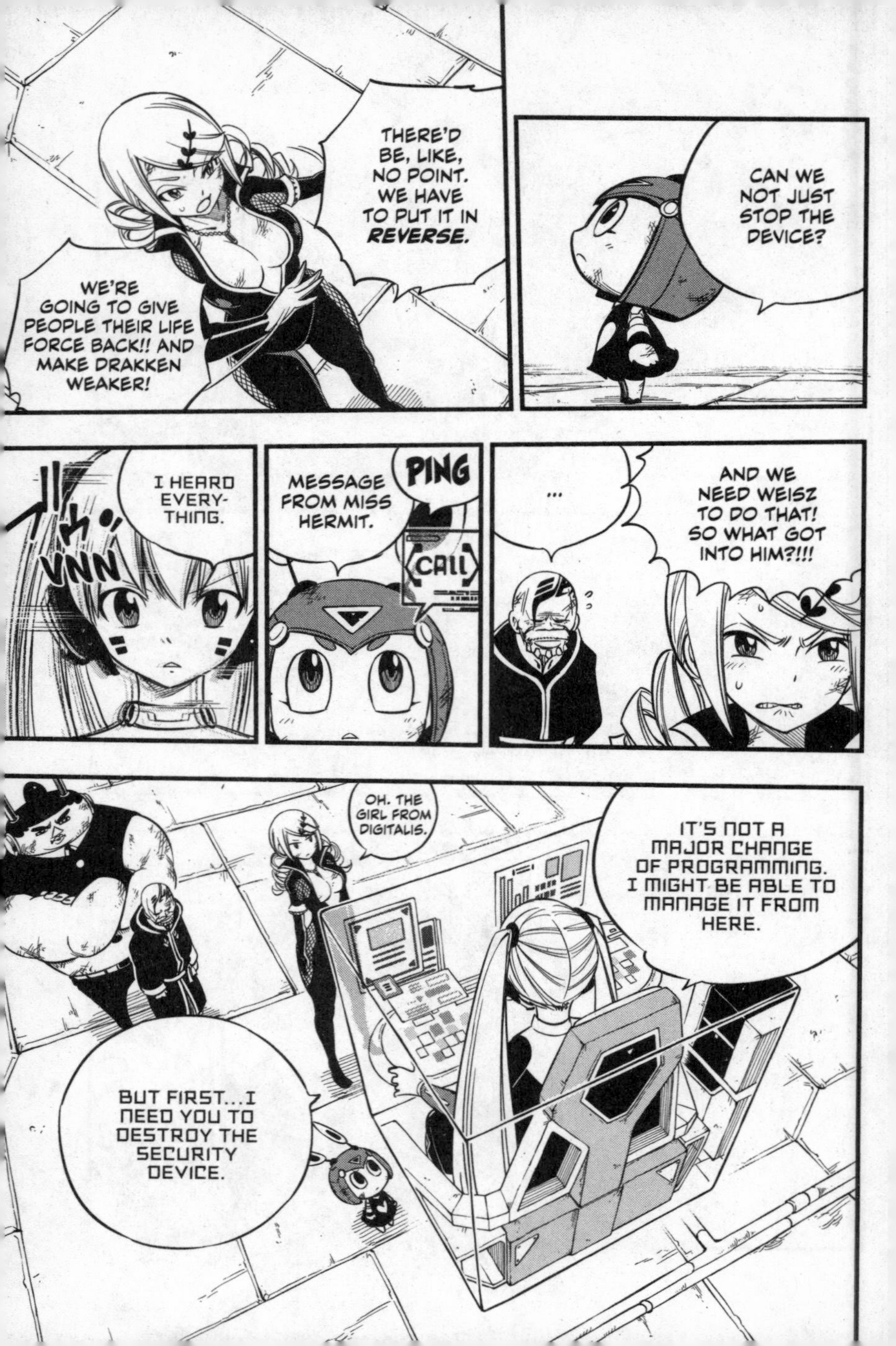
CAN WE NOT JUST STOP THE DEVICE?
THERE'D BE, LIKE, NO POINT. WE HAVE TO PUT IT IN *REVERSE.*
WE'RE GOING TO GIVE PEOPLE THEIR LIFE FORCE BACK!! AND MAKE DRAKKEN WEAKER!
AND WE NEED WEISZ TO DO THAT! SO WHAT GOT INTO HIM?!!!
...
PING
CALL
MESSAGE FROM MISS HERMIT.
VNN
I HEARD EVERY-THING.
IT'S NOT A MAJOR CHANGE OF PROGRAMMING. I MIGHT BE ABLE TO MANAGE IT FROM HERE.
OH. THE GIRL FROM DIGITALIS.
BUT FIRST...I NEED YOU TO DESTROY THE SECURITY DEVICE.

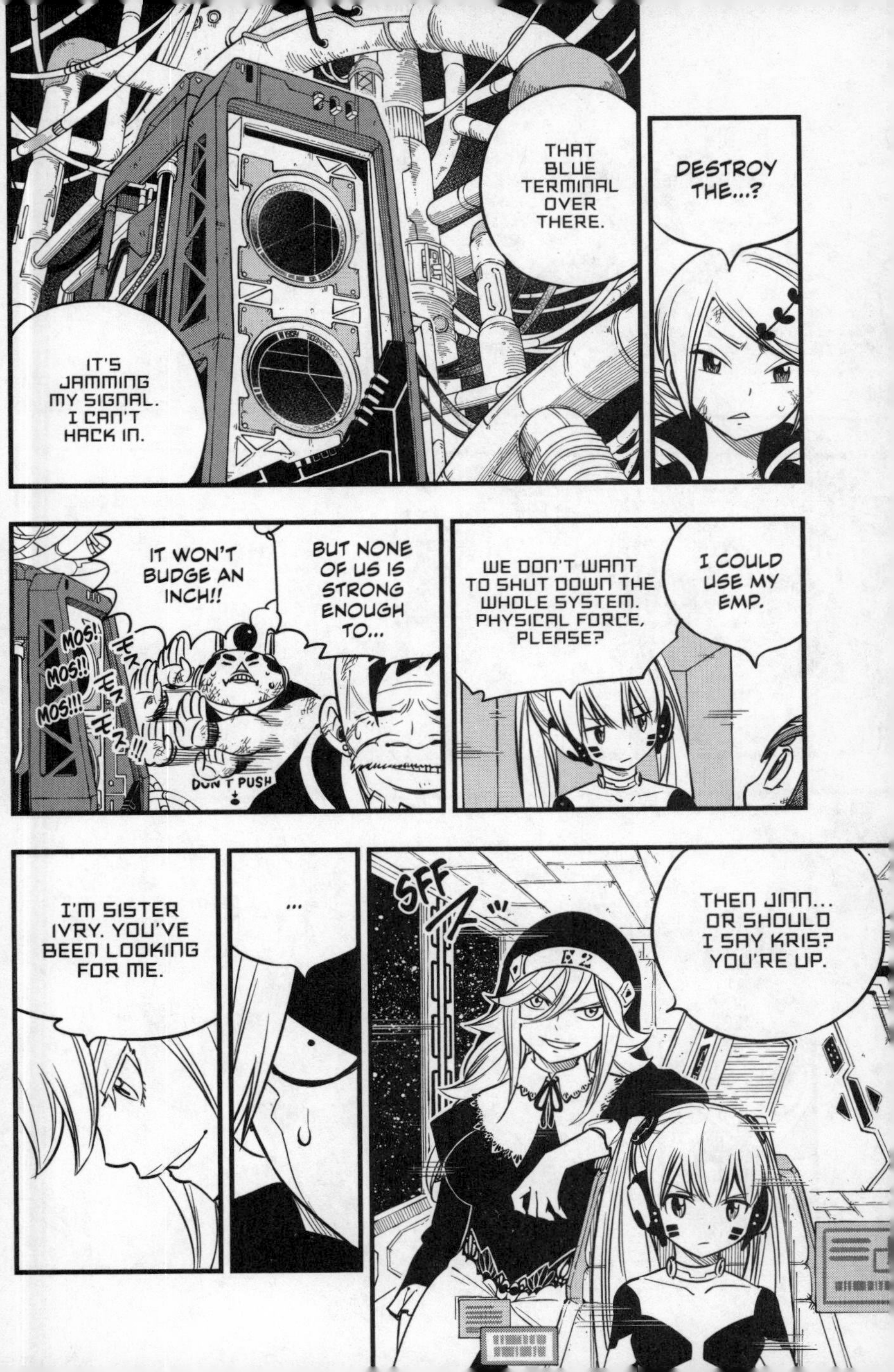
DESTROY THE...?
THAT BLUE TERMINAL OVER THERE.
IT'S JAMMING MY SIGNAL. I CAN'T HACK IN.
I COULD USE MY EMP.
WE DON'T WANT TO SHUT DOWN THE WHOLE SYSTEM. PHYSICAL FORCE, PLEASE?
BUT NONE OF US IS STRONG ENOUGH TO...
IT WON'T BUDGE AN INCH!!
MOS!
MOS!!
MOS!!!
DON'T PUSH
THEN JINN... OR SHOULD I SAY KRIS? YOU'RE UP.
SFF
...
I'M SISTER IVRY. YOU'VE BEEN LOOKING FOR ME.

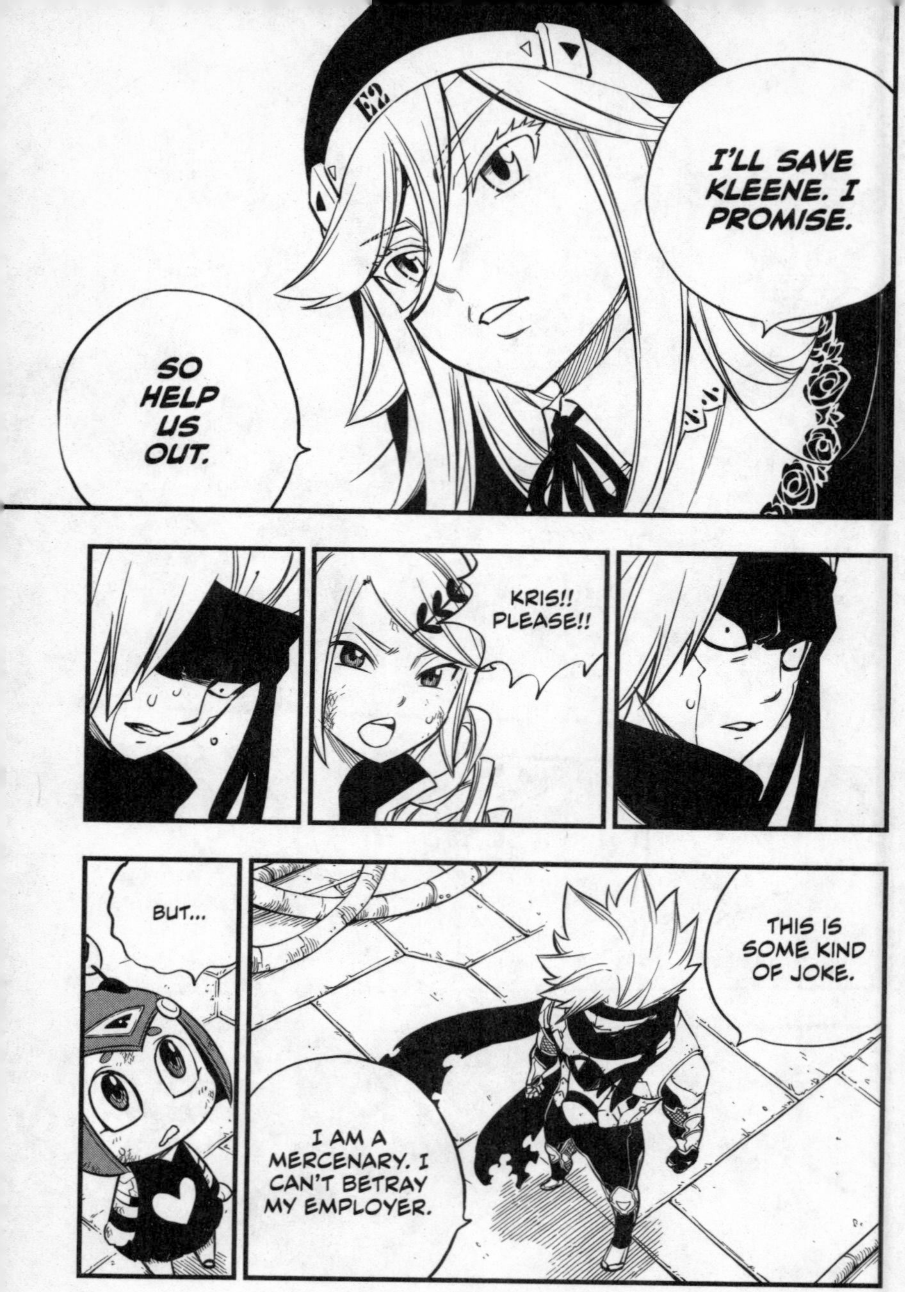
I'LL SAVE KLEENE. I PROMISE.
SO HELP US OUT.
KRIS!! PLEASE!!
THIS IS SOME KIND OF JOKE.
I AM A MERCENARY. I CAN'T BETRAY MY EMPLOYER.
BUT...

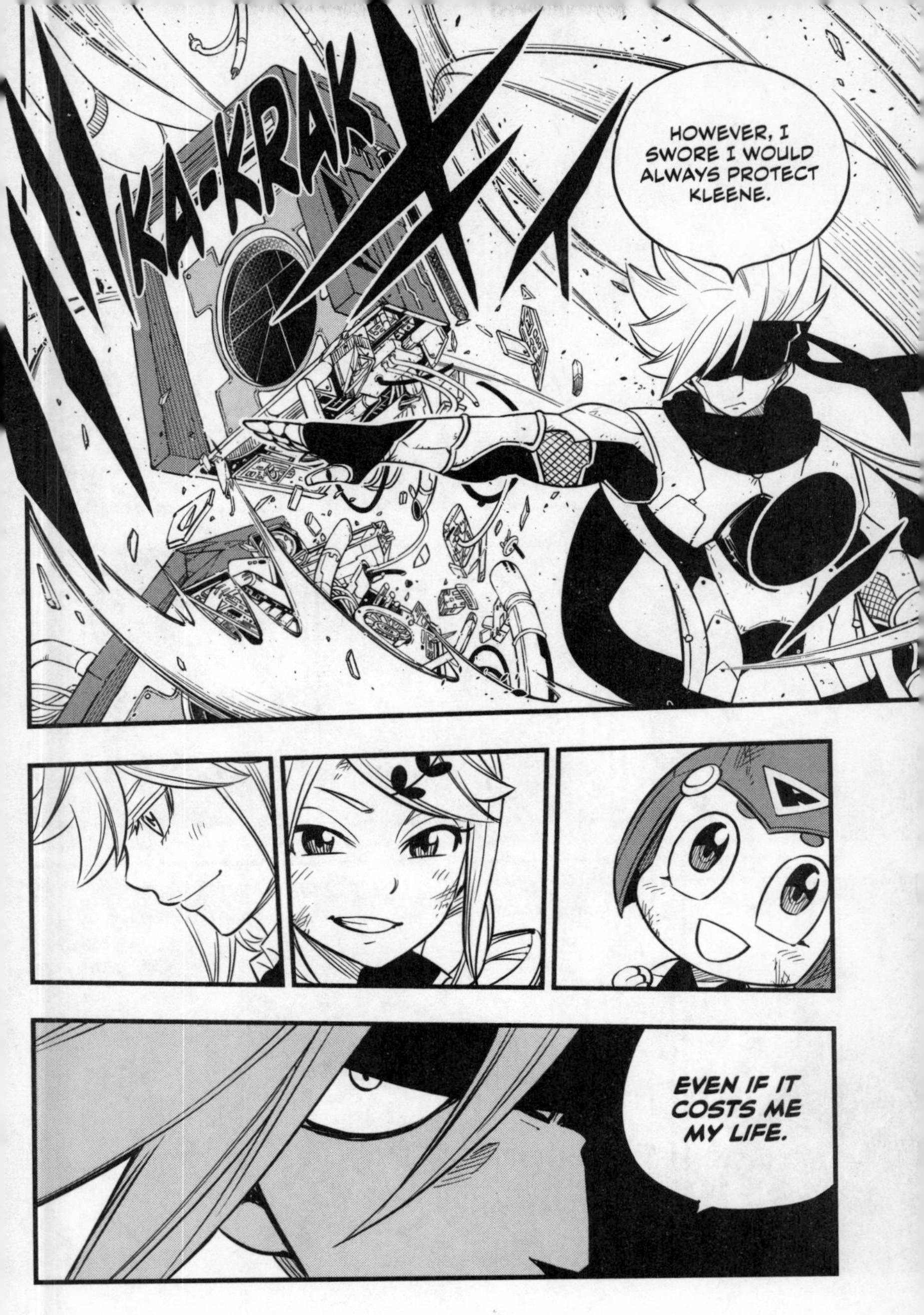
HOWEVER, I SWORE I WOULD ALWAYS PROTECT KLEENE.
KA-KRAK
EVEN IF IT COSTS ME MY LIFE.

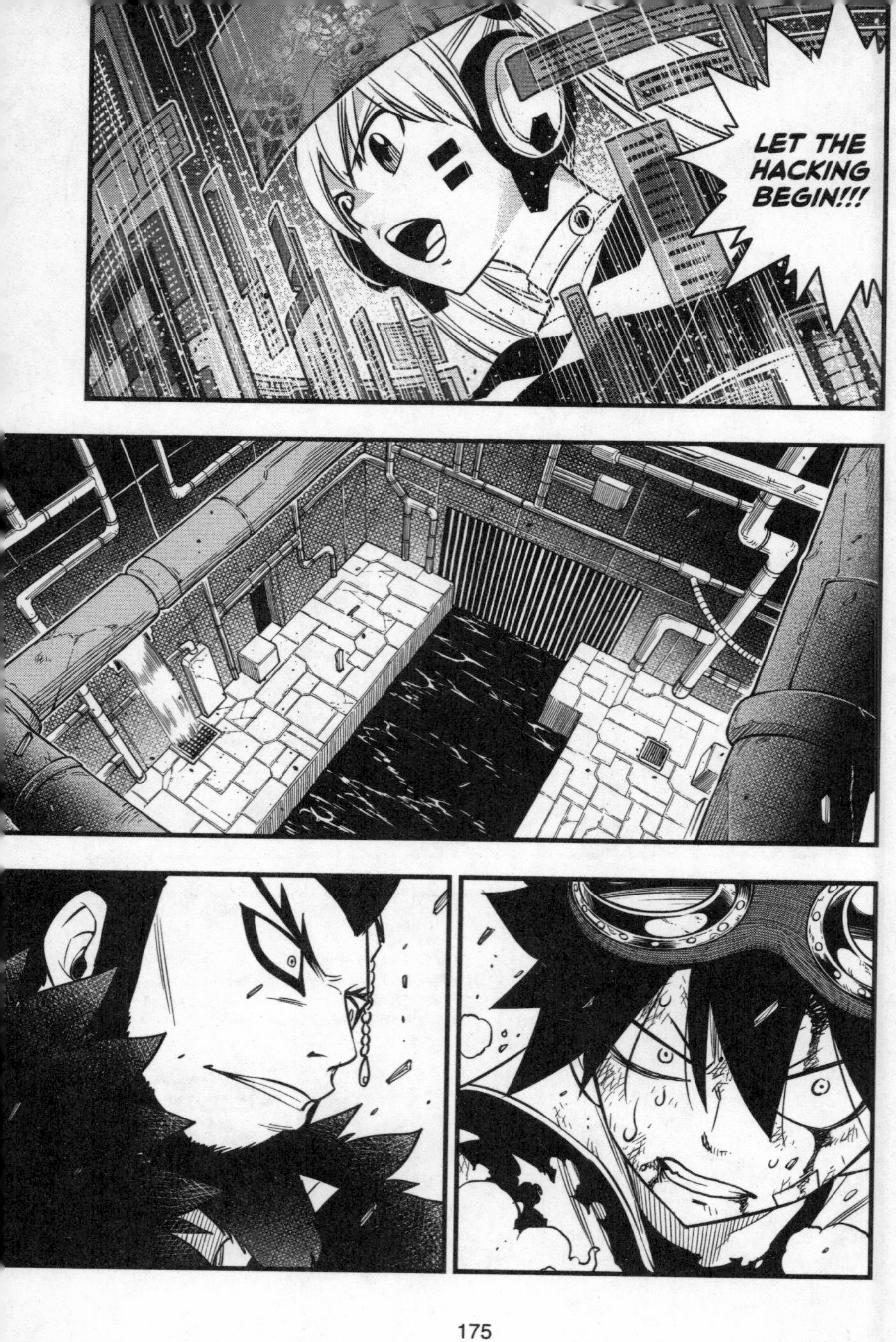
LET THE HACKING BEGIN!!!

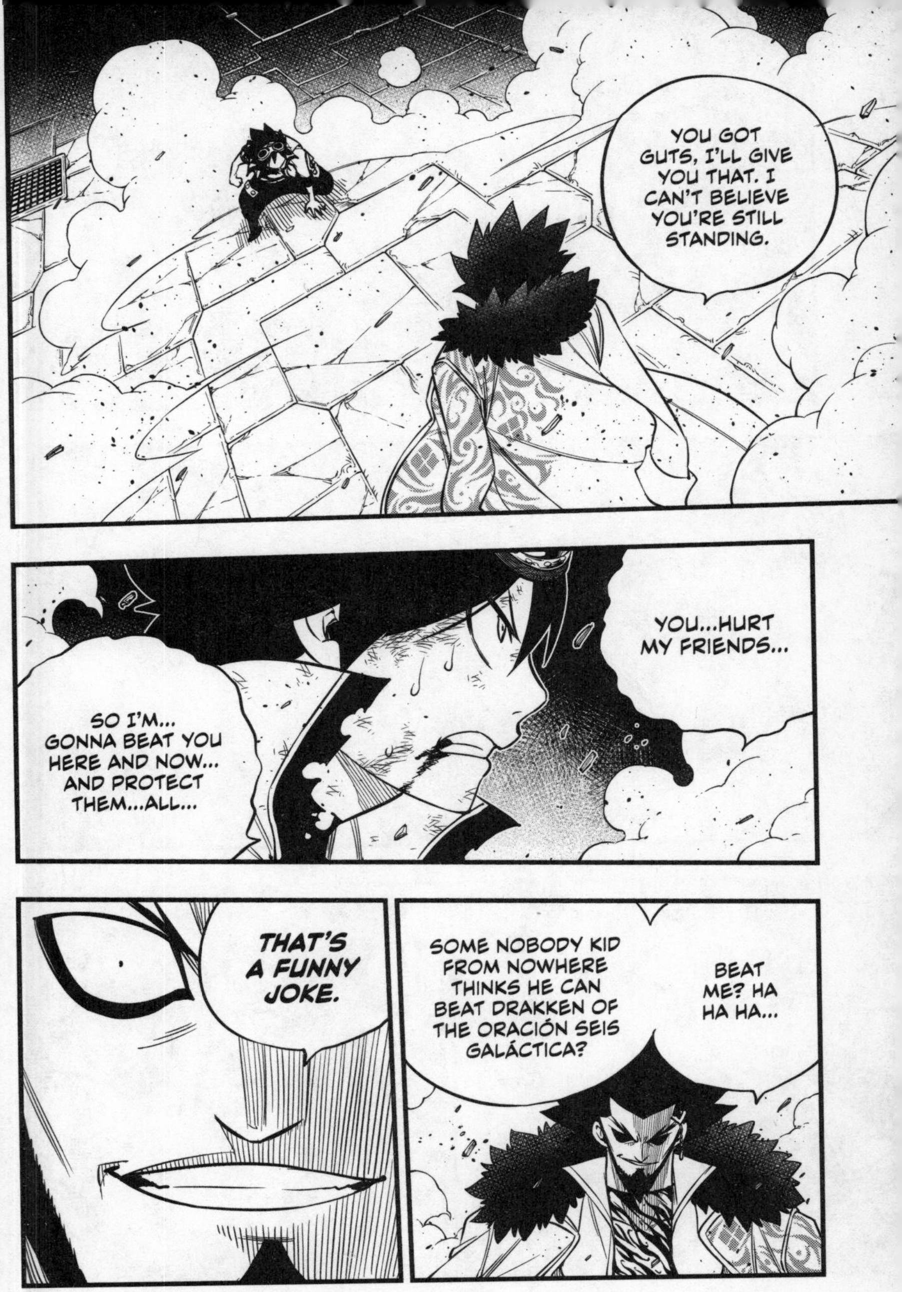
YOU GOT GUTS, I'LL GIVE YOU THAT. I CAN'T BELIEVE YOU'RE STILL STANDING.
YOU...HURT MY FRIENDS...
SO I'M... GONNA BEAT YOU HERE AND NOW... AND PROTECT THEM...ALL...
BEAT ME? HA HA HA...
SOME NOBODY KID FROM NOWHERE THINKS HE CAN BEAT DRAKKEN OF THE ORACIÓN SEIS GALÁCTICA?
THAT'S A FUNNY JOKE.

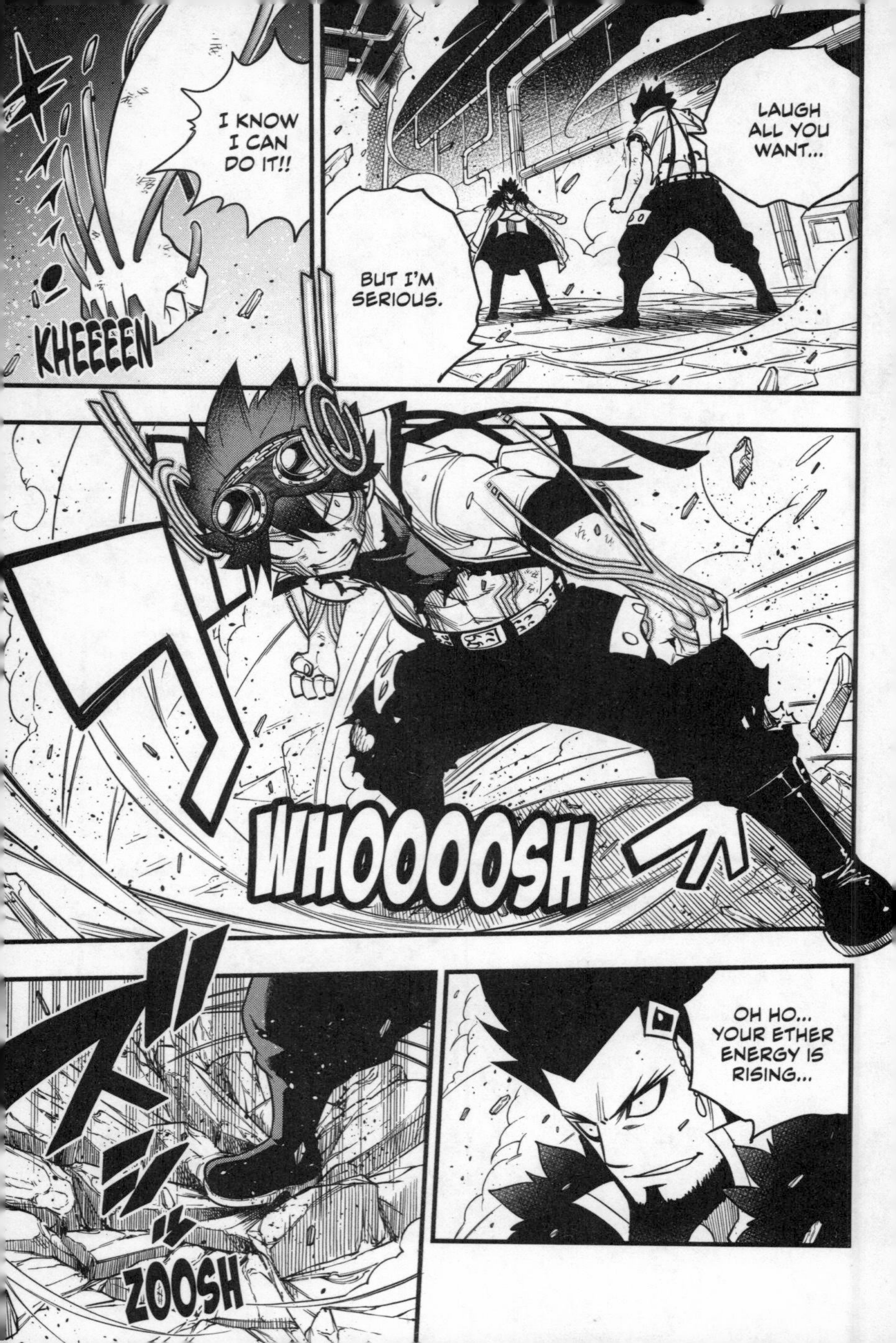
LAUGH ALL YOU WANT...
BUT I'M SERIOUS.
I KNOW I CAN DO IT!!
KHEEEEN
WHOOOOSH
OH HO... YOUR ETHER ENERGY IS RISING...
ZOOSH

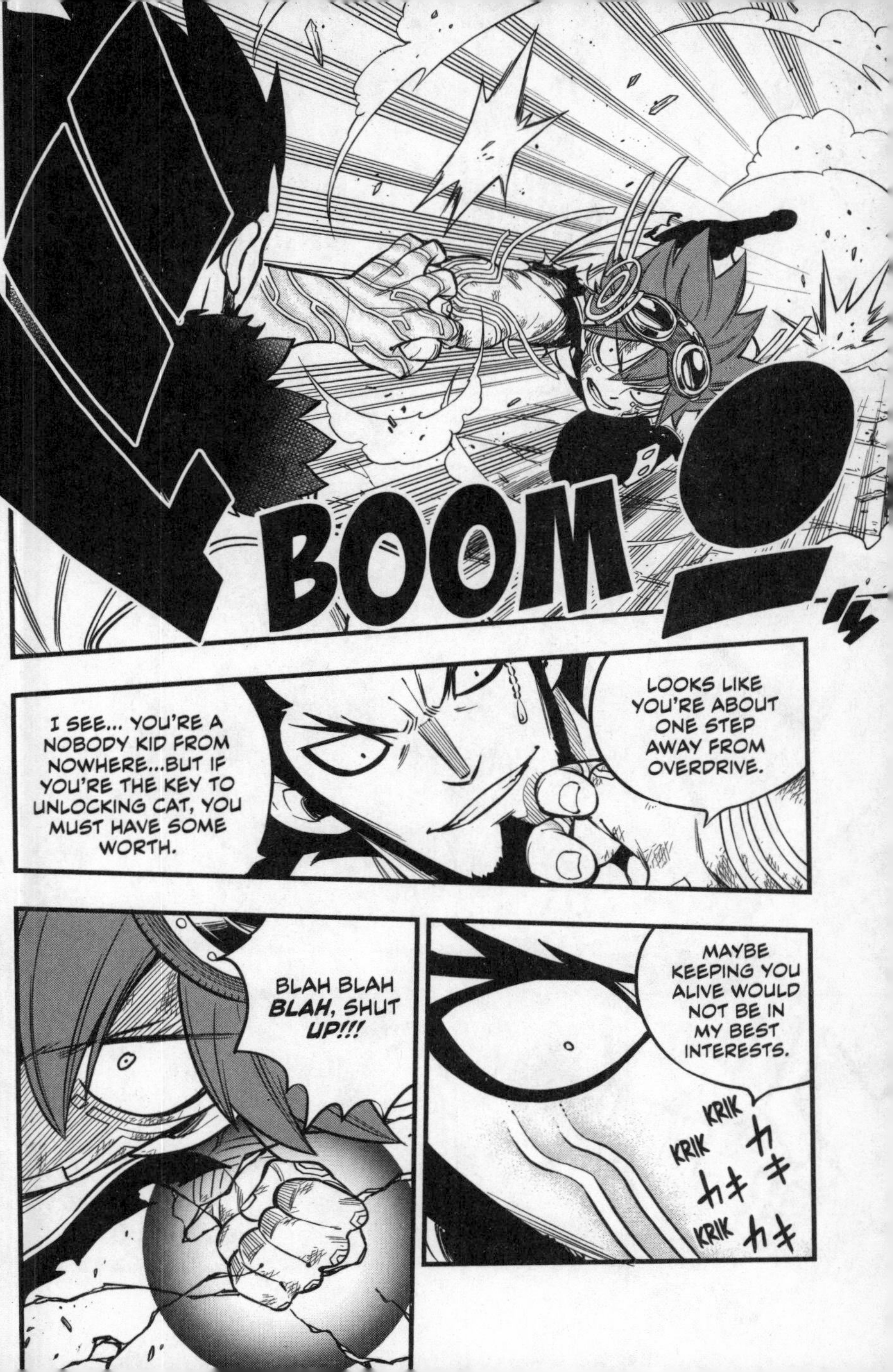
BOOM
LOOKS LIKE YOU'RE ABOUT ONE STEP AWAY FROM OVERDRIVE.
I SEE... YOU'RE A NOBODY KID FROM NOWHERE...BUT IF YOU'RE THE KEY TO UNLOCKING CAT, YOU MUST HAVE SOME WORTH.
MAYBE KEEPING YOU ALIVE WOULD NOT BE IN MY BEST INTERESTS.
KRIK KRIK KRIK
カキ カキ カキ
BLAH BLAH ***BLAH***, SHUT ***UP!!!***

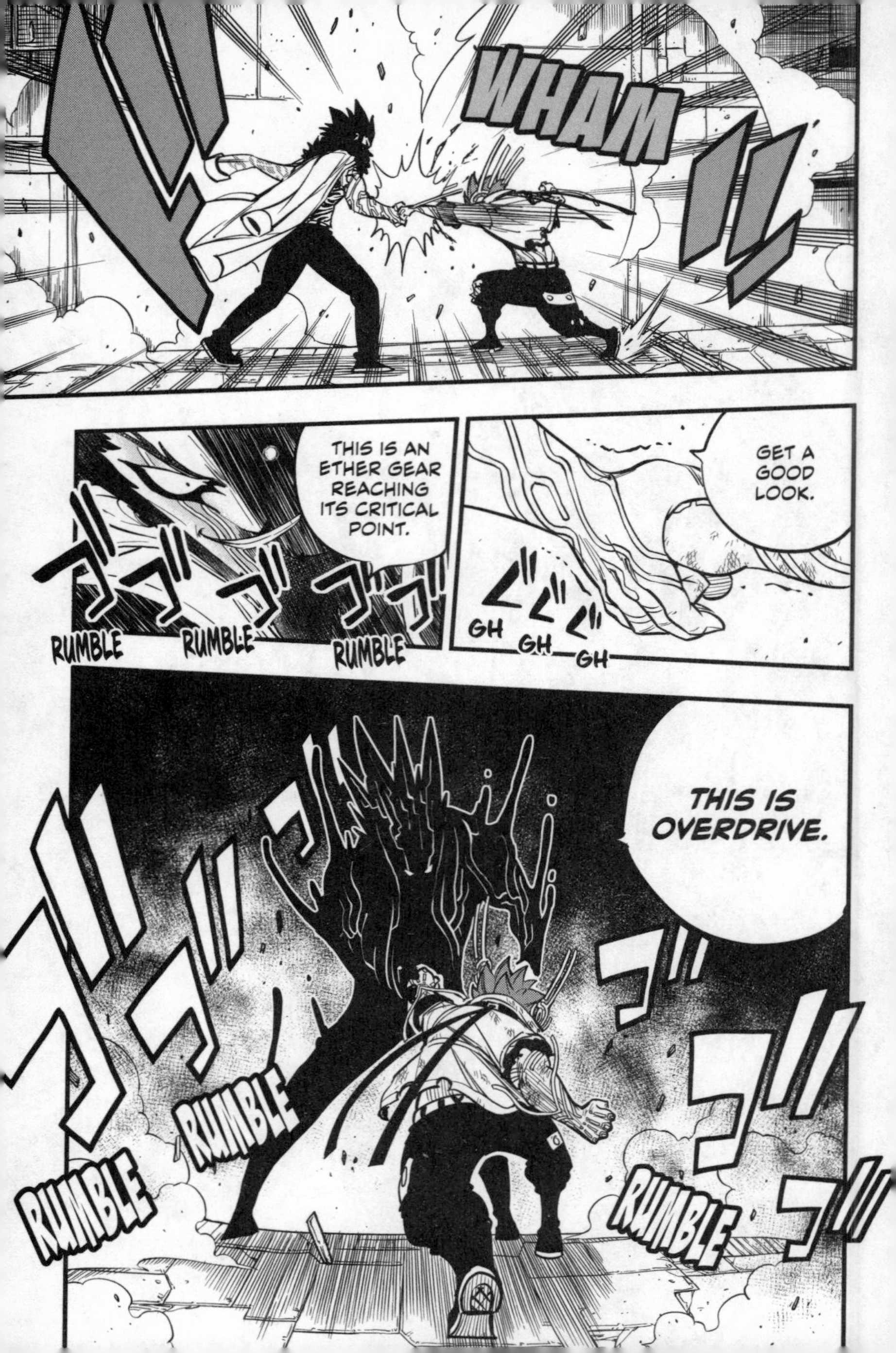
WHAM!!
GET A GOOD LOOK.
GH
GH
GH
THIS IS AN ETHER GEAR REACHING ITS CRITICAL POINT.
RUMBLE
RUMBLE
RUMBLE
THIS IS OVERDRIVE.
RUMBLE
RUMBLE
RUMBLE

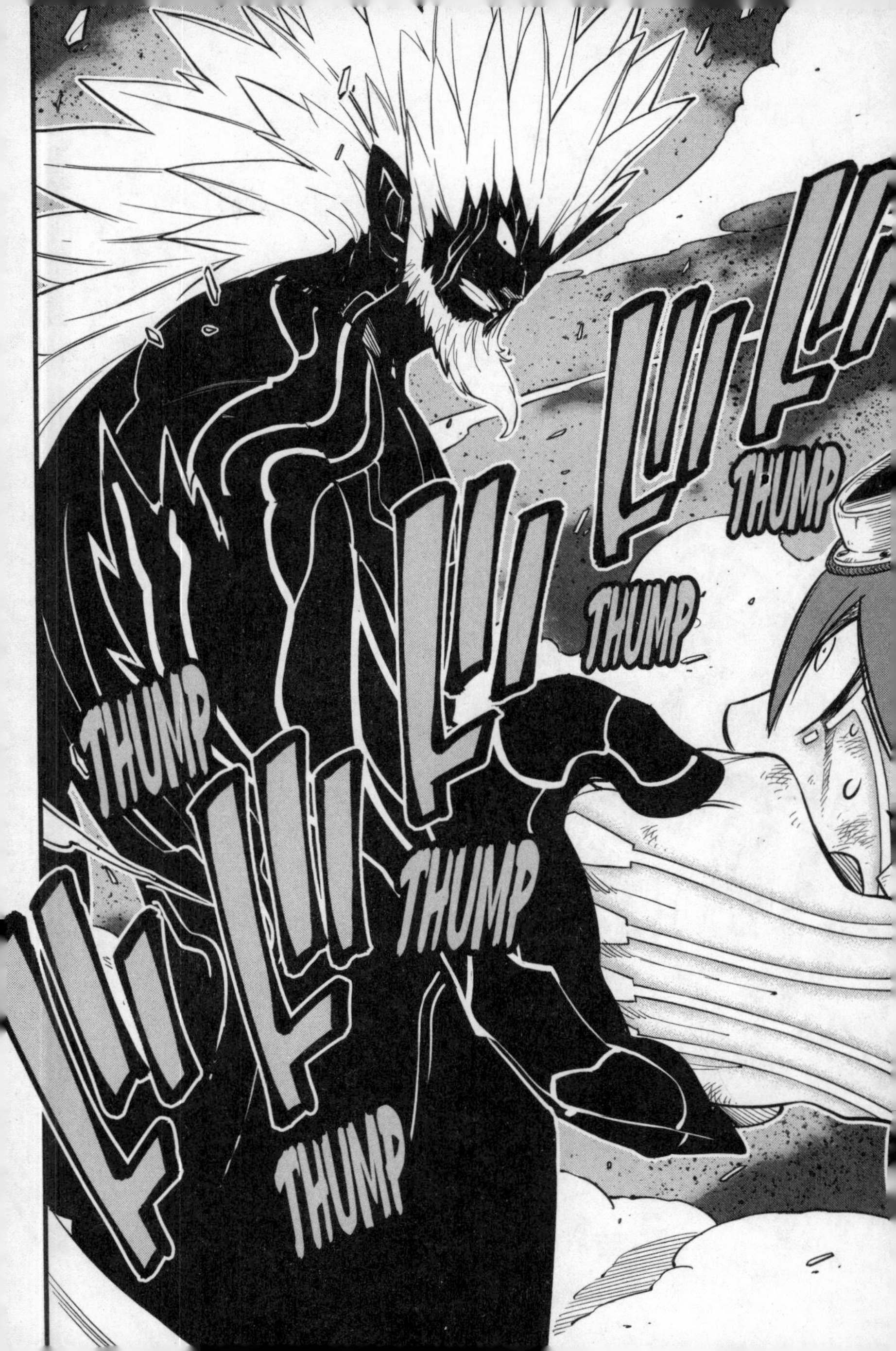
THUMP
THUMP
THUMP
THUMP
THUMP

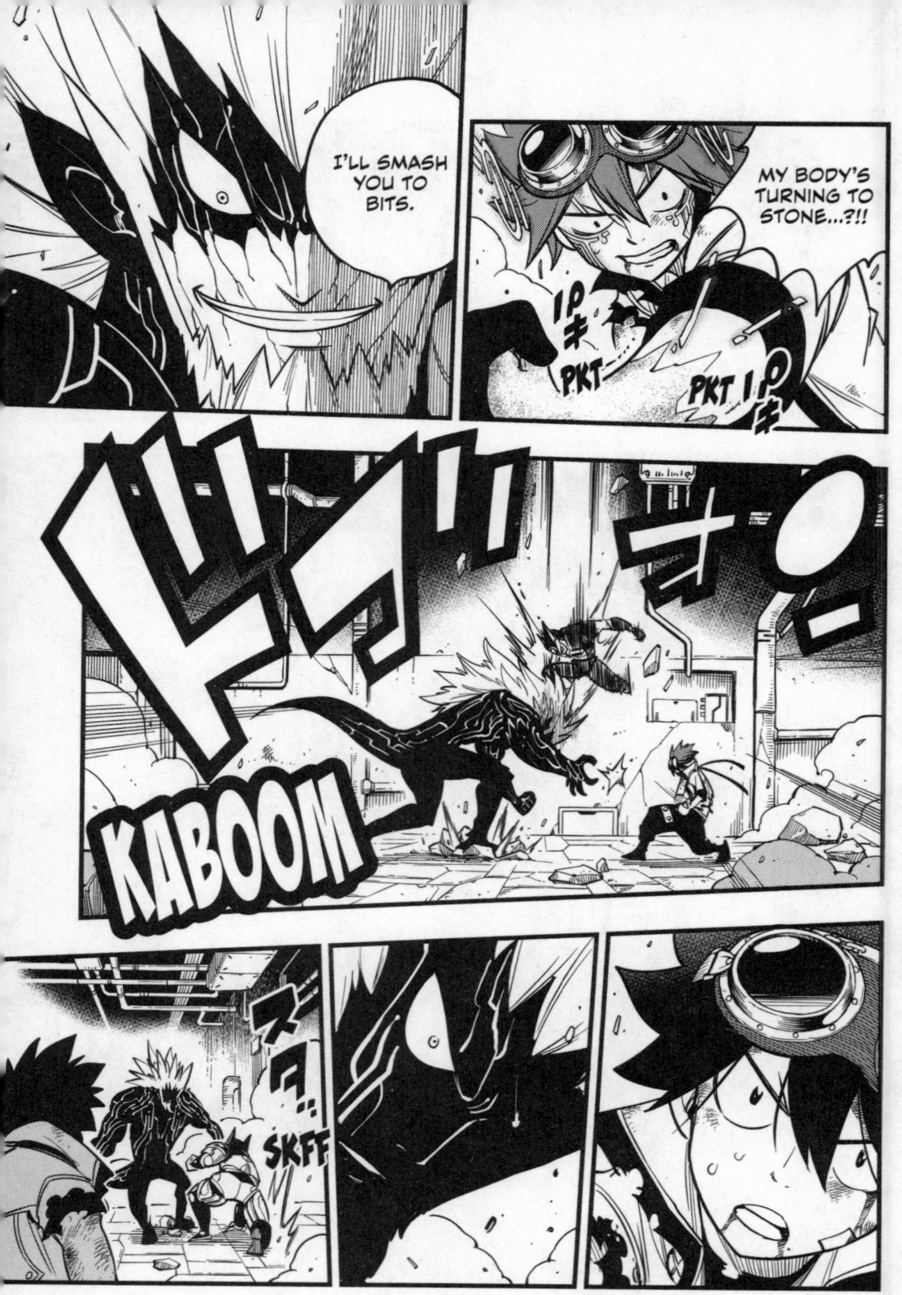
MY BODY'S TURNING TO STONE...?!!
PKT
PKT
I'LL SMASH YOU TO BITS.
KABOOM
SKFF

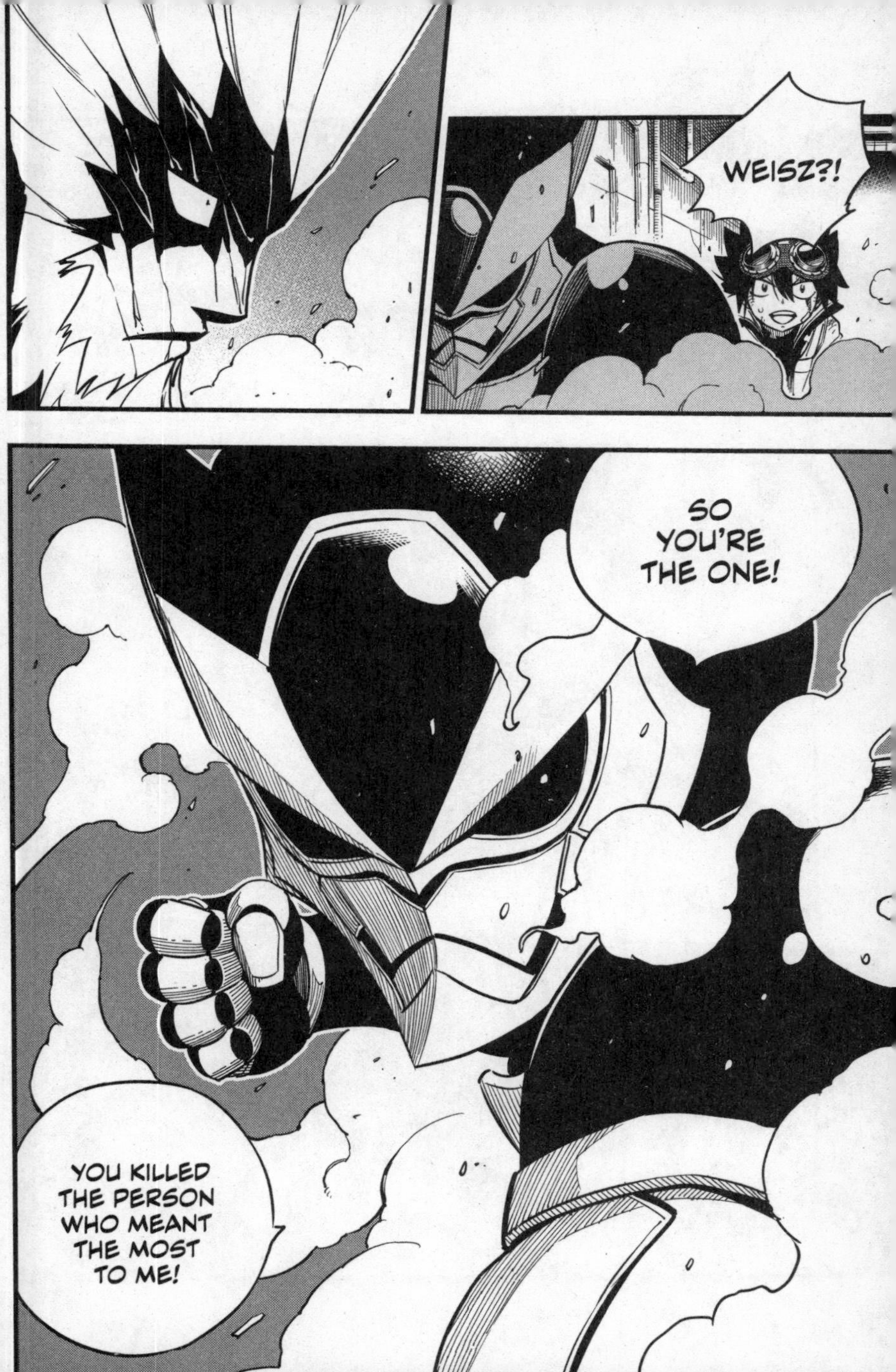
WEISZ?!
SO YOU'RE THE ONE!
YOU KILLED THE PERSON WHO MEANT THE MOST TO ME!

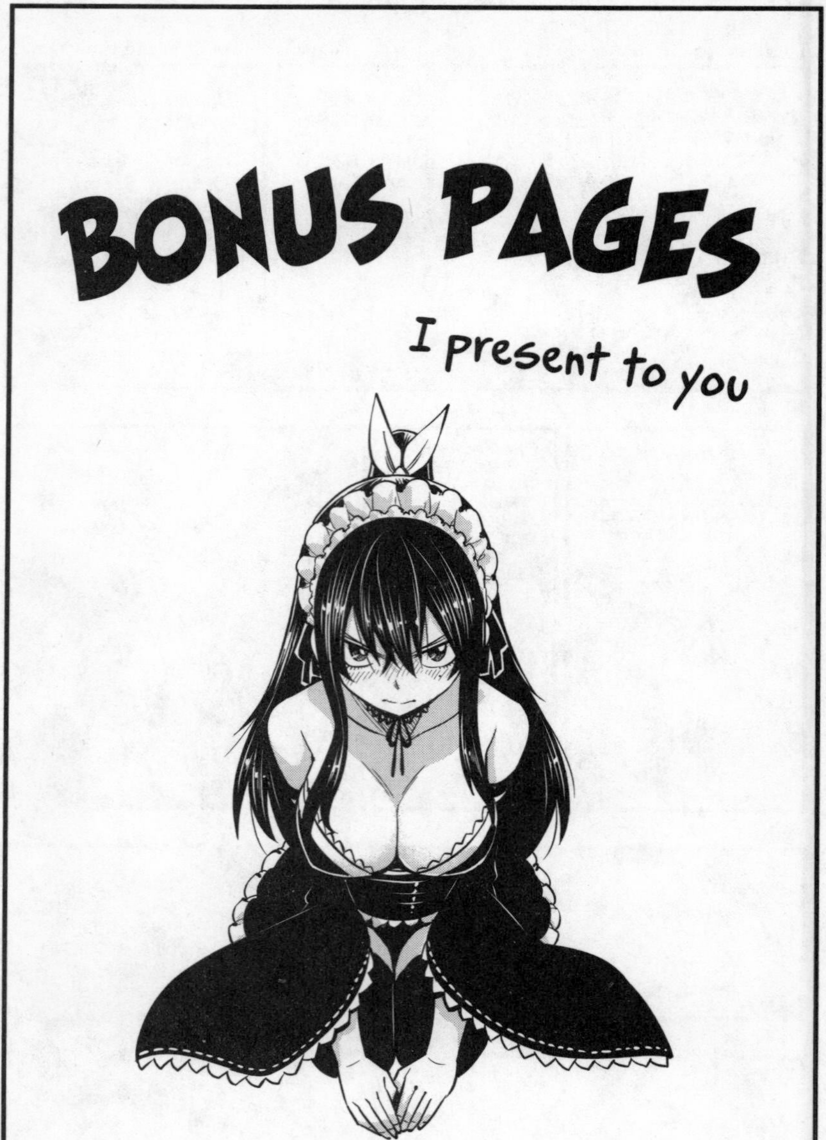
BONUS PAGES
I present to you

SPOT THE DIFFERENCE

There are 10 differences on this page compared to page 132! See if you can find them!!

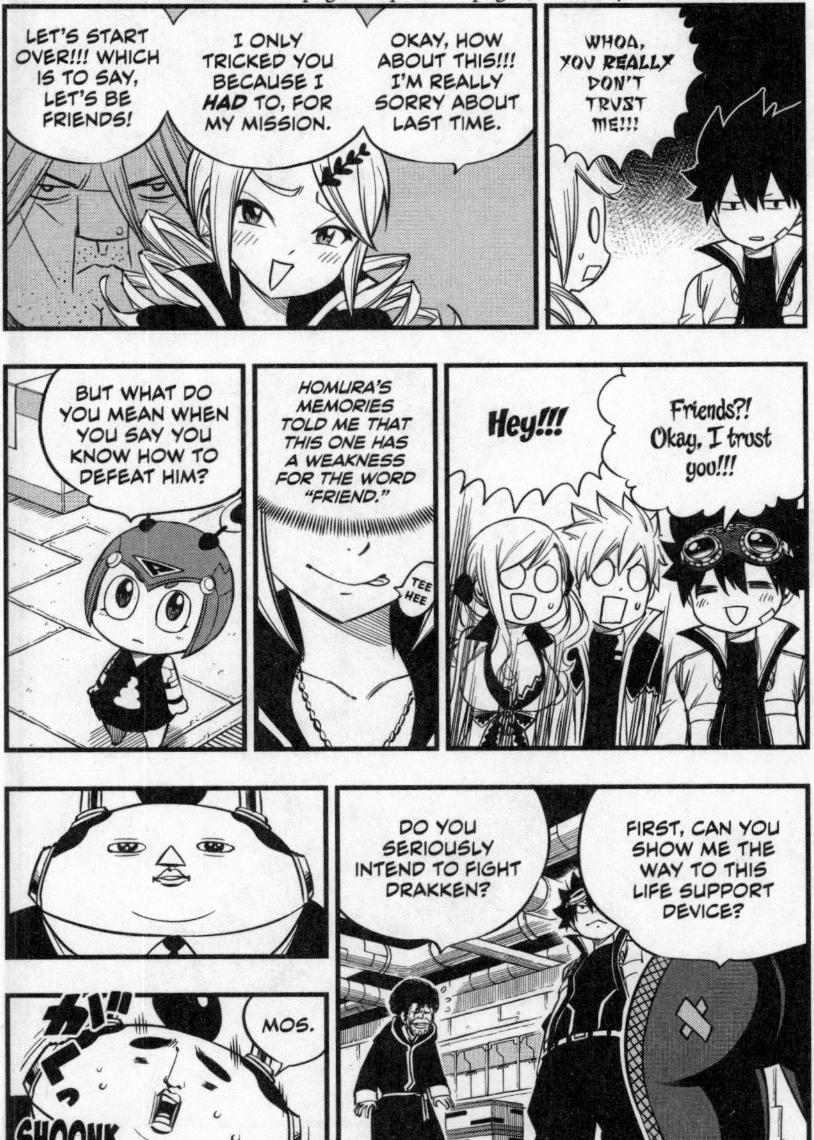

WHOA, YOU REALLY DON'T TRUST ME!!!
OKAY, HOW ABOUT THIS!!! I'M REALLY SORRY ABOUT LAST TIME.
I ONLY TRICKED YOU BECAUSE I HAD TO, FOR MY MISSION.
LET'S START OVER!!! WHICH IS TO SAY, LET'S BE FRIENDS!
Friends?! Okay, I trust you!!!
Hey!!!
HOMURA'S MEMORIES TOLD ME THAT THIS ONE HAS A WEAKNESS FOR THE WORD "FRIEND."
TEE HEE
BUT WHAT DO YOU MEAN WHEN YOU SAY YOU KNOW HOW TO DEFEAT HIM?
FIRST, CAN YOU SHOW ME THE WAY TO THIS LIFE SUPPORT DEVICE?
DO YOU SERIOUSLY INTEND TO FIGHT DRAKKEN?
MOS.
SHOONK

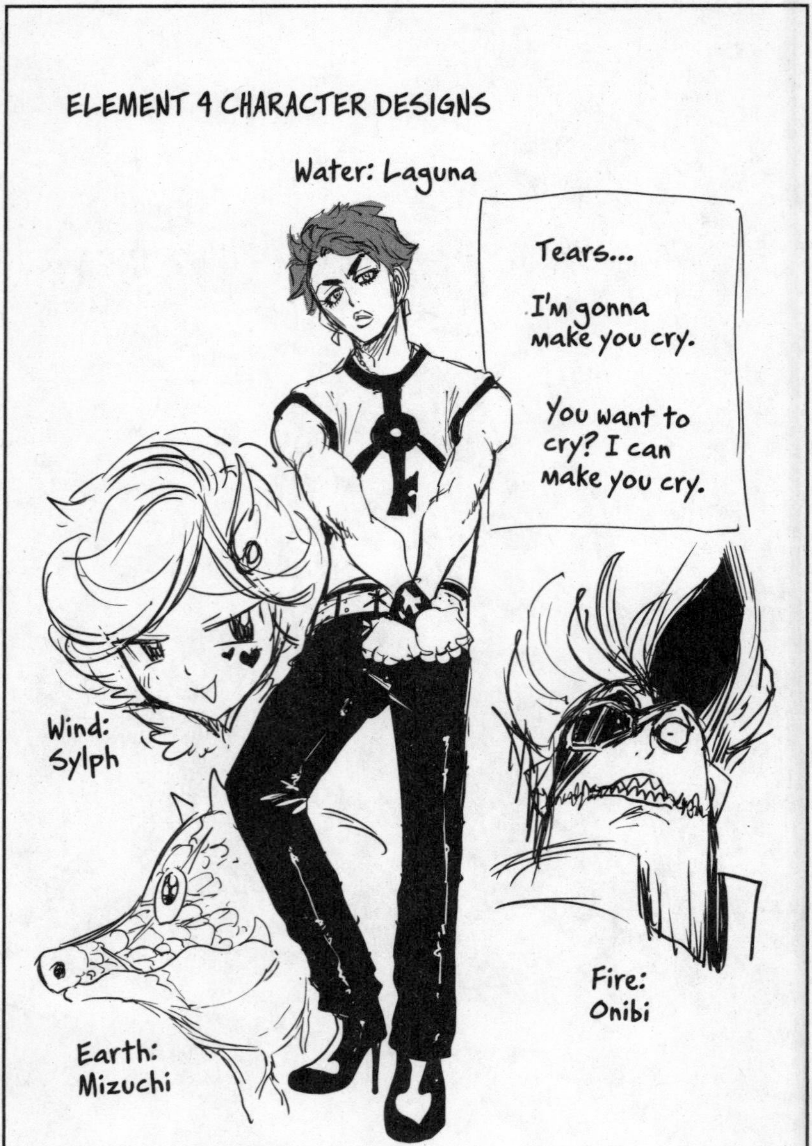
ELEMENT 4 CHARACTER DESIGNS
Water: Laguna
Tears...
I'm gonna make you cry.
You want to cry? I can make you cry.
Wind: Sylph
Fire: Onibi
Earth: Mizuchi

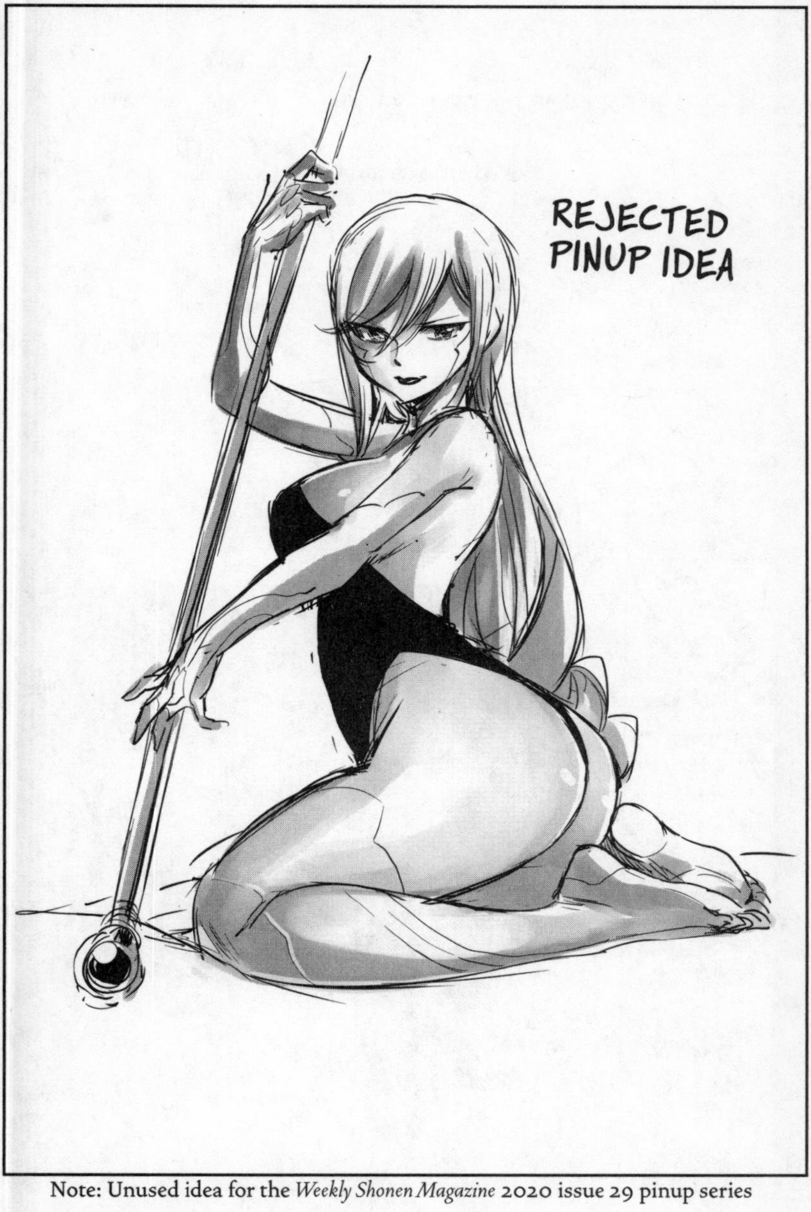
REJECTED
PINUP IDEA
Note: Unused idea for the *Weekly Shonen Magazine* 2020 issue 29 pinup series

AFTERWORD

The afterword corner. I've been doing it since my debut, so I've written a total of more than 100. It started because I was under the mistaken impression that a compiled graphic novel always has an afterword, and then I just couldn't stop, and now here we are. I'm actually pretty terrible at writing essays (not that I hate it), and it's extremely laughable that someone like me would try to convey anything with words, but I'm pretty sure these are going to continue.

Now, sometimes I want to give a brief commentary on individual chapters.

· **Chapter 87** ····· I wanted to draw the Four Shining Stars in their Battle Dress! I like each of the designs quite a bit, and I used them again for the cover of this volume.

· **Chapter 89** ····· This was Hermit's first battle scene, so I tried to figure out how Hermit would fight, and this is how it turned out. Stuff like the scene where she's creating Hologram Hermit is really SF, don't you think? And I know I've said this a billion times, but this series is not "science-fiction" SF, it's "space fantasy" SF.

· **Chapter 92** ····· I drew this chapter because I wanted a scene where Homura identifies herself as a member of the Shining Stars. I think that her strategy against Sylph's attacks was kind of sloppy, but this chapter is more about feelings than plot.

· **Chapter 94** ····· This is one chapter where Mosco is just utterly adorable(?). He's an extremely useful character, and he always comes in handy when I want to throw in a little gag. Really, I just have to have him say, "Moscoy" whenever (ha ha). But I do actually put some thought into his placement in the scene. I like to think I've come up with all possible variations, but when I actually place him in the scene, a new variation will come up. I feel like he still has a lot of funny visuals to give us.

· **Chapter 95** ····· The Belial Gore arc is reaching its climax, and this chapter takes us a long way towards the battle against Drakken. What happened in Weisz's past? I hope you'll stay tuned and find out in the next volume.

That reminds me, the names of Weisz's (Arsenal's) special moves have something in common. He actually uses the parts of names of the dragons that show up in my last series, *Fairy Tail*.

Anyway, I hope to see you next time.

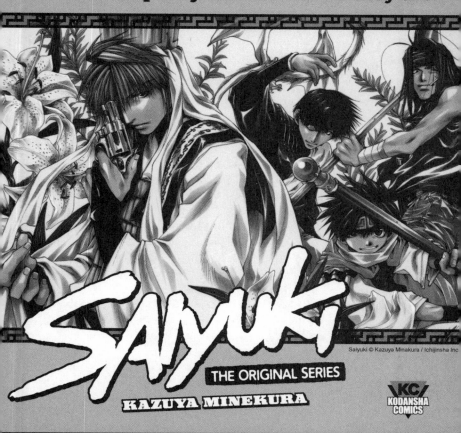

Young characters and steampunk setting, like *Howl's Moving Castle* and *Battle Angel Alita*

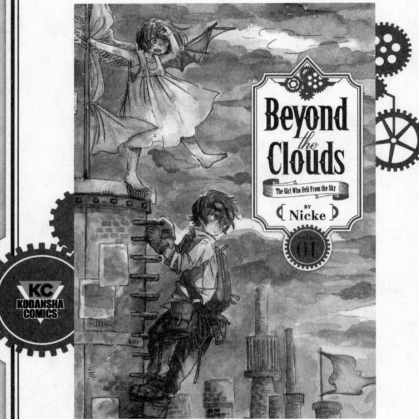

Beyond the Clouds © 2018 Nicke / Ki-oon

A boy with a talent for machines and a mysterious girl whose wings he's fixed will take you beyond the clouds! In the tradition of the high-flying, resonant adventure stories of Studio Ghibli comes a gorgeous tale about the longing of young hearts for adventure and friendship!

PERFECT WORLD 1

Rie Aruga

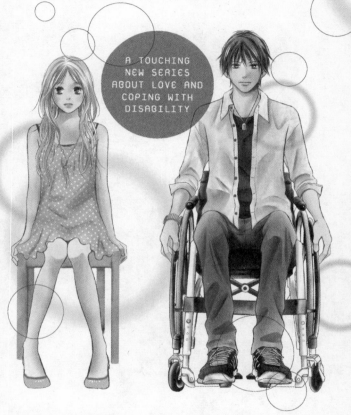

A TOUCHING NEW SERIES ABOUT LOVE AND COPING WITH DISABILITY

An office party reunites Tsugumi with her high school crush Itsuki. He's realized his dream of becoming an architect, but along the way, he experienced a spinal injury that put him in a wheelchair. Now Tsugumi's rekindled feelings will butt up against prejudices she never considered — and Itsuki will have to decide if he's ready to let someone into his heart...

"Depicts with great delicacy and courage the difficulties some with disabilities experience getting involved in romantic relationships... Rie Aruga refuses to romanticize, pushing her heroine to face the reality of disability. She invites her readers to the same tasks of empathy, knowledge and recognition."
—Slate.fr

"An important entry [in manga romance]... The emotional core of both plot and characters indicates thoughtfulness... [Aruga's] research is readily apparent in the text and artwork, making this feel like a real story."
—Anime News Network

Perfect World © Rie Aruga/Kodansha Ltd.

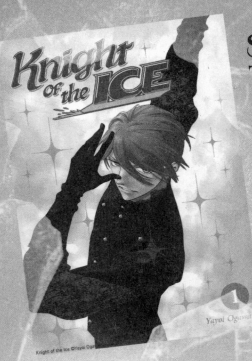

Knight of the Ice ©Yayoi Oga...

Knight of the ICE

Yayoi Ogawa

SKATING THRILLS AND ICY CHILLS WITH THIS NEW TINGLY ROMANCE SERIES!

A rom-com on ice, perfect for fans of *Princess Jellyfish* and *Wotakoi*. Kokoro is the talk of the figure-skating world, winning trophies and hearts. But little do they know... he's actually a huge nerd! From the beloved creator of *You're My Pet* (*Tramps Like Us*).

Chitose is a serious young woman, working for the health magazine *SASSO*. Or at least, she would be, if she wasn't constantly getting distracted by her childhood friend, international figure skating star Kokoro Kijinami! In the public eye and on the ice, Kokoro is a gallant, flawless knight, but behind his glittery costumes and breathtaking spins lies a secret: He's actually a hopelessly romantic otaku, who can only land his quad jumps when Chitose is on hand to recite a spell from his favorite magical girl anime!

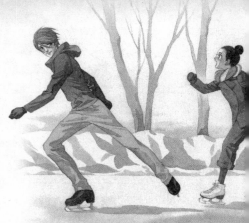

KC KODANSHA COMICS

A Kodansha Comics Trade Pap[...]
EDENS ZERO 11 copyright © 202[...]
English translation copyright © 20[...]

Published in the United States by Kodansha Comics, an imprint of
Kodansha USA Publishing, LLC, New York.

Publication rights for this English edition arranged through
Kodansha Ltd., Tokyo.

First published in Japan in 2020 by Kodansha Ltd., Tokyo.

ISBN 978-1-64651-038-2

Original cover design by Narumi Miura (G x complex).

Printed in the United States of America.

www.kodanshacomics.com

9 8 7 6 5 4 3 2 1
Translation: Alethea Nibley & Athena Nibley
Lettering: AndWorld Design
Editing: David Yoo
Kodansha Comics edition cover design by Phil Balsman

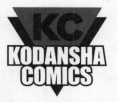

Publisher: Kiichiro Sugawara

Director of publishing services: Ben Applegate
Associate director of operations: Stephen Pakula
Publishing services associate managing editor: Madison Salters
Assistant production manager: Emi Lotto, Angela Zurlo